MONSTROUS BIRTHS AND VISUAL CULTURE IN SIXTEENTH-CENTURY GERMANY

Religious Cultures in the Early Modern World

Series Editors: *Fernando Cervantes*
Peter Marshall
Philip Soergel

Titles in this Series

1 Possession, Puritanism and Print: Darrell, Harsnett, Shakespeare and the Elizabethan Exorcism Controversy
Marion Gibson

2 Visions of an Unseen World: Ghost Beliefs and Ghost Stories in Eighteenth-Century England
Sasha Handley

3 Diabolism in Colonial Peru
Andrew Redden

4 Sacred History and National Identity: Comparisons between Early Modern Wales and Brittany
Jason Nice

Forthcoming Titles

The Religious Culture of Marian England
David Loades

www.pickeringchatto.com/religious

MONSTROUS BIRTHS AND VISUAL CULTURE IN SIXTEENTH-CENTURY GERMANY

BY

Jennifer Spinks

MUNDUS INTELLECTUALIS

LONDON
PICKERING & CHATTO
2009

Published by Pickering & Chatto (Publishers) Limited
21 Bloomsbury Way, London WC1A 2TH

2252 Ridge Road, Brookfield, Vermont 05036-9704, USA

www.pickeringchatto.com

BRITISH LIBRARY CATALOGUING IN PUBLICATION DATA

Spinks, Jennifer
Monstrous births and visual culture in sixteenth-century Germany. – (Religious cultures in the early modern world)
1. Visual communication – Germany – History – 16th century 2. Abnormalities, Human, in art 3. Monsters in art 4. Prints, German – 16th century 5. Art and religion – Germany – History – 16th century 6. Reformation and art – Germany
I. Title
760'.0449616043'0943

ISBN-13: 9781851966301
e: 9781851969654

This publication is printed on acid-free paper that conforms to the American National Standard for the Permanence of Paper for Printed Library Materials.

Typeset by Pickering & Chatto (Publishers) Limited
Printed in the UK by the MPG Books Group

CONTENTS

ACKNOWLEDGEMENTS

Many people have generously offered their help and advice during the years that I have worked on this project. Chief amongst them is Charles Zika, and I owe him a great debt for his support, encouragement, inspirational character and intellectual rigour. For various kinds of support, advice or useful comments on my research over the years, I also owe particular thanks to Michael Bennett, Sue Broomhall, Megan Cassidy-Welch, Liam Connell, Patricia Crawford, Heather Dalton, Julie Davies, Dagmar Eichberger, Elise Grosser, Claudia Guli, Yasmin Haskell, Catherine Kovesi, Dolly MacKinnon, Peter Matheson, Grantley McDonald, Leigh Penman, Michael Pickering, Lyndal Roper, Rainer Schoch, Peter Sherlock, Larry Silver, Charlotte Smith and Karl Vocelka.

I am very grateful to the editors of this book series – Fernando Cervantes, Peter Marshall and especially Philip Soergel – for their initial interest in my work, as well as to Daire Carr, Mark Pollard and Julie Wilson at Pickering & Chatto for their patient and friendly assistance. Within the School of Historical Studies at the University of Melbourne, I owe special thanks to Erica Mehrtens and Joy Damousi for their help. Publication of this work was assisted by a publication grant from the University of Melbourne; by the School of Historical Studies; and by a grant from the Research and Research Training Committee, Faculty of Arts, the University of Melbourne.

Sections of the book have appeared or are forthcoming in the following three articles: 'Wondrous Monsters: Representing Conjoined Twins in Early Sixteenth-Century German Broadsheets', *Parergon*, 22:2 (2005), pp. 77–112; 'Jakob Rueff's 1554 *Trostbüchle*: A Zurich Physician Explains and Interprets Monstrous Births', *Intellectual History Review*, 18:1, special issue on *Humanism and Medicine in the Renaissance*, ed. S. Broomhall and Y. Haskell (2008), pp. 41–59; and 'Monstrous Births and Counter-Reformation Visual Polemics: Johann Nas and the 1569 *Ecclesia Militans*', *Sixteenth-Century Journal* (forthcoming 2009). I am grateful to the journal editors for permission to use revised material from these articles for this book.

My research has been aided by a number of scholarships and fellowships. I am grateful for the support of an Australian Postgraduate Award; a scholarship from the DAAD (German Academic Exchange Service); Harold Wright and Sarah and William Holmes scholarships for research in the British Museum; a Norman Macgeorge travelling scholarship; a scholarship from the ÖAD (Austrian Academic Exchange Service); a Grete Sondheimer fellowship at the Warburg Institute; a humanities travelling fellowship from the Australian Academy of the Humanities; and most recently a research fellowship at the Herzog August Bibliothek in Wolfenbüttel. All have provided wonderful opportunities to pursue research in stimulating and enjoyable environments.

I owe thanks to the staff of the following libraries and institutions visited during the course of my research: the University of Heidelberg libraries; the Bayerische Staatsbibliothek in Munich; the Staatliche Graphische Sammlung in Munich; the library of the Germanisches Nationalmuseum in Nuremberg; the British Library and the Warburg Institute in London; the Department of Prints and Drawings at the British Museum; the Staatsbibliothek in Berlin; the University of Vienna; the Österreichische Nationalbibliothek in Vienna; the Herzog August Bibliothek in Wolfenbüttel; and the Zentralbibliothek in Zurich. Staff at the University of Melbourne libraries have been a great source of help, most particularly staff in the inter-library loan and rare books sections. I also wish to thank those institutions, acknowledged in the figure captions, which provided images for the book.

My greatest thanks go to those closest to me. My first debt is to my parents, for their unwavering support and love over many years. My final thanks go to Ted Colless, for making all things better in many different ways.

This book is dedicated to Ted, with much love.

LIST OF FIGURES

INTRODUCTION: WONDERS AND MONSTERS IN EARLY MODERN EUROPE

Monstrous births were a source of fascination and fear in early modern Europe. In the first half of the sixteenth century they were of particular importance in the German-speaking territories of the Holy Roman Empire that became caught up in religious conflict, the Reformation and the Counter-Reformation. During this period intellectual and theological debates, widely circulated publications and visual culture reflected a preoccupation with phenomena that were simultaneously natural and unnatural. These ranged from showers of blood to strange comets and included the topic of this book: monstrous births. One of the most dramatic and iconic publications to report such wonders may well be a 1578 German-language broadsheet from Strasbourg. It informs the reader and viewer about the separate births in Italy of a seven-headed child and a horned child in January 1578 (Fig. I.1).[1] The child with seven heads had been born in Evorizo (Eusrigo), in the vicinity of Milan, to a woman of good repute in the community.[2] The other child, with four horns and a kind of loose skin cap, was born in Piedmont. How might people at the time have viewed these children? The seven-headed child would very likely have recalled for viewers the seven-headed beast of the Apocalypse, with the child's satyr-like legs adding an additional demonic element. For those people disposed to interpret the scene along apocalyptic lines, the child on the left-hand side of the image could also easily be associated with the second beast of the Apocalypse, marked by the horns on its head.

Not only are these children themselves both demonic and apocalyptic in appearance, but they are shown here in the context of a destructive storm and flood of biblical proportions. The town is clearly identified in the text as the 'town of Horb on the [river] Neckar'.[3] That is, this is a German town that lies in ruins behind the two Italian monstrous births. The broadsheet text further reports that Horb was the site of a great flood and storm on 15 May 1578; events witnessed by the anonymous author of the broadsheet. The flood and storm had caused great devastation, killing and injuring many people and animals, destroying twelve houses and damaging many more. Perhaps most shockingly, however, the weather conditions had unearthed the headstones and the contents of graves

Warhaftige vnd schröckliche bildnuß vnd gestalt zwoer neuer leydigen vngewonlichen Mißgeburt/ dises gegenwärtige Jar außkom̃en. Sampt der beschreibung des Erbärmlichen Wassergusses/ jüngst zu Horb im Land Wirtenberg/ den 15. Tag Maij/ dises LXXVIII. Jars vorgangen

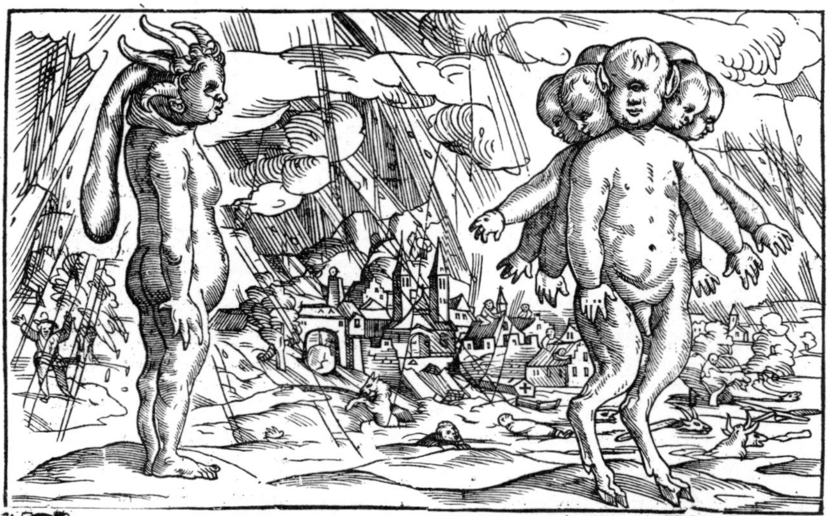

NIcht vnfüglich mag dise nun gegenwärtige zeit wol eyne rechte Wunderzeit heyssen: seiteynmal inn kurtzem also vil Wunder vnd zeychen auff eynander kom̃en vnd folgen: das es frommen Hertzen eyn schrecken machet. Vnd warlich/ das sie nicht gar on bedeutnus vnd würckung seien/ sihet man leyder täglich hin vnd wider/ ferr vnd nahe/ an den wunderlichen vnruhen/ empörungen/ kriegen vnd Blutvergiessen/ verfolgungen/ verhergungen/ verrhätereien/ Meuchelmördereien/ falschen Lehren/ einfallen frembdes Volcks Kriegsgeschrey/ plünderung fürnemmer Stätt/ vngewonhten kranckheyten vnd Seuchen/ absterben hoher Leut/ Vngewittern/ wütenden Winden/ schwären Wassergüssen/ Mißgewächssen/ vnd endlich allenthalben vm̃ sich herum̃ an der Vnmenschlichen vntreu vnd mißtrauen/ an den vnchristlichen händeln/ dem vbersatz/ schinden/ Judentzen vnd Vorkauff/ an allerhand schand vnd lastern/ Gottslästerungen/ verachtung vnd verkerung GOttes Worts/ verspottung fromer Leut warnung/ vngehorsam gegen Obern vnd Fürgesetzte/ vnd kurtzum̃/ an heutiger grosser sicherheyt/ vnd erkaltung aller Lieb. Vnd das man nun der jüngstvergangenen Wunder/ die doch auch noch jre würckung zuvollrichten haben/ geschweige/ Als der erscheinung frembder Sternen/ Cometen/ Wundergesicht/ vnd Himelsflam̃en/ der verfinsterung Sonn vnd Mons/ der Erdbidem/ vnd anderer schröcklichen fällen.

So besehe vnd erwige man alleyn dise beyde hie vorgebildete scheutzliche Wundergeburten. Deren die eyne des nächsten verschinenen Jenners/ dises gegenwärtigen Jars 78. zu Evorigo/ im Novareser Land/ des Meyländischen Gebiets/ ist von eyner zimlich gestandenen Matronen an die Welt gebracht worden/ oberhalb mit siben händen/ sampt so vil Köpffen gestaltet/ vnter welchen der fürnemist Kopff nur eyn Auge mitten inn der stirn hatte/ vnd zwey Schweinsoren daran. Vnterhalb aber hat es Füs wie eyn ander Viech oder Thier.

Die ander Mißgeburt oder Scheusal ist gleichsfals auch im Jenner/ dises 78. Jars/ inn gestalt/ wie hie im gemäl angezeygt/ geboren worden/ vnd dasselbig von eynem Weib inn Piemont.

Es hat auch der Ehrwürdig vnd Hochgelehrt Herr Doctor Simon Pauli/ Superintendens zu Rostock/ inn der jungstverloffenen Franckforter Fastenmeß/ auch eyn dergleichen erschröcklich vnnatürlich Geburt/ so bald zu angang des Neuen Jars zu Grevesmülen im Land zu Mechelburg von eyns Schneiders Weib an tag gebracht worden/ inn truck ausgehn lasen/ vnd darbei eyne schöne Erinnerung vnd vermanung angehenckt/ dahin wir dan die Leut wöllen gewisen haben.

Vber diß haben wir auch neulich den 15. tag des Mayens/ inn der Statt Horb am Necker gelegen/ eyn Erbärmlich Gewässer erfaren/ allda es durch eyn Wolckenbruch von den nächsten Bergen grose Steyn gerissen/ vnd durch die Statt gefüret vnd alles/ was es angetroffen/ hinweg geschwället vnd geflötzet hat. Auch/ als man jm etwas zuwehren/ die Statthor zusperrte/ hat es durch die Maur hinder dem Spital eynen einpruch gethan/ vnd also vnversehen/ Leut vnd Viech/ Getreyd vnd vnd frucht verfürt/ zwölff Häuser gar hingeflötzt/ die andern verterbt/ das Wisenthal gantz zerrissen/ die Broñen eingeworffen/ die Grabsteyn vor der Statt aufgehebt/ vnd sie inn die Statt geschweiñet/ also das die Todten vnter den Lebendigen sint geschwoñen/ sonderlich hat man vnter denselbigen eyner Kindbetterin wargenoñen/ die man kurtz zuvor begraben hatte. Auch hat es andern jamer mehr angericht/ der hie zu lang wer zuerzelen. Aber aus erzeltem hat man genug den zorn Gottes zuersehen/ wie schwärlich es abgange/ wann er eynmal entbrinnet: Derhalben wer es grose zeit/ solche warnungen bußfärtiglich zuerkennen/ ehe man noch greulichers erfahre/ vnd Gott bewegt werde/ seinen Griñ gar vber vns auszuschütten: Darvor vns Gott gnädiglich beschütze. Amen.

Getruckt zu Straßburg/ Anno M. D. LXXVIII.

Figure I.1: Two Italian monstrous births from 1578 against a German landscape, from Anon., *Warhaftige vnd schroeckliche bildnuß vnd gestalt zwoern neuer leydigen vngewonlichen Mißgeburt ...* (Strasbourg: n.p., 1578). Photo courtesy of the Zentralbibliothek Zürich, shelfmark PAS II 15/33.

from the graveyard, and both a body in a shroud and a coffin are visible in the centre of image. The graves were disturbed, giving up the dead, 'just as the earth swam [i.e., moved] under the living'.[4] The unearthing of graves lends a decisively apocalyptic air to the scene, recalling for audiences the events of the coming Day of Judgement when the dead would rise from the ground. However, the scene is not overseen by a merciful Christ, but instead by two looming and demonic monstrous births. It is the anger ('zorn') of God that dominates here. The author advises readers that they must pay close and penitent attention to 'warnings like these ... before one experiences something much more gruesome'.[5] Several elements – two monstrous births, and a destructive storm and flood – are combined in this broadsheet with great graphic impact. They are intended to demonstrate that such signs were proliferating,[6] and that they were 'not without meaning and effect'.[7] The unlikely birth of a seven-headed baby, viewed by contemporaries as a real event, or at least an event with real significance, is presented here in a highly dramatic way that could scarcely have been imagined at the beginning of the sixteenth century.

Decades before this broadsheet from 1578, monstrous births had appeared in German print culture in a variety of forms. Cases that achieved notoriety ranged from twin girls born joined at the forehead near the town of Worms in 1495, to the hybrid-bodied Papal Ass that appeared in Rome in 1496 and later became an important figure in Reformation polemic. The great variety and plenitude of monstrous births were part of their appeal, and also, as the sixteenth century progressed, increasingly something to be feared and decoded as a sign of the coming Apocalypse. Monstrous births fascinated people at all levels of society, and were reported in both popular and learned publications throughout the sixteenth century. Broadsheets, pamphlets and books analysed and argued for the possible meanings of such phenomena, and in doing so tell us about the interests and concerns of early modern societies. In the last several decades there has been a revival of interest in the monstrous as an important element of the cultures of medieval and early modern European societies.[8] The monster – variously defined – was not merely a marginal figure, but one that was richly symbolic and often utilized to represent and debate issues of morality, religion and politics, thereby putting them into concrete and easily grasped terms.

This book examines widely circulated representations of monstrous births that appeared in illustrated German-language printed publications from the very late fifteenth through to the late sixteenth century. It traces how this material developed in the context of the extraordinary religious and social changes that unfolded in German lands during the Reformation and its aftermath. While monstrous births were of interest across Europe in the early modern period, printed reports of their appearance were especially numerous in German lands. While some of the individual cases of child and animal misbirths examined here may seem fantastic and physically unfeasible to modern readers, at the time they were reported and discussed as specific, real events. These children and animals were represented and perceived as tangible and immediate, both spatially and chronologically.

Early modern European monstrous births were almost exclusively represented in print. Indeed, monstrous births were almost never depicted in paintings in the sixteenth century, and there are few extant drawings.[9] These different types of illustrated printed publications – books, pamphlets and broadsheets – often served different sorts of audiences: religious and secular, local and geographically dispersed, popular and elite, literate and illiterate. Nonetheless they also formed part of a shared culture and a close examination reveals many intersections between them. German publications of this kind undoubtedly formed a large part of a broader trend. Paula Findlen has observed that there was:

> a rich publishing history of broadsheets, natural histories, and encyclopedias of the strange and unfamiliar that characterized the sixteenth-century love affair with the marvelous, and that catalogued the many pleasurable and terrifying ways in which nature made manifest the hand of God in the world.[10]

Findlen's study focuses on Italian materials, and her remark captures the vigorous programme of publication but not the political and social urgency of the religious context that became so distinctive in German publications.[11] Crucially, this story of the representation of monstrous births is inescapably bound up with a shift in the interpretation of monstrous births that occurred over the course of the Reformation. Robert Scribner pointed to the fundamental complexity of the monstrous birth when he asserted that 'the monster was an ambivalent figure, for it was both a sign and a direct revelation'.[12] Monstrous births occupied a strange place mid-way between the secular and the religious. Nonetheless, they were overwhelmingly interpreted as signs from God, and increasingly drawn into religious polemic.

This book argues for a growing, not decreasing, religious emphasis in understanding monstrous births during the sixteenth century; that, in fact, the representation of monstrous births became increasingly more apocalyptic in tone, or more likely to reference apocalyptic themes, over this period.[13] To draw on Stuart Clark's definition, apocalyptic ideas at this time were 'based on beliefs concerning the appearance of the Antichrist, the second advent, the resurrection of the dead, the end of the world, and the Last Judgement'.[14] This was a fundamentally conservative apocalypticism, distinct from the revolutionary, socially disruptive forces associated with millenarianism. In his classic study, Jean Delumeau also distinguished carefully between millenarianism and an apocalypticism tied up with the Last Judgement.[15] Despite this conservative aspect, apocalypticism was certainly a theme that could be both vitriolic and divisive, and it was strongly associated with Lutheranism and with Reformation debates and battles.[16] As Clark argues, apocalypticism intensified 'the themes of warning, punishment and repentance'.[17]

While the representation of monstrous births flourished as a result of print culture, and developed in various ways, authors and artists were drawing upon a body of existing ideas, both classical and early Christian, and their medieval development. The most important and commonly cited early authors on monstrous births were Aristotle, Cicero, Pliny the Elder, the lesser-known but significant Julius Obsequens, and Augustine.[18] Early views on monstrous births fitted into three systems. Aristotle proposed entirely natural explanations, and is distinctive for demonstrating no interest in the idea of monsters as portents. He ascribed the formation of foetuses, including deformed ones, to entirely physical causes and gave a primary role to semen. The concept of a perfect form, from which all creatures deviated to greater or lesser degrees, was the cornerstone of his theory. This concept contained an implicit moral condemnation of bodies that were furthest from the ideal, and especially of monsters.[19] Cicero, on the other hand, emphasized the divinatory (prodigious) function of monstrous births and showed little interest in their physical causes. His book *De divinatione* considers monsters in the course of a dialogue that presents the case for and against divination.[20]

Pliny and Augustine viewed the phenomenon as an aspect of nature's (and, in Augustine's case, also therefore God's) wondrous and essentially unknowable qualities.[21] These two authors were particularly influential on late medieval and early modern thought on this topic, in which monstrous births were part of a divinely authored 'book of nature'.[22] In his thirty-seven book *Natural History*, Pliny emphasizes the remarkable nature of multiple births – more than three children at once was considered a portent, 'except in Egypt, where drinking the water of the Nile causes fecundity'.[23] The deviations from normal births that Pliny discusses are relatively mild, and are not characterized by the fascination with extreme physical deformity in the human races and domestic animals characteristic of the early modern period. Instead, he primarily demonstrates a desire to enumerate the great and wondrous variety of possible types in the world, rather than fully accounting for their cause or meaning.[24] Several centuries later, the fourth- or fifth-century Roman author Julius Obsequens prepared his *Liber de prodigiis*, which reported wondrous and prodigious events that had taken place in Rome between 249 and 212 BC. Obsequens's book was enthusiastically taken up by humanists in the sixteenth century.[25] He viewed monstrous births and other wonders as portents and, like Pliny, was particularly concerned with enumerating their great variety. This focus on the marvellous variety of natural wonders helped fundamentally to shape late medieval and early modern attitudes to monstrous births.

Augustine was certainly the most influential early author to have written on monstrous births, above all because his *City of God* placed them within a Christian framework.[26] He emphasized that, while many people considered portents to be outside nature, they were in fact part of God's creation: 'an occurrence contrary not to nature, but to nature as we know it'.[27] For Augustine, monsters were strikingly visual phenomena:

> just as it is not impossible for God to create whatever nature He chose, so it is not impossible for Him to change those natures which He has created in whatever way He chooses. This is why there has sprung up so great a multitude of those marvels which are called 'monsters', 'signs', 'portents' or 'prodigies'. If I chose to recall and mention them all, would this work ever come to an end? The word 'monster', we are told, clearly comes from 'to demonstrate' [*monstrare*], because monsters are signs by which something is demonstrated. 'Sign' [*ostentum*] comes from 'to show' [*ostendere*]; 'portent' from 'to portend', that is, 'to show in advance' [*praeostendere*]; and 'prodigy' from 'to speak of what is far away' [*porro dicere*], that is, to foretell the future.[28]

In the seventh century Isidore of Seville echoed Augustine but gave a more explicitly negative meaning to monstrous births:

> Portents and omens [*ostenta*], monsters and prodigies are so named because they appear to portend, foretell [*ostendere*], show [*monstrare*] and predict future things ... For God wished to signify the future through faults in things that are born, as through dreams and oracles, by which he forewarns and signifies to peoples or individuals a misfortune to come.[29]

There was an intense interest in human and animal monstrosity in the medieval period, but it was more commonly directed towards the monstrous races[30] rather than the individual human or animal monstrous births that Isidore refers to here. Nonetheless, stories about individual births were recorded in diaries and, in a modest way in comparison to later print culture, were also circulated, mostly through personal correspondence.[31] Several cases of conjoined twins were even visually recorded as simple stone relief sculptures in Vézelay and Florence.[32] Monstrous births featured in historical annals, where they played a role, along with meteorological and other prodigies, as portents of dramatic political events or natural disasters.[33] Some preachers incorporated monstrous births into moralizing stories that formed part of sermons.[34] In the *Gesta Romanorum*, a collection of stories and exempla compiled early in the fourteenth century for use by English Franciscans, the birth of conjoined male twins is given a positive symbolic value:

> There was a male child born, divided from the navel upward. Thus he had two heads and breasts, and a proper number of sensitive faculties to each. While one slept or ate, the other did neither. After two years, one part of the boy died, and the other survived about three days. ... My beloved, the child represents the soul and body of man.[35]

Another fourteenth-century author, Nicole Oresme, wrote that variety was a normal part of nature and such creatures were not to be wondered at. Lorraine Daston and Katharine Park argue that attitudes like these were an exception to the more common understanding of monstrous births as negative portents.[36] Biblical passages influenced these negative medieval and early modern understandings of the origin, purpose and interpretation of monstrous births. The monsters that appeared in the Bible were generally not monstrous births like the child in the *Gesta Romanorum*, but singular monsters rich with prophetic meaning, like the four hybrid beasts that emerged from the sea in the dream of Daniel 7:1–28. In the Apocrypha, 2 Esdras 5:8 tells of how 'menstruous women shall bring forth monsters', amongst other signs of the coming Apocalypse.[37] Most important were the beasts of the Apocalypse in the New Testament Book of Revelation; the seven-headed beast became one important reference point for understanding monstrous births during the sixteenth century, as the 1578 monstrous birth of Eusrigo indicates. Daniel, Esdras and especially the Book of Revelation had been amongst those texts most often translated into German in the late medieval period.[38]

Representations of biblical monsters were widely circulated in the sixteenth century, both textually and visually, thanks to a programme of translation and illustration fostered by the Reformation and the printing revolution, and monstrous births and biblical monsters were juxtaposed in the increasingly accessible print culture of post-Reformation sixteenth-century Europe.

In their exceptionally rich and stimulating co-authored study, *Wonders and the Order of Nature 1150–1750*, Daston and Park locate monstrous births at the heart of their history of wonder. They revise their earlier view that interpretations of monstrous births had progressed in a teleological fashion from a religious, or 'superstitious', system to one that was based on new scientific principles and a desire to observe and classify.[39] In their new study, they describe a world in which scientific and religious explanatory systems co-exist throughout the early modern period. Daston and Park's remarkable study has opened up the topic in a way that invites new interpretations. The more detailed study of German materials in this book leads to some new conclusions and emphases. In particular, this book seeks to demonstrate that there was an unexpected number of positive representations of monstrous births clustered in the period before the onset of the Reformation. In addition, religious interpretations of monstrous births not only co-existed with scientific interpretations, as Daston and Park emphasize, but actually seem to have grown in strength during the sixteenth century and become increasingly apocalyptic in tone.

Robert Scribner's seminal work on printed Reformation propaganda, *For the Sake of Simple Folk*, includes examples of monstrous births in the context of Reformation polemic.[40] In his essay 'The Reformation, Popular Magic and the

"Disenchantment of the World"', Scribner noted that phenomena like monstrous births were, prior to the Reformation, part of a 'moralized universe' in which 'moral deviance, both individual and collective, was reflected in natural deformity'.[41] While this widely held but overly general view will be nuanced in this book, the statement clearly delineates the nexus between morality, religion and the physical world in the early modern period. Scribner goes on to argue that this viewpoint was deepened and expanded by Protestants, to create a world view in which moral failings, individual and collective, incurred terrible and wondrous punishments.[42] As this book will demonstrate, Catholics, too, participated in the formation of this newly imagined world, shaped by religious disorder and the rise of print and with the specific reference point of monstrous births.

Scribner's emphasis on visual culture when discussing monstrous births is particularly valuable for understanding the specifically visual aspects of their representation. The vigorous, graphically engaging visual images of the sixteenth century are central to this study. The etymological link between the word 'monster' and the verb *monstrare* (to show) goes back at least as far as Augustine, who saw monstrous births as demonstrating something significant in a visual form. Nonetheless, the relationship of monstrous births to the visual culture of the early modern period is little understood, perhaps because the topic has been neglected by art historians. Indeed, monstrous creatures were often represented during this period in prints that are, by the standards of the time, artistically crude, mass-produced and derivative. Yet these graphically forceful images are deserving of more detailed iconographic and stylistic analysis, as this book aims to demonstrate.

The sixteenth century offers a rich array of visual and textual materials for understanding natural wonders and prodigies. Indeed, the visual culture of early modern monstrous births is often best encountered through illustrated print catalogues.[43] These materials were first brought to scholarly attention by Aby Warburg's seminal essay on prophecy and astrology in Martin Luther's time, although monstrous births appear in it only incidentally.[44] The essay focuses upon the culture of prophecy and prodigies in late fifteenth- and early sixteenth-century German lands. Warburgian art historians including Rudolf Wittkower and Fritz Saxl also developed an interest in signs and prodigies.[45] Wittkower, in particular, was nonetheless dismissive of the appeal of 'popular pamphlets' to the 'largest, worst educated and most superstitious section of the population ... After the invention of printing this method was chosen to advertise monstrosities far and wide'.[46] His comments underline the fact that it is only relatively recently that crudely printed and mass-produced broadsheets and pamphlets have received acceptance as useful sources for understanding widely held cultural attitudes.[47] More recent cultural and intellectual studies emphasize that monstrous births are capable of illuminating important social preoccupations.[48]

This book is concerned with German-language materials, and recent German scholarship has demonstrated some aspects of the complexity of these sources, their great abundance and their relationship to broader social, cultural, political and religious issues.[49] Rudolf Schenda's work forms a crucial bibliographical foundation, and evidence of the widespread nature of the phenomenon.[50] In other European scholarly traditions, Jean Céard's groundbreaking French study of 1977 is oriented towards French material and towards literary culture, but is woven through with analyses of the Renaissance revival of interest in the culture of prodigies in the classical world, and the pan-European intellectual understanding of monstrous births during the sixteenth century.[51]

The incorporation of Warburgian visual analysis into cultural history has contributed to a broader sense of the possible sources available to historians, and encouraged the increasing use of images as historical sources.[52] The last several decades have seen the rise of a new mode of cultural history in which, as Peter Burke urges, the historian might think of 'cultures' in the plural; work with a considerably broadened and loosened definition of culture; focus more on the adaptation and the active reception of culture than on tradition; and give more weight to representation, invention and imagination as social forces.[53] A significant aspect of this type of cultural history has been the rise of interest in the methods of the Warburg school of image analysis and a concomitant cultural history that is both social and intellectual in character. Scribner's work on crude but powerful woodcut images in the German Reformation, on the polemics of visual print culture, and also the affective power of the visual in this culture, have been a key element of the reassessment of early modern printed images as historical sources.[54] More recent work on the nexus between visual culture, religious change and the natural world (both wondrous and everyday) during this period advance still more complex models of the visual as a significant historical force.[55]

Some of the most innovative recent scholarship examines religious art, especially work produced during periods of religious conflict, and pays less attention to aesthetic qualities than to the work's devotional and affective power.[56] Images of monstrous births have a peculiar relationship to religious images, as their content is primarily secular. Yet they become so connected to the religious debates of the period that their relationship to religious visual culture is undeniable. Daston and Park have revised existing narratives about a 'progression' from religion to science by arguing for the co-existence of the two in relation to wonders. Scribner has taken issue with the traditional Weberian idea that the Reformation led to a 'disenchantment of the world', and as such was the harbinger of modern society.[57] In a similar vein, Peter Parshall has recently observed – in relation to the interpretation of natural events in an eschatological climate – that although there is a temptation to separate scientific interpretations from those based upon a theological world view, in the final analysis 'the dictates of reason and manifest evidence of the irrational were in a constant state of tension'.[58]

Not only images but also texts are crucial components of sixteenth-century publications on monstrous births. This book examines sources that were often consciously aimed at a variety of readers and viewers of varying levels of literacy and education. Formerly more sharply drawn distinctions between 'high' and 'low' culture tend to have been blurred in recent examples of cultural history.[59] Popular print culture is no longer necessarily regarded as low or unsophisticated culture.[60] Intersections between popular and elite or learned culture are underscored by the very broad cultural fascination exerted by monstrous births. Most of the sources examined here are of the sort that were not inventoried or otherwise recorded, and it is difficult to ascertain their reception. However, through close and contextualized examinations it is possible to see how they appropriated and responded to earlier publications, current events and important themes in sixteenth-century German lands. The great variety within the sources is the best testimony to the broad appeal and cultural significance of monstrous births.[61]

This book is a cultural history of monstrous births in print culture during a period of intense religious change and conflict. It is for the most part a chronological study, and structured as a series of analyses of different types of printed publications. These sources combine images and German texts, and were aimed at very wide audiences and markets.[62] They range from the crudest prints to the most accomplished, and those with cursory descriptive texts as well as complex inter-textual polemics. Cumulatively, the book analyses the most significant types of representation to emerge between the late fifteenth and late sixteenth centuries. It examines single sheet and pamphlet publications by humanists, physicians, artists and Reformers; the emergence of illustrated books dealing with the theme of monstrous births and other wonders; a Counter-Reformation reworking of a theme more commonly associated with Protestants; and proliferating reports that emphasized the great and disturbing multitude of such births.

Above all, this book is concerned with the meanings that people of the time ascribed to monstrous births and how these meanings can be understood by examining printed sources. It places considerably more weight than any previous study on the positive interpretations given to monstrous births in the period immediately preceding the Reformation. It argues for a rise in negative and apocalyptic readings as the sixteenth century progressed, and proposes that this reached a peak just past the middle of the century following a decisive turning point during the Reformation, to be followed by publications that injected new life and new topical concerns into the theme of monstrous births. Chapter 1 examines a series of broadsheets published in the 1490s that combined poems by the humanist Sebastian Brant with crude but dynamic images of monstrous births. Brant's broadsheets demonstrate a relatively new interest – given impetus by developments in printing technology – in individual, locally-born monstrous creatures; and how these creatures were quite distinct from the exotic monstrous races that were depicted in enduringly popular publications like John Mandeville's *Travels* and Konrad von Megenberg's *Buch der Natur*. Brant's humanist colleagues also contributed to this newly intensified interest in monstrous births, associated with the reign of Holy Roman Emperor Maximilian I (1493–1519).

Broadsheet representations that were aimed at increasingly wider audiences flourished from the turn of the sixteenth century. The imagery of monstrous births published in the early decades of the century forms the focus of Chapter 2, and especially prints created by leading artists including Albrecht Dürer and Hans Burgkmair the Elder. This was a famously fertile period in the history of German art, and especially graphic art. Nonetheless, images of monstrous births have been relatively neglected in studies of visual culture during this period. The chapter situates these images within contemporary artistic debates and trends, including Dürer's own writing. Through a focus on the representation of conjoined twins, the chapter demonstrates the great variety of approaches that were adopted by artists and authors in representing monstrous births. It draws out the complexity of these images, in which an urge towards naturalistic representation was combined with an evident deployment of artistic artifice and trends drawn from the broader visual culture of the period.

Monstrous births took on overwhelmingly negative overtones as they became part of Reformation polemic. They simultaneously became more directly and frequently linked with apocalyptic imagery. Chapter 3 looks at two of the most important examples of monstrous births from the first half of the sixteenth century: the Monk Calf, born in Freiberg in 1522, and the more visually bizarre Papal Ass, washed up on the banks of the Tiber in Rome in 1496. These creatures were polemically analysed in a 1523 pamphlet written by Martin Luther and Philipp Melanchthon, who allegorically interpreted the creatures' body parts as they lambasted the Catholic church. The bodies of the monsters became texts to be read and argumentatively decoded using highly visual language.

These singular monsters gave way to a great multitude as the century progressed. Chapter 4 examines the proliferation of books depicting monstrous births and other wonders that appeared in a wave in the 1550s. These books were produced with a variety of purposes in mind: as medical and midwifery manuals, as natural history studies, and above all as books of wonders. This chapter closely examines three early and richly illustrated examples by the Protestant authors Jakob Rueff, Job Fincel and Konrad Lycosthenes. While these books used broadsheets as sources, they moved away from the tendency within broadsheets to present monstrous births as individual and unique phenomena, and towards a focus on the cumulative effect of such events. In particular, Fincel and Lycosthenes developed a strongly Lutheran account of the history of the world.

This was one in which prodigies like monstrous births, dramatically multiplying in numbers in their own lifetimes, were signs of the coming Last Days.

German print publications on monstrous births are often characterized as almost exclusively produced by Protestants during this period. Chapter 5 examines a highly complex, understudied broadsheet that presents an unusual Catholic interpretation of the theme. Titled the *Ecclesia Militans*, and published in 1569, it combines a polemical poem by the Catholic exponent of Counter-Reformation polemic, Johann Nas, with an extraordinary image in which well-known monstrous births from throughout the century are jumbled together in an almost carnivalesque sequence which includes biblical figures overwhelmingly drawn from the apocalyptic Book of Revelation. This broadsheet draws together previously circulating ideas about monstrous births, tumultuous religious changes and apocalypticism, in a graphically dramatic format that appropriates and inverts themes previously developed by Lutheran authors. By this point of the century, monstrous births and the apocalyptic Book of Revelation were closely enmeshed, and overwhelmingly presented as such in German Reformation and Counter-Reformation print culture.

As second- and third-generation Protestantism became stressed and fractured during the later decades of the sixteenth century, new publications appeared that still interpreted monstrous births in apocalyptic terms. Many of these publications depicted events that took place in towns and cities under special strain: those in which Calvinism and Lutheranism struggled for ascendancy, for example, or from border towns in Inner Austria under threat during the Habsburg-Ottoman War of 1593–1606. Monstrous births still offered ways to make sense of a disordered world, and to continue religious debates. But by this stage monstrous births were increasingly more likely to be presented alongside other misbirths or wonders. A greater focus on children born with multiple heads, on multiple births, and on the capacity of some monstrous births to speak, led to new and often more complex narratives about and representations of monstrous births. The world of the wondrous had grown in iconographic variety, imaginative complexity and political, religious and social significance by the close of the sixteenth century to become a rich cultural resource. Print culture and religious turmoil had turned monstrous births into iconic figures in a world teeming with disturbing wondrous signs. The trajectory of that process is traced in the following pages.

1 FROM MONSTROUS RACES TO MONSTROUS BIRTHS: SEBASTIAN BRANT AND THE INTERSECTION OF HUMANISM, PRINT CULTURE AND MONSTROUS BIRTHS AROUND 1500

In the 1490s, Basel-based author Sebastian Brant published a series of works intended to gain the praise of fellow humanists, the interest of a much wider public audience and the political patronage of Holy Roman Emperor Maximilian I. This chapter examines how a group of broadsheets by Brant, published in both German and Latin and illustrated with vigorous woodcuts, gave a new place in public life to singular, local monstrous births. It will also examine the ways in which these monstrous births were perceived as quite distinct from the exotic monstrous races that had been the most frequently represented form of monstrous body in medieval culture. Sebastian Brant utilized short publications to promote his interpretations of monstrous births. Broadsheets and pamphlets, with their potential to reach large audiences, were at a critical early stage of development during this period.[1] While short publications aimed at wide audiences had not yet reached the dramatic explosion in numbers of the early Reformation,[2] writers like Brant were working together with publishers to create products with a wide appeal. These were publications that combined text and image in dynamic ways to inform the public, literate and illiterate alike, about current events. Their development coincided with the early stirrings of a flourishing and consciously self-confident period in German art, especially graphic art.[3] These broadsheets incorporate illustrations that range from crude but graphically dynamic to technically and conceptually sophisticated. They testify to the range of possible approaches during this period of innovation.

The late fifteenth and early sixteenth centuries occupy a distinctive point at the close of the medieval period and prior to the dramatic changes set in motion by the Reformation. As printing technologies became increasingly accessible, the subsequent Reformation and post-Reformation periods saw a larger number of broadsheets and pamphlets reporting monstrous births, while from the middle of the sixteenth century a new wave of compendium-style books also began to appear. Accordingly, the wealth of sources from the 1520s onwards has tended to sideline the earlier material and the pre-Reformation period has received little attention in recent studies. Yet, while the sources from around 1500 are fewer in number and less easy to link to major social and intellectual changes, they are notably diverse and often complex in content. In fact, the years around 1500 are precisely the period when it is possible to see a tangible shift of interest from the monstrous races that lived at the margins of the world, to individual monstrous births that might have occurred in a nearby village.[4] Hartmann Schedel's 1493 *Weltchronik*, produced at considerable expense in both German and Latin by the major Nuremberg publisher Anton Koberger, was one rich contemporary source of knowledge on matters religious, geographical, political and historical, and it provides a compelling example of the shift that Brant exemplifies. This chapter traces that shift and the new ideas and context that it provided for innovators like Brant.

The monstrous races entered the publications of medieval and early modern Europe via classical authors.[5] Ktesias of Knidos, a royal physician in fourth-century BC Persia, as well as Megasthenes, who was sent to India in *c.* 303 BC by Seleucus Nicator in the wake of Alexander the Great's campaigns, both prepared influential texts incorporating passages on monstrous races. Megasthenes's observations were diffused through the work of other classical authors, and above all those of Pliny the Elder.[6] Authors like Pliny, Augustine and Isidore, who discussed monstrous births, also related tales of the monstrous races as examples of natural wonders, and they became a regular source of entertainment and instruction.[7] Despite their far-flung locations, the monstrous races were increasingly drawn into a Christian world view. One group of Middle High German Poems known as the *Vienna Genesis* (1060–1170) proposes, for example, that Adam had a number of children who were born with physical deformities.[8] These children subsequently generated further corruptions in the human race:

> Some had heads like those of dogs; some had their mouths on their breasts, their eyes on their shoulders; they had to make do without a head. Some had such large ears that they covered themselves with them. One had a single foot, very large; with it he ran quickly as the animals in the forest. Some bore children which went on all fours like cattle. Some completely lost their beautiful coloring: they became black and disgusting, and unlike any people. Their eyes shone, their teeth glittered. Whenever they revealed them, they made even the devil terrified. The descendants displayed on their bodies what the forebears had earned by their misdeeds. As the father had been inwardly, so the children were outwardly.[9]

In narratives like this, ideas about unique monstrous births become intermingled with ideas about the origins of monstrous races. Distant monstrous races were increasingly represented during the later medieval period in travel narratives. These manuscripts fostered the rise of visual representations of the monstrous races, providing a pool of imagery that could be drawn upon as printed images were developed. Various versions of the travels of Alexander appeared, often illustrated, as did editions of the apocryphal twelfth-century letter by Prester John, an equally apocryphal Christian king who ruled a marvellous kingdom in India and told of it in this text.[10] One of the most famous and enduring travel narratives was John Mandeville's well-known *Travels*, examined below. It made a highly successful transition into widely available printed sources and in doing so touched on monstrous births. The *Itinerary* of contemporary author John Witte of Hesse, which details his journey to the Holy Land that commenced in 1389, did not make such a dramatically successful or enduring transition to print.[11] However his records of monstrous races, including Pygmies, Cyclopes and men with two faces, place him within the same tradition, and indicate something of the popularity of this theme.

The monstrous races were represented, too, in late fifteenth-century encyclopedic compilations about the natural world. Konrad von Megenberg's *Buch der Natur*, for example, was a staple of manuscript editions and was also prepared as an illustrated printed book published in October 1475 by Johann Bämler in Augsburg.[12] The final chapter, on 'wondrous springs and strange humans',[13] dealt specifically with the monstrous races, and the associated wonder of magical springs (Fig. 1.1).[14] The accompanying woodcut illustration shows a dynamic parade of various members of the monstrous races, including the dog-headed

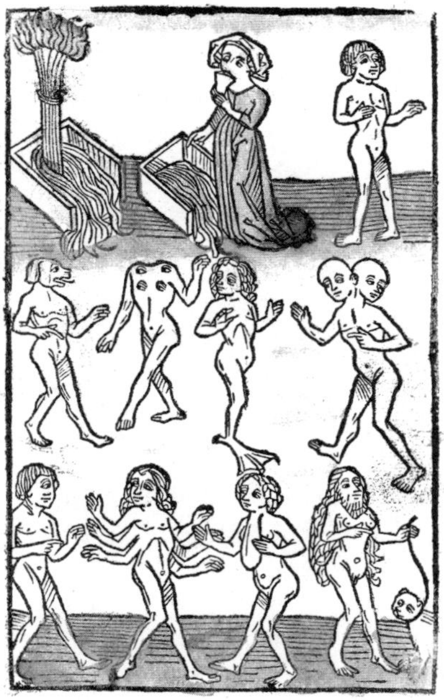

Figure 1.1: Wondrous springs and strange humans, from K. von Megenberg, *Hie nach volgt das buch der Natur* (Augsburg: Schönsperger, 1499), sig. E i v. Photo courtesy of the Herzog August Bibliothek Wolfenbüttel, shelfmark A: 45.1 Phys. 2°.

Cynocepahali, a member of the headless Blemmyae race, and a man with a single eye. Some are less well known: the man with six arms, the woman with a large goitre ('Kröpfe') and the bearded woman who, as the text makes clear, is taking her pet leopard for a walk, right out of the border of the image. The text, straightforwardly descriptive and derivative of sources such as Pliny, explains that these are all representations of monstrous races from distant lands. As the final chapter of the *Buch der Natur*, they form a kind of diversion and counterpart to the more domestic knowledge presented in the preceding chapters. No mention is made of individual natural creatures like monstrous births, whether human or animal: their appearance in print was still to come.

John Mandeville's *Travels*

John Mandeville's *Travels* recounts a marvellous journey to the Holy Land and beyond, and is notable for the strong narrative presence of Mandeville himself. He claims to be an English knight who has spent much of his life travelling the world after leaving England in 1322. Yet the true nationality of the story's author and his country of residence have been particularly vexed questions, with Mandeville sometimes even posited as the pen-name of an armchair traveller. There are a number of early manuscript versions, the original most likely being either French or Anglo-French, and written in 1356 or 1357.[15] German translations appeared in the 1390s, and were widely circulated in illustrated print versions in the second half of the fifteenth century. Michael Velser (given as Felder) translated the first of the two early German printed versions of the *Travels*, or, in German, *Reisen*. It was published in Augsburg by Anton Sorg in 1481 and contained over one hundred woodcuts.[16] A second German translation appeared in the same year. The translator was Otto von Diemeringen, a canon of Metz, and this edition, equally richly illustrated, was published by Bernard Richel in Basel.[17]

In one passage, the *Reisen* brings together monstrous births, monstrous races and biblical history in a manner reminiscent of the *Vienna Genesis*. An unillustrated section tells of Noah's son Cam (normally Cham), who was allocated Asia when the world was divided up after the flood. The text relates the story of Cam's descendants. These include his grandson Nimrod, whose wife, the story tells, lay with the devil and subsequently gave birth to deformed children who then formed a new race:

> from Cam's son was Nimrod born, the first king that ever was ... and to his wife the devil often came, and had his way with her, and from this she gave birth to humans that were against nature, one without a head, another with only one leg and truly wondrous ... they all came from Cam.[18]

While Mandeville demonstrates a deep fascination with the monstrous races, this passage is the closest that he comes to mentioning monstrous births. There is, however, an intriguing additional section in Michel Velser's German translation of the 1390s. Velser occasionally adds his own comments and observations to the text, as is the case in one extended passage that describes how an Egyptian family hatched chicken eggs by warming them in an oven.[19] Velser concludes this story by reporting a more recent event that he saw as equally wondrous. A bird had laid three eggs, and from the third of these a dog was 'hatched'. Velser had seen this dog with his own eyes: 'I, Michael Velser, who translated this book into German, saw it myself'.[20] He also saw the bird, 'the size of a goose', which was kept in the garden.[21] The addition of a contemporary and singular wonder in this revised German edition of Mandeville indicates that interest in such singularities, as distinct from the monstrous races, was starting to become a significant part of the world of monsters and marvels.

The Nuremberg *Weltchronik*

These connections are evident in different and more substantial ways in the richly illustrated Nuremberg World Chronicle or *Weltchronik*, one of the landmark book publications of the late fifteenth century. It was published in Nuremberg in 1493 by the printer Anton Koberger following a complex collaboration with author Hartmann Schedel and designers Michael Wolgemut and Hans Pleydenwurff.[22] The *Weltchronik* is structured as an account of the six ages of the world, in which the events of the Old and New Testament lead into more recent history.[23] The book is particularly interesting in terms of the printed representation of the monstrous birth for two reasons. First, it gives a very clear sense of the differentiation between and even shift of interest from monstrous races to monstrous births in a major publication of the late fifteenth century. Second, it includes some of the first known printed and widely available representations of monstrous births in Germany. While the accompanying textual passages are often brief, the images of both monstrous races and monstrous births that appear in the *Weltchronik* are distinctive because each is used only once. Many of the other woodcut illustrations, in contrast, are used repeatedly to illustrate quite different places and people.[24] An unillustrated broadsheet in Latin text advertising the *Weltchronik* – carefully kept by its author Hartmann Schedel – indicates how people of the time might have seen monstrous births, and what interest they held for them. The book is described and praised in both prose and poetry, and the poem promises to inform the reader about 'heavenly, terrible signs / Comets, and many gruesome misbirths'.[25] Wondrous natural signs could provide entertainment as well as being a retrospective marker of significant historical turning points, a commentary on current events or a guide to the future, and nearly all representations of monstrous births fulfilled several of these qualities.

The images of monstrous races in the *Weltchronik* are condensed into only two pages, and are chronologically located in the second book, 'Das ander alter der werlt': the age of Noah and the second of the six ages described in the book. They appear in three vertical strips with twenty-one figures in total (Fig. 1.2); the third strip borders a world map.[26] These often naked, adult, dynamically-posed figures include the headless Blemmyae, the dog-headed Cynocephali and the Sciapod sheltering underneath his single huge foot. The text presents them as the descendants of Noah, much as was the case in Mandeville's *Travels*, although the details of the lineage are glossed over. The *Weltchronik* monstrous races are both metaphorically and literally pushed to the margins or borders. Structurally, they take on the role of border decorations, so often composed of literally grotesque bodies in which the play of artistic fantasy acted as a counterpoint to more sober visual information conveyed in the centre of a picture. The meaning of marginal images, and hence, creatures, was by no means certain. Entertaining and diverting, they could lead the viewer's imagination off on tangents.[27] Like the demonic, fantastic church decorations that were condemned in the twelfth century as distractions to piety by Bernard of Clairvaux, monstrous creatures evaded clear and unambiguous definition and prompted wonder.[28] Geographically marginal, too, these members of the monstrous races were far removed from the lives of European *Weltchronik* readers.

By the late fifteenth century, the two distinct phenomena of monstrous races and monstrous births might lead to similar imagery and indeed appeal to similar audiences for similar reasons, but were nonetheless characterized as ontologically distinct and were to become even more so. This separation primarily took place because the monstrous races remained distant inhabitants of faraway lands represented in travelogues. Unlike many of the marvellous animals that were recorded by travellers and eventually brought back to Europe – dead or alive – most of the monstrous races were never given any sort of concrete verification. John Block Friedman notes an increasing scepticism towards the monstrous races from the Renaissance onwards, despite the continuing fascination that they exerted.[29] The 'savages' of the New World might partly fill this increasing gap. However, the unique monstrous birth which could be verified and documented in the new broadsheets appears to have best met a need to experience the marvellous as something tangible, and particularly as a sign of God's working in the world. Lorraine Daston and Katharine Park argue that a feature of the late medieval period is a growing emphasis on 'verification through personal experience and oral report'.[30] That is, the marvels of the East, the monstrous creatures of strange lands, are described in narratives that emphasize the personal engagement and

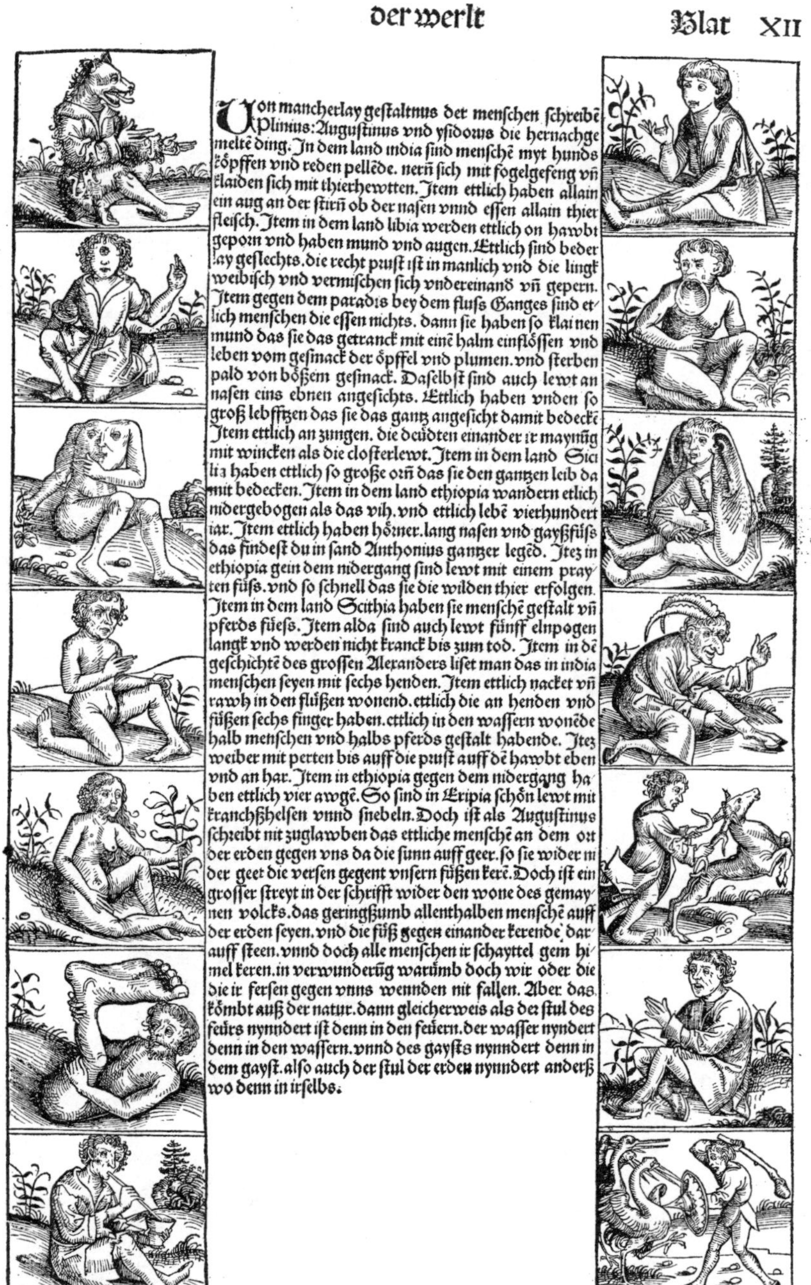

der werlt Blat XII

Von mancherlay gestaltnus der menschen schreibẽ
Plinius: Augustinus vnd ysidorus die hernachge
meltẽ ding. In dem land india sind menschẽ myt hunds
köpffen vnd reden pellẽde. nerñ sich mit fogelgefeng vñ
klaiden sich mit thierhewtten. Item ettlich haben allain
ein aug an der stirñ ob der nasen vnnd essen allain thier
fleisch. Item in dem land libia werden ettlich on hawbt
gepom vnd haben mund vnd augen. Ettlich sind beder
lay geslechts. die recht prust ist in manlich vnd die lingk
weibisch vnd vermischen sich vndereinand vñ gepern.
Item gegen dem paradis bey dem fluss Ganges sind et-
lich menschen die essen nichts. dann sie haben so klainen
mund das sie das getranck mit einẽ halm einflössen vnd
leben vom gesmack der öpffel vnd plumen. vnd sterben
pald von bössem gesmack. Daselbst sind auch lewt an
nasen eins ebnen angesichts. Ettlich haben vnden so
groß lebffitzen das sie das gantz angesicht damit bedeckẽ
Item ettlich an zungen. die deudten einander ir maynũg
mit wincken als die closterlewt. Item in dem land Sici
lia haben ettlich so große orñ das sie den gantzen leib da
mit bedecken. Item in dem land ethiopia wandern etlich
nidergebogen als das vih. vnd ettlich lebẽ vierhundert
iar. Item ettlich haben hörner. lang nasen vnd gayßfüss
das findest du in sand Anthonius gantzer legẽd. Itez in
ethiopia gein dem nidergang sind lewt mit einem pray-
ten füss. vnd so schnell das sie die wilden thier erfolgen.
Item in dem land Scithia haben sie menschẽ gestalt vñ
pferds füess. Item alda sind auch lewt fünff elnpogen
langk vnd werden nicht kranck bis zum tod. Item in dẽ
geschichtẽ des grossen Alexanders liset man das in india
menschen seyen mit sechs henden. Item ettlich nacket vñ
rawh in den flüßen wonend. ettlich die an henden vnd
füßen sechs finger haben. ettlich in den wassern wonẽde
halb menschen vnd halbs pferds gestalt habende. Itez
weiber mit perten bis auff die prust auff dẽ hawbt eben
vnd an har. Item in ethiopia gegen dem nidergang ha-
ben ettlich vier awgẽ. So sind in Eripia schön lewt mit
kranchßhelsen vnnd snebeln. Doch ist als Augustinus
schreibt nit zuglawben das ettliche menschẽ an dem ort
der erden gegen vns da die sunn auff geer. so sie wider ni
der geet die versen gegent vnsern füßen kerẽ. Doch ist ein
grosser streyt in der schrifft wider den wone des gemay-
nen volcks. das geringßumb allenthalben menschẽ auff
der erden seyen. vnd die füß gegen einander kerende dar-
auff steen. vnnd doch alle menschen ir schayttel gem hi-
mel keren. in verwunderũg warũmb doch wir oder die
die ir fersen gegen vnns wennden nit fallen. Aber das
kömbt auß der natur. dann gleicherweis als der stul des
feürs nynndert ist denn in den feüern. der wasser nyndert
denn in den wassern. vnnd des gaysts nynndert denn in
dem gayst. also auch der stul der erden nynndert anderß
wo denn in irselbs.

Figure 1.2: Monstrous races, from H. Schedel, *Register des buchs der Croniken vnd geschichten* [the *Weltchronik*] (Nuremberg: Anton Koberger, 1493), f. XII r. Photo courtesy of the Herzog August Bibliothek Wolfenbüttel, shelfmark A: 1.4 Hist 2°.

experiences of a trustworthy narrator. This desire on the part of audiences grew even stronger, they argue, when it came to monstrous births.

The *Weltchronik*'s monstrous births are much more carefully integrated into a chronology of historical events than the monstrous races at the beginning of the book. The first illustrated example in the *Weltchronik* dates from the year AD 614 and is concerned with two children, shown engagingly juxtaposed with a comet and remarkable rainbow (Fig. 1.3). The children are described as one aspect of a range of 'various wondrous and shocking things [that] appeared during this time in Greece'.[31] The 'great rainbow' ('großer regenpoge[n]') is, perhaps surprisingly, the event that is linked specifically to a contemporary (that is, seventh-century) fear that the end of the world was coming.[32] All these events take place in the time of Muhammad and his 'vbeltat' or evil deeds. The children are cherubic in appearance, child-like and therefore distinct from the more adult bodies of the monstrous races depicted at the beginning of the *Weltchronik*. One child has a double set of arms and legs. The other has two heads. However, the text only mentions the first, four-footed, child. The second child, with two heads, seems to be an addition by the book's designers and certainly adds visual and conceptual symmetry to the arrangements of woodcuts on this page. The double heads balance the double limbs, and each child is seated on a grassy patch of ground below an illustration of turbulent events in the sky overhead. The decision to add this image seems to have been a deliberate one, as the block is not used anywhere

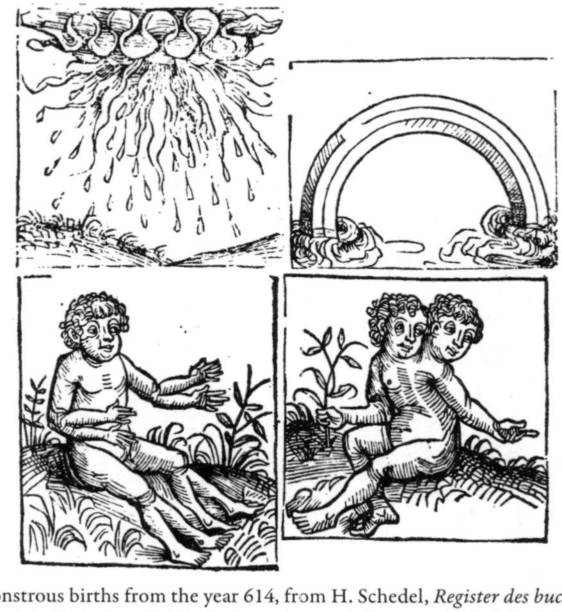

Figure 1.3: Monstrous births from the year 614, from H. Schedel, *Register des buchs der Croniken vnd geschichten* [the *Weltchronik*] (Nuremberg: Anton Koberger, 1493), f. CLI r. (detail). Photo courtesy of the Herzog August Bibliothek Wolfenbüttel, shelfmark A: 1.4 Hist 2°.

else in the book. It is the first of a number of examples in the present book of the ways in which text and image could deviate from one another. This is the most complex arrangement of misbirth images in the *Weltchronik*. The next is an unchildlike figure with one lower body, and – above the waist – two fully-formed bodies, born in 1004 in 'dem land vasconia', or Gascony (Fig. 1.4). Each of the two figures drinks from a cup, and gestures with his free hand. Despite the symmetry of pose, gesture and appearance, the brief text, as well as describing the body, draws a distinction between them, stating that 'and when one of them ate the other slept'.[33] Similar cases of conjoined twins will be examined soon; cases in which the meaning of dissonant actions in conjoined twins is given metaphorical value. Here, however, it remains simply a subtle difference between the image and the text.

The *Weltchronik*'s next example of a misbirth, born in 1128, is accompanied by even less textual information. Schedel simply writes of how 'a woman gave birth to a wondrous shape with a double body. In front it was human and behind a dog' (Fig. 1.5).[34] It is a similar figure to the previous example, with two highly symmetrical, outward gesturing conjoined twins, although with the notable difference that one has the head of a dog. This enigmatic birth is included in a passage which describes the unhappy events that took place during that year, against the background of unrest in the kingdom of Aragon during the reign of Alfonso I (depicted on the same page). Two final illustrated examples date from 1277 (Fig. 1.6). The first of the two images on this page represents a figure with the head of a child and the body of a lion. The child was born to 'a nobleman's wife in the bishopric of Constance'.[35] Perhaps because of this elite status,

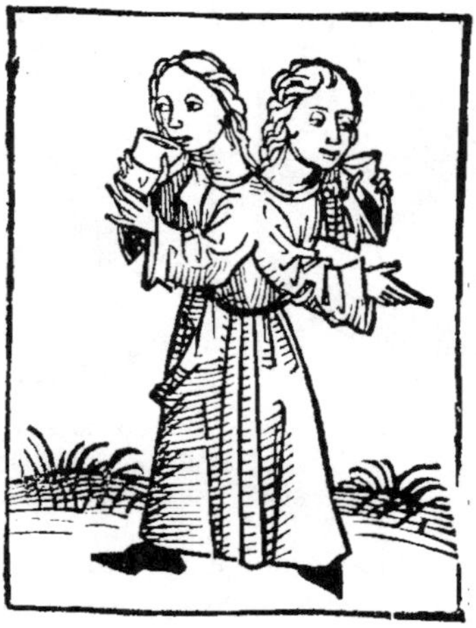

Figure 1.4: Monstrous birth from the year 1004, from H. Schedel, *Register des buchs der Croniken vnd geschichten* [the *Weltchronik*] (Nuremberg: Anton Koberger, 1493), f. CLXXXII v. (detail). Photo courtesy of the Herzog August Bibliothek Wolfenbüttel, shelfmark A: 1.4 Hist 2°.

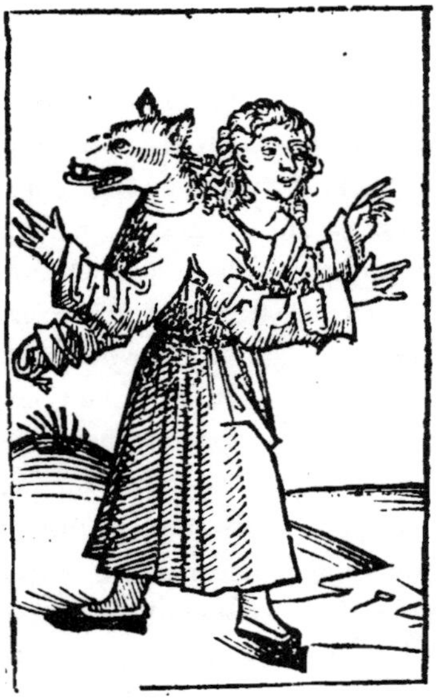

Figure 1.5: Monstrous birth from the year 1128, from H. Schedel, *Register des buchs der Croniken vnd geschichten* [the *Weltchronik*] (Nuremberg: Anton Koberger, 1493), f. CXCVIII r. (detail). Photo courtesy of the Herzog August Bibliothek Wolfenbüttel, shelfmark A: 1.4 Hist 2°.

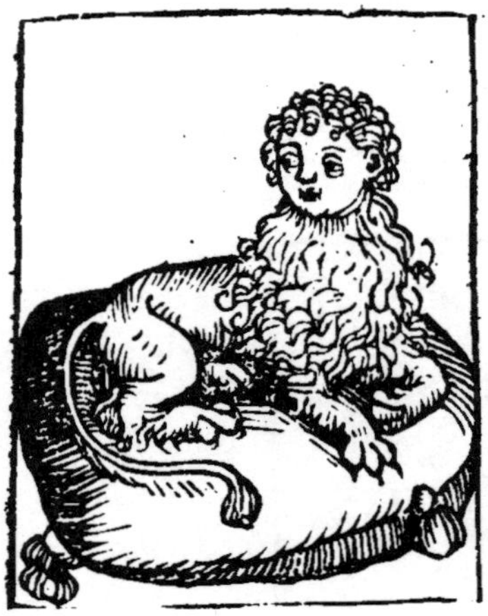

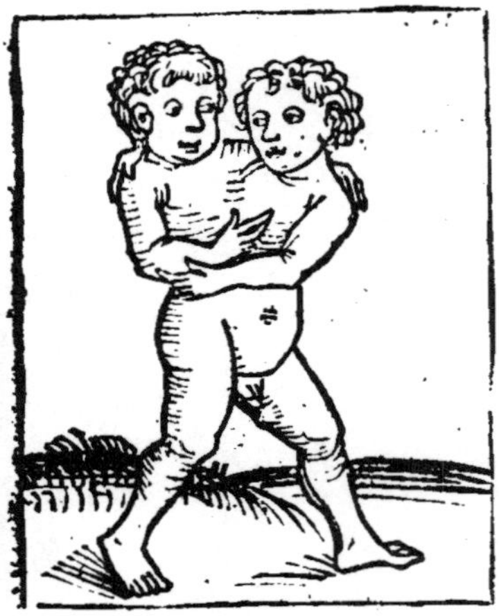

Figure 1.6: Monstrous births from the year 1277, from H. Schedel, *Register des buchs der Croniken vnd geschichten* [the *Weltchronik*] (Nuremberg: Anton Koberger, 1493), f. CCXVII r. (two details). Photo courtesy of the Herzog August Bibliothek Wolfenbüttel, shelfmark A: 1.4 Hist 2°.

it is shown elegantly posed on a cushion like a favourite pet. The second illustration depicts conjoined twins born in Esslingen, briefly described in the text with the added information that the children died within an hour of their birth. The illustration shows them standing unaided, unnaturally strong and apparently smiling at each other. While none of the misbirths reported in the *Weltchronik* are given extended analysis or commentary, they are certainly differentiated and located within varying historical contexts in the way that the monstrous races in the book were not. They provide a way of understanding monstrous births as historically significant events of local relevance. Here, they are presented in a lavishly produced book that would have had a limited audience. But they were soon appropriated and adapted for inexpensive, rapidly produced and more accessible publications by Sebastian Brant.

The Culture of Prodigies during the Early Reign of Maximilian I

For *Weltchronik* readers in 1493, the history presented by the book was in a continuum with the present. That year marked the beginning of the reign of Emperor Maximilian I (1493–1519). Although this period is frequently seen through the prism of the coming Reformation, it was marked by distinctive events of its own. These included civil disturbances like peasant uprisings, local alliances and violent conflicts in Swabia and Bavaria in particular, and disruptive external factors like the growing Turkish threat.[36] Increasingly, these events and fears were reported and discussed in broadsheets and pamphlets, just as monstrous births were, and people at all levels of society often saw them as intimately connected.

Daston and Park identify three major responses to the monstrous birth in the early modern period: horror (or terror), repugnance and pleasure.[37] Negative readings would appear to have dominated interpretations of monstrous births in the classical, medieval and early modern periods. Only the third category of response – pleasure – indicates a positive reading of the monstrous birth. Daston and Park's discussion of the category of 'pleasure' is focused on the later sixteenth and seventeenth centuries, and on monsters understood as having at least partly natural causes.[38] While they have established more clearly than earlier scholars the distinctive features of the monstrous birth, their concept of a positive response seems open to both nuancing and expansion through a close study of sources from the early sixteenth century. Negative interpretations of the phenomenon of monstrous births were not nearly so certain in the years leading up to the Reformation, as Klaus Littger has recently noted.[39] The majority of broadsheets in this chapter and the next represent conjoined twins – textually and visually – in a variety of ways that indicate an understudied diversity of responses to human monstrous births in the years around 1500. The children in a number of these publications could be described in various positive ways: as omens of good fortune; as ordinary, appealing babies placed in a domestic setting; or as metaphors for political unity. Some broadsheets do, in fact, present the children in ways that are not only positive, but move the viewer, going beyond a sense of pleasure at seeing something literally marvellous to a sympathetic acknowledgement of the children's humanity.

Wondrous natural signs took on special significance during the reign of Maximilan I. During this period many scholars analysed biblical dates and looked for natural and other signs of the Last Days. The year of 1484 was marked by the great conjunction of Saturn and Jupiter in Scorpio, and the expectation of dramatic events that would flow from this conjunction. The concept underlying this activity was astrological, and focused on the actions and influences of the stars and the planets. However other natural phenomena, including monsters, were drawn into these interpretative efforts. Johann Lichtenberger's prophecies, first published in 1488 as the *Prognosticatio*, drew on the 1484 writings of Paulus van Middleburg, amongst others.[40] Lichtenberger's *Prognosticatio* was frequently republished from 1490 and dominated thinking on the nature and interpretation of prophecies and wondrous signs.[41] It brought together astrology and prophecy, and in the tradition of Joachim of Fiore, looked for signs of a Last World Emperor. Lichtenberger had been resident at the court of Emperor Frederick III in the 1470s as the court astrologer, although he later fell out of favour.[42] Lichtenberger's *Prognosticatio* was apocalyptic in tone, although not directed towards any kind of social conflict or upheaval. He identified Friedrich III and then, when Friedrich proved disappointing, his son Maximilian, as the great leader of the End Times.[43]

Authors associated with the court circle of Emperor Maximilian I produced compilations of astrological signs and wondrous natural phenomena, which sometimes included monstrous births. The cultural historian Aby Warburg drew a useful distinction between what he characterized as 'artificial' and 'miraculous' divination (astrology being the former, monsters and other portents the latter), while nonetheless demonstrating how in practice the two forms of divination intersected in many texts from this period.[44] In an illustration for a 1501 manuscript on prodigies by the humanist Joseph Grünpeck, a variety of monstrous births are shown in a bizarre audience with Maximilian I, who surveys a varied range of wonders that had appeared during his reign (Fig. 1.7).[45] They include the conjoined twins of Worms, the eight-legged Landser sow and the double-headed Guggenheim goose. This manuscript illustration is a reminder that elite publications, produced primarily for an elite audience, could be, and were, influenced by broadsheets, as the artist is primarily drawing upon broadsheets from the 1490s by Sebastian Brant, discussed below. Grünpeck joined Maximilian's Innsbruck court in 1497, and is best known as the Emperor's biographer and secretary.[46] Grünpeck was involved in the supply and preparation of astrological documents for Maximilian, although he left the court in late 1501 or 1502 ill with syphilis. He was heavily influenced by the work of Lichtenberger.[47] His 1501 manuscript reports the best-known misbirths of the preceding decade,

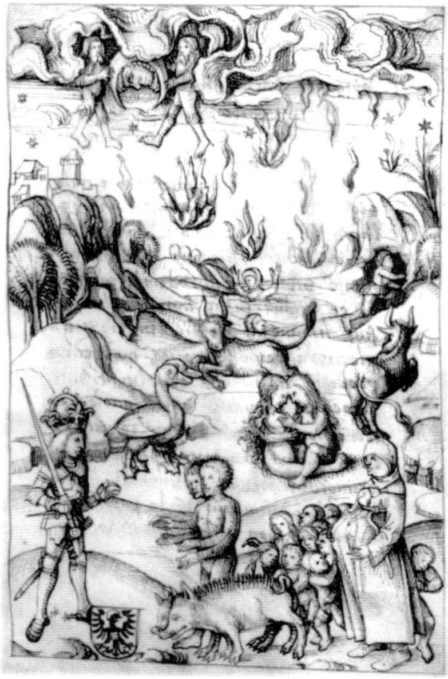

Figure 1.7: Monstrous births and natural wonders shown with Emperor Maximilian I, from J. Grünpeck, 'Prodigiorum, ostentorum et monstrorum quae in saeculum Maximilianeum inciderunt, interpretatio' (1501), Universitäts- und Landesbibliothek für Tirol, Cod. 314, f. 6 r. Photo courtesy of the Universitäts- und Landesbibliothek für Tirol.

although he was considerably more interested in astrological explanations for such phenomena than in the political interpretations that Brant preferred, as discussed below.[48] He suggests that the birth of multiple children, for example, is governed by Venus in conjunction with Scorpio, while births with additional heads are governed by the position of Jupiter or Mars.

Another humanist at Maximilian's court who wrote on the topic of wonders and monstrous births, Jakob Mennel, seems effectively to have taken over Grünpeck's role.[49] Between 1501 and 1503 in particular, Mennel reported upon and publicized wondrous and strange signs in the region. His most substantial work on the topic is the 1503 manuscript titled 'De signis, portentis atque prodigiis' ('Of Signs, Portents and Prodigies') which includes several small illustrations of monstrous births by the so-called 'Mennel master'.[50] There was a very pragmatic reason for the preparation of this manuscript and related activities: Maximilian was keen to publicize the occurrence of such signs to gather support for his plans to conduct a crusade against the Turks.[51] In this the manuscripts echoed Brant's broadsheets, which had also been created to serve political (amongst other) purposes, as the remainder of this chapter demonstrates. Relatively few people saw these manuscripts, although they are important reminders of how wonders were increasingly fashionable as well as politically significant in the early years of Maximilan's reign.

Sebastian Brant's Broadsheets

While the *Weltchronik* includes monstrous births, it was the publication of a number of broadsheets on monstrous births in 1495 and 1496 by humanist Sebastian Brant that cemented their place in print culture and gave them a much wider audience. Basel- and later Strasbourg-based Brant prepared verse texts in both German and Latin, and analysed the significance of the births in some detail.[52] Brant is today remembered primarily for his 1494 *Narrenschiff* ('Ship of Fools'), a moralizing and satirical collection of poems on the theme of human folly. This richly illustrated publication achieved great popularity and led to many translations and new versions, including a Latin translation by Jakob Lochner published in 1497 with a new preface by Brant. The combination of witty but misanthropic text with images that harshly satirized human folly touched a popular nerve. The *Narrenschiff* took full advantage of the new medium of print, reaching a large and receptive audience. Brant's richly illustrated 1501 edition of Aesop's *Fables* is another vivid combination of text and image.[53] The book is in two parts, the first a collection of the fables from Aesop as well as other authors, and the second a collection of anecdotal descriptions of many unusual things, drawing upon Ovid, Homer, Aristotle and Pliny, and including descriptions of the monstrous races.[54] One passage is concerned with abnormal births, and more precisely the bearing of many children in one pregnancy.[55] Citing Aristotle, Brant relates the case of a woman who had given birth to five children, all of whom had rapidly sickened and died, as did the mother. Brant tops this with:

> a still more astounding and perhaps previously unknown natural wonder: a woman from eastern Franconia (which is a part of Germany) has in the year in which we are writing, that is in the year 1500, over the course of eighteen months given birth to fifty-two children, who (excepting nine miscarriages) were all properly formed and received baptism.[56]

Just as Michel Velser added his story of the bird egg that contained a dog to Mandeville's *Reisen*, Brant expands his compilation of earlier, classical sources with a reference to a contemporary wonder. The picture that accompanies this passage combines the two stories. The woman from the earlier story is shown in bed surrounded by her five babies. To her side, the German woman who had given birth to fifty-two children in the year 1500 is shown sitting with her hands raised as though in prayer. A deliberately uncountable mass of babies clusters on the floor around her. Two have been differentiated, however: one points at the first birth scene, while the other gestures to his praying mother. The reader or viewer is evidently being offered a comparison here. In the past, an important multiple birth had involved five children. In the reader's own time, this number had escalated to the dramatic total of fifty-two. The text and especially the image tells the reader and viewer that they live in extraordinary times, full of signs from God; an idea also being deployed for Maximilian's use by Joseph Grünpeck and Jakob Mennel at just this time.

Manuscripts and even books were not, of course, accessible to the great majority of people. Brant's broadsheets from the 1490s, however, were aimed at a larger audience. Brant helped to shape the print culture in which dramatic, localized, polemical events and debates could be rapidly diffused to a large audience. He used illustrations to dramatize his texts and make them more appealing or meaningful to a wide variety of readers and viewers. Indeed, Brant took a special interest in the illustration of his works. This led to his involvement in book publication projects with artists of great talent, including Albrecht Dürer.[57] In her recent study of several of Brant's broadsheets, Vera Sack emphasizes Brant's special interest in the illustrations for his texts. She notes that he regularly claimed to have 'gemalt' (painted or represented) his illustrations himself. Such claims are clearly not intended to mean that he literally drew up the images.[58] Rather, they should be taken to mean that Brant conceived and planned the pictorial elements: the figures; the background elements; the incorporation of text; and perhaps the composition of the images. Brant's contribution to the development of the representation of the monstrous birth through the medium of the broadsheet is hard to overestimate, in particular through his ability to bring together words and images in ways designed to appeal to the widest possible audience.[59]

The Conjoined Twins of Worms

Brant's earliest broadsheet reporting a natural wonder dates from 1492 and reports the dramatic case of a meteor that had landed in the town of Ensisheim.[60] The broadsheet is dedicated to Maximilian, the 'Romischen kuning' (Roman king), or Holy Roman Emperor-in-waiting. However, Brant's first broadsheet on a monstrous birth dates from 1495. It was prompted by the birth of conjoined twins on 10 September 1495 in Bürstadt, 7 km east of the free imperial city of Worms, which lies on the Rhine in the Rhineland-Palatinate. The broadsheet is known as *Von der Wunderbaren geburt des Kindes bei Wormß* ('On the Wondrous Birth of the Child near Worms'), and was published in Augsburg in 1495 by Johann Schoensperger (Fig. 1.8).[61] The twins were born shortly after the 1495 Worms *Reichstag* or Diet, partly accounting for their notoriety, and they were rapidly and closely associated with Worms rather than their birthplace, Bürstadt.[62] This was a tumultuous period in the Empire. Maximilian I had been the uncrowned Holy Roman Emperor and King of the Romans since 1486,

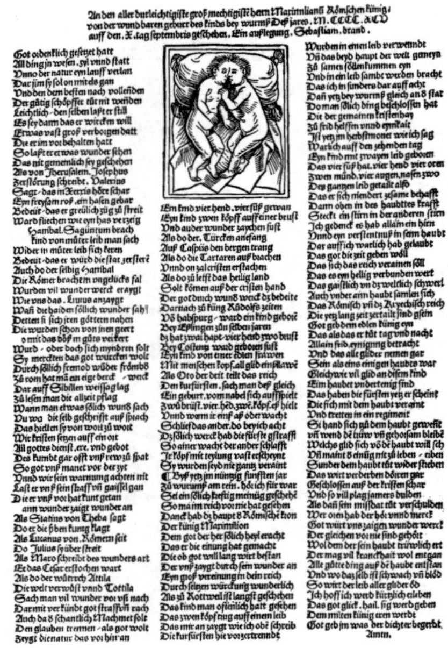

Figure 1.8: Conjoined twins born near Worms, from S. Brant, *Von der Wunderbaren geburt des Kindes bei Wormß* (Augsburg: Johann Schoensperger, 1495). Photo courtesy of the bpk / Staatsbibliothek zu Berlin / Inkunabelsammlung, Inc. 253.

effectively ruling jointly with his father until the latter's death in 1493. Like his father before him, he was engaged in difficult negotiations with the Estates.[63] Led by Berthold von Henneberg, Elector, Archbishop of Mainz and arch-chancellor of the Empire, they demanded greater political and financial control in return for the funds that Maximilian was so desperate to levy to aid his various war campaigns and to defend his lands against the Turkish threat. The Diet took place from March to August of 1495, although Maximilian did not reach an agreement of sorts with the Estates until 1497. These wrangles – complicated by reluctance on the part of the princes for reform – were a feature of his reign. Late 1495, in the wake of the Diet, was a particularly dramatic time, and Sebastian Brant makes a number of references to the unrest in his poem. It runs to three columns of text, and is in fact dedicated to Maximilian I. This dedication is more than formulaic, as Brant addresses many of his arguments directly to the Emperor.

Brant begins by asserting that 'God has arranged in an orderly manner / All things in existence, purpose and condition'.[64] Sometimes, however, he must disorder the natural world as a warning in times of great need. This is a point restated a number of times in the poem. Brant differs from many other early modern authors of broadsheet texts on misbirths by bringing to his analysis knowledge of the use of portents and prodigies in the ancient world. References to classical authors and political leaders including Livy, Valerius, Xerxes, Hannibal, Caesar and Attila testify to Brant's humanist knowledge and also to his understanding of the importance that the correct analysis of natural prodigies had played in the course of history. He includes cases of towns and cities attacked and devastated – Jerusalem, Saguntum, Thebes – and emphasizes that God's warning signs were not always acted upon: 'often repentance comes to us too late'.[65] In some cases, the worship of heathen gods had exacerbated disasters. The ultimate purpose of wondrous signs, in Brant's view, was to advance the spread of Christianity. Brant effectively appeals to Maximilian to make himself one of the great figures of history; one who performs deeds to the glory of God. The poem is imbued with his sense of urgency about the Turkish threat, a pressing issue in Maximilian's Austrian lands.[66] The polemical interpretation and deployment of wonders remained central to Maximilian's political aims over the next several years, as Mennel's 1503 manuscript – intended to shore up support for a campaign against the Turks, discussed above – demonstrates.

In the second column of his 1495 Worms broadsheet Brant begins to discuss specific cases of monstrous births. These seem to be almost certainly based upon illustrated descriptions of misbirths in the 1493 Nuremberg *Weltchronik*. The closeness of the intellectual world and print cultures occupied by the makers of the *Weltchronik* and Sebastian Brant is striking. Brant's earliest broadsheet on a natural wonder, reporting the 1492 comet of Ensisheim, was owned by Hartmann Schedel and was the basis for a passage in the *Weltchronik* reporting the meteor.[67] The first misbirth described in Brant's broadsheet is a child with four hands, four feet and two heads born during the reign of the 'shameful Muhammad' ('schantlich Machmet'). Dating from the seventh century, Brant's inclusion of this pair emphasizes to the reader his view of the long-standing nature of Islam's threat to the Christian world.[68] The second example is a child born in Esslingen with two heads, four hands and two chests during the thirteenth-century reign of Rudolf I, the first German Habsburg king. It is immediately followed by the case of a child with a human head and a lion's body, born to a 'noble woman' ('edeln frawen') in Constance.[69] A further example records the birth of a child who had two chests, four arms and two heads, and was born during the reign of Emperor Otto III (980–1002). Otto, called 'Oroder drit' by Brant, had put particular effort into expanding and unifying the Empire, ultimately unsuccessfully, and was responsible for the election of the first German Pope, Gregory V. The *Weltchronik* records that this birth took place 'in dem land vasconia' (Gascony) in 1004. It seems likely that there was some confusion here, as the *Weltchronik* relates the birth to 'Bishop Odo' rather than to Otto III.[70] Brant is either correcting what he sees as a mistake, or deliberately twisting his source to bring in the example of another Emperor with a particular interest in unification.[71] These children, Brant points out in line with the *Weltchronik*, do not act in a unified way; when one eats, the other sleeps, and so on. Finally, he refers to the case of a child recently born in Rottweil with two heads and one body. This case, he argues, is like the electoral princes ('kurfürsten') who would like to have one body with two heads; that is, dispersed leadership of the Empire that would reduce the power of the Emperor.

These last two cases in particular are implicitly compared to the case of the Worms twins, discussed in some detail in the third column. Brant is at pains to establish fully the physical appearance of what he describes as one child, not two:

> One child born with two bodies
> With four feet, four hands, four ears
> Two mouths, four eyes and two noses
> The whole body thus apportioned[72]

Brant speculates on the implications of the conjoined foreheads, concluding that the child had only one brain, and therefore only 'eyn verstentnuß' (one understanding, or more literally, mind). This is not a simple observation, but instead an opportunity for Brant to draw out an extended and very contemporary political metaphor. He notes that the twins were born in the same place as the recent discussions on the structure of the Empire (that is, Worms, rather than Bürstadt). He then goes on to argue how the child, with many limbs gathered together under one ruling head, is an apt metaphor for the correct way to organize and rule the Empire itself.[73] This is clearly intended as a message to those members of the Estates who had sought to negotiate a reduction in the Emperor's power at the 1495 Diet. Brant even suggests that the child provides a model for the reconciliation of the western and eastern (that is, Greek) Christian churches; a challenge that he also hopes Maximilian will rise to.[74] His support for Maximilian is absolute, and one of the final lines of the poem observes that 'all good things come from the head'.[75] There is no doubt that for Brant piety is a crucial part of the response to the twins, but so too is engaged political action and policymaking.

Two quite different images were used for the German and Latin editions of Brant's broadsheets on the Worms twins. The German edition shows the girls lying together on a single cushion. While the image is simple, it has an air of tenderness and the children are entirely unthreatening. Its odd, self-enclosed domesticity seems removed from the dramas of history, religion and politics that Brant's poem conjures up. However, it was possibly constructed as a metaphor for the ideal of unity that Brant is so concerned to express and argue for in his poem. In the same year of 1495 a Latin edition was published in Basel by J. Bergmann von Olpe (Fig. 1.9).[76] The text is in most respects similar, although

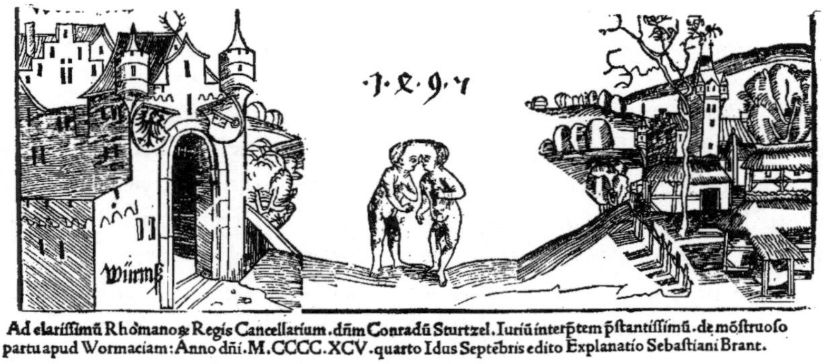

Figure 1.9: Conjoined twins born near Worms, from S. Brant, *De Monstruoso partu apud Wormacium* (Basel: J. Bergmann von Olpe, 1495), detail. Photo courtesy of the Universitätsbibliothek, Basel.

certain differences point to its narrower and more elite audience. The most notable differences are the inclusion of a brief discussion of the influence of the stars on current events, and a passage that encourages the princes – in any case more inclined at this time to uphold the status quo – to support Maximilian.[77] Brant's tone is conciliatory and he urges the need for unity in the empire. Finally, perhaps to make room for these additions, he includes fewer examples of misbirths from earlier periods in the Empire. The poem is dedicated to Konrad Stürtzel, Maximilian I's court chancellor. While the content and political intention of this poem is fundamentally similar, the image accompanying it seems quite different. This woodcut illustration creates a sense of veracity, political significance and currency that seems more in tune with the text. The children stand at the centre of the horizontal panel, their bodies opening out in a mirror-like, upright pose that is physically quite unfeasible for newly-born children though typical of many later broadsheet images of monstrous births. They are joined at the forehead, and so lean intimately towards each other, and appear to look deeply into one another's eyes. The year is printed prominently above them, emphasizing to purchasers and readers of the broadsheet the currency of the event. To the left and right of the twins, relatively detailed landscapes are depicted. These make up the city of Worms and its surroundings, the status of the city confirmed by the coats of arms at its gate. One, representing a key, is the lesser arms of the city of Worms, a reference to the fact that Peter was its patron saint, while the second is the imperial coat of arms.[78] The village on the right of the image most likely represents Bürstadt, the actual birthplace of the twins. The broadsheet image informs the reader or viewer that the monstrous birth is not only very recent chronologically, but also very close geographically. Unlike the monstrous races that lived at the margins of the world, this monstrous birth is an event, the image suggests in tandem with the text, which demands attention.[79] These separate and quite different images for different editions of Brant's poem show how diverse approaches to representing monstrous births could be.

The Worms twins were made famous through publications like Brant's, and even appear in another of his broadsheets, discussed below. The new medium of the broadsheet fostered the rapid circulation and copying of news and visual models. The twins appear, for example, in a broadsheet published in Erfurt in 1500 by Hans Sporer (Fig. 1.10).[80] The text is considerably shorter than Brant's erudite poem, and the image is, in both design and cutting, cruder than the images for his broadsheets. Like Brant, the author here refers to the twins as singular, 'such a child' ('Eyn. soelich. kint'), and notes that this child still lives ('lebt noch'). The relative longevity of the Worms twins was a remarkable thing, and worth the issuing of a broadsheet five years after the original birth.[81] The broadsheet emphasizes this fact with a rather startling image that is a reminder of the diversity of possible representations: the twins, by this time only about five years old, are represented as fully-grown women. The text also reports that Maximilian I gave the girls ten guldin. This adds weight, retrospectively, to Brant's 1495 attempt to link the children's appearance with the actions of the new ruler. Another striking representation of the Worms twins can be found in theologian Thomas Murner's 1499 *Inuectiua contra Astrologos* ('Invective against Astrology'; Fig. 1.11).[82] Here, they stand alongside the double-headed imperial eagle, echoing, in perverted, reversed form, its heraldic, symbolically abnormal body. Murner uses the twins to attack astrology, following Augustine who was one of the commentators to have queried why twins born at the same time might lead such different lives despite their matching astrological profiles. The logic of using conjoined twins to make this argument is not entirely clear, but certainly furnishes Murner with a graphically compelling example that would attract attention to his pamphlet.[83]

Thanks to such a wide variety of publications, the Worms twins did not disappear into obscurity. Indeed, they appeared over half a century later in Sebastian Münster's 1550 *Cosmographia*, amongst other compilations of wonders and similar books that became popular around mid-century. Münster claimed personally to have seen them in Mainz in 1501, when 'they were six years old. They were two girls and did not live to be more than ten years old.'[84] Evidently, the death of the girls around 1506 was also well known. This celebrated case of twins joined at the forehead seems to have contributed to the visual representation of the idea that conjoined twins possessed a particular emotional bond, and not merely a shared physical destiny. A broadsheet reporting the birth of twins in Strasbourg on 6 May 1511 is one example that represents two girls joined at the stomach but clasped in one another's arms and staring intimately into one another's eyes.[85] They have long, plaited hair and unchildlike bodies, possibly also suggesting that

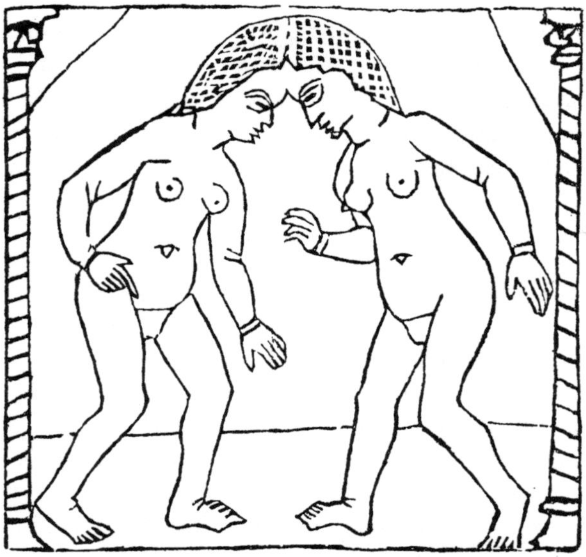

Figure 1.10: Conjoined twins born near Worms, from Anon., *Eyn. soelich kint ist geboren ein meil von W[o]rms* (Erfurt: Hans Sporer, 1500), detail, in A. Schramm, *Der Bilderschmuck der Frühdrucke*, 23 vols (Leipzig: Karl W. Hiersemann, 1922–43), vol. 13 (1930), fig. 319. From the collection of the author.

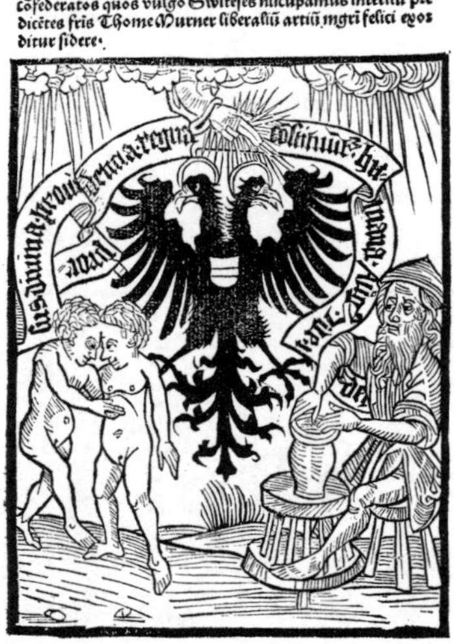

Figure 1.11: Conjoined twins born near Worms, from T. Murner, *Inuectiua contra Astrologos* ([Strasbourg]: [Hüpfuff], 1499), title page. Photo courtesy of the Herzog August Bibliothek Wolfenbüttel, shelfmark A: 70 Quod (10).

the unusually long-lived Worms twins had helped shape a trend to represent misbirths as considerably older than their age.[86] The distinctive nature of conjoined twins and their representation in pre-Reformation German print culture will be returned to in the next chapter. This chapter, however, concludes with another facet of Brant's broadsheets: his interest in animal rather than human misbirths, and their political value during Maximilian's reign.

The Landser Sow

The following year, Brant prepared new broadsheets publicizing and analysing the birth of the wondrous sow of Landser on 1 March 1496. The creature was born with one head and two bodies, just like the Worms twins. The broadsheet was published in two editions: one German (Fig. 1.12), and a Latin edition.[87] Both were illustrated with the same woodcut, in which the animal looks, as Colin Eisler so memorably writes, as though it is 'fox-trotting' with itself.[88] The extended accompanying poem, recently the subject of a careful study by Sack, goes some way towards explaining the almost comical and certainly unsubtle image.[89] The text begins with a reference to the great number of wondrous events or 'wunderwercks' appearing in the world. The hand of God lies behind them, Brant writes, although this point is made with considerably less emphasis than in the Worms broadsheet. He moves swiftly to an overview of monstrous children born recently, and places them within the context of other natural phenomena like meteors and earthquakes. Brant also reminds his readers at this point of the twins born in Worms in 'recent days' ('kurtzen tagen'). In the second column Brant turned to the specific case of the Sow of Landser, and records that 'herr Cristoffel von hattstat' (Christoph von Hattstatt, the magistrate with responsibility for Landser), had brought the sow to his attention.[90] In a personalized reminiscence, Brant describes the creature, which 'was gruesome enough to see'. It had four ears, eight feet, one head and 'from one throat two tongues'.[91] Brant

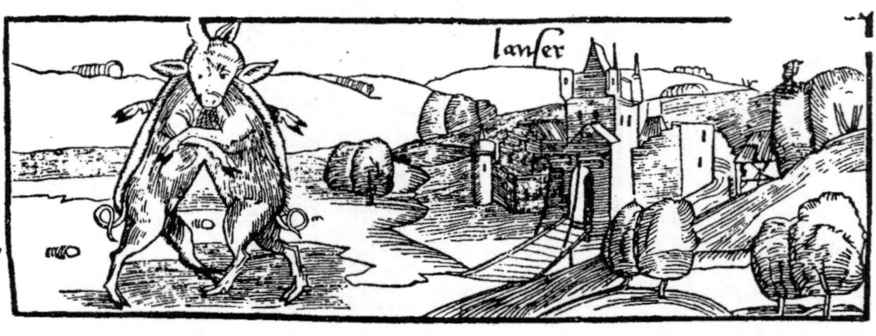

Figure 1.12: The wondrous sow of Landser, from S. Brant, *An den grosmechstigsten aller durchlichtigsten herren Maximilianu[s] … Von der wuderbaren Su zuo Landser* (n.p., 1496), detail, in P. Heitz (ed.), *Flugblätter des Sebastian Brant* (Strassburg: Heitz und Mündell, 1915), fig. 10. From the collection of the author.

does not draw any positive meaning from its physical similarity to the Worms twins. Indeed, this broadsheet demonstrates a rather different attitude to a monstrous birth on Brant's part, although with a similar political goal. He poses the key issue: 'but what will this sow bring us?', then immediately answers 'but what this sow means / I don't entirely know'.[92]

Despite Brant's seeming reluctance to extract meaning from the birth, he does make it clear that he sees it in a negative light. In particular, he writes that 'It doesn't please me / that it has this two-part tongue'. He explicitly compares the sow to the Worms twins, who, despite their deformities 'nonetheless had human shapes and ways'.[93] They had suggested to him the positive metaphor of the harmonious joining together of diverse elements within the Empire under Maximilian I's leadership, as well as the possible reconciliation of the Western and Eastern Christian churches. The sow is quite different, however, and Brant decides at this point: 'I fear that this sow represents / power in the hands of sow-like people'.[94] He therefore uses the sow of Landser to point to a disordering of political affairs. Following this, he argues for a concerted approach to external political dangers, above all the Turkish threat, and also domestic issues, notably the disruptions threatened by the *Bundschuh* peasant uprisings.[95] Fundamentally, Brant finds it hard to extract a positive meaning from this birth because the pig is such an ignoble animal, a 'repulsive unclean animal / that searches in dirt for all its delights'.[96] He immediately compares the pig to 'the Turks' ('der Türcken') who live, he writes, in a similar state. He then takes the argument a step further: 'the sow is brother to the Turk', and, finally, both are the same as the Antichrist ('dem endkrist').[97] The coming of the Antichrist was a sign of the Last Days, although Brant adds that only God can know the exact time that this will happen.[98] Brant's text places the Landser sow within an explicitly apocalyptic framework. This seems to be a relatively uncommon association for a monstrous birth in the late fifteenth and early sixteenth centuries, although it was to become formulaic from the Reformation onwards.

Sack has recently argued that the poem should be read as a satire, albeit one that addresses the serious political issues outlined above.[99] Brant does not take the monstrous birth seriously as a prodigy, she suggests, in distinction to his earlier broadsheets. Sack rests her argument particularly upon Brant's observation that he is pleased to discover that 'this wondrous swine ... did not live for long'. Indeed, it survived 'no more than one night'.[100] That is, if it had lived longer, Brant might have taken it more seriously.[101] There is an implied comparison here with the Worms twins, whose remarkable longevity (already six months old at the time the sow was born) was highly unusual. However, most misbirths did die immediately upon being born, and could be regarded as prodigies nonetheless. Brant's opinion on this point does not reflect the prevailing opinion, nor does it seem to have been influential.[102] Brant's broadsheets demonstrate the range of interpretations of monstrous births possible at this time. Indeed, his attitude in this particular case seems to be equivocal. While he concludes that the sow is not a prodigy, he discusses it as if it were for the purpose of promoting his political agenda and support for Maximilian I. Sack's argument that the broadsheet was a satire aimed at pleasing a small group of political and humanist allies seems somewhat overstated, given the larger audience for wonders addressed and partly generated through broadsheets like these.[103]

In June 1496 Sebastian Brant wrote that monstrous births 'appear to me to represent the common course of nature in our time'.[104] He was responding to the Strasbourg official Johannes Sigrist who had asked him to comment upon yet another misbirth, this time a child born with two heads. Brant declined. Indeed, there is only one more publication by him from the 1490s on monstrous births, and it lacks the political engagement of the previous examples. Brant's sense of the plenitude of monstrous births is, however, underlined by this new publication, which appeared in 1496 in both German and Latin editions. Each illustrated and reported four different misbirths: the Worms twins, the Landser sow, and conjoined geese and pigs (or rather piglets or 'Ferkel') born in Guggenheim in Alsace, 'two miles distance from Strasbourg'.[105] The broadsheet is dedicated to Albrecht, Duke of Bavaria and Bishop of Strasbourg. The Guggenheim pigs are represented twice, flanking the geese at the centre of the image and adding a graphically arresting edge to the image, as well as increasing the sense of a multitude of monstrous births. In the accompanying poem, Brant reflects in fairly general terms on the great number of monstrous, or wondrous, births that had appeared recently. He notes his own role in publicizing and discussing such cases 'that nature shows us / as I have often earlier written'.[106] For Brant, as for his contemporaries, it was ultimately the hand of God that lay behind nature in both its everyday and extraordinary forms, and it is this rather general conclusion that dominates his final broadsheet on monstrous births.

Brant virtually invented the genre of broadsheets reporting the birth of strange creatures as well as other natural wonders. His publications prepared the ground for the large number of publications on monstrous births that appeared in the sixteenth century. They demonstrate the variety of possible understandings of monstrous births at the close of the sixteenth century, while their engaging, graphically dynamic combinations of image and text underline the visual nature of the fascination exerted by monstrous births. The next chapter examines the phenomenon more closely, and its connection to the artistic culture of the early sixteenth century.

2 VISUAL CULTURE AND MONSTROUS BIRTHS BEFORE THE REFORMATION: ALBRECHT DÜRER, HANS BURGKMAIR AND CONJOINED TWINS

Sebastian Brant's richly textual broadsheets are illustrated with images that are crude in execution but possess an engaging vigour. From the 1490s onwards an increasing number of images of individual monstrous births were published in single sheet prints. Some of these were illustrated by leading artists, such as Albrecht Dürer and Hans Burgkmair the Elder. While the previous chapter established the shift from the monstrous race to the monstrous birth, this chapter examines representations of monstrous births in the context of developments in the artistic and broader visual culture of the period. It utilizes a variety of sources including Albrecht Dürer's own writing, and examines his attitudes towards natural wonders, monstrosity and artistic creativity. Lastly, it uncovers the variety and complexity of images of monstrous births in the years immediately preceding the Reformation. Many of the monstrous births discussed here are conjoined twins, and a number are even represented as propitious signs. Indeed, some monstrous births from this period were visually identified with one of the most revered figures imaginable in early modern culture: the infant Christ. This startling iconographic implication has gone unremarked in earlier studies, and positive representations of misbirths have in general received comparatively little attention. They are, therefore, the focus of this chapter. Yet negative representations of monstrous births, however, should not be overlooked, and this negative imagery, as the next chapter argues, finds a fuller and fundamentally apocalyptic expression during the Reformation.

The early sixteenth century is a celebrated period in the history of German art, and was perceived as exceptional even by contemporaries. There was a wave of optimism about German cultural accomplishment that endorsed the increasingly self-consciously creative abilities of German-speaking artists.[1] The rise of a deeply Christian humanism in northern Europe at this time had a profound impact on artists like Dürer, Burgkmair and Lucas Cranach.[2] These northern European artists became more artistically self-aware and their work demonstrates, as Craig Harbison expresses it, 'an attention to peculiar imaginative and personal experience'.[3] The flourishing artistic environment saw the rise of realistic genres, notably the landscape, the still-life and the portrait.[4] Visual verisimilitude or realism was a crucial component of these developments but it was a realism that was still heavily inflected by medieval spirituality.[5] In the field of printmaking – an area of dramatic development at the turn of the century and the following several decades – vast strides in technical capabilities advanced this complex visual realism.

Visual images were viewed in a context that extends well beyond our modern experiences of sixteenth-century visual culture, which is often preserved in hushed and sedate museums, churches and palaces. In early modern Europe, paintings, sculptures, textiles, drawings and especially prints were encountered in taverns, in fairs, in processions and in other environments that are lost to us today. This entwinement of visual culture with aspects of daily life, from high to low, increasingly interests historians as well as art historians.[6] Part of the vigour of early sixteenth-century visual culture was due to the growth of widely available printed images, particularly of secular subjects. Religious images for private devotion formed a major part of the new market for cheap, or at least affordable, prints. Secular images that had similar graphic qualities and an equally broad reach depict military parades, peasant festivals, moral and sexual relations between men and women, clothing, the new world and many other subjects.[7] These prints, while secular, are often bound up with ideas about morality, decorum and the transgression and inversion of social and bodily boundaries. The dramatic bodies of monstrous births form part of this vigorous graphic visual culture.[8] Robert Scribner emphasized the varieties and functions of visual experience when he observed that 'the emergence of naturalism and rationalism in German art ... had the effect of intensifying the emotional and moralising features of visual representation, indeed may even have heightened the magical power of the image'.[9]

In early sixteenth-century German art the representation of monstrosity, realism and fantasy could be intertwined. Nature, closely observed, was full of strange things that held the power to astonish. As a potentially deceptive sense, sight prompted suspicion, and the more realism and naturalism achieved by artists, the greater the potential for trickery.[10] The complex notion of realism in visual art is particularly important to this book and its concern with children and animals perceived as real but also as unnatural or monstrous. As 'witness' to these creatures, visual artists tried to represent both the reality and the preternatural drama of monstrous births. Veracity, or perhaps more precisely immediacy, was not always conveyed by sober, naturalistic documentation, but instead by artistic invention. The broadsheets examined in this chapter demonstrate a frequent interplay of naturalism (the artist's attempt to faithfully mimic nature) and fantasy (the artist's knowing deviation from natural models in the pursuit of invention).

Albrecht Dürer's Wondrous Sow

The wondrous sow of Landser, which featured prominently in several Brant broadsheets, also attracted the attention of Nuremberg artist Albrecht Dürer. He made an engraving of the creature that was published in 1496 (Fig. 2.1). This image almost certainly drew upon the Brant broadsheet because, despite the very different styles of representation, Dürer's engraving includes the castle in Landser that is also represented in Brant's publication.[11] Rainer Schoch cautions that the relationship of Dürer's engraving to the Landser sow is not absolutely clear, although the connection is extremely likely.[12] While Brant's broadsheet should be considered Dürer's most important source, he may also have been prompted or otherwise inspired by a stuffed conjoined pig that was on show in Nuremberg that Easter. According to Heinrich Deisler's *Nuremberg Chronicle* of 1488 to 1506:

> Item: during Easter two sows came here that had grown together and had only one head, and one of them had beneath its body four feet; altogether there were ten feet as the other sow had six feet.[13]

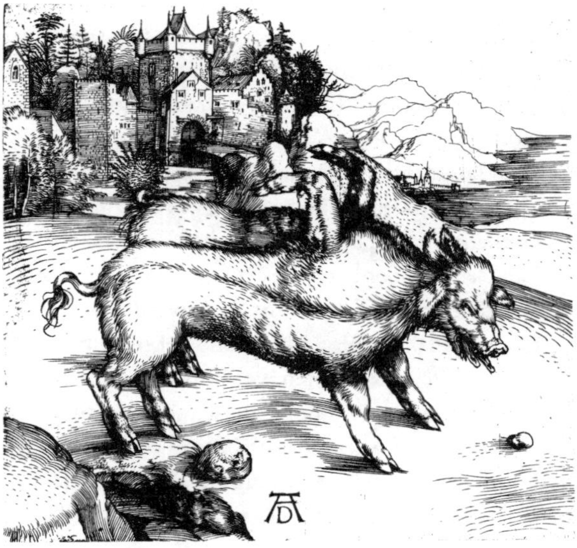

Figure 2.1: Albrecht Dürer, a pair of conjoined pigs, known as the monstrous pig of Landser (engraving, 1496). Photo courtesy of The British Museum, Department of Prints and Drawings, registration no. E,2.157. © The Trustees of the British Museum.

Dürer's engraving of the sow provides a rare opportunity to compare the representation of a specific monstrous birth created by an anonymous artist with one by a celebrated artist. In comparison with the crude woodcut images accompanying Brant's texts, Dürer's representation of the wondrous sow of Landser is without question the more accomplished and sophisticated, although not necessarily the more interesting; the two images engage the viewer in different ways. Dürer's print is in many ways the antithesis of the broadsheet images. It is finely rendered, naturalistic and indicates his fascination with and respect for the natural world. The creature stands on six legs, certainly a more feasible pose than in Brant's broadsheet image, although, unrealistically, it is depicted as larger and older than it would actually have been. The print contains no text at all, apart from Dürer's prominently placed monogram. It is only possible to speculate on why this might be so. Possibly the animal had become so notorious that Dürer felt that text was unnecessary. Possibly he felt the composition was sufficiently powerful without explanatory material. There is also another, more pragmatic explanation. This image is an engraving, while Brant's broadsheets were illustrated with woodcuts, in which the integration of text and image was more expected. Dürer's choice of engraving over woodcut is intriguing, and indicates that he intended from the outset to prepare a very detailed image. The print dates from the same year as Dürer's prodigal son engraving of 1496,[14] and the two projects may have been connected. The lively pigs and piglets in the prodigal son print were no doubt based on studies from life, and Dürer may have been intrigued enough by the case of the Landser sow to have produced this image at the same time. Clearly, there was a pragmatic factor to his interest, and he must have hoped to profit from the climate of fascination with portents and monstrosity that had become so important during the reign of Maximilian I. Despite the artist's fame, this image was not particularly influential. The choice of engraving as a medium, the lack of explanatory or polemical text, and the realism, detail and modelling of the figure, all combine to make this image unique.

The sow of Landser is the only printed image by Dürer in which the principal subject is a locally-born monstrous birth. Around this time, *c.* 1496–7, he also made a woodcut print that places the theme of monstrous births in a classical context. The image represents Hercules in triumphant combat with a pair of conjoined twins, although it is difficult to see that the twins, fallen together in combat and dressed in bulky armour, are indeed conjoined.[15] This is a highly unusual subject, not part of the normal range of Herculean iconography, and a particularly striking one for Dürer to select for his first print depicting a classical subject.[16] Dürer possibly returned again to the theme of monstrous births. A painting from 1527 of disputed authenticity, the *Head of a Bearded Child*, depicts the head of a child floating against a dark background. Its angelic face is framed with short curly hair and long, wispy side-whiskers and beard that are delicately traced against the dark background. Erwin Panofsky aptly and simply describes this image as 'enigmatical'.[17] It is a highly unusual image, not least because wondrous children like this were almost never represented in paintings.

It was during the earlier period of his artistic career that Dürer produced many of his detailed and sensitive nature studies.[18] The sow of Landser might strike the viewer, in the context of these sketches, as one more expression of Dürer's exceptionally close study of the natural world and his unprecedented attempts to capture the particularities of nature. Dürer's self-conscious conception of his own role as an artist was bound up with his belief that artists should look to nature as the most important source and model.[19] For Dürer, this was explicitly connected to the veneration of God, who had given artists special powers to depict his own creation, the natural world.[20] In 1512 Dürer began writing his theoretical work on human proportion, *Die lehre von menschlischen Proportion*, and completed it in 1528. The passages on aesthetic theory at the end of book three are rich in examples that explicate his ideas about creativity, the natural world and divine authority.[21] In one passage, Dürer exhorts his readers: 'don't diverge from nature in your imaginings, thinking that you want to find things for yourself; in that way you will be led astray'.[22]

This might sound restrictive. Yet Dürer's understanding of what nature encompassed was both broad and complex. His fascination with the natural world extended to bizarre natural phenomena, as his engraving of the wondrous sow of Landser makes clear. Whether in widely circulated prints or in sketches that remained in his personal collection, Dürer repeatedly gave visual form to connections between the natural, the fantastic, the monstrous, and the play of the imagination. In *Die lehre de menschlischen Proportion*, Dürer warned the reader:

> Yet let every man beware that he make nothing impossible and inadmissable in Nature, unless indeed he would make some fantasy (*Traumwerck*) in which it is allowed to mingle creatures of all kinds together.[23]

He also wrote, however, that artists are able 'every day to have fresh figures of men and other creatures to make and pour out which no one has seen or thought of before'.[24] Dürer's theoretical interests in *Traumwerck*, and more generally in artistic inventiveness, provide a context for his approach to the monstrous. He maintained an interest in representing and interpreting the significance of strange but nonetheless natural events. In 1503 he produced an annotated sketch recording how blood fell from the sky and left cross-shaped stains on the clothing of a female servant.[25] He wrote that this was 'the greatest wonder-work that I have seen in all my days', while the servant herself feared that 'she must die of it'.[26] In 1525 Dürer had a terrifying dream in which huge volumes of water fell from the sky, striking the earth with great force and causing him to wake in terror. His annotated sketch of this dream landscape concluded with the sentiment that 'God turns all things to the best'.[27] Dürer's understanding of nature as rich with mysterious signs evidently contributed to his desire to depict the natural world in its beautiful but also monstrous manifestations. However, his enthusiasm for monstrous births seems to have declined later in his life. In the third book of *Die lehre von menschlischen Proportion*, he writes:

> Take the images of the blind, the lame and withered cripples and cover them up. Everything is ugly in these due to the flaws. Also flee from excess; when you want to depict someone with three eyes, three hands and feet.[28]

Despite Dürer's early interest, it was his colleagues who went on to produce more startling and original images of monstrous births in the 1510s and 1520s, discussed later in this chapter.

The Conjoined Twins of Ertingen

Dürer certainly took up the theme of current and local misbirths in 1512 with a drawing of conjoined twins born on 20 July 1512 in Ertingen near Riedlingen, close to the Danube river in Swabia (Fig. 2.2). It is an image that underscores his interest in natural prodigies. As a drawing that does not seem to relate to any finished work, it points to a more private interest. Several broadsheets prepared by

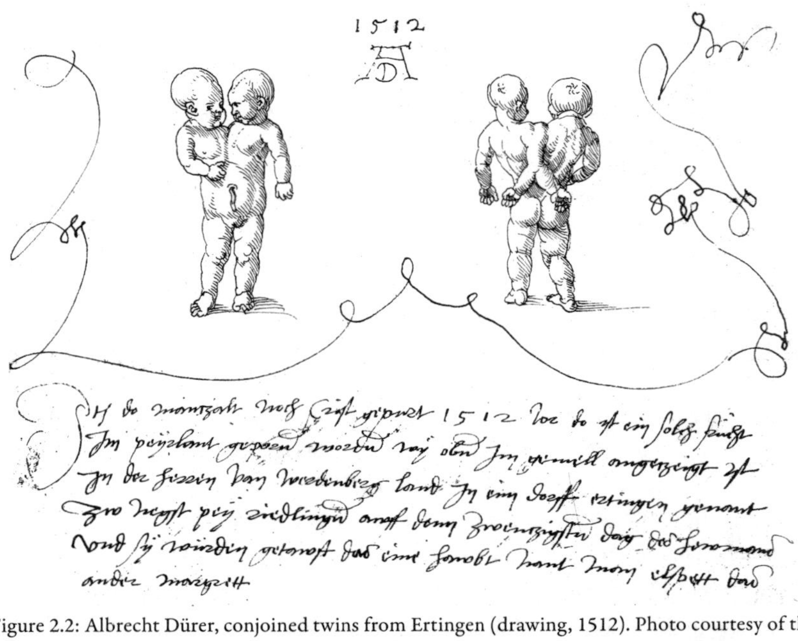

Figure 2.2: Albrecht Dürer, conjoined twins from Ertingen (drawing, 1512). Photo courtesy of the Ashmolean Museum, University of Oxford, registration no. WA1855.102 PI291.

lesser-known artists for much wider audiences also represent the Ertingen twins, and this cluster of connected materials is examined here. These broadsheets demonstrate a range of visual approaches and indicate the scope of interpretations attached to monstrous births in the period leading up to the Reformation. Dürer briefly annotated his sketch of the Ertingen twins, and the text is similar in style and content to the type of factual information that was to become increasingly common in broadsheets:

> Item: In the year after Christ's birth, 1512, a fruit [foetus] as shown in the above drawing was born in Bavaria, on the land of the Lord of Werdenberg, in a village named Ertingen near Riedlingen, on the twentieth of July. They were baptized and one head was named Elisabeth, the other Margaret.[29]

The sketch itself is a mixture of the probable and improbable. The dangling remnant of the umbilical cord is the most lifelike touch, and the most noticeable difference from the broadsheets of the twins that will be discussed shortly. But the pose of these excessively symmetrical bodies, with firmly planted feet and, in the rear sketch, over-defined musculature, is entirely fanciful. Dürer gives the impression that he is charmed rather than horrified by or fearful of these children, an impression underscored by the casual arabesque that decorates and frames the sketch. Dürer gives no indication that he personally saw the children, although the birth occurred in Bavaria and therefore reasonably close to home; a fact that may have sparked his interest. It is likely, however, that he instead based his drawing on a broadsheet depicting the same twins, a publication with two columns of text that are supplemented by an attached image (Figs 2.3 and 2.4).[30] Printed on both sides of the paper and intended to be turned over, the woodcut illustration shows the twins from both front and back. Double representations of monstrous births, although more often printed side by side, became fairly common in the sixteenth century.[31] Images like these could present the maximum amount of visual information about the body of a misbirth. Here, the girls are shown as impossibly sturdy and muscular. They are labelled Elisabet and Margareta, although this information is of dubious value, as these labels – unlike the clumps of flowers below – are not adjusted to correspond correctly on the reverse image. Elisabet and Margareta interact a little, particularly in the rear view on the reverse of the sheet where they look towards one another. The anonymous author establishes the location and date of the birth, and provides a new, shared name – Elßgred – for the twins. They were born, the author tells the reader, 'in the lands of the lord of Werdenberg',[32] a point repeated on each of the broadsheet dealing with this birth, and underlining the territorial nature of the Holy Roman Empire during the period. From the outset, the author presents misbirths in an ambiguous light and declares that they can have both positive and negative implications:

> Misbirths frequently take place
> They have two meanings
> To be misshapen means to be unlucky
> That which is properly formed has a good destiny[33]

The author presents several examples of misbirths that had occurred within the last several decades. First, the poem tells of two children born in Rain in Bavaria just before the 'Bavarian war' ('bayrischen krieg'), most likely a reference to the Landshut War of Succession of 1504 and 1505. The second misbirth described

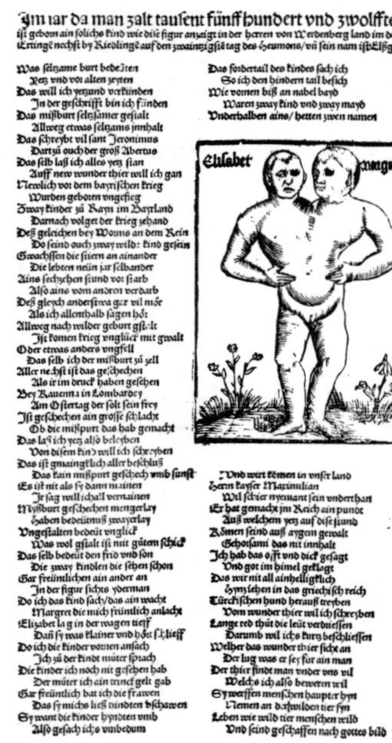

Figure 2.3: Elßgred, from Anon., *Im iar als man zalt tausent fünff hundertvnd zwolften ist geboren ain solichs kind ...* (n.p., 1512). Photo courtesy of The British Museum, Department of Prints and Drawings, registration no. 1876,0510.619. © The Trustees of the British Museum.

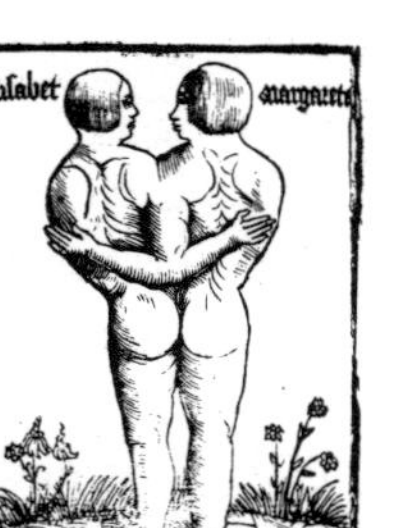

Figure 2.4: Elßgred, from Anon., *Im iar als man zalt tausent fünff hundertvnd zwolften ist geboren ain solichs kind ...* (n.p., 1512), detail. Photo courtesy of The British Museum, Department of Prints and Drawings, registration no. 1876,0510.619. © The Trustees of the British Museum.

is the case of the Worms twins, who – Brant's relatively positive contemporary interpretation notwithstanding – are considered as precendents for 'War, violent disasters / Or some other disaster'.[34] The reference was most likely to the localized, ongoing conflicts that took place in Swabia and Bavaria during this time, and which saw alliances formed and reformed primarily through the Swabian League.[35] As this broadsheet notes, the birth occurred in the lands of count Christoph of Werdenberg, a relatively important member of the Swabian League with extensive family connections and interests.[36]

The poem also reports the case of the notorious monster of Ravenna, born in Italy on 8 March 1512, and heralding what the author calls a 'great battle' ('grosse schlacht'), although he does not actually provide dates or other details. The battle was almost certainly the sacking of Ravenna by French, Spanish and papal forces on 11 April 1512. This case demonstrates how widely and also rapidly broadsheets showing monstrous births must have circulated. The author confidently refers to this very recent, foreign case, as one that 'you have seen in print'.[37] The birth of the monster of Ravenna had been recorded by a number of observers and chroniclers of the city of Florence including Marino Sanuto and Luca Landucci.[38] It quickly reached an interested public across Europe, with printed reports appearing in Latin and French in 1512, and Spanish in 1513.[39] The monster of Ravenna also became well known in German-speaking lands, as the Ertingen broadsheet indicates. Two extant German broadsheets individually record the birth, one dating it to 1506 and the other to 1512.[40] One represents the monster of Ravenna alone on barren ground, and its birthplace is given as Florence rather than Ravenna. The most important information conveyed is that 'our Holy Father the Pope' (at this time Julius II) was aware of the birth and had directed that the child should not be fed, but rather 'without food be allowed to die'.[41] As a handwritten annotation across the second broadsheet indicates, the print was acquired by Tegernsee Abbey, as was another broadsheet representing the Ertingen twins, discussed below.[42] The child's birth is described as 'a wondrous and shocking thing'.[43] It was born to a nun ('Closter frawen') in a nunnery close to Florence, lived only forty days, was fed and in fact showed a preference for 'confectionaries made of sugar and other sweet things'.[44] The various elements of and marks upon the child's hybrid body are noted, including three letters over its heart (IX and V) and an image of three flames below; a leg covered in scales; an eye on the knee; and how growing from its head was 'one horn just as Moses had two'.[45] While the child was interpreted in negative terms in Italy, and also in German lands later in the century, here there is a noticeable lack of interpretation, with the exception of the horn, which is in any case related to Moses rather than interpreted as devilish or otherwise disturbing.[46] Schenda rightly observes that 'horn, winged ears, scaley thighs and bird's claws are attributes of the devil'.[47] Yet the author of this broadsheet hesitates. First, no one knows 'whether it is a boy or a girl'.[48] Neither 'learned doctors of sacred scripture or the unlearned'[49] could read the letters on the monster's chest. Ultimately, writes the broadsheet author, 'one also cannot know whether it means good or evil'.[50] The diabolical possibilities of this monstrous birth remain undeveloped in the German context in this period – something that certainly changes with the Reformation.[51]

The Ertingen twins are like the more bizarre hybrid-bodied monster of Ravenna, the writer is presumably suggesting, because they, too, are dramatic natural signs that cannot and should not be ignored. In this Ertingen broadsheet, the nature of the girls' physical deformities is described in some detail, and the author recounts having given the mother a tip or 'trinkgelt' so that she would turn them over, much as the reader or viewer of the broadsheet is encouraged to turn over the image to see the children front and back. This anecdotal, personalized moment is echoed in another passage, which also indicates a level of sympathy for the twins and an apparent desire to represent them very much like ordinary babies:

> The two children indeed looked
> In a friendly way at each other
> As the picture shows everyone
> When I saw the child and one awoke
> Margret gave me a friendly smile
> Elizabeth lay deep in the basket
> She was smaller and fast asleep[52]

The text, in this case, differentiates between the two girls – here given separate names again – much more than the images. Margret is bigger, and smiles at the author, while tiny Elizabeth sleeps. Indeed, there are several shifts between references to one and two children, typical of this type of publication. Despite the intimacy of the scene, Klaus Walter Littger notes that it has ambiguous and potentially negative implications: because the actions of the twins are not alike, they might herald negative events.[53] The author of the broadsheet is sure that their birth heralds misfortune, although admitting 'no-one knows what disaster will come after this'.[54] Nonetheless, the author suggests that it will concern the conflicts between princes ('Fürsten') and lords ('herren') in the Empire; the inability of Maximilian to raise sufficient funds; and the subsequent incapacity to deal with the threat posed by the Turks, who at that time were holding the upper hand ('gantz überhand'). Like Brant, this anonymous author urges the reader to support Maximilan, but ends pessimistically with a condemnation of the 'wild beast' ('wilden tier') that lives under the surface of man, despite his creation in God's image.

Looking again at the image after reading the complex poem, the clumsy strength and aggressiveness of the twins, hands on hips, starts to seem less like poor artistry and more like an attempt to represent an ultimately negative view of the children. This must remain a tentative point, however, not least because another broadsheet of the same year uses a very similar image. Evidently one is either based upon the other, or else there is an unknown common source (Fig. 2.5). In a subtle and less aggressively posed detail, the hands of the girls in this broadsheet image lightly touch in front. The reversed, double image is printed on one sheet, and is integral to the broadsheet rather than being attached. The text is briefer, and in both Latin and German. It establishes the facts of the event, including, in the Latin passage, the names of the parents: Paulo Mandelin and Barbara Engelhartin. The twins are repeatedly referred to as one child, not two, and the reader is assured that they appeared 'as this image shows'.[55] Then, in conclusion, the anonymous author briefly but firmly offers a positive interpretation that contradicts that of the other broadsheet. The twins look at each other face to face, and for that reason do not have the negative, warning value of most misbirths:

> All misbirths have the meaning
> Both now and in the past
> Of misfortune, war, and great discord
> But this child does not
> As everyone can certainly see
> Since they are looking at one another[56]

The shift between one child and two is particularly confusing in this passage, but the positive message is clear. The suggestion that this is one child, not two,

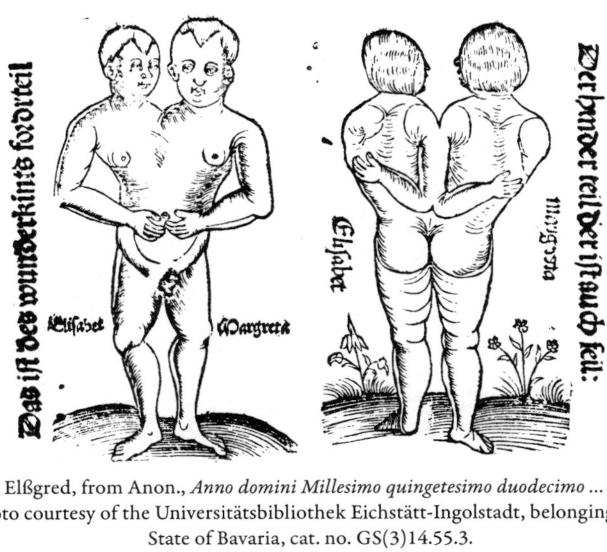

Figure 2.5: Elßgred, from Anon., *Anno domini Millesimo quingetesimo duodecimo ...* (n.p., 1512), detail. Photo courtesy of the Universitätsbibliothek Eichstätt-Ingolstadt, belonging to the Free State of Bavaria, cat. no. GS(3)14.55.3.

may be an aspect of emphasizing the unity argued for by the author. The action of the twins who look at each other is reminiscent of the Worms twins, and the political unity symbolically represented by the joined head that Brant developed as a political metaphor. The importance of these six lines is underscored by their placement at the base of the broadsheet, where they form an emphatic final statement.

The fact that different attitudes could be and were expressed towards cases of conjoined twins (and, more generally, misbirths) during this period is demonstrated by these two broadsheets on the Ertingen twins, publications that seem initially similar but are quite different in attitude. Two further extant broadsheets represent the Ertingen twins, and the different aesthetic qualities of these publications underscore the diversity of the medium and visual subject in the early sixteenth century. They are undated but most likely appeared soon after the event, as publications of this type generally did. Both sheets show the twins once only. The first has a simple image and German text by an author named Biglin, who notes the date and location of the event, including its occurrence in the land belonging to the Werdenberg counts, and labels the children 'Elsbeth' and 'Elisabethen' (Fig. 2.6).[57] The girls are flanked by two heraldic shields: on the left the Werdenberg family arms, and on the right the arms of the Cistercian

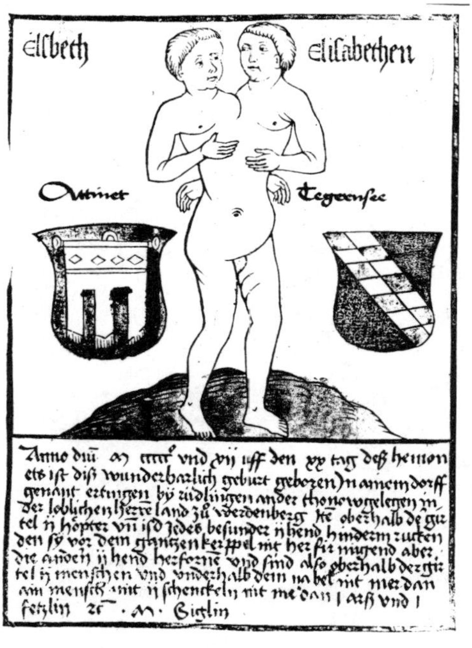

Figure 2.6: Elsbeth / Elisabethen, from Biglin (?), *Elsbeth / Elisabethen* (n.p., 1512). Photo courtesy of bpk / Kupferstichkabinett, Staatliche Museen zu Berlin / Jörg P. Anders, cat. no. 328–10.

order.[58] Klaus Walter Littger argues that this is a reference to a dramatic event in the Werdenberg family that had occurred in 1511: Christoph's brother Felix had murdered a rival from the noble Sonnenberg family, and then gone into hiding in the female Cistercian abbey of Heiligkreuztal, close to Ertingen.[59] Given the broader political upheavals that are referred to in the broadsheets discussed above, it seems possible that another, or additional, association is likely. Heiligkreuztal was under the direction of the large and wealthy abbey at Salem, east of Ertingen and very close to Heiligenberg, the seat of the Werdenberg family.[60] The abbot of Salem was a powerful figure in the region, especially in the years preceding this birth.[61] During the years when the Swabian League was particularly involved in regional conflicts, and also during the division of the Empire into twelve *Kreise* or circles in 1512, many alliances were under renegotiation. The visual analogy of two bodies joined together could be a reference – approving or even satirical – to an arrangement between the Werdenberg family and the abbey. The possibility of satire is suggested by the irreverent language of the accompanying text, which includes a fairly graphic description of the physical characteristics of the girls in earthy language. It finishes with a confirmation that they share one 'arß', or arse, and 'fetzlin', crude slang for female genitalia. Whatever the specific meaning of the Cistercian coat of arms, this broadsheet further demonstrates just how broad in scope and audience the print culture of misbirths was in this period, and also how visual aspects of a broadsheet could and did offer additional information to that supplied by the text.

One final broadsheet on the Ertingen twins has text in both German and Latin, and again reports the circumstances of the birth, including the names of the parents (Fig. 2.7).[62] It adds that the father is now a sad ('trurig') man – a rare reference to the effect that such an event may have had upon parents.[63] It does not provide any physical description at all, and piously concludes: 'What that means the almighty God knows / [He] who comes to our aid both early and late'.[64] It is the image that is particularly compelling, and suggests, if not a positive interpretation of the twins, at least a desire to treat them as individuals. Their gesturing hands frame their distinctively individual faces as they stare, one sadly, the other rather accusingly, out at the viewer. The idea that monstrous births could be represented in a dignified manner is rarely canvassed, but is clearly a feature of these sources. They offer an opportunity to open up a considerably expanded understanding of the perception of monstrous births before the Reformation.

Wolf Traut and the Misbirth at Spalt

The year before the birth of the Ertingen twins, conjoined girls had also been born at Spalt in the vicinity of Nuremberg in Bavaria. The only known broadsheet to report the birth was published in Munich in 1511 (Fig. 2.8) and includes a

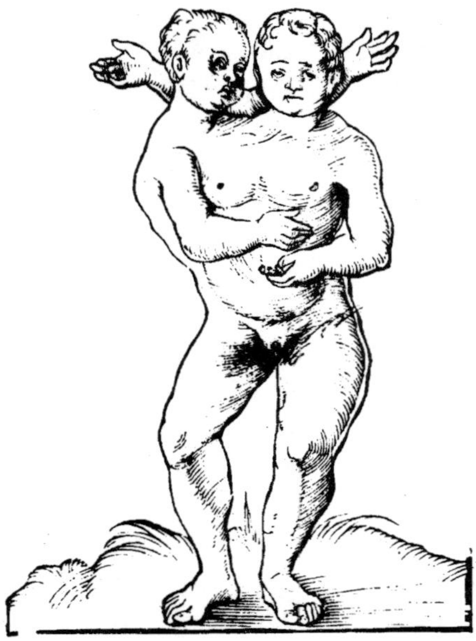

Figure 2.7: Elisabet / Margret, from Anon., *Anno domini Millesimo quingetesimo duodecimo ...* (n.p., 1512), detail. Photo courtesy of the Universitätsbibliothek Erlangen, Einblattdruck A IV, 3.

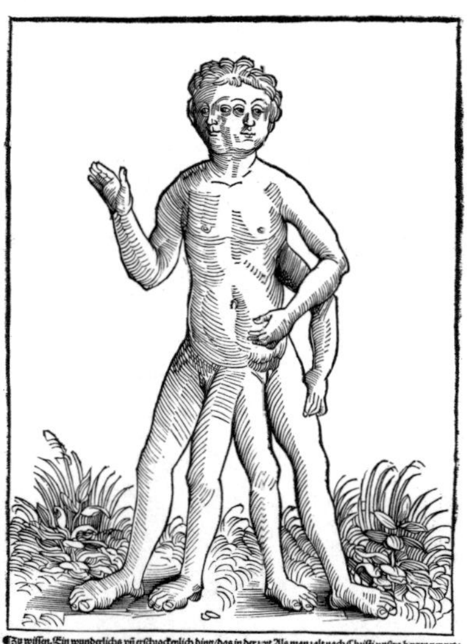

Figure 2.8: Wolf Traut, Monstrous birth of Spalt, from Anon., *Zu wissen. Ein wunderlichs vn[d] erschrockenlich ding ...* (n.p., 1511). Photo courtesy of The British Museum, Department of Prints and Drawings, registration no. 1876,0510.603. © The Trustees of the British Museum.

woodcut by Wolf Traut, the Nuremberg artist and associate of Albrecht Dürer.[65] The accompanying text characterizes the event as a 'wondrous and shocking thing',[66] locates it in time and place, and describes the girls' deformities:

> ... the child was born from the wife of a shepherd. It had one head with two faces; three hands with two stretched out from each side in a normal way. The third hand lay between the shoulders on the back. There was one body down to the two individual private parts on each side, with four human legs and feet.[67]

The broadsheet text does not seem to have been concerned with drawing a moral or political message from the event, but simply with reporting it as the newsworthy appearance of a 'wonderful creature' ('wunderbarliche Creatur'). A number of reliable witnesses had seen the child, including 'master Heinrich von Porperg, at that time the priest of the above-named town of Spalt'.[68] Spalt, the text reports, is 4 miles (6.5 km) from Nuremberg, although it cannot be certain that artist Traut saw the child personally. The writer emphasizes, however, that the image accompanying the text shows the child as she truly appeared: the image is 'abkunderfeth' (counterfeit or 'from the life').[69]

Despite this assurance, the girl is represented by Traut in a highly symmetrical, unrealistic fashion. Of her three arms, one, on the right-hand side, is raised in a poignant gesture, almost of benediction, while the other two hang on the left. The three arms disturb the sense of symmetry, but it is quickly re-established by her single head with its double face. Traut utilizes formal means – an unnatural symmetry – to create an arresting effect. Such formal, stylized approaches were increasingly used to amplify or nuance the messages conveyed by the physical characteristics of a monstrous birth. That is, these aspects make the images stranger, more foreboding or unsettling, or simply more visually arresting. A sense of realism is simultaneously visually intensified and conceptually undermined for the viewer when the bodies of new-born, physically deformed infants are presented as dramatically strong, unnaturally posed and symmetrically formed. There is a sense of confusion in many of these images between similar or 'twinned' bodies and a play of unnatural symmetry, repetition and exaggeration that can also be found at this time in the emerging visual vocabulary of the decorative grotesque. A mode of decorating walls and ceilings with fanciful, fantastic vegetal and animal forms that flowed into one another and through architectural elements, the decorative grotesque was influenced by medieval illuminations as well as more directly by classical sources. It was taken up with enthusiasm across Europe. A border decoration by the German artist Daniel Hopfer, utilized in a 1518 edition of the Bible published by Silvan Otmar in Augsburg in 1518, is one apt example of the trend.[70] The image grows out symmetrically, or mirror-like, from a central point, and strange creatures striking unnatural poses appear to be straining to break away from the patterned web that holds them. At the base of the grotesque, a head with multiple faces is uncannily similar to the shared face of the conjoined twins of Spalt depicted by Traut in 1511.

The bodies of conjoined twins seem particularly suited to a stylized form of representation, as a further graphically striking example demonstrates.[71] It is a mid sixteenth-century copy after a 1513 original by the important artist Hans Burgkmair the Elder, as the annotations on the drawing indicate (Fig. 2.9).[72] It depicts conjoined twins girls born in Bleiburg in Kärnten, in modern-day Austria. The text, presumably copied from a broadsheet illustrated by Burgkmair, describes how the girls were still-born, and that the birth was verified by important people, including the local lord, the Grafen von Ladron. The brief text does not attempt a positive or negative assessment of the meaning of the event. The girls are shown front and back, and – despite being still-born – their multiple limbs spread out unnaturally and with dramatic visual effect, indicating the extremes to which the effect could be taken. Traut had also decided to pose the 1511 child from Spalt in a way that underlined her distinctiveness. Against nature, his newly-born child is represented as much older and stands upright on grassy ground. Also against nature, the child is preternaturally calm, and dignified and authoritative in pose, in contradistinction to the Bleiburg twins, who are ominous but certainly not dignified in aspect. The most unexpected aspect of Traut's image is certainly the hand raised as though in benediction. Connections are seldom, if ever, drawn between holy figures and individual monstrous

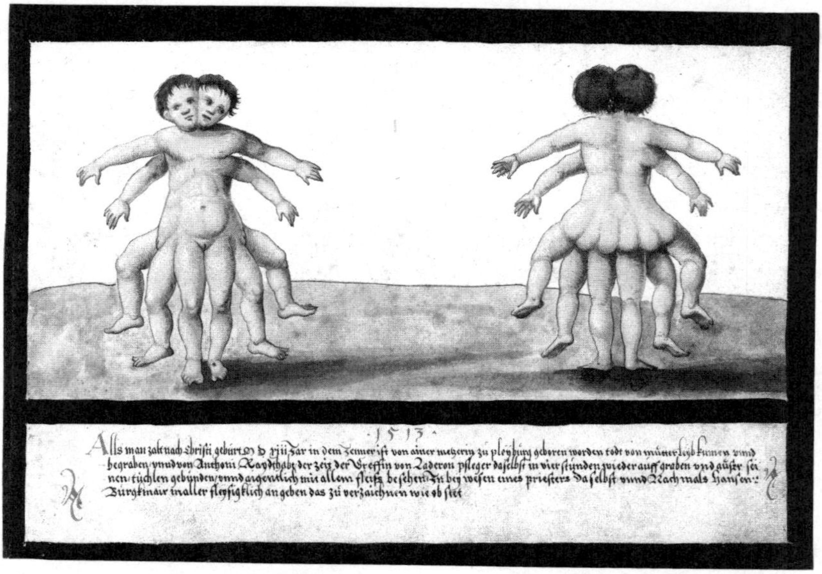

Figure 2.9: After Hans Burgkmair the Elder, conjoined twins girls born in Bleiburg in Kärnten in 1513 (drawing, [*c.* 1550]). Photo courtesy of the Staatsgalerie Stuttgart, Graphische Sammlung, Inv.Nr. C 1992/4097. © Foto: Staatsgalerie Stuttgart.

births. Given the negative interpretations that dominate most studies of the topic, this is not surprising. This unexpected gesture, however, is not unique. It was repeated several years later in another, still more visually innovative image by Burgkmair.

Hans Burgkmair's Tettnang Twins

Hans Burgkmair of Augsburg, like his colleague and rival Dürer, was one of the pre-eminent printmakers of this period.[73] In the first decade of the century he had completed the innovative multi-block frieze 'Natives of Africa and India' (1508), the first image on this scale made in northern Europe.[74] He had worked for Maximilian I on prestigious book illustration commissions including the *Theuerdanck* (*c.* 1509–12) and the *Weisskunig* (*c.* 1514–18), and was starting to work on the multi-sheet print known as the *Triumphzug* ('Triumphal Chariot', *c.* 1516–18). In a sure sign of the artist's status, in 1516 Maximilian bestowed on Burgkmair his own coat of arms.[75] That same year, a broadsheet incorporating a woodcut by Burgkmair reported the birth of conjoined twins on 8 April 1516 in Tettnang, close to the Bavarian imperial city of Lindau on the shores of Lake Constance (Fig. 2.10).[76] Tettnang itself, however, was part of the landholdings of

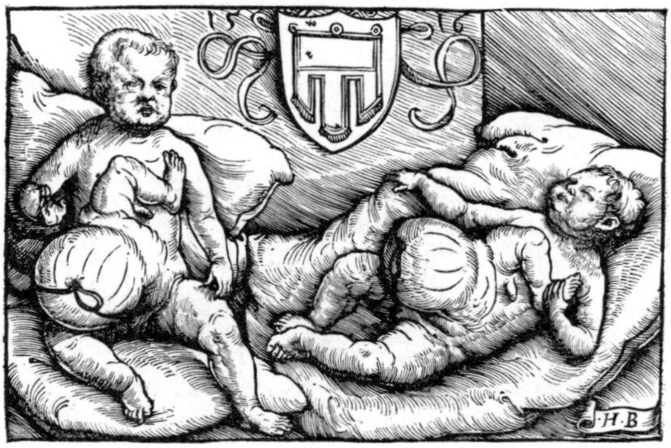
Diſz künd iſt geboren worden zu Tettnang

Uff den Achten tag des monats Apprillen von der geburt Jhesu Christi/ als man zalt/ fünfftzehenhundert vnd Sechtzehen Jare/ jnn der halben ſtunnd als nach mit nacht die glock ains geſchlagenn hat iſt in des wolgebornenn Herren herrn Vlrich Graue zü Muntfort vnnd ſtat Tettnang vonn ainer frawen mit namen Anna Bingerin / Conradenn Millers da ſelbs Eewirtin ain ſolch künd wie ob ſtet/ mit dem fieſzlin vnnd ſchwentzel an ſeiner prüſt auch groſſem plaſarben gewechs an ſeinem bauch auſſen her vñ Ain Retin vñ Rotfarbe ſtraumen darüber wie ain geſchwer geborn worden/ So des/ ſelbig künd wachend/ ſeine Bain von ain ander/ vnnd ſo es ſchlaffend auch der maſſen gelegen/ aber alwegen das fieſzlin in der hand haltend vnd iſt ain döchterlin vnnd biſz an/ den Neünden tag lebendig geweſen/ ſolich künd hat der ob beſtimbt Herr vnnd Grauff ſeinen maller Mayſter Matheyſen miller Maler burger zü Lindaw mit fleyſz hayſen verzaychnen oder konterfenn vnd zü trucken ver ortnen wie oben geſehen wirt.

Figure 2.10: Hans Burgkmair the Elder, monstrous birth of Tettnang, from Anon., *Disz künd ist geboren worden zu Tettnang* (n.p., 1516). Photo courtesy of the Staatliche Graphische Sammlung, Munich, H. 728, Inv.-Nr. 154318.

the count of Montfort-Tettnang, at that time Ulrich VII. The illustration depicts the nameless children lying beneath the prominent arms of Ulrich VII: arms shared with his close relations, the Werdenbergs, who were Montfort in origin. The accompanying text states that the Lindau painter Mathis Miller had made a sketch of the twins (no longer known) on commission for Ulrich VII:

> the lord and Count, referred to above, ordered his painter Matheysen Miller, painter and citizen of Lindau, to take pains to sketch or counterfeit this child, and have it printed in the prescribed manner as seen above.[77]

The text emphasizes that the count ordered his painter to record the birth, and indicates that he may well have seen the value of publicizing its occurrence in his lands, following the well-known and in many ways positively received births in Worms and especially Ertingen. On 29 July 1516 Ulrich concluded an agreement with eight relations and close associates to form a three-year alliance of mutual co-operation and protection within the larger context of the Swabian League.[78] The birth had occurred less than four months earlier, and Ulrich may well have wished to record it as a potentially auspicious omen and way of advertising and increasing his own status during the negotiations. The prominent appearance of the Montfort-Tettnang coat of arms in the published broadsheet, created by a leading artist closely associated with Maximilan I, indicates that Ulrich orchestrated its publication in an act of deliberate self-promotion during a politically turbulent period.

Political issues are not the only interesting aspect of this broadsheet, which also includes a particularly complex and detailed representation of the children. The expression counterfeit (here 'konterfenn') is used as it is in many other broadsheets to indicate that the image is taken 'from the life'. The text records the place and date of the birth, the names of the parents, a brief physical description, and the sober fact that the children died after only nine days. There is also a rather humanizing descriptive element. The 'döchterlin' (daughter or little girl) sleeps 'holding [her brother's] little foot in her hand'.[79] Burgkmair depicts the children twice, although 'child' is perhaps more accurate a term here, as the male twin is so partially formed in comparison to his sister. Certainly, the broadsheet text refers to only one child. At first glance, the style of the image is relatively naturalistic. However, a closer examination of the picture complicates this apparent naturalism. On the left, the girl sits up on a cushion, in line with a detail in the text: 'as the child herself was awake her legs were held apart'.[80] Her face is grave and watchful, and her right hand is raised in a gesture that is distinctly reminiscent of benediction, and as such similar to the blessing gesture from Traut's 1511 Spalt image. More specifically, it recalls Christ's gesture in the guise of the *Salvator mundi* (saviour of the world). Although the girl's final two fingers are not shown turned down, the effect is certainly similar, with the visual focus thrown onto the two central raised fingers. Christ was depicted as *Salvator mundi* both as an adult and as a child. Lucas Cranach the Elder's *c.* 1505 woodcut of *The Infant Christ as Redeemer* forms a useful comparison and may well have been known to Burgkmair.[81] Another possible source is the images of the infant Christ on a cushion in the guise of *Salvator mundi*, used in almanacs and as new year's images during this period (Fig. 2.11).[82] The growth of sculptures in fifteenth- and sixteenth-century Germany representing the infant Christ without Mary are also relevant. These are sculptures that generally represent Christ making a blessing gesture with his right hand.[83] It seems quite astonishing that an explicit parallel could be drawn between the Christ child and a monstrous birth, but this certainly seems to be what the visual evidence suggests. Given that these representations of the infant Christ were developed in a German artistic context, it may well have been a localized iconographic phenomenon. It was evidently rooted in the kind of positive representations of misbirths discussed here, and did not survive the more polemical and generally negative representations that developed in the Reformation and are examined in the following chapter.

In Burgkmair's image, the child's left hand rests very lightly on her thigh, in a poised gesture that indicates control, as does the extended left leg, resting over the edge of the pillow. The pose and gesture are unnatural, particularly in the sense that they are beyond the physical capacity of the new-born child. Yet there

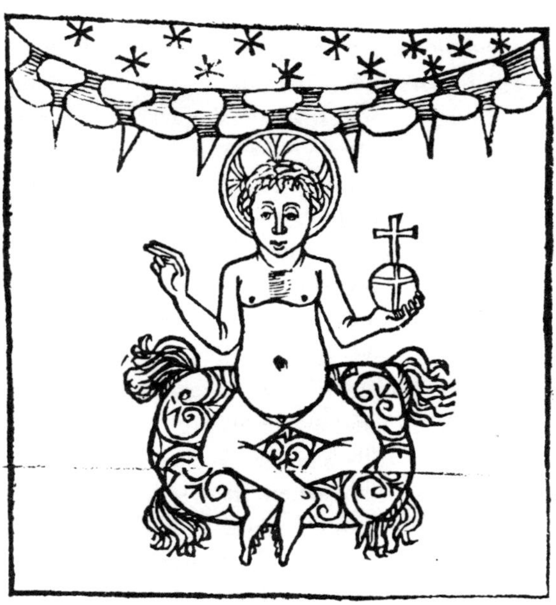

Figure 2.11: New years' child ('Neujahrskind') (woodcut from almanac, 1491). Photo courtesy of the bpk / Staatsbibliothek zu Berlin / Inkunabelsammlung, Inc. 1882.5.

also seems to be a level of naturalism in the depiction quite different in effect to the representation of the Spalt and Ertingen twins. The boy twin's leg and penis are distinctly formed, but the rest of the body is simply a kind of shapeless, swollen bag that ends in the umbilical cord. There is no attempt to give this featureless area a more recognizable shape, or indeed to give it a more symmetrical relationship to the whole body of the female twin, as was frequently the case in broadsheet images of conjoined twins.[84] The image and text both record the fact that the birth included both male and female in one joined body; this may well have seemed more wondrous to contemporaries than most conjoined twins from this period, who shared the same gender.[85] However, the female child is visually dominant – indeed, the true subject of the image – in a way that makes the association with the infant Christ still more astonishing and intriguing. The right-hand representation of the girl is also striking, but in a different way. Here, it seems entirely natural. She lies asleep, with closed eyes. Her right hand curls gently over the left edge of the pillow. Her left hand clasps the foot of the leg that grows from the chest with a gesture that seems entirely natural and unforced, as though gripping a mother's finger. It is both a charming and pathetic detail in the image, and one that is, again, echoed in the text.

Burgkmair's image, then, shows the child twice, but not, as would be more common in such publications, to show the front and back, and therefore fully display the child's bodily structure.[86] The purpose here seems to be quite different. She is shown twice but in each case in a frontal pose. It is a pose that seems intended to convey different aspects of the meaning and effect of this birth: that is, it is an extraordinary and mysterious event, and it is also a pathos-filled domestic scene. Although Burgkmair is a major artist of the period, this print has received little attention and its unusual nature has gone unremarked. Yet it is a structurally complex image that recalls double portraiture, uncommon at this time although of interest to Burgkmair.[87] Double portraits of the same figure often seem to have – or at least to imply – an extra edge of psychological intensity and desire to literally portray the multi-faceted personality and character of one person. Speculatively, this seems to be the case in Burgkmair's Tettnang print. Of course, it is not possible to know the extent to which Burgkmair was reliant on the no longer known sketch (or possibly sketches) made by the minor Lindau artist Mathis Miller. Certainly, the issues of the artist as witness are complex here. The text refers to Miller's image as 'counterfeit' or 'from the life'. Yet, of course this print itself is not based on first-hand observation, as Burgkmair has worked from a sketch by another artist. How closely has he followed it? Lacking the sketch, it is not possible to say. A question mark must remain over whether the decisive features of this woodcut can be attributed to Burgkmair or to the artist Miller, whose work is today unknown. It is, however, worth noting that Burgkmair displays his initials prominently in this woodcut. An artist of

Burgkmair's talent, reputation and working methods would be unlikely to copy without modification a model by a minor artist.[88]

Fundamentally, the issue here is not the identity of the author of the concept underlying this print, but instead the nature of the image itself. It is certain that the image presents the Tettnang birth in a complex way, and one that expands considerably on the information contained in the accompanying text. The child is shown on the right as an ordinary child in a domestic setting, eliciting pity and empathy from the viewer. On the left, she appears in the guise of a wonder sent by God, and, most strikingly, as reminiscent of the infant Christ. This radically positive image is not typical of later images in the sixteenth century, which generally emphasized the fearful aspects of such children. Burgkmair's approach did not establish a pattern of representation, but is nonetheless, like the other broadsheets surveyed here, an important example of attitudes in the pre-Reformation period. Both of Burgkmair's representations, the domestic and the wondrous, fundamentally approve of the child, and as such form part of a broader collection of imagery that shows us how misbirths could be welcomed by the societies in which they appeared. Publications like this indicate what a complex and varied range of ideas had developed around the theme of monstrous births since the 1490s. Print culture, political patronage and artistic innovation would seem to have been crucial components of this development. Another factor – religious crisis – was about to dramatically change the face of German society and culture. Monstrous births were affected by it, too, and would become a tool for reformers and their enemies engaged in public and polemical debate.

3 REFORMATION VISUAL CULTURE AND MONSTROUS BIRTHS: LUTHER'S MONK CALF AND MELANCHTHON'S PAPAL ASS

The most notorious and still best-known monstrous births of the early modern period are two creatures known as the Papal Ass and Monk Calf. Their images are emblematic of the printed propaganda wars of the Reformation.[1] The Papal Ass, washed up on the banks of the Tiber in Rome in 1496, and the Monk Calf, born in Freiberg in 1522, were polemically analysed in a 1523 pamphlet written by Martin Luther and Philipp Melanchthon. Monstrous births could be viewed in positive and sympathetic terms, as the previous chapters have demonstrated. Yet this 1523 pamphlet by the two most important figures of the Lutheran Reformation forms a decisive shift in attitude, in which interpretation and representation became not only more polemical – and particularly anti-papal – but took on a notably apocalyptic aspect. This chapter therefore shifts in approach from the previous chapters, which surveyed many different cases, and instead takes a very close look at one single pamphlet, its broader publication context in Reformation thought, and its afterlife in the following decades.

Natural Prodigies in the Early Lutheran Reformation

In a commentary on Genesis 30, Luther discussed examples of women who had been affected by a fright or other external stimuli during pregnancy and consequently gave birth to deformed children.[2] One woman gave birth to a child with a face like a corpse after she had seen a corpse; others transferred 'bloody spots' (presumably birthmarks) to their unborn children when they touched those parts of their own bodies after being suddenly frightened. Most strikingly, one woman gave birth to a dormouse:

> I remember that when I was a boy at Eisenach, a beautiful and virtuous woman gave birth to a dormouse. This happened because one of the neighbours had hung a little bell on a dormouse in order that the rest might be put to flight when the bell made a sound. This dormouse met the pregnant woman, who, ignorant of the matter, was so terrified by the sudden meeting and sight of the dormouse that the fetus in her womb degenerated into the shape of the little beast.[3]

Luther's aim in telling such stories was pragmatic: he warned that pregnant women are vulnerable and should be protected for the sake of their unborn children.[4] Clearly, like some of his contemporaries, he believed in the power of the maternal imagination. This attitude was not a hallmark of earlier publications on monstrous births – or indeed Luther's own writing on the Monk Calf – although later in the century it became more common to attribute deformities in children at least partly to a pregnant woman's overactive imagination.[5]

The Reformation had given fresh impetus to interest in monstrous births and other natural wonders.[6] Publications like Johann Carion's illustrated *Prognosticatio*, which appeared in 1521, revived some of the issues from the turn of the century publications surveyed in Chapter 1, and incorporated new aspects such as the 'great flood' scare of 1524.[7] Publications like Carion's were as much concerned with entering into contemporary debates about religious (and by association, social and political) changes as they were with enumerating astrological, meteorological and other signs. This entwinement of the wondrous and prodigious within current debate continued in a publication of 1527, in which Johann Lichtenberger's late fifteenth-century book of prophecies was republished as *Die Weissagunge*, with a foreword by Martin Luther.[8] Luther is quite explicit here about his belief that God is responsible for abnormal phenomena, writing:

> above the earth, God gives his signs in the heavens, when some disaster impends: he sends comets, or causes the Sun and Moon to lose their light, or some other uncommon figure to appear. Likewise, on earth, monstrous prodigies are born, both human and animal; and this is not done by the angels but by God himself. Through such signs, he threatens the ungodly and displays the future ills that will smite the rulers and the land, as a warning to them. Such things are not sent for the godly; they have no need of them. For which reason, as Jeremiah says, let them not be dismayed by these signs of heaven: these are not meant for them but for the ungodly.[9]

Monstrous births, then, were to be seen as negative signs with apocalyptic significance, but the pious should not fear them (just as they should not fear the Last Days). The issue of whether or not natural signs conveyed discernable meanings continued to engage Luther and also his follower and collaborator Philipp Melanchthon. Their interests diverged at some points: Melanchthon held a strong and ongoing belief and intellectual interest in astrology, which Luther consistently dismissed as an inexact science.[10] In one telling phrase he declared 'that art of theirs is so much shit'.[11] Luther was, however, emphatic about the importance of what he called 'terrible things and portents', which included eclipses and monstrous births:

> the stargazers, and those who seek to prophesy and foretell from the stars what the future holds, imagine that these things [stars] darken the earth, and trouble it, and are harmful. For all God's creations are good, and are created by God only to be put to good

> use; but man makes them evil by his ill use of them. These are signs, but not portents or terrible things. Eclipses are terrible things and portents, as are monstrous births.[12]

As H. C. Erik Midelfort observes, Luther was concerned that people might become caught up in seeking physical explanations of such phenomena rather than heeding God's warnings.[13] Nonetheless, Luther did sometimes relate them to important current events. In a letter of 23 May 1525 to Johann Rühel, Luther observed that the death of the elector Frederick the Wise was foretold by a rainbow, and 'a child born here in Wittenberg without a head, and another with its feet reversed'.[14] An explicitly eschatological attitude was most typical of Luther's approach, one in which monstrous births and other wonders were best understood as signs of the coming End Times. Reflecting on the period of Holy Roman Emperor Maximilian's reign, Luther writes:

> And under the reign of this Maximilian there were wondrous signs in the heavens, and many of them; also on earth and in the waters; of which Christ speaks: 'There shall be great signs', etc. So much so, that we read of no age in which there have been more or greater signs. And these give us a certain hope that the blessed day is close upon us.[15]

Luther's reference to 'the blessed day', identified earlier in this passage as the Day of Judgement, is a reminder of the complexities of Lutheran eschatological thought.[16] Reformers viewed the birth of monstrous creatures as negative events, and part of the disasters that must precede the Day of Judgement.[17] A crucial aspect of the meaning of the Papal Ass and Monk Calf is the close association of the Pope or papacy with the Antichrist, one of the figures whose coming will signal the Last Days.[18] Yet Luther makes clear that the Day of Judgement was ultimately desired as much as feared, and the events that would precede it were therefore to be interpreted in a simultaneously negative but also hopeful light.[19]

Polemical Pamphlets

There was nothing passive about this period of waiting for the imminent Apocalypse and Day of Judgement. Particularly in the period leading up to the Peasants' Revolt of 1525, heated debates between supporters of Luther, reformers who disagreed with him on particular issues, and others who were entirely against the movement for reform, took place in many parts of German-speaking Europe. These debates were often conducted in print, between authors located in different regions, who sought not only to counter their specific enemies but also to sway a broader audience. The years between 1520 and 1526 saw an outpouring of Reformation-linked publications mostly written in German (rather than Latin) and in pamphlet form: these were known as *Flugschriften*.[20] While it has been estimated that approximately 10,000 pamphlets were published in German-speaking areas in the first three decades of the sixteenth century, nearly three-quarters of this total appeared between 1520 and 1526 alone.[21]

Luther and Melancthon's combined pamphlet of 1523 was illustrated with striking images of the Monk Calf and Papal Ass, and titled the *Deuttung der czwo grewlichen Figuren, Bapstesels czu Rom und Munchkalbs zu Freijberg ijnn Meijszen funden* (the 'Meaning of Two Gruesome Figures, the Papal Ass of Rome and the Monk Calf of Freiberg found in Meissen').[22] Published the year following the September 1522 publication of Luther's German translation of the New Testament, it shares a crucial feature with the Luther Bible, many polemical Reformation pamphlets and the great majority of sixteenth-century publications on monstrous births, as it is written in German[23] and makes full use of its wide vernacular appeal as well as its graphically arresting illustrations.[24]

The Monk Calf and the Papal Ass

This publication generated two of the best-known visual images of Reformation polemic: those of the Papal Ass and Monk Calf.[25] The Papal Ass, washed up on the banks of the Tiber in Rome in 1495, made its way to Germany in visual form via an engraving by the Bohemian artist Wenzel von Olmutz, published in the late fifteenth century (Fig. 3.1). Several decades later, and perhaps prompted by his colleague Melanchthon (see below), Luther first became intrigued by the then-nameless monstrous birth and sought to incorporate it into his eschatological world view. He wrote a homiletic epistle that year (on the second Sunday in Advent, concerning Luke 21:25–33) titled 'A Christian and well-substanti-

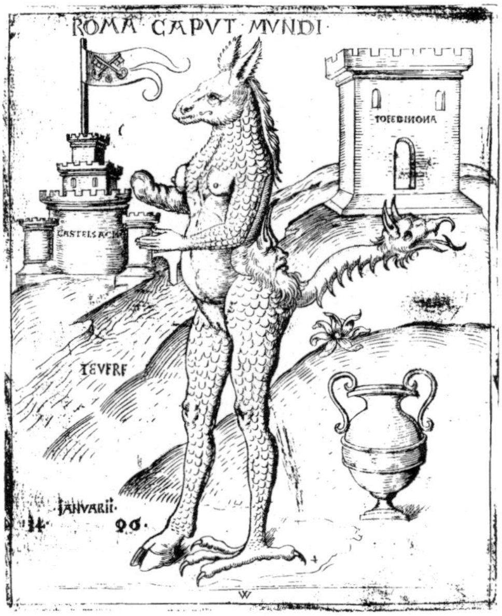

Figure 3.1: Wenzel von Olmutz, monstrous birth in Rome (engraving, [*c.* 1495–1500]). Photo courtesy of The British Museum, Department of Prints and Drawings, registration no. E,1.15. © The Trustees of the British Museum.

ated proof of the Day of Judgement, and of the signs that it cannot now be far off'.[26] In line with his sceptical views on astrology, he notes the great number of signs that had appeared but were unpredicted by astrologers. These signs were emphatically not part of the natural order. Although they were not referred to in Luke, Luther explicitly added monstrous creatures to his list and framed this addition as an attack on Rome and the papacy:

> let no astrologer dare to say that the natural course of the heavens foreshadowed the fearful monster that was cast up dead by the River Tiber, in Rome, a few years since: it had an ass's head, a woman's breast and belly, and elephant's foot in the place of the right hand, fish scales on its legs, a dragon's head on its hinder parts, etc. By which it signifies the papacy, and God's great wrath and punishment. Such a succession of signs will bring something greater than reason can conceive.[27]

The Monk Calf, also known as the monster of Saxony, was a deformed calf foetus discovered in the town of Waltersdorf near Freiberg in Saxony on 8 December 1522 – at just the time of Luther's writing on the Papal Ass, and perhaps even prompting his interest. Printed images of the creature quickly began circulating.[28] One very simple woodcut from 1522 represents the calf in the form and pose which were to become best known (Fig. 3.2).[29] The anonymous text is very

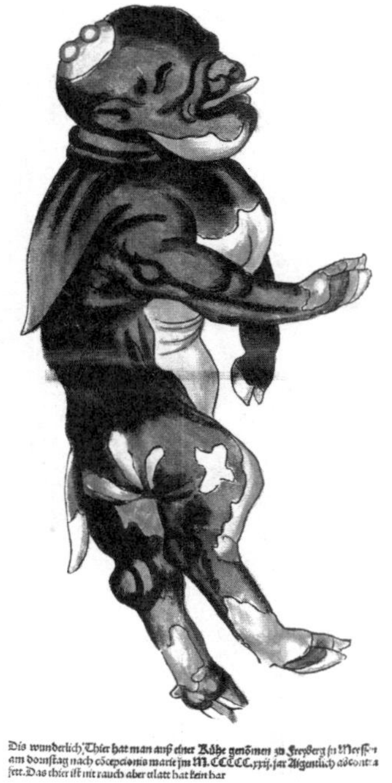

Figure 3.2: Monstrous calf, from Anon., *Dis wunderlich Thier hat man auß einer Kuehe geno[m]men ...* (n.p., 1522). Photo courtesy of the Herzog August Bibliothek Wolfenbüttel, shelfmark A: 118.4 Quod. (12).

simple; it records the date and place of birth of the 'wondrous animal' ('wunderliche Thier'), and states that the image here is 'truly from the life' ('Aigentlich abcontrafett'). The woodcut includes a small additional detail: the beast has no fur and is smooth all over. Due to various physical features, including a flap of skin that resembled a monk's cowl and a tonsure-like mark on its head, the creature could be and was interpreted both as a sign of the degeneracy of Catholicism, and, more rarely in opposition, as a 'Lutheran monster' that revealed the former Augustinian monk Luther's purported heresy.[30]

In 1523 Luther and Melanchthon jointly prepared their pamphlet interpreting the messages conveyed by the unusual bodies of the two creatures. Luther discussed the Monk Calf, while Melanchthon wrote about the Papal Ass. Lucas Cranach and his workshop provided updated prints to illustrate the texts (Figs 3.3 and 3.4). Cranach was one of the most important and well-established artists in Germany during this period, and closely (although not exclusively) associated with the Lutheran cause.[31] His woodcuts for this pamphlet were substantially similar to previous versions, although with subtle points of difference that will be examined below. His woodcuts became the definitive versions, and the two creatures were from then on irrevocably linked, both to each other and to the Lutheran cause. Many pamphlets by Luther from this period were published

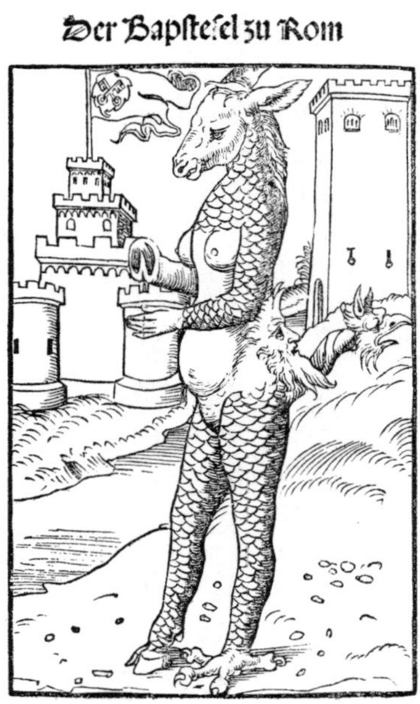

Figure 3.3: Lucas Cranach the Elder and workshop, Papal Ass, from P. Melanchthon and M. Luther, *Deuttung der zwo grewlichen Figuren Bapstesels zu Rom vnd Munchkalbs zu Freyberg jn Meyssen funden* (Wittenberg: [Rhau-Grunenberg], 1523), sig. A i v. Photo courtesy of the Herzog August Bibliothek Wolfenbüttel, shelfmark A: 118.4 Quod. (10).

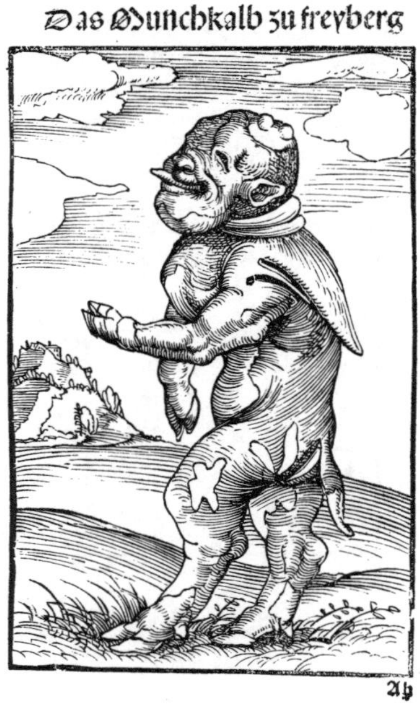

Figure 3.4: Lucas Cranach the Elder and workshop, Monk Calf, from P. Melanchthon and M. Luther, *Deuttung der zwo grewlichen Figuren Bapstesels zu Rom vnd Munchkalbs zu Freyberg jn Meyssen funden* (Wittenberg: [Rhau-Grunenberg], 1523), sig. A ij r. Photo courtesy of the Herzog August Bibliothek Wolfenbüttel, shelfmark A: 118.4 Quod. (10).

with title pages with decorative borders. Most editions of this 1523 pamphlet have a simple, text-only cover page, and then the two single full-page images of the Papal Ass followed by the Monk Calf.[32] There is a sense that this is a particular kind of illustration, reminscent of earlier monstrous birth broadsheets that sought to record a real but bizarre event; one that is intended to help the reader understand Melanchthon and Luther's analyses, and also conceptually akin to the illustration of apocalyptic imagery in Luther's 1522 New Testament, explored later in this chapter. Variations were, of course, also possible. An edition of the text from 1523, from an unknown publisher in Wittenberg, presents the Papal Ass and Monk Calf in a way that will become more typical of images of monstrous births later in the century. It combines two disparate births from different decades and locations into one woodcut image in which the drama is increased through an encounter between the two creatures (Fig. 3.5). This opening page adds a new phrase to the title of the book: 'with signs of the Day of Judgement' ('mit anzaygung des jungstentags'). The text of the pamphlet remains the same. It is the frame and context that are amplified to emphasize the apocalyptic meaning of these creatures, a trend that will continue in the following decades. In this title page image, the Papal Ass and Monk Calf stand as though in conversation,

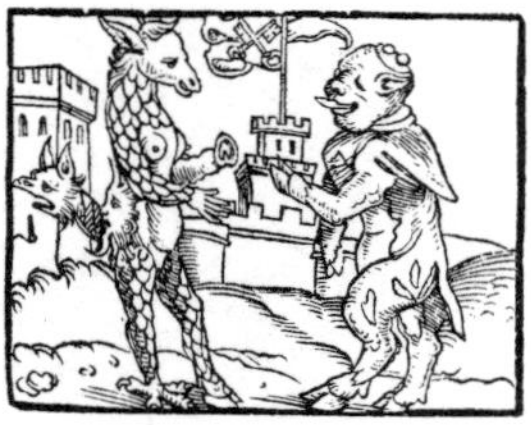
Deuttung der zwo grewlichen Figuren Bapstesels zu Rom vnnd Munchkalbs zu Freyburg in Meyssen funden/mit an= zaygũg des jung stentags.

Philippus Melanchthon.
Doctor Martinus Luther.

Wittemberg
M.D.xxiij.

Figure 3.5: Papal Ass and Monk Calf, from P. Melanchthon and M. Luther, *Deuttung der zwo grewlichen figuren Bapstesels zu Freyburg in Meyssen funden, mit anzaygu[n]g des jungstentags* (Wittenberg: n.p., 1523), title page. Photo courtesy of the Herzog August Bibliothek Wolfenbüttel, shelfmark A: 151.40 Theol. (29).

the papal keys flying on the flag behind them. The image itself is a composite, just as their bodies are composite. Versions of the pamphlet were reprinted, and also translated during the century into French, Dutch and English.[33] It was possibly Melanchthon who had provided a model and the impetus for the pamphlet. An earlier (undated) publication directed at the 'Antichrist' papacy and its 'synagogue' (*Figur des Antichristen Bapsts vn[d] seiner Synangogis*) was another version of Melanchthon's text, although published anonymously.[34] Melanchthon revised the text for the joint 1523 pamphlet, translating biblical quotations from Latin to German and in other relatively minor ways making it more accessible to a wider audience. Luther then provided his own analysis of the Monk Calf.

Philipp Melanchthon's Papal Ass

Melanchthon analyses the creature one body part at a time, utilizing biblical references, and conveying a central message about the corruption of the church in Rome as revealed by its bizarre physical structure. He begins his analysis of the Papal Ass with a reference to the Book of Daniel: 'God has always indicated his grace or wrath by many signs, and in particular He has used such miracles for speaking to the rulers, as we see in Daniel'.[35] Melanchthon implicitly addresses the highest levels of society, and aims at the widest possible audience. Melanchthon's text, as noted above, is a revised version of an earlier publication. In addition to translating various Latin passages into German, Melanchthon seems to have sought to make his text more accessible to a larger audience in several other ways. For example, each new paragraph is numbered; 'Auffs erst ...' (firstly), and so on, matching Luther's following text. This is a subtle difference, but it seems better suited to a text that may, for instance, be read out loud to a group rather than be read privately and individually. There are other differences, including the addition of entirely new sentences. One particular addition is especially pertinent to the function of the visual in Reformation polemic, especially with respect to monstrous births, as Melanchthon writes:

> And so in fact all creatures of the papal empire 'paint' and exemplify something that no human could create. Instead one must say that God himself has represented [or created] this image of horror.[36]

The term 'counterfeit' was used frequently in broadsheets to testify to the realism of their imagery, as previous examples show. Melanchthon uses a variant of the word here: 'abcontrofeyt'.[37] But instead of the artist Cranach being the one who has created the 'counterfeit', Melanchthon presents God in the guise of an artist who uses his creations to convey visual messages. That Melanchthon added this passage to his revised version indicates that he saw this especially visual metaphor as one that would be accessible and meaningful to a broader audience. Luther uses the verb to paint ('malen') in his text, and the world of visual culture seems to have had special resonance for these Reformers and – at least in their estimation – for their audiences, a point to be returned to later in this chapter.

Melanchthon's analysis plays up the visually dramatic aspects of the creature. The monstrous body parts of the Monk Calf – those details that distinguish it from an ordinary calf – are rather vague in outline. The Papal Ass, however, as represented by Cranach as well as by Wenzel von Olmutz in an earlier image, has an almost jarring, collage-like combination of sharply delineated but ill-matching body parts. Step by step, Melanchthon describes and interprets these individual elements. He begins with the polemical and direct statement that 'Firstly, the head of the ass represents the Pope'.[38] The Pope, he indicates here, has brought the church into a worldly and physical, rather than spiritual, state. The low state of the ass in the animal kingdom is underscored through a reference to Exodus 13:13, in which first-born children and animals are consecrated to God: 'but every first-born donkey you will redeem with a lamb or kid; if you do not redeem it, you must break its neck'. That is, God does not value donkeys (or asses) as he does other creatures. That the head of the Papal Ass is formed in this way is a true sign of the creature's low state.

Next, Melanchthon addresses one hand, which 'like an elephant's foot represents the spiritual regime of the Pope'. As forcefully as an elephant, the Pope's 'regime' makes its way into and corrupts souls with innumerable and intolerable laws. Melanchthon adds, in a metaphor that it is easy to imagine seizing the imagination of audiences: 'like the great heavy elephant it tramples and grinds down everything that it comes across'. The human-shaped other hand of the Papal Ass, in turn, represented the Pope's worldly 'regiment'; that is, those secular rulers who gave support to the papal office.[39] In Cranach's woodcut accompanying the text, these hands are neatly displayed one above the other, emphasizing through contrast the peculiarity of the elephant hand.

The right foot of the creature, in the form of the foot of an ox, is aligned by Melanchthon with the elephant-shaped right hand. The foot represents the servants of the church: 'the papal teachers, preachers, priests and confessors, and particularly the scholastic theologians'. That is, it refers to those responsible, in the Pope's name, for oppressing the 'poor folk' ('arme volck') with their activities. Identifying papal supporters with the End Times, Melanchthon refers the reader to Matthew 24:4: 'There will come false Christians and false prophets'. The other foot, in the shape of a claw, is aligned with the human-shaped hand. It represents canons, as worldly servants of the popes.[40] Melanchthon's language becomes still more physical in the next section, in which the female belly and breasts of the Papal Ass are described:

> [these] represent the body of the papacy: that is Cardinals, bishops, clerics, monks, students ... their life is simply guzzling food, boozing, unchaste lechery, and leading the 'good life' on earth.[41]

Melanchthon's understanding of the belly and breasts as especially potent symbols was to be intensified in a revised 1535 edition of the pamphlet, discussed below.[42] In this 1523 version, however, he turns fairly rapidly to the arms, legs and back of the creature, with a metaphor that is a little less obvious: the scales on these body parts represent secular rulers, who tolerate the failings of the papal system, effectively protecting it as they cling on to its 'body'.[43] This passage makes a particularly intriguing visual appeal to the reader or listener. The innocuous scales represented in the woodcut must be imaginatively reconfigured by the reader into a multitude of earthly rulers. Much more anthropomorphic in form are the faces of the old man and dragon ('trach') that emerge from the Papal Ass's backside. The man represents the coming end of the papacy, already growing old; the dragon represents the bulls and books published by popes with the purpose of universally enforcing their will.[44]

Melanchthon's tenth and final point shifts away from the body of the creature and to the location where it was found: Rome. In the image of the Monk Calf, the background landscape is unimportant and included no distinguishing elements. In the case of the Papal Ass image, the background is crucial. The distinctive shape of the Castel Sant Angelo in Rome is carefully delineated, and for those not familiar with the famous tower, the fluttering flag with the crossed papal keys could inform even the least educated of the connection with Rome and the papacy. The tower to the right is the Tor di nona, used as the papal prison.[45] Dramatically, in his final point, Melanchthon claims that finding the creature dead, 'confirms that the papacy is coming to an end'.[46]

Martin Luther's Monk Calf

Luther begins his text with the disclaimer: 'I will leave aside the prophetic meaning of this monk calf, since I am no prophet'. Nonetheless, he asserts that God has sent this creature in order that it might act as a sign for those in German or 'deuttsch' lands. In explicating the meaning of this sign Luther provides a very close analysis of the meaning of the different parts of the Monk Calf's body. He hopes, above all, that the creature is a sign of the coming Day of Judgement: 'My wish and hope is that the Day of Judgement is coming'.[47] His text is explicitly directed at monks (and nuns), and, as Robert Scribner puts it, is intended to reveal 'the false appearance of spiritual and godly life found in the monkery'.[48] It is also intended to attract the attention of social elites, although its warning polemic is implicitly directed at a much wider audience. Luther refers to prophetic episodes in the Bible (the Book of Daniel), as well as Old Testament stories in which calves play a role (Isaiah and Exodus). However, the majority of the text is taken up with an attentive, analytical and polemical reading of the visual appearance of the animal. This section begins with strong words:

> Firstly and in summary let there be no debate about this sign: God has dressed this calf in clerical clothing, in the [monk's] habit. In doing so he has without doubt intended to represent something significant: that it must soon be clear how all monks and nuns are nothing other than false liars who appear externally to lead a spiritual life.[49]

Luther reminds the reader of the biblical golden calf, worshipped as a god by the Israelites (Exodus 32).[50] He then asks rhetorically: 'What is this calf then? It is the false idol in their lying hearts.'[51] Later in the text, he also emphasizes that this creature does not represent one single figure, but instead the failings of a whole group of monks.[52] Luther proposes individual body parts as symbols for these failings. The creature's blindness demonstrates their ignorance of the true nature of God.[53] The large ear is an attribute of the priest who hears confession: 'As the ear and the habit means the intolerable tyranny of confession'. The deformities around the neck are also rich with meaning. The monk's 'cowl' is tightly wound around the neck, signifying the stubbornness of the monks. The two bumps on the creature's head are, Luther warns, deceptive. Superficially similar to Moses's horns, they might appear to signify the Gospel and its preaching, but this is purely a false appearance.[54] The mouth is particularly important, and also complex. The lower jaw is human, the upper bestial, and, as Robert Scribner writes, 'instead of God's Word, they preach the calf's snout, that is, their own good'.[55] Even the bald skin reveals the slippery smoothness of the monk's tonsure.[56]

Luther also ascribes meaning to the pose of the creature. The previous chapter examined publications that depicted monstrous births in unnatural poses, impossible for new-born children: dancing, embracing or even gesturing in a Christ-like way. The Monk Calf is similarly unnatural. It stands commandingly, with an outstretched arm (or, more accurately, hoof), and with its tongue hanging out. In fact, there is a difference here from the first broadsheet of 1522, in which the hooves are twisted forward, as though the creature were actually recorded lying down. Here, Cranach swivels the hindquarters back so that the trotters appear to stand firmly on the ground. The difference is subtle but decisive. Luther interprets the pose metaphorically:

> The calf conducts itself in the manner of a preacher: it extends the rear legs as though standing and stretches out its right hoof just as a preacher stretches out his right hand and keeps the left close by his side; it throws back its head and has a tongue in its mouth [that is, it appears to speak]; and entirely has the appearance of standing and preaching.[57]

That is, the creature is a perverted version of a preacher. It should be noted that in the woodcut the Monk Calf stretches out its left hoof, rather than the right hoof referred to by Luther in the text. The same reversal occurs in Melanchthon's discussion of the Papal Ass below, and indicates that both were likely working from preliminary drawings for the woodcut rather than the final, reversed image.[58] Visuality was absolutely central to Luther's interest in and polemical use of the Monk Calf.[59] He treats the body of the Monk Calf as a kind of picture that can be broken down into its component parts and symbolically analysed. Here, the body of the creature forms the entirety of the picture. The background of the actual image is inconsequential. This idea of the monster's body as a kind of picture can be expanded in two ways. First, Luther did not see the creature with his own eyes; the beast he interpreted was already an artistic interpretation. Second, Luther explicitly refers to the image and the creature by way of a painting metaphor:

> Because as the Papal Ass 'paints' the papacy, so this Monk Calf 'paints' the apostles and students of the popes, in order the whole world might truly see what sort of preachers and teachers it had previously listened to and continues to listen to.[60]

That is, the Papal Ass (and this is one of Luther's few comparative points in the text) represents, or more literally has 'painted' ('abmallt') the Pope, while the Monk Calf visually represents his followers and students. The fuller meaning of the verb 'abmalen' incorporates the idea of acting as a sign (although emphatically a very visual one): the Papal Ass and Monk Calf visually represent and act as signs for the papacy and its followers.[61] The creatures embody these aspects, and they represent them to a wide audience.

Luther's text on the Monk Calf was almost immediately rebutted, notably by Hieronymus Emser, who wrote a pamphlet on the animal published in 1524.[62] Another broadsheet that was most likely published late in 1523 demonstrates that Luther and Melanchthon's pamphlet influenced other publications. This broadsheet was almost certainly published in Saxony, with anonymous text and illustration (Fig. 3.6).[63] It depicts a calf born in Landsberg near Halle that is not notably deformed, but does have a bald patch on its head as well as ass's ears ('Esels oren'). The broadsheet explicitly makes a connection with the Monk Calf, noting that 'the other one at Freiberg is also in this way born'.[64] Indeed, the birth of a creature like this – hardly a dramatic misbirth – would not have made it into print without the precedent of the Monk Calf and the sensational debates that surrounded it. The Landsberg calf is depicted almost as though gesturing; indeed – with open mouth and raised hand – almost as though it is orating the column of text that appears to its right. Whether intended or not, this effect reminds the modern reader of the oral and visual environment that these 'textual' publications appeared in; one in which the greater part of the audience for

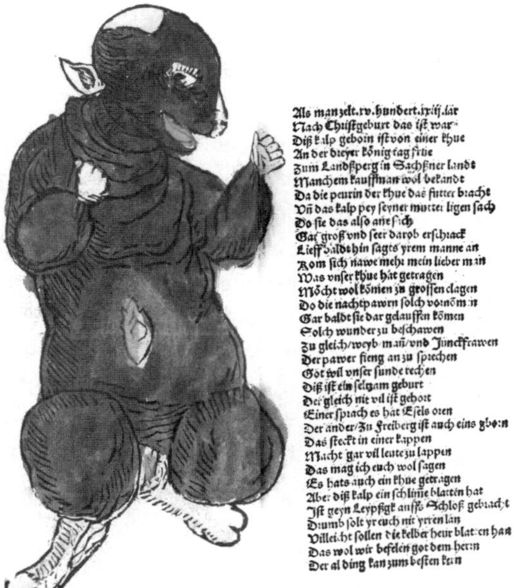

Figure 3.6: Monstrous calf, from Anon., *Als Man zelt. xv hundert. xxiij iar* (n.p., 1523). Photo courtesy of the Herzog August Bibliothek Wolfenbüttel, shelfmark A: 118.4 Quod. (11).

the broadsheet could see the image well enough for themselves, but would have the text read to them by someone else.[65]

Visual Culture in the German Reformation

Both Melanchthon and Luther use very visual metaphors in analysing the Papal Ass and Monk Calf, and they also treat the bodies of the Monk Calf and Papal Ass as images that can be broken down into individual segments and interpreted. The image of the composite monstrous birth has a peculiar relationship to the accompanying text in which the creature becomes itself a kind of text that can be sequentially read. It is not coincidental that the creatures they discuss are animal rather than human misbirths, as there seems more scope, at least at this early point in the century, to discuss an animal rather than a human infant, however deformed, in entirely damning terms. Their composite structure has echoes in the visual culture of the period, where the composite body is used, for example, in moralizing allegories as well as in mnemonic imagery.[66] Wondrous signs other than monstrous births could take on similar forms. A broadsheet from *c.* 1490–1 describes how fire from the sky destroyed a village near Constantinople, and was immediately followed by a wondrous vision in the sky of a knight – his triple face composed of a moon, sun and star – holding a woman with eagle's wings and an unnatural lower body.[67] Composite bodies like these mostly date from the pre-Reformation period, and form part of the visual culture that was appropriated and adapted according to the new needs of the Reformers and their opponents. Much closer to the period of Luther and Melanchthon's pamphlet, Anton Woensam's *c.* 1525 woodcut *The Good Wife* is an example of a deliberately constructed version of the composite body, didactic in flavour and presenting the body as a text to be sequentially 'read'; her hoofed feet, for example, unexpectedly represent her steadfastness.[68]

Some pre-Reformation publications had ascribed specific meanings to individual body parts in monstrous births, like the conjoined foreheads of the Worms twins. Yet none had so rigorously and polemically done so as Luther and Melanchthon's publication. This pamphlet is at the heart of a tangible shift in the representation and interpretation of monstrous births, and one that fitted the aggressively polemical culture of the early Reformation. That this polemic took visual as well as textual form is now well recognized. This period saw the rise of vigorous debates and fundamental shifts in visual culture. The most famous of these developments was the wave of iconoclasm, which saw the destruction of religious images and objects. More moderate 'reforms' of imagery included a move to remove any hint of lasciviousness (especially in female figures) in the images on church walls.[69] Martin Luther had a pragmatic attitude towards the use of religious images, and contributed to a culture of visual propaganda that stood on the borderline of the religious and the secular.[70] One of the most important aspects of the visual culture of the Reformation was the vigorous use of printed propaganda, deployed by Lutherans with remarkable success. Robert Scribner observed that 'Luther and other reformers spoke of pious images as masks (*larvae*) behind which the devil lurked, hoping to lure souls to damnation'. This did not mean that Luther rejected the use of images, and Scribner provided examples of how what he called the 'semiology of arousal' (which went well beyond the sensual) could be 'employed also for its revelatory effect, especially in Reformation propaganda, putting into practice Luther's notion of the masks of the devil disguising diabolical reality'.[71] Examples of this could include a broadsheet depicting Pope Alexander VI with a flap that lifted to reveal a devil, the 'true' Pope. While images like these are some of the most memorable of the era, the majority of the images created in response to the new religious context were less startling, and often drawn from the Bible.[72]

Religious imagery nonetheless increasingly moved outside relatively controlled environments like church walls and elite manuscripts, and into the turbulent new world created by the widely available printed image. The Reformation focus on making the word of God more widely and personally known, partly through the tool of the vernacular Bible, increased the number of biblical illustrations exponentially. Luther's 1522 translation of the New Testament, illustrated by Cranach, played an important role in this development. While this famous translation included twenty-one illustrations, they were all images from one single, and singularly monstrous, book of the New Testament: the Book of Revelation.[73] Luther's ideas about visual images are closely bound up with his views on the apocalyptic Book of Revelation – a connection seen in microcosm in the 1523 pamphlet.

The Apocalypse

While Albrecht Dürer had created what many regard as the definitive illustrated series of the Apocalypse in 1498, a flood of other versions appeared in the first half of the sixteenth century.[74] The increasing popularity of the Book of Revelation as a subject for illustration during the sixteenth century was evidently connected to the growth of an apocalyptic world view, especially amongst followers of the Lutheran Reformation. The Book of Revelation prophesied the terrible events that would precede the Last Days (war, famine, plague and various disasters) that many feared but also hoped were fast approaching. In this environment there was a tangible value in giving shape to apocalyptic imagery, and a ready audience for the new editions that came onto the market. As Bernd Moeller has identified, the End Times ('Endzeit') were one of the four most popular subjects for sermons preached in German towns in the early Reformation period.[75]

Also known as the Revelation of Saint John the Divine, or, more simply, as the Apocalypse, the Book of Revelation is one of the most confusing and debated books of the New Testament.[76] The prophetic visions that make up the majority of the book include the ritualistic opening of the book closed with seven seals, which releases chaos; the marking of the 144,000 faithful in order that they might be saved in the tumult; the violent destruction of the city of Babylon (identified from the earliest days of this text with Rome); the city's personification, the figure of the whore of Babylon; the celebration of the marriage of the Lamb; the chaining up of the devil for a thousand years; and the dazzling and very materialist vision of the New Jerusalem. The Book of Revelation is particularly notable for its monstrous beasts. A creature emerges from the ground, two horns on its head and roaring like a dragon; this is the beast notoriously numbered 666 (Revelation 13:11–18). A dragon from the Abyss wreaks havoc on humanity (Revelation 11:7). Most striking of all is the seven-headed beast, which first appears in Revelation 12:2–6, where it waits to attack the male child born to the woman clothed in the sun, and is foiled by God's intervention in lifting the child up to heaven. It is then attacked by Michael (Revelation 12:7–9), ridden upon by the Whore of Babylon (Revelation 17:3–14), and finally cast into a pit of brimstone (Revelation 19:20). The seven-headed beast of the Apocalypse was taken up with particular enthusiasm in the visual culture of sixteenth-century Germany. An image by Hans Brosamer depicts a seven-headed Luther on the title page of a 1529 pamphlet by Johann Cochlaeus, the *Sieben Kopffe Martini Luthers* (Fig. 3.7).[77] The heads represent Luther in various guises, some obviously negative in meaning and others requiring Cochlaeus's explanatory text. Luther is represented as a doctor of theology, as a monk, as a Turk, as a (populist) priest, as a fanatic, as a church visitor (seeking to usurp the papacy) and as the thief Barabbas, shown as a wild man.[78] However, the iconography of seven heads was much more commonly associated with anti-papal propaganda and the seven-headed beast with the Pope himself.[79] As such parodies indicate, the bizarre imagery of the Book of Revelation secured it a central place in the visual culture of this period.

Precisely, too, because of the fantastic, visionary nature of its imagery, Luther decided that clarifying illustrations for the Book of Revelation would be helpful to the reader and included them in his New Testament translation. Yet Luther questioned the canonicity of the Book of Revelation in his preface to it, considering it 'neither apostolic nor prophetic'.[80] 'My spirit cannot accommodate itself to this book', he writes, 'I stick to the books which present Christ to me clearly and purely'.[81] It is clear that Luther was troubled by the literally visionary nature of this book:

> the Apostles do not deal with visions, but prophesy in clear and plain words, as do Peter and Paul, and Christ in the gospel. For it befits the apostolic office to speak clearly of Christ and his deeds, without images and visions. Moreover there is no prophet in the Old Testament, to say nothing of the New, who deals so exclusively with visions and images.[82]

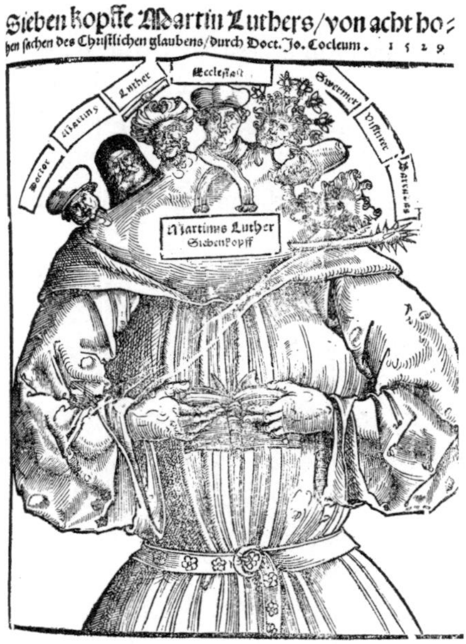

Figure 3.7: Seven-headed Luther, from J. Cochlaeus, *Sieben kopffe Martin Luthers* ([Dresden]: [Wolfgang Stöckel], 1529), title page. Photo courtesy of the Herzog August Bibliothek Wolfenbüttel, shelfmark A: 236.22 Theol (10).

Rosemarie Bergmann notes Luther's insistence on 'simple, correct illustration of the text, [and] the elimination of all symbolic and extraneous matter'.[83] The illustrations, prepared by Cranach and his workshop, draw upon Dürer's images of 1498. However, they are distinguished by a greater faithfulness to the text, a less tumultuous approach to composition, and are given greater clarity by being produced over twenty-one images rather than the fifteen in Dürer's series.[84] These well-known images also, in the September Testament or first edition, introduce the specific visual association of the Pope with monstrous elements of the book through the attribute of the papal tiara. The beast from the abyss which threatens the two prophets by the temple (Revelation 11:7) unmistakably wears this triple crown. The whore of Babylon who rides on the back of the seven-headed beast (Revelation 17:3) also wears the tiara, thrown into sharp relief by the open sky behind her. Explicitly anti-Catholic, too, is the depiction of the beast with two horns, here with a monk's cowl hanging from its neck (Revelation 13:11).[85] By the second edition of the New Testament, published in December 1522, these details had been deleted. They were regarded by many as excessively provocative, and influential figures like Duke George of Albertine Saxony pressed for their removal.[86] Yet they did not disappear entirely. In the first half of the sixteenth century a number of artists produced Apocalypse illustrations, notably Hans Schäufelein, Hans Burgkmair, Hans Holbein the Younger and Sebald

Beham.[87] These all drew upon both Dürer and Cranach to some extent, and a number retained the anti-papal imagery that had been excised from Luther's second edition.[88] Holbein's 1523 illustration of the whore of Babylon for a Basel edition of Luther's September Testament, for instance, represents her wearing the papal tiara, and with a highly voluptuous body emphasizing her sinful nature and projecting in polemical form the image of a corrupt and worldly papacy (Fig. 3.8).[89]

Luther's doubts about the authenticity and usefulness of the Book of Revelation diminished through the course of the 1520s. By 1530, he had reversed his original opinion, influenced by the upheavals of the Peasants' Revolt of 1525; the revocation of the recess of the 1526 Diet of Speyer at the 1529 Diet of Speyer (leading to the formation of the Schmalkaldic League); the Sack of Rome of 1527; and the renewed Turkish threat in the wake of the siege of Vienna of 1529.[90] He wrote a new preface for the Book of Revelation presenting it as serious prophecy. He discusses the obscure imagery of the text in terms of the historical figures and events that are, he argues, represented within it. One of the most important aspects of this new preface is his specific equation of the Pope with the whore of Babylon.[91] This is underscored by the return of the anti-papal and anti-monkish elements in the illustrations for his eventual 1534 edition of the entire Bible.[92] Luther makes very topical political use of the Book

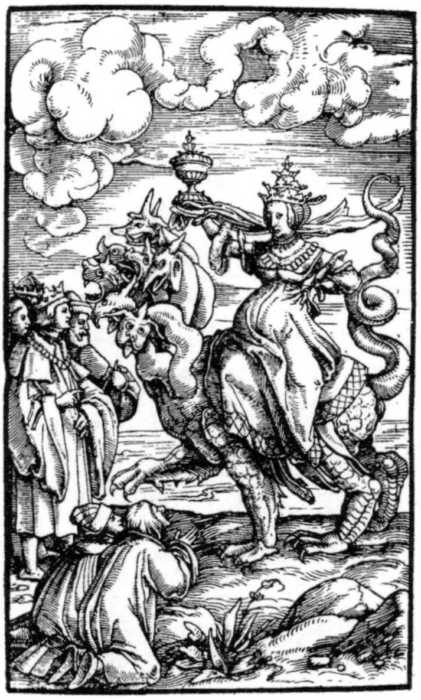

Figure 3.8: Hans Holbein the Younger, the Whore of Babylon, from *Das gantzs neuw Testament yetz klärlich auß dem rechten grundt teuscht* (Basel: Thomas Wolff, 1523), f. CLXXXIII v., detail. Photo courtesy of the Württembergischen Landesbibliothek, Stuttgart, shelfmark B deutsch 1523 03.

of Revelation in this new preface, underlining his pragmatic understanding of it despite the strangeness of the imagery. Indeed, he engages further with it, using the Book of Revelation as a vehicle for developing his ideas about the relationship of the visual to prophecy. This process seems likely to have been influenced by his preparation of the Monk Calf and Papal Ass pamphlet in 1523, and the ideas that it contained about visuality and the interpretation of mysterious signs sent by God. In the new preface, Luther described a type of biblical prophecy (listed third in the passage cited below) that foretells events that are not elsewhere explicitly explained in the Bible:

> this prophecy is of three types. The first expresses itself simply in words, without images and without figures – as Moses, David, and others of the prophets prophesy about Christ, and as Christ and the Apostles prophesy about Antichrist, false teachers, etc. The second type does this with images, but alongside them it supplies their interpretation in specific words – as Joseph interprets dreams, and Daniel both dreams and images. The third type does it without either words or interpretations, exclusively with images and figures, like this book of Revelation and like the dreams, visions, and images that many holy people have had from the Holy Spirit – as Peter in Acts 2[:17] preaches from Joel [2:28], 'Your sons and your daughters shall prophesy, and your young men shall see visions, and your old men shall dream dreams'. So long as this kind of prophecy remains without explanation and gets no sure interpretation, it is a concealed and mute prophecy and has not yet come to the profit and fruit which it is to give to Christendom.[93]

Luther's control over the illustrations for the translated Bible underlines his concern for the visual, and care to distinguish between what he characterized as appropriate and inappropriate imagery.[94] Robin Barnes observes that the rise of printing changed people's thinking about the Apocalypse in that it allowed more sophisticated readers to reflect further upon the text, and provided them with concrete visual images in naturalistic settings. Consequently a new sense of reality and specificity became attached to the Book of Revelation. However, Barnes also notes a simultaneous yet contrary tendency towards confusion engendered by the plurality of imagery, esoteric source material and scholarly speculation that could be attached to it, and argues that this tendency grew as the sixteenth century progressed.[95]

The Return of the Papal Ass

These increasingly entrenched themes form a background to the Papal Ass's return in the following decades. As the Reformation unfolded, the Papal Ass – due to its location in Rome and its distinctive iconography – remained an emblematic figure in Luther and Melanchthon's deployment of polemic in print. In 1535 Melanchthon prepared a new edition of his text on the Papal Ass, still illustrated by the original Cranach image.[96] Melanchthon's expanded text takes sharper, more polemical aim at the papacy in a number of short new passages, including one on the ass's head as a demonstration of the foolishness of the Pope, and another on the human hand as a sign the worldly, aggressive ambitions of the Pope.[97] Two particularly substantial new sections dramatically increase the anti-papal and also the apocalyptic import of the Papal Ass. Several new pages on the breasts and belly of the creature emphasize the themes of whoring and sin (and implicitly, perhaps, refer to the whore of Babylon), while the 'shameless female belly' ('vnuerschampt frawen bauch') represents the Antichrist's worst excesses.[98] A final passage, about the location of the creature in Rome, excoriates the Catholic church in Rome for failing to correctly read God's signs, depicted or painted ('gemalet') by God himself, even when they are as strikingly visual and terrible as the Papal Ass.[99] This new passage by Melanchthon is followed by an 'Amen' by Luther. The very visual metaphors employed by Luther and Melancthon in the 1523 pamphlet are further underscored in this short text by Luther. He writes:

> The Papal Ass is itself a dreadful, ugly, terrifying picture, and the longer one looks at it, the more terrifying it seems. However nothing is so completely terrifying as the fact that God himself made and revealed such a wonder and such a monstrous image. If a human had invented, carved or painted it, one would scorn or laugh at it. However since the highest Majesty himself created and depicted it, the whole world should be dismayed and quake, for from it one fully understands what he thought of and intended.[100]

Here, Luther further draws out the idea of God the artist creating an image ('Bilde') in the form of the Papal Ass. Luther acknowledges the potentially comic aspects of the creature; if a man had made this image, it would be laughed at. But since God has created it, the proper response is to try to understand its intended and divine message.

Luther returned to the Papal Ass in 1545, when he commissioned a series of nine images from Cranach for a short pamphlet (with brief captions) generally known as the *Depiction of the Papacy*.[101] In this publication, Cranach's earlier illustration is very lightly reworked, with a little more free space around the upper body to emphasize the creature's more prominent female breasts.[102] The womanly stomach bulges out further, and is emphasized by a prominent belly button. (Although it must be noted that none of the sixteenth-century versions emphasizes the female genitalia to the extent of the Wenzel von Olmutz engraving of the 1490s.) Gizzards have been added to the neck of the dragon, increasing the bulging, pendulous quality of the figure, and a forked tongue flickers from the dragon's open mouth. The Papal Ass opens a sequence of nine images, which were published in the immediate aftermath of Luther's vitriolic text *Wider das Babstum zu Rom vom Teufel gestifft* ('Against the Papacy at Rome, Founded by the Devil') of 1545.[103] This lengthy pamphlet presents the papacy in vehement terms as the Antichrist and harbinger of the Last Days. As Mark U. Edwards, Jr, notes, the Pope is caustically and memorably referred to at one point as 'Her Sodomitical Hellishness Paula III'; the papacy is intrinsically entwined within Lutheran polemic not just as the Antichrist, but also as the whore of Babylon.[104]

The new 1545 illustration of the Papal Ass by Cranach, this time along with Melanchthon's Papal Ass text, appeared again in 1549 (three years after the death of Luther), and with additional text by Matthias Flacius Illyricus.[105] Despite Melanchthon's status here as primary author, the publication was almost certainly not approved by him, but instead initiated by Flacius. The two were in bitter conflict at the time over the issue of adiaphora (that is, matters of church ritual and theology argued by some to be 'indifferent' in terms of salvation, and therefore not worth fighting about), and the Leipzig Interim, accepted by Melanchthon but vigorously opposed by Flacius. It was published the year that the latter left Wittenberg, where he had been professor of Hebrew, for Magdeburg – the location of this edition.[106] Flacius uses the 1523 version of Melanchthon's text, and adds several new passages.[107] These include a transcription of a text by Melanchthon on the issue of adiaphora, and apparently opposing the Interim.[108] This text reflects Melanchthon's opposition to the Augsburg Interim, before his acceptance of the compromise Leipzig Interim in December 1548, and is included by Flacius to undermine Melanchthon's more recent – and in Flacius's eyes appalling – compromise.

Flacius therefore uses Melanchthon's text on the Papal Ass, with its highly graphic condemnation of the papacy, as a springboard to oppose any religious compromise through the Leipzig Interim. In an introductory text, Flacius argues that the papacy can be represented in both words and images as worse than the devil or the whore of Babylon from the Book of Revelation. He maintains the highly visual language used by Luther and Melanchthon, and even concludes by claiming that the arts of geometrical and arithmetical proportions are inadequate for the present times, which demanded instead a 'new swinish art' ('newen Sewkunst').[109] Later in the pamphlet, Flacius adds additional texts that talk of the disastrous events leading up to the Last Days, specifically identifying the Pope as the Whore of Babylon, holding up her goblet, drunk on the blood of Christ, and seated on the back of the seven-headed beast which represented Rome itself (and also the 'Roemische Reich', or Roman Empire) and its support of the papacy.[110] The increasingly voluptuous body of the Papal Ass accords with this emphasis on the Babylonian woman. This combination of monstrous births and the Revelation imagery of the whore of Babylon will return again in sixteenth-century polemic, although in the unexpected form of a Catholic broadsheet by Franciscan Johann Nas, the subject of Chapter 5. First, though, the new genre of wonder books, which would eventually place a great multitude of monstrous births within an apocalyptic world view, will be examined.

4 WONDER BOOKS AND PROTESTANTS: JAKOB RUEFF, KONRAD LYCOSTHENES AND JOB FINCEL

The Monk Calf and Papal Ass continued to play a role in German publications on monstrous births as the sixteenth century progressed. The latter half of the century saw the rise of publications that moved well beyond reporting singular, and in the main contemporary monstrous births, and towards a new genre called the wonder book. These collected together monstrous births and various other wonders and disasters across decades, centuries or even millennia. The Monk Calf and Papal Ass took a central place amongst a group of increasingly iconic monstrous births. The most important authors to produce illustrated German wonder books were Job Fincel and Konrad Lycosthenes, and their precursor Jakob Rueff, and they are the focus of this chapter. Negative and also apocalyptic rhetoric about monstrous births became still more deeply entrenched in this genre. The increasing number of cases circulating in print fostered an accompanying polemic of multiplicity as well as a desire to identify and single out emblematically bizarre new cases. Chief amongst these in the middle of the century was the visually demonic monster of Krakow, examined in some detail later in this chapter.

The attitudes of Rueff, Fincel and Lycosthenes towards the Monk Calf and Papal Ass are a useful introduction to these authors' wider interest in monstrous births. In 1554, the Zurich physician Jakob Rueff included the Monk Calf in his book *Ein schön lustig Trostbüchle von den empfengknussen vnd geburten der menschen* ('A Cheerful Consolation Book on the Generation and Birth of Humans', Fig. 4.1). This creature was less a human-animal hybrid than a monstrous animal birth with exceptional qualities, although Rueff refers to it as a child ('kind') rather than an animal, presumably in an attempt to legitimize its inclusion in his book on human generation and birth. The illustration makes it appear rather smaller and less dramatic than it had in Lucas Cranach's version for Martin Luther. Rueff notes its birth in Saxony in 1522, 'the year and beginning of Martin Luther's preaching of the gospel'[1] – most likely a reference to Luther's translation of the New Testament, first published in 1522. Rueff therefore demonstrates his allegiance to the Protestant Reformation by including this case and accompanying it with a positive reference to Luther. The Monk Calf is a central figure in a 1557 illustrated wonder book by the eventual physician and enthusiastic follower of the Reformation, Job Fincel. His compilation of wondrous phenomena begins in 1517, the year that Luther had decisively set the Reformation in motion with his 95 Theses. Fincel directs the curious reader both to Luther's collected writings and also to Rueff's book, in both cases – unusually – giving a page number as reference.[2] Here, the Monk Calf stands commandingly in front of the town of Freiberg (Fig. 4.2). On the facing page, a woodcut shows two deformed children born in Wittenberg: one lacking a head, and the other with his legs reversed. They stand here in front of remarkable suns seen in Hungary and a rainbow seen in Wittenberg. The rainbow and the children had been identified by Luther in 1525 as foretelling the death of elector Frederick the Wise.[3] In the same year of 1557, Basel humanist Konrad Lycosthenes included the Monk Calf in his massive compilation of wonders, the *Wunderwerck*, with a brief comment noting that this was the creature 'about which Luther had written a great deal' (Fig. 4.3).[4]

The Monk Calf, despite its origins as a vehicle for vitriolic anti-papal polemic, is presented in these books in almost positive, commemorative terms as a milestone of Luther's early career. What of the Papal Ass? Rueff does not include or in any way discuss it. While he does use the Monk Calf to make a point-

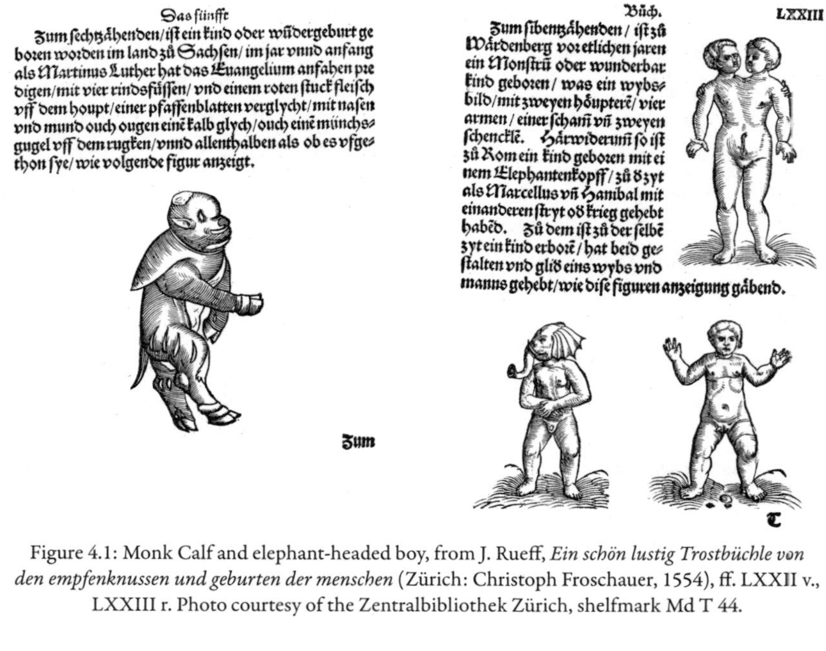

Figure 4.1: Monk Calf and elephant-headed boy, from J. Rueff, *Ein schön lustig Trostbüchle von den empfenknussen und geburten der menschen* (Zürich: Christoph Froschauer, 1554), ff. LXXII v., LXXIII r. Photo courtesy of the Zentralbibliothek Zürich, shelfmark Md T 44.

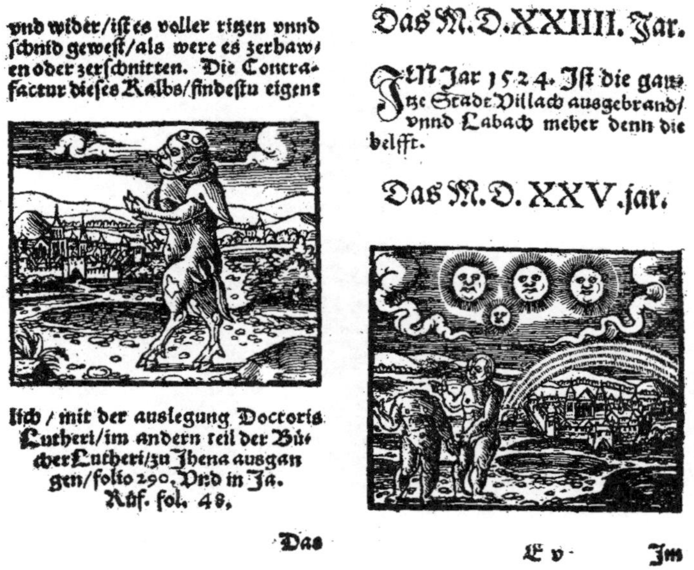

Figure 4.2: Monk Calf and monstrous children born in Wittenberg, from J. Fincel, *Wunderzeichen mit figuren* (1557), sigs E iiij v., E v r. Photo courtesy of the Universitäts- und Landesbibliothek Sachsen-Anhalt, Halle (Saale), shelfmark Pon Vc 1036 b (2).

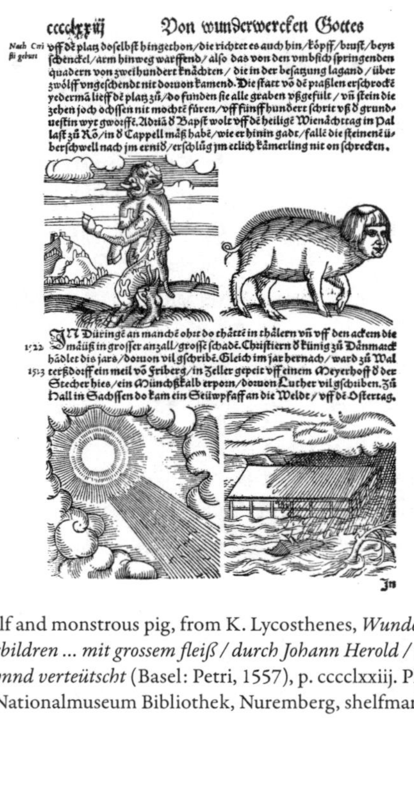

Figure 4.3: Monk Calf and monstrous pig, from K. Lycosthenes, *Wunderwerck Oder Gottes vnergrundtliches vorbildren ... mit grossem fleiß / durch Johann Herold / vffs treüwlichst inn vier Buecher gezogen vnnd verteütscht* (Basel: Petri, 1557), p. cccclxxiij. Photo courtesy of the Germanisches Nationalmuseum Bibliothek, Nuremberg, shelfmark NW. 3350h.

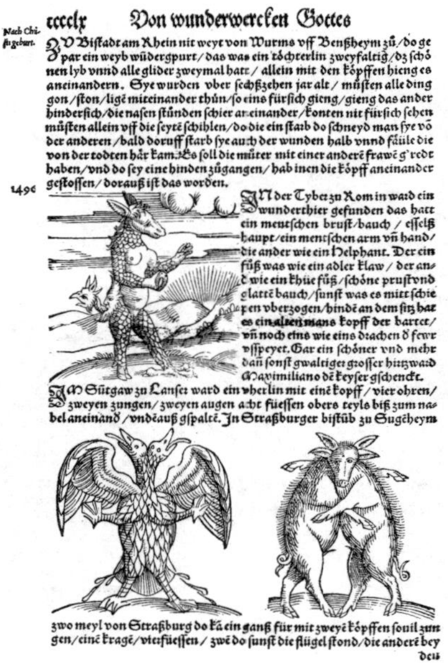

cccclx Von wunderwercken Gottes

Nach Christi geburt. ZV Biſtadt am Rhein nit weyt von Wurms vff Benſzheym zů / do ge par ein weyb wūdergpurt / das was ein tóchterlin zweyfaltig / dz ſchó nen lyb vnnd alle glider zweymal hatt / allein mit den kópffen hieng es aneinandern. Sye wurden vber ſechſzehen jar alt / műſten alle ding gon / ſton / ligē miteinander thůn / ſo eins fürſich gieng / gieng das ander hinderſich / die naſen ſtůnden ſchier aneinander / konten nit fürſich ſehen műſten allein vff die ſeytē ſchihlen / do die ein ſtarb do ſchneyd man ſye vō der anderen / bald doruff ſtarb ſye auch der wunden halb vnnd fäüle die von der todten hār kam. Es ſoll die műter mit einer anderē frawē g'redt haben / vnd do ſey eine hinden zůgangen / hab inen die kópff aneinander geſtoſſen / dorauſz iſt das worden.

1496 IN der Tyber zu Rom in ward ein wunderthier gefunden das hatt ein mentſchen bruſt / bauch / eſſelſz haupt / ein mentſchen arm vñ hand / die ander wie ein Helphant. Der ein fůſz was wie ein adler klaw / der an der wie ein khüe fůſz / ſchóne pruſt vnd glattē bauch / ſunſt was es mitt ſchie pen vberzogen / hindē an dem ſitz hat es ein alten mans kopff der bartet / vñ noch eins wie eins drachen d' fewr vſſpeyet. Gar ein ſchóner vnd mehr dañ ſonſt gwaltiger groſſer hitz ward Maximiliano dē keyſer gſchenckt.

IM Sütgaw zu Lanſer ward ein vherlin mit einē kopff / vier ohren / zweyen zungen / zweyen augen acht füeſſen obers teyls biſz zum na bel aneinand' / vndē auſz gſpaltē. Jn Straſzburger biſtūb zu Sugēheym

zwo meyl von Straſzburg do kā ein ganſz für mit zweyē kópffen ſovil zun gen / einē kragē / vierfüeſſen / zwē do ſunſt die flügel ſtond / die anderē bey den

Figure 4.4: Papal Ass, from K. Lycosthenes, *Wunderwerck Oder Gottes vnergrundtliches vorbildren ... mit grossem fleiß / durch Johann Herold / vffs treüwlichst inn vier Buecher gezogen vnnd verteütscht* (Basel: Petri, 1557), p. ccccclx. Photo courtesy of the Germanisches Nationalmuseum Bibliothek, Nuremberg, shelfmark NW. 3350h.

edly pro-Lutheran observation, he does not engage in anti-Catholic polemic. Lycosthenes includes the Papal Ass in immediate proximity to other monstrous births of the 1490s, and therefore prioritizes its pre-Reformation chronological context, rather than stressing its role within Reformation polemic (Fig. 4.4). Fincel should perhaps not even have discussed the Papal Ass, given that his chronology begins in 1517.[5] Yet he opts to conclude his book with a discussion of the creature, describing its physical characteristics and emphasizing its hybrid body, although not giving an interpretation in the style of Philipp Melanchthon or even including an illustration. Instead, he refers the reader directly to Melanchthon's own interpretation, even giving the page number.[6] The Papal Ass's importance for Fincel, however, is underlined by its location at the end of the book. For Fincel, the most self-consciously Protestant of the three authors here, the Papal Ass 'in actuality describes the papacy'. He states that God is sending warnings that should be heeded, that Martin Luther was part of his plan to save the faithful, and that the 'Godless' ('Gottlosen') must be responsible for their own ends.[7]

Rueff, Fincel and Lycosthenes were seminal authors who shaped a genre that became known as the wonder book.[8] Their own books were produced with a variety of purposes in mind: as medical and midwifery manuals, as natural history studies and as books of wonders. These publications underscore the tremendous growth of interest amongst publishers and readers during this period in monstrous births and natural wonders as topics for book-length studies. Several compilations of natural wonders had appeared earlier in the century, and Robin Barnes describes two Latin works, one by Joachim Camerarius and another by Friedrich Nausea, as the 'first true German wonder-books', while noting that 'their influence seems to have been quite limited'.[9] Perhaps this was partly because these earlier books had relatively little to offer the reader interested in the monstrous births that were appearing in their own times. The German-language books intended for a wide audience, and published from the 1550s, were full of such cases.[10] Towards the end of the century, further (unillustrated) German wonder books appeared by Protestant authors such as Christoph Irenaeus and Andreas Engel.[11] Similar publications by French authors, notably Pierre Boaistuau and Ambroise Paré, also appeared from the 1560s and formed a substantial group in their own right, although a comparative study is beyond the scope of this work.[12] Publications in England and Italy followed, including the translation and revision of Lycosthenes into English by Stephen Batman as *The Doome Warning All Men to Judgement* of 1581 and works that appeared in Italy in the seventeenth century authored by Ulisse Aldovandri and Fortunio Liceti.[13] The first wonder book by a German Catholic author – the Jesuit Caspar Schott – did not appear until the 1660s.[14]

The first wave of sixteenth-century Protestant German wonder books examined here appeared against the background of a great rise in the number of publications on natural history, astronomy and geography by authors including Girolamo Cardano, Conrad Gessner and Sebastian Münster; works that often emphasized the wondrous properties of the natural world.[15] In the wake of Luther's death in 1546, this period also saw the fracturing of Lutheranism into two groups: the Philippists (following Melanchthon, in various respects more inclined to accommodation, and particularly interested in the interpretation of the natural world as rich with interpretable signs from God); and the gnesio-Lutherans (who saw themselves as direct upholders of Luther's legacy, and adhered to a more strictly biblical understanding of God's plans).[16] The wonder books examined here are part of an important trend and point of conflict within later sixteeth-century Protestant culture about the correct interpretation of the natural world, particularly in understanding the coming of the Last Days.[17] This activity took place in the wake of the dramatic escalation and fragile resolution of confessional difference between the Schmalkaldic War of 1546–7, the Augsburg and Leipzig Interims of 1548, and the 1555 Peace of Augsburg.

Visually and thematically, the books that appeared in the 1550s emphasized the great number and great variety of monstrous births. They offered a new and graphically dynamic visual representation of monstrous births and their meanings. All three of the authors examined in this chapter interpreted monstrous births as warning signs from God, although Lycosthenes and, above all, Fincel took this considerably further than Rueff and unequivocally interpreted them as signs of the coming Last Days. Fincel argues that the fact that such a great *number* of signs had appeared since 1517 was in itself a testimony to their significance.[18] That is, in their dramatic forms and sheer proliferation, monstrous births were one phenomenon of the violent and turbulent Last Days that would precede the Day of Judgement.[19] Rueff, Fincel and Lycosthenes also demonstrated a greater concern to establish patterns and types of monstrosity than was possible in the broadsheets that were the most important sources for these new authors. Scholars sometimes therefore discuss these books from the 1550s as part of a shift in understanding monstrous births; from seeing them primarily as signs from God to viewing them more as medical curiosities or puzzles.[20] That is, some scholars see these books as prefiguring a future science of teratology, the systematic study and classification of physical monstrosities. While this has an evident connection with Rueff's work, it has relatively little relevance to the publications by Fincel and Lycosthenes, who wrote eschatological and polemical histories that sought to situate wonders in a world shaped by the Reformation and textually and visually conveyed their ever-increasing number.

Jakob Rueff

Rueff's *Trostbüchle* is highly significant for the development of the genre of wonder books that reported cases of monstrous births. Nonetheless, it cannot be properly considered a wonder book. It is, instead, a book on the generation and birth of children. Yet it evidently influenced later authors – including Rueff's immediate contemporaries Fincel and Lycosthenes – in its inclusion of an entire and richly illustrated chapter on the topic of monstrous births, more normally the province of broadsheet publications at that time.

Zurich resident Rueff (*c.* 1505/6–58) was a physician specializing in wounds and various types of simple surgery, a friend of naturalist Conrad Gessner, and even held the position of Zurich's *Stadtartzt*, or city doctor, for several years, despite not being technically eligible for the position.[21] An enthusiastic supporter of religious reform, Rueff also wrote religious plays in addition to his *Trostbüchle* of 1554, primarily intended for midwives.[22] As such it was influenced by a considerably shorter and equally popular publication from earlier in the century, Eucharius Rößlin's *Der Swangern Frauwen und hebammen Rosegarten* ('The Pregnant Woman and Midwife's Rose Garden'), first published in Strassburg in 1513.[23] A Latin edition of Rueff's text translated by the Zurich minister Wolfgang Haller, *De Conceptv et Generatione Hominis*, appeared in the same year of 1554.[24] The two editions indicate an attempt to gain the widest possible audience for the work. Rueff's book was reprinted and also translated a number of times through the following century.

Rueff traces the development of the foetus from the moment of conception, and follows Galen in describing the process of conception as one in which male and female 'seed' mingle together. However, despite his preference for Galen, Rueff prefaces his discussion of conception with an acknowledgement that the Aristotelian model (in which the male seed was dominant) was regarded as valid by many commentators. Indeed, Aristotelian theories of generation seem to have been more in favour through the sixteenth century.[25] The nature of female seed is given a slightly Aristotelian cast in the Latin edition, in that it is described as menstrual. However, the generative power of female seed remains important. It seems possible that Rueff's implicit preference for the Galenic model might reflects the then-recent appearance of two additional publications. Two Latin translations of Galen's *De foetum formatione* ('On the Formation of the Foetus') had appeared in 1536, one in a Basel edition by Janus Cornarius (Hagenbut) and one in the Paris *Opera diversa* by Johannes Guinterius (Johann Guinther).[26] Rueff's friend Gessner was deeply interested in Galen, and prepared several editions of Galen's collected works.[27] The engaging woodcut illustrations by Jos Murer in Rueff's book show an embryonic child becoming recognizably human in form over a series of pages, while another section, of more value to midwives, shows the various positions that babies may take in the womb.[28] This draws upon earlier medical texts and advice manuals, notably Rößlin's *Rosegarten* of 1513. The illustrations represent twins as well as single births. Rueff did not, however, follow Rößlin in the earlier author's inclusion of an illustration of conjoined twins in the womb (Fig. 4.5).

Rueff's interest in monstrous births evidently predated the publication of his *Trostbüchle* by at least a decade, as a broadsheet by 'I.R.' published by the Frosch publishing house in Zurich in 1543 is certainly by Rueff (Fig. 4.6).[29] This broadsheet reports the case of conjoined twin girls born in Schaffenhausen in Switzerland. Unusually for a broadsheet, it is written in Latin and discusses the possible natural causes, including astrological, of the birth. The illustration accompanying the text is also unexpectedly realistic, in comparison to many other broadsheet illustrations that tended to prioritize the dramatic representation of a birth over naturalistic depictions.[30] Rueff included the case again in his *Trostbüchle*, situating it in the context of a number of similar cases. He notes there that 'the same (type of) two children grown together' were born in the Swiss town of Einsidlen (Einsiedeln) in 1553.[31] This was only a year before the publication of the *Trostbüchle*, and indicates the contemporary circulation of reports of misbirths. There are two additional illustrated cases of conjoined twins on the facing page. One pair is joined at the stomach, and the other at the back. No location or date of birth is given for either of these sets of twins.

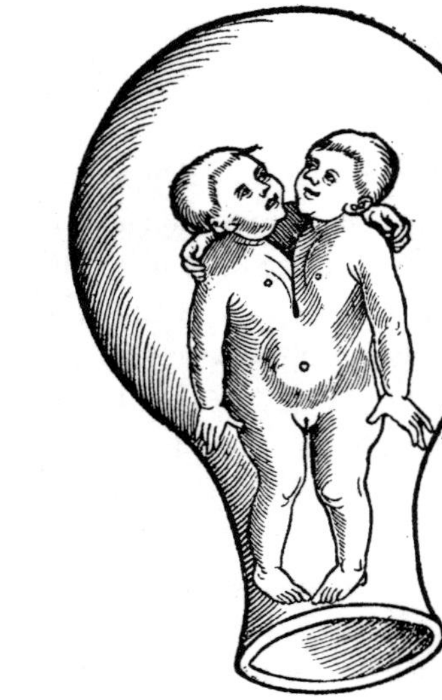

Figure 4.5: Conjoined twins in the womb, from E. Rößlin, *Der swangern Frauwen vnd Hebamen Rosegarten* (Argentine: Martinus Flach, 1513), sig. Cij v., detail. Photo courtesy of the Herzog August Bibliothek Wolfenbüttel, shelfmark 25.1 Med.

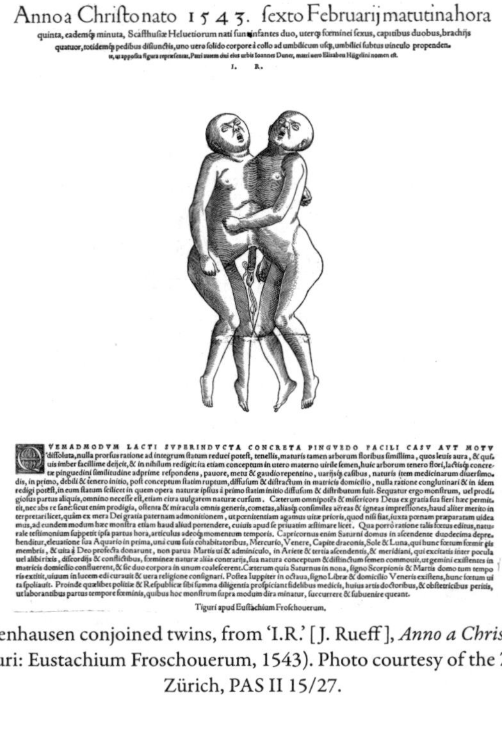

Figure 4.6: Schaffenhausen conjoined twins, from 'I.R.' [J. Rueff], *Anno a Christo nato 1543. sexto Februarij ...* (Tiguri: Eustachium Froschouerum, 1543). Photo courtesy of the Zentralbibliothek Zürich, PAS II 15/27.

Lycosthenes reported the case of the Schaffenhausen conjoined twins briefly in his *Wunderwerck* of 1557, which uses a very similar illustration to that in Rueff's broadsheet and the *Trostbüchle*, albeit with subtle differences. However, the striking naturalistic qualities are retained and are thrown further into relief in this compendium through comparison with many other images (Fig. 4.7). The image is repeated several times: its sense of singularity and careful observation is quite lost, giving way to an emphasis instead on the pathos of the figures, with their thrown-back heads and open mouths.[32]

Rueff discusses these monstrous births and others (thirty-two in total) in the third chapter of the fifth book of his *Trostbüchle*. He generally describes the physical deformities in simple terms, and provides brief contextual details including the date and location of particular births. As well as reporting contemporary cases, he also used a series of classical examples from the Roman author Julius Obsequens. Rueff was familiar with this material because Lycosthenes had prepared an illustrated edition published in 1552, thereby indicating some level of mutual intellectual influence between the two Swiss authors.[33] In Rueff's *Trostbüchle*, these are some of the most summarily described cases in the chapter on monstrous births, and he repeatedly and simply notes that the children were

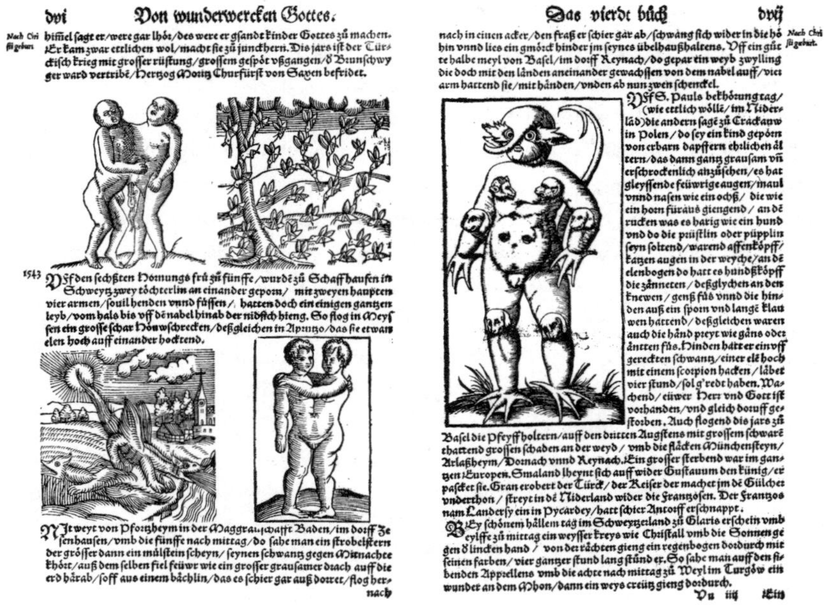

dvi Von wunderwercken Gottes.

Nach Christi geburt

hiffiel sagt er/were gar lhôr/des were er gsandt kinder Gottes zů machen. Er kam zwar ettlichen wol/macht sie zů junckherrn. Dis jars ist der Türckisch krieg mit grosser rüstung/grossem gespôt vßgangen/d' Brunschwyger ward vertribẽ/Hertzog Moritz Churfürst von Sayen befridet.

1543 Vff den sechßten Hornungs frů zů fünffe/wurdẽ zů Schaffhausen in Schweytz zwey tôchterlin an einander gepom/ mit zweyen haupten vier armen/souil henden vnnd füssen/ hatten doch ein einigen gantzen leyb/vom hals bis vff dẽ nabel hinab der nidsich hieng. So flog in Meyssen ein grosse schar Hôuwschrecken/deßgleichen in Apruzzo/das sie etwan elen hoch auff einander hocktend.

Nit weyt von Pfortzheym in der Maggraueschafft Baden/im dorff Zesenhausen/vmb die fünffe nach mittag/do sahe man ein strobelstern der grôsser dann ein mülstein scheyn/ seynen schwantz gegen Mitnachte kôrt/auß dem selben fiel feüwr wie ein grosser grausamer drach auff die erd hårab/soff aus einem båchlin/das es schier gar auß dorret/flog hernach

Das vierdt bůch dvij

nach in einen acker/den fraß er schier går ab/schwång sich wider in die hôhin vnnd lies ein gmôrck hinder jm seynes übelhaußhaltens. Vff ein gůtte halbe meyl von Basel/im dorff Reynach/do gepar ein weyb zwylling die doch mit den lånden aneinander gewachssen von dem nabel auff/vier arm hattend sie/mit hånden/vnden ab nun zwen schenckel.

Nach Christi geburt.

Vff S. Pauls bekhôrung tag/ (wie ettlich wôllẽ/im Niderlåd)die andern sagẽ zů Crackauw in Polen/do sey ein kind gepôrn von erbarn dapffern ehrlichen ål tern/das dann gantz grausam vñ erschrockenlich anzůsehen/es hat gleyssende feüwrige augen/maul vnnd nasen wie ein ochß/ die wie ein horn füraus giengend/ an dẽ rucken was es harig wie ein hund vnd do die prüstlin oder püpplin seyn soltend/warend affenkôpff/ katzen augen in der weyche/an dẽ elenbogen do hatt es hundßkôpff die zånneten/deßglychen an den knewen/genß fůs vnnd die hinden auß ein sporn vnd langẽ klauwen hattend/deßgleichen waren auch die hånd preyt wie gåns oder åntten fůs. Hinden hatt er ein vffgereckten schwantz/einer elẽ hoch mit einem scorpion hacken/låbet vier stund/sol g'redt haben. Wachend/eüwer Herr vnd Gott ist vorhanden/vnd gleich dorauff gestorben. Auch flogend dis jars zů Basel die Pfeyffholtern/auff den dritten Augstens mit grossem schwarẽ thattend grossen schaden an der weyd/ vmb die flåcken Münchenstein/ Arlaßheym/Dornach vnnd Reynach. Ein grosser sterbend war im gantzen Europen. Smaland lheynt sich auff wider Gustauum den künig/er paschet sie. Gran erobert der Türck/der Keiser der machet jm dẽ Gülcher vnderthon/streyt in dẽ Niderland wider die Frantzosen. Der Frantzos nam Landersy ein in Pycardey/hatt schier Antorff erschnappt.

Bey schônem hållem tag im Schweytzerland zů Glaris erschein vmb eylffe zů mittag ein weysser kreys wie Christall vmb die Sonnen gegen d' lincken hand/ von der råchten gieng ein regenbogen dordurch mit seinen farben/vier gantzer stund lang stůnd er. So sahe man auff den sibenden Apprellens vmb die achte nach mittag zů Weyl im Turgôw ein wunder an dem Mhon/dann ein weys creütz gieng dordurch.

Vu iiij Ein

Figure 4.7: Schaffenhausen conjoined twins and the monster of Krakow (or the Netherlands), from K. Lycosthenes, *Wunderwerck Oder Gottes vnergrundtliches vorbildren ... mit grossem fleiß / durch Johann Herold / vffs treüwlichst inn vier Buecher gezogen vnnd verteütscht* (Basel: Petri, 1557), pp. dvi, dvij. Photo courtesy of the Germanisches Nationalmuseum Bibliothek, Nuremberg, shelfmark NW. 3350h.

born in 'Roemer land'. There is one poignant variation in his borrowing from the Lycosthenes edition: a boy whose stomach gapes open to reveal his internal organs is replaced by a girl, and a view of her womb (Fig. 4.8). She forms an apt but subtly unsettling counterpoint to the anatomical image of a pregnant woman used earlier in Rueff's book (Fig. 4.9). Huldrych M. Koelbing notes that Rueff borrowed several images from the 1543 Basel edition of Vesalius, and the opened-up female body certainly recalls a similar image in that edition.[34] In a style deliberately reminiscent of classical statuary, however, the Vesalius illustration omitted the woman's arms, legs and head, as well as the elaborate chair and the tiny foetus in her womb, which all form such striking elements in the Rueff illustration.[35]

Rueff's sequence of monstrous births emphasizes the physical variety of the phenomenon, and particularly cases of additional or missing limbs.[36] This type of deformity is an evident focus of his interest in the natural causes of physical monstrosity in human children. The lack or excess of limbs is for Rueff an opportunity to demonstrate his interest in 'uberflussigkeit', or the excess of seed, as well as the 'weakness' ('schwachheit vn[d] bloedigkeit') contained within semen. The result, he says, was most commonly 'children with twisted limbs, without all their limbs, or instead having too many'. This passage is from the first chapter of book five, on the topic of the 'Molam' where no child develops in the womb, but instead a formless mass of flesh. In the same section Rueff explains how 'toads, worms, or other poisonous animals' inside the womb could gnaw away at and damage the child; how bestiality could cause deformities; and how a lack of heat in the womb combined with weak semen could have ill consequences where the child was, metaphorically speaking, 'not cooked, prepared, and made into a real child'.[37] Nonetheless, he firmly describes the most dramatic and unusual forms of monstrous births as coming 'from God'.[38] Rueff's unusually pronounced interest in natural causes does, however, substantially differentiate his book from the broadsheets that it drew upon, and also the wonder books that would follow it, all more concerned with the moral, social or political message conveyed by a misbirth.[39] In the sixteenth century few German authors displayed interest in the natural causes of physical deformity.[40]

Alongside the many human misbirths in Rueff's book, he also includes four human-animal hybrids, difficult both to categorize and to account for. These evidently helped to provide a model of encyclopedic variety for later wonder book authors.[41] One of these creatures is the Monk Calf, discussed above. Another, on the facing page, is a male child with an elephant's head, born in Rome 'during the time that Marcellus and Hannibal battled or waged war against one another' (see Fig. 4.1).[42] Implicitly, for the educated reader, the deformity recalls Hannibal's military feat of bringing elephants across the Alps. This seems to have been a well-known classical example of a misbirth, and Rueff's source was evidently

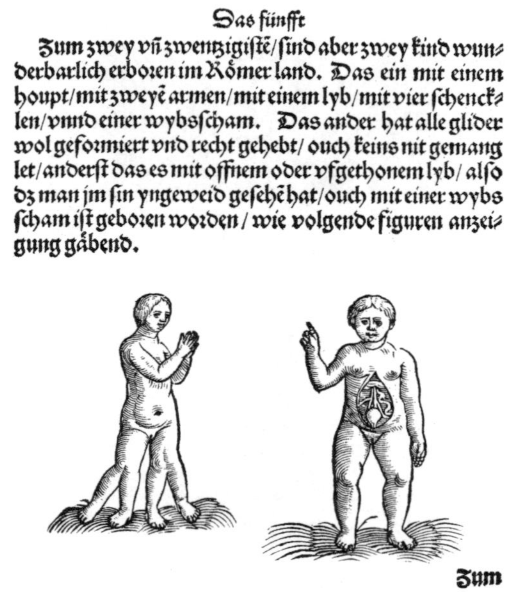

Das fünfft

Zum zwey vñ zwentzigistẽ/sind aber zwey kind wunderbarlich erboren im Römer land. Das ein mit einem houpt/mit zweyẽ armen/mit einem lyb/mit vier schencklen/vnnd einer wybsscham. Das ander hat alle glider wol geformiert vnd recht gehebt/ ouch keins nit gemanglet/anderst das es mit offnem oder vfgethonem lyb/ also dz man jm sin yngeweid gesehẽ hat/ouch mit einer wybsscham ist geboren worden/ wie volgende figuren anzeigung gäbend.

Zum

Figure 4.8: Girl with a gaping-open stomach, from J. Rueff, *Ein schön lustig Trostbüchle von den empfenknussen und geburten der menschen* (Zürich: Christoph Froschauer, 1554), f. LXXV v. Photo courtesy of the Zentralbibliothek Zürich, shelfmark Md T 44.

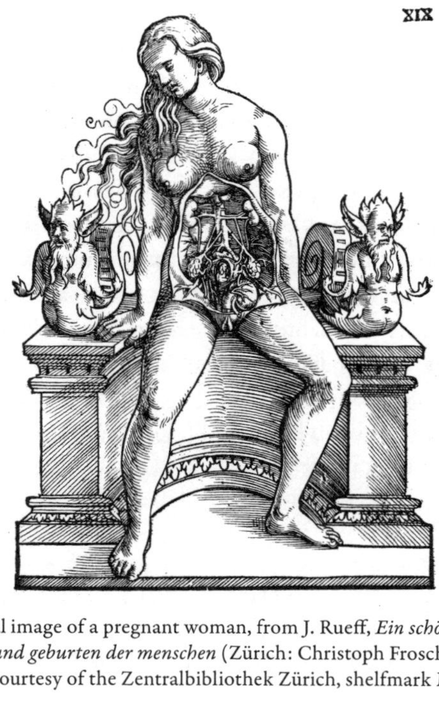

Figure 4.9: Anatomical image of a pregnant woman, from J. Rueff, *Ein schön lustig Trostbüchle von den empfenknussen und geburten der menschen* (Zürich: Christoph Froschauer, 1554), f. XIX r. Photo courtesy of the Zentralbibliothek Zürich, shelfmark Md T 44.

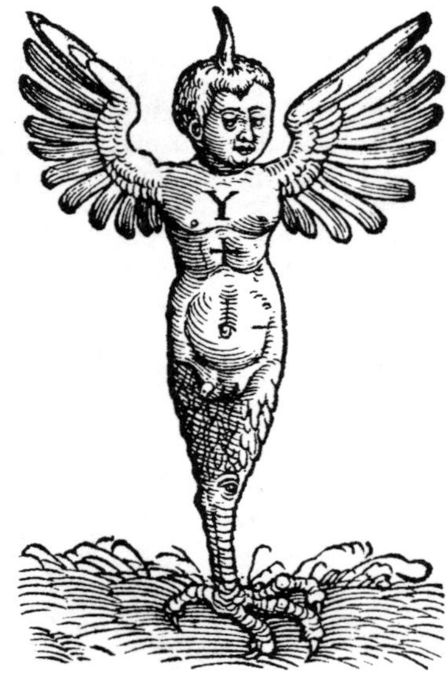

Figure 4.10: Monster of Ravenna, from J. Rueff, *Ein schön lustig Trostbüchle von den empfenknussen und geburten der menschen* (Zürich: Christoph Froschauer, 1554), f. LXXVI v., detail. Photo courtesy of the Zentralbibliothek Zürich, shelfmark Md T 44.

again Lycosthenes's 1552 edition of Obsequens.[43] Third, Rueff included the 1512 Italian monster of Ravenna, which was one of the more notorious monstrous births of the sixteenth century (Fig. 4.10). Indeed, Rueff completes his chapter on monstrous births with this particular example. While he describes the physical characteristics of the child, he does not ascribe any specific meaning to its deformities. Instead, he concludes with the more general idea that many more similar births would take place, and that 'we should learn [from] the eternal God's wonder works, and take on [these messages] to better ourselves'.[44] At this point, Rueff prioritizes a divine understanding of monstrous births, a reminder that his interest in natural causes fitted within a typical and uncontroversial view of the world. Finally, Rueff includes the monster of Krakow, an extraordinary hybrid creature with various animals' head growing from its body, born in the 1540s. This intriguing and – for Rueff and his peers – very contemporary case is examined later in this chapter as an exemplification of the extraordinary variety of forms that monstrous births could now encompass within one body.

Job Fincel

Several years later, Fincel made good use of the work of his precursor Rueff when writing his own book on wondrous signs: the *Wunderzeichen*. Fincel (1526/30–89) grew up in a Lutheran family, studied in Erfurt and then in Wittenberg, where he became part of Melanchthon's circle.[45] He became a doctor of medicine in 1562, lectured at the university in Jena, and was active later as a physician in Weimar and Zwickau. Beyond his (ultimately three-volume) *Wunderzeichen*, Fincel also published poetry and a study of the plague. He included over one hundred cases of monstrous births in the first volume of his *Wunderzeichen*, published in 1556. Although he rarely discussed individual cases in any detail, he was consistent and clear about their primary role as warning signs from God. Fincel displayed limited interest in the possible physical causes of misbirths (much more important to Rueff), although in the second volume of his 1566 edition he did write that 'excessive or too few limbs in births, etc., happen naturally, and are therefore not wondrous signs'.[46] Most authors writing on wonders in the sixteenth century saw these explanatory systems as part of a continuum, not as opposed alternatives. Divine and natural causes co-existed.[47] Nonetheless, different authors prioritized particular causes within that continuum. Fincel does maintain, therefore, that wondrous signs can have both natural and unnatural causes, but repeats that their ultimate cause is always one thing, 'namely God' ('nemlich Gott').[48] It is hard to overemphasize how much more importance Fincel lays on the religious, political and social meanings of monstrous births than on discovering their possible natural causes.

The three volumes of the *Wunderzeichen* appeared between 1556 and 1562, and drew on Fincel's personal notes as well as broadsheets and other publications on wondrous events. They were clearly well received, as the multiple editions and three volumes demonstrate. At the Frankfurt book fair in 1569, the bookseller Michael Harder had 171 copies of the *Wunderzeichen* for sale, even more than his 158 copies of Thüring von Ringoltingen's popular German edition of the story of Melusine.[49] The 1557 edition of the first volume of Fincel's *Wunderzeichen* is the focus here as it was published in an illustrated edition that demonstrates a new approach to the relationship between text and image in the reporting and analysis of monstrous births.[50] That is, the illustrations generally combined several unrelated wonders, creating a dramatic effect that emphasized the great number, variety and cumulative impact of wonders.

Fincel himself had no doubt that these signs were becoming more numerous in his own lifetime.[51] In an extended foreword to his book, he makes explicit the framework in which he views the increasingly prevalent and terrifying wonders and disasters occurring in the natural world.[52] He recalls for the reader, at some length, the story of the city of Sodom, destroyed by God in punishment for the sins of the city's inhabitants. For Fincel, monstrous births, floods, fire, plague and other disturbing natural phenomena are warnings to a sinful or 'Godless world' ('Gottlose Welt') that reminds him increasingly of Sodom.[53] He is very specific about the location of the modern-day Sodom: it is the seat of the papacy, which is 'covered and filled up with sodomitic sins'.[54] His Reformation polemic continues with the declaration that 'the holy man Doctor Martin Luther has led us out of this damned Sodom'.[55] The Turkish threat is another symptom of the state of crisis. Fincel reminds his readers of the dramatic natural events, including floods and earthquakes, which had appeared around the time of the coming of 'Mahomet'.[56] However, the papacy is the greater threat, and the terrible events that Fincel describes are often characterized as representing the papacy.[57] They form part of the general tendency towards disruptive wars that Fincel observes in his own time, including the terrible local events of the 1546–7 War of Schmalkalden.[58] So too are new waves of disease, especially plague, which Fincel compares to the coming of the pestilence in chapter sixteen of the Book of Revelation.[59] Current events related to religious reform and its associated civil conflicts form the backbone of the book. In 1553, for example, the battle between various princes is described as being accompanied by the sounds of the cry 'Weh/ Weh/ Weh', a reference to chapter eight of the Book of Revelation. Fincel continues, 'such a lamentation is also in the last few years often to be heard here'.[60]

Fincel's chronological structure and tendency in the accompanying illustrations to combine phenomena and events from different times and locations, like monstrous births, earthquakes, storms and plagues of insects and disease, into one single image adds to the sense of drama and urgency. One woodcut, used for the year 1536 and repeated for 1544, depicts a male child with four arms and four legs standing against the background of a town invaded by locusts and pelted by fiery stones (Fig. 4.11). In the year 1537, a child with no feet watches as the castle in Heidelberg is bombarded by hailstones in the course of a terrible storm.[61] The tower containing gunpowder (the 'puluerthurn') has been hit with resulting fire and devastation. In 1551, Fincel reports the birth of child or 'Kind' born in the forests near Wittstock, not far from Wittenberg. The child looks suspiciously like a devil, and stands before three unnatural suns seen in Magdeburg that same year (Fig. 4.12). Like the considerably more famous monster of Krakow, discussed later in this chapter, this demonic-looking monstrous child, born during the decade in which Fincel was writing, adds an increasingly sinister aspect to the phenomenon of the monstrous birth.

Fincel discusses the issue of whether wondrous phenomena are sent by a wrathful God as punishment, or by a merciful God as signs to the pious and sinners alike and a warning to overcome sin. He ultimately concludes that God is showing his anger but simultaneously also his mercy by allowing sinners to repent. Through repentance, the faithful could rebalance the order of the world and redirect God's righteous anger towards the Turks and the papacy. Believers could be saved, just as Lot was led out of the city of Sodom.[62] The coming Day of Judgement would then become a source of solace ('trost') rather than fear.[63] Variations of the phrase, 'the Day of Judgement is at the door' appear regularly throughout the book.[64] This aspect of his work increased rather than decreased

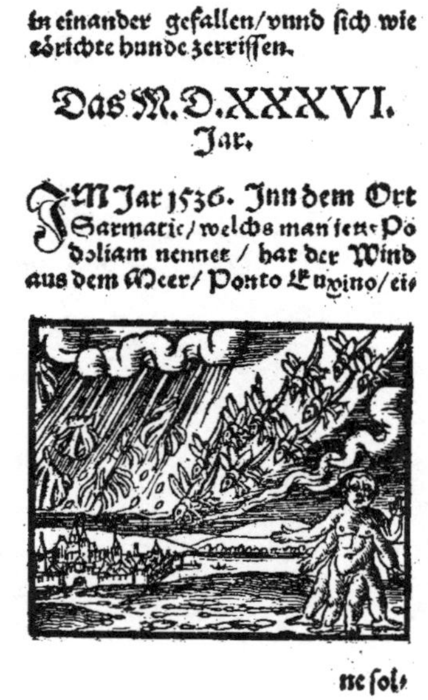

zu einander gefallen/vnnd sich wie
töricht hunde zerrissen.

Das M.D.XXXVI.
Jar.

IM Jar 1536. Inn dem Ort
Sarmatie/welchs man jetzt Po
dolien nennet / hat der Wind
aus dem Meer/ Ponto Euxino/ei

ne sol

Figure 4.11: German monstrous births in Italian landscape, from J. Fincel, *Wunderzeichen mit figuren* (1557), sig. H vi v., repeated at sig. M viij v. Photo courtesy of the Universitäts- und Landesbibliothek Sachsen-Anhalt, Halle (Saale), shelfmark Pon Vc 1036 b (2).

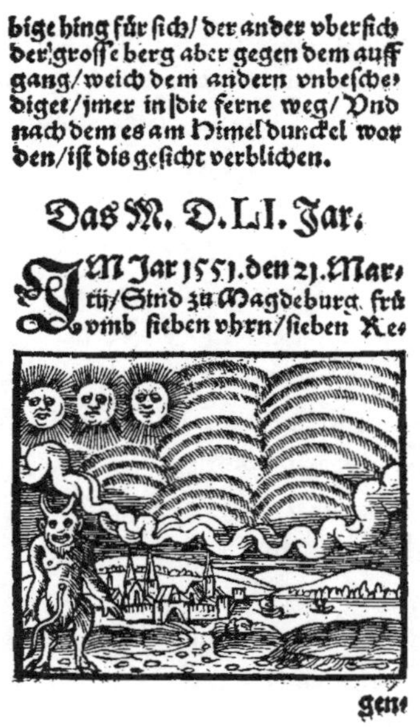

dige hing für sich/ der ander vber sich
der grosse berg aber gegen dem auff
gang/weich dem andern vnbesche
diget/jmer in die ferne weg/ Vnd
nach dem es am Himel dunckel wor
den/ist dis gesicht verblichen.

Das M. D.LI. Jar.

IM Jar 1551. den 21. Mar
tij/Sind zu Magdeburg frü
vmb sieben vhrn/sieben Re

gen

Figure 4.12: Monstrous birth from Wittstock, in landscape showing three suns in Magdeburg, from J. Fincel, *Wunderzeichen mit figuren* (1557), sig. R vi v. Photo courtesy of the Universitäts- und Landesbibliothek Sachsen-Anhalt, Halle (Saale), shelfmark Pon Vc 1036 b (2).

between the first, unillustrated edition of 1556 and the illustrated edition of 1557. This edition includes several additional concluding sections, notably an eight-page closing text which deals with the prophecy of the coming of the Antichrist in Revelation 13. Utilizing Lutheran themes, this text contains a series of reflections on the Apocalypse, on prophetic imagery, on numerical calculations concerning the timing of the Last Days (although Fincel, like Luther, does not attempt to predict when the Day of Judgement will come) and the identification of the papacy with the Antichrist.

Konrad Lycosthenes

The best-known sixteenth-century wonder book author is Konrad Wolffhart (1518–61), more frequently known by his Latin name, Lycosthenes. His *Prodigiorum ac ostentorum chronicon* ('Chronicle of Prodigies and Signs') appeared in 1557. In the same year a German-language version, the *Wunderwerck* ('wonder work'), was carefully translated by Lycosthenes's associate Johann Herold.[65] Herold's role was more important than that of translator, as he also wrote an additional preface for the volume, which further clarified the categorization of monstrous births, as well as reflecting on the value of making them widely known through a vernacular translation.[66] The *Wunderwerck* is an ambitious book of over five hundred pages that relates the occurrence of wondrous events through history.[67] Like Hartmann Schedel's *Weltchronik*, Lycosthenes's book canvassed the periods of the Old and New Testaments as well as recent history. Each of the individual 'books' or chapters in Lycosthenes's volume begins with a historical turning point, notably the birth of Christ and the coronation of Charlemagne. All these structural elements distinguish Lycosthenes's approach significantly from Fincel's, which focused upon events beginning in 1517 and the onset and unfolding of the Reformation in northern Germany.

Lycosthenes studied in Heidelberg, where he was awarded his doctorate in 1539. He spent his professional life in Basel, where he was a church deacon, and worked on publications including the *Wunderwerck*.[68] This project was evidently inspired in part by his earlier work on the fourth- or fifth-century wonder book by Julius Obsequens, the *Liber de prodigiis*, which appeared as an illustrated edition in 1552 and reported wondrous events that had taken place in Rome between 249 and 212 BC.[69] Lycosthenes was a whole-hearted supporter of religious reform, although his religious affiliations are not as explicitly drawn as Fincel's are in the *Wunderzeichen*, and were likewise not shaped by the bitter debates between followers of Luther and Melanchthon in the aftermath of Luther's death, but instead by the Swiss as well as the Lutheran Reformation.[70] Many of the phenomena that Lycosthenes reports, at least those from the sixteenth century, concern either Swiss regions or Saxony, indicating that he utilized material supplied by friends and acquaintances including reformers in northern Germany.

The *Wunderwerck* is remarkable for its breadth and for its compilation of materials from many different sources. Lycosthenes certainly consulted Fincel, Luther, Melanchthon, Brant and Rueff, as well as many classical, early Christian and humanist authors, and he also utilized broadsheets, pamphlets, year-books and chronicles.[71] Lycosthenes places a much greater priority on what these wondrous events and creatures can actually communicate to the reader, and the significance of their increasing occurrence (emphasized through the chronological structure), than on the process of their creation. Sometimes Lycosthenes explicitly connects these wonders to major events: a multiple birth might mean a coming famine, for instance; and in the manner of Sebastian Brant, conjoined male and female twins born in Rohrbach near Heidelberg in 1486 are discussed alongside the crowning of Maximilian as King of the Romans ('Keyser').[72]

What message, then, did these events convey? Lycosthenes sees monstrous signs as forming part of the disintegration of a sinful world, and therefore warning of the Last Days. These ideas are given further emphasis for a wider audience in Johann Herold's German-language preface. Like Job Fincel, Lycosthenes places great emphasis on the sheer number of wonders that appeared in his own lifetime. Prior to 1484, the *Wunderwerck* reports eighty-four cases of monstrous births. In the years between 1485 and 1555, one hundred and six cases are reported. There is a much greater volume of wondrous events in Lycosthenes's book than in any previous text, and this is reinforced visually. First, this aspect is emphasized in the frontispiece. Almost like a cabinet of wonders or scientific curiosities, the woodcut presents a neatly arranged array of phenomena (Fig. 4.13).[73] These include a flood; a vision of a battle in the sky; a comet; a storm; an earthquake; a harpy; a hydra, a merman and merwoman; conjoined twins; a centaur; and the monster of Krakow, examined in more detail later in this chapter. The core of the image incorporates four scenes from the life of Christ and a central, dominant image that underscores the apocalyptic message of the book by showing Christ seated on a rainbow presiding over the Day of Judgement. These wondrous phenomena are divine in origin and warn of the Last Days; a point therefore conveyed in concise but complex pictorial form at the outset of the book. This image conceptually and structurally builds upon the simpler frontispiece with multiple wonders that Lycosthenes had used five years earlier for his edition of Julius Obsequens (Fig. 4.14). The great variety of natural wonders is also visually underlined in the *Wunderzeichen* through the book's large number of illustrations (many of which are repeated). Only eight pages contain no illustrations, most pages have more than one, and some have as many as five.

Rather than inserting single images that bring together several events in the style of Fincel's *Wunderzeichen*, Lycosthenes juxtaposes his imagery to build up

Wunderwerck

Oder

Gottes vnergründtliches vorbil-
den/das er inn seinen gschöpffen allen/so Geystlichen/so
leyblichen/in Fewr/Lufft/Wasser/Erden/auch auß den selben vier vrhaben/
ineingfügtem stuck dem Menschen/in Gflügel/Vieh/Thier/Visch/Gwürm/
von anbegin der weldt/biß zů vnserer diser zeit/erscheynen/hören/brieuen las-
sen. Zů gwiser anmhanūg seiner Herlicheit/zů abschröckung sündtlichs lebens.
Oder aber sonst verhängt hatt/den Ausserwöltē zůr übung vnd Christenlichem
nachsinnen. den bösen zůr straaff jres vnglaubens / mit sonder
wunderbarer geheymnus vnd bedeüttung.

Alles mit schönen Abbildungen gezierdt/vnnd an den Leser einer Vor-
rede/in dero/ der entscheyd/ hafft/betrug/füg vnd vrtel so hierinnen zů
erlernen vnd zůhaben/in kurtze/eygentlich fürgeschribē vnd abgemalt.

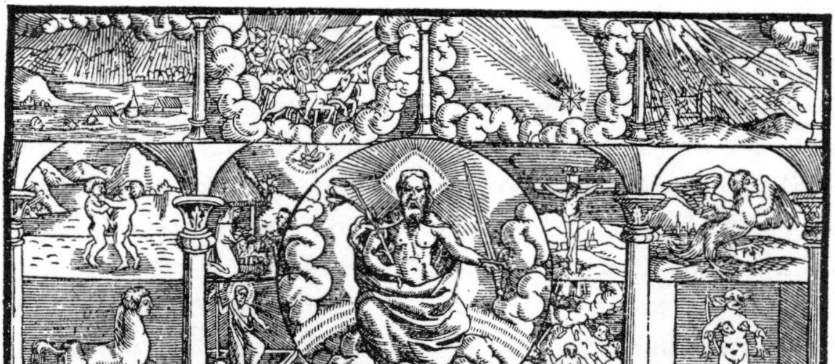

Auß Herrn Conrad Lycosthenis Latinisch zůsammen getragner beschrey-
bung/mit grossem fleiß/durch Johann Herold/vffs treüw-
lichst inn vier Bücher gezogen vnnd Verteütscht.

Mit Rö. Key. May. Freyheyt vnd Priuilegien.

Figure 4.13: K. Lycosthenes, *Wunderwerck Oder Gottes vnergrundtliches vorbildren ... mit grossem fleiß / durch Johann Herold / vffs treüwlichst inn vier Buecher gezogen vnnd verteütscht* (Basel: Petri, 1557), title page. Photo courtesy of the Herzog August Bibliothek Wolfenbüttel, shelfmark H: QuH 22.2 (1).

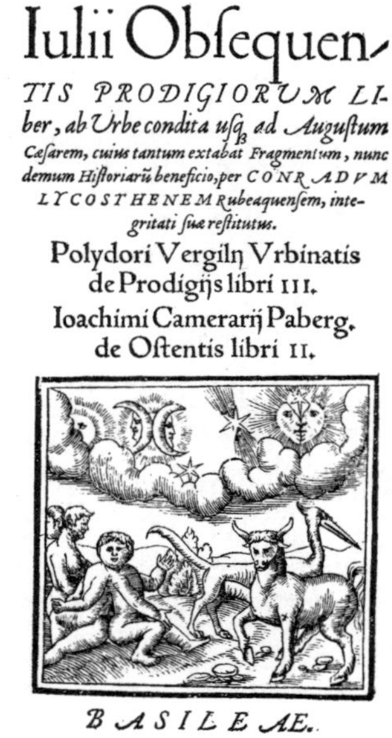
Iulii Obſequen-
TIS PRODIGIORUM LI-
ber, ab Urbe condita uſq; ad Auguſtum
Cæſarem, cuius tantum extabat Fragmentum, nunc
demum Hiſtoriarũ beneficio, per CONRADUM
LYCOSTHENEM Rubeaquenſem, inte-
gritati ſuæ reſtitutus.
Polydori Vergilij Vrbinatis
de Prodigijs libri III.
Ioachimi Camerarij Paberg.
de Oſtentis libri II.
BASILEAE.

Figure 4.14: Obsequens, *Prodigiorum liber*, ed. K. Lycosthenes (Basel: Oporinus, 1552), title page. Photo courtesy of the Herzog August Bibliothek Wolfenbüttel, shelfmark M: Lh 1497.

foreboding scenes of a world descending into or already experiencing the Last Days. As was the case in Fincel's *Wunderzeichen*, stories of devilish, Antichrist-like figures underscore this approach.[74] Due to the proliferation of illustrations, many pages combine images of devilish creatures, misbirths and dramatic weather conditions in a process of juxtaposition that is cumulatively more dramatic than single images could be.[75] Lycosthenes's book does not build to a grand finale, but simply reports the latest wonders to have occurred as he was completing the book and briefly admonishes the reader to heed God's warnings.[76] For the modern reader, this prompts a mental image of the sixteenth-century reader uneasily closing the book and awaiting the next wonder to further escalate the dramatic warning signs. Lycosthenes's book was taken up and appropriated for Catholic ends in a broadsheet by the Franciscan Johann Nas in 1569, examined in considerable detail in the following chapter and providing more examples of Lycosthenes's vivid and visually and textually dense publication. Lycosthenes's reader can sometimes visually identify his most important examples by judging the relative size of the imagery and the amount of space given to it. One of the most significant and up-to-date monstrous births in Lycosthenes's work – the 1540s monster of Krakow – repays closer examination and demonstrates some significant new emphases in the representation and conceptualization of monstrous births in sixteenth-century German print culture. It is illustrated on a larger scale (see Fig. 4.7) and also takes a key place in Lycosthenes's frontispiece. Both Rueff and Fincel also considered it an unusual and noteworthy case, albeit for rather different reasons.

The Monster of Krakow

The monster of Krakow, born in 1547, was a terrifying demonic figure in appearance, with webbed claws instead of hands and feet, a forked tail, flaming eyes, a sharp trunk-like nose and lion-like mouth, and animals' heads at its armpits, elbows and knees. Like the Papal Ass, the Krakow monster was born outside German-speaking lands. Its foreign origins enhanced its strangeness, and it was also connected by commentators with various political upheaval and battles. In some sources it had an alternative birthplace and birthdate: 1543 in the Netherlands. The 1543 monster was, in all important physical respects, identical to the better-known monster of 1547.[77]

Despite the physical improbability of this monster to the modern viewer, contemporaries emphasized its reality. The wonder book author Christoph Irenaeus wrote in 1584 in his unillustrated *De monstris* that 'it really was a loathsome monster or wondrous birth'.[78] The Krakow monster is undoubtedly more artificial in its physical construction than many other monstrous births from the sixteenth century, and is reminiscent in this respect, too, of the Papal Ass, as well as the 1512 monster of Ravenna. The creature's body draws upon the medieval and Renaissance visual tradition of representing devils and demons with clawed feet, with tails, and quite often with the odd faces at joints or other body parts that are so distinctive on this monstrous birth.[79] Lorraine Daston and Katharine Park observe that contemporaries tended to see the Krakow monster as demonic in origin (therefore somewhat different from normal monstrous births), and devilish in appearance.[80]

Did Rueff, in his seminal chapter on monstrous births, see the monster of Krakow as a demonic monstrous birth? Surprisingly, he did not. Yet the monster of Krakow is the most visually demonic monstrous birth in his *Trostbüchle* (Fig. 4.15), and Rueff was interested in the issue of whether or not demons could engender children. Later in the book, he pursues the question of the devil's capacity to generate semen and engender children.[81] Rueff did not, in fact, believe that this was physically possible, and relates the tale of the magician Merlin's birth to a mother who had, in Rueff's opinion, merely dreamed of a demonic lover. However, Rueff notes that such dreams could be caused by the devil, even if a pregnancy could not.[82] He also tells the story of a woman who had believed that she was pregnant, but – thanks to the work of the devil – gave birth to nails, glass, pieces of hair, stones, 'and such-like things'.[83] Despite his rejection of the power of the devil to generate semen and physically engender children, Rueff's strategy of loosely juxtaposing theories of conception, images of visually demonic monstrous births and discussions of the activities of demons does reflect broader cultural anxieties about the devil.[84] Even in his rejection of the idea of demonic generation, Rueff discusses topical issues, reinforcing his point that God is ulti-

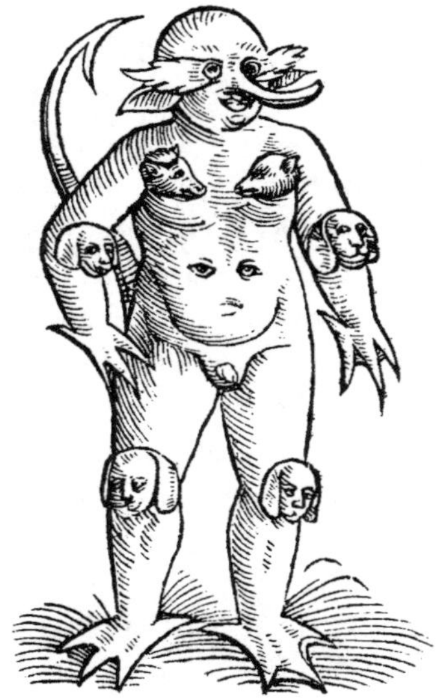

Figure 4.15: Monster of Krakow, from J. Rueff, *Ein schön lustig Trostbüchle von den empfenknussen und geburten der menschen* (Zürich: Christoph Froschauer, 1554), f. LXXII r., detail. Photo courtesy of the Zentralbibliothek Zürich, shelfmark Md T 44.

mately responsible for the wondrous deviations of the natural world, but also throwing attention back onto the natural causes of monstrous births.

Despite its demonic appearance, then, it was the physical causes of the monster of Krakow that most interested Rueff. He describes its various body parts, but does not attempt to interpret them. The iconographic tradition described above marked the Krakow monster as visually demonic, particularly because of the extra heads disposed about its body. Rueff notes the existence of these animal heads, and that they grow from the body of a child who has 'a human shape, fully formed'.[85] That is, it was the fact that there were animal heads on a human body that intrigued him: why did a human body have animal parts? He locates the origins or 'vrsachen' of the child as the work of God, who may be punishing unnaturally spilled semen.[86] This recalls the 'sodomitische' sins that will preoccupy Fincel, but it is not deployed with the same vitriolic and anti-papal intent. Instead, Rueff continues with an extended reference to Pliny, who, according to Rueff, had reported that in Africa there were 'many strange forms' ('mancherley seltzame[n] gstalten') that were the product of semen that had been 'mixed' ('vermischt').[87] The result was 'unusual births and monsters against the normal course of nature'.[88] Rueff, then, effectively proposes a physical explanation for the monster of Krakow precisely because it mixed together human and animal in one body, while God nonetheless remains the final cause of the 'wonderful monster' ('wunderbarlich Monstru[m]').[89] While he does not countenance the mixing together of human and demonic seed, the perverse sexual mingling of human and animal seed certainly seemed a feasible cause of monstrosity to Rueff. Apart from its horrifying appearance, the greatest sign of its exceptional nature in most sources would be the fact that it spoke, and warned of the Last Days. However, this is a point that Rueff leaves out of his account. Rueff was conventionally pious, but the case of the Krakow monster demonstrates how he was more concerned with disordered seed than with the coming Apocalypse. This was neither because he was a physician – so too was Fincel – nor because of his humanist leanings, which were stronger still in Lycosthenes. Instead, it seems to reflect the distinctive focus of the *Trostbüchle* on human generation and birth.

With his focus on natural causes, Rueff's intriguing but untypical discussion of the monster of Krakow differs substantially from the analyses by Fincel and Lycosthenes as well as later sixteenth-century attitudes. Fincel places the Krakow monster next to a representation of the 1512 monster of Ravenna (Fig. 4.16), despite the decades separating the two births. He interprets each distinctive feature on the body in negative, moralizing and politically current terms.[90] (In what seems to be a reprise of his interest in the destruction of Sodom, Fincel argues of the monster of Ravenna that because 'it was an androgyne, [it] represents the most shameful sodomitic fornication'.[91]) Wondrous signs appear in the sky above, and Fincel writes that when the monster of Krakow was born 'it lived three hours and said, Awake, your God is at the door'. Fincel emphasizes that 'the

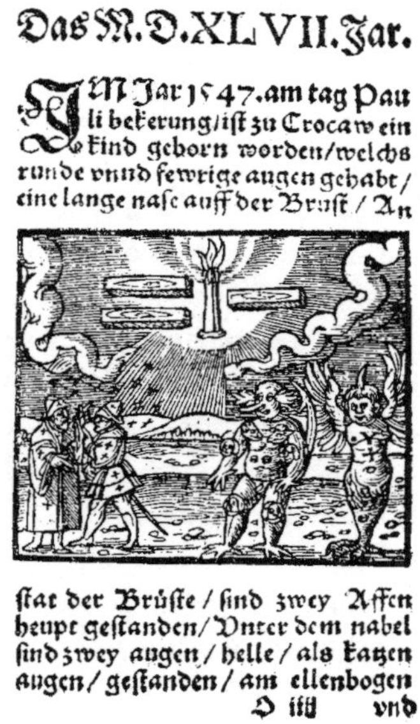
Das M.D.XLVII.Jar.

IM Jar 1547. am tag Pauli bekerung/ist zu Crocaw ein kind geborn worden/welchs runde vnnd fewrige augen gehabt/ eine lange nase auff der Brust / An

stat der Brüste / sind zwey Affen heupt gestanden/ Unter dem nabel sind zwey augen / helle / als katzen augen / gestanden / am ellenbogen

O iiij vnd

Figure 4.16: Monster of Krakow and monster of Ravenna, from J. Fincel, *Wunderzeichen mit figuren* (Leipzig: Jacob Bärwald, 1557), sig. O iiij r., detail. Photo courtesy of the Universitäts- und Landesbibliothek Sachsen-Anhalt, Halle (Saale), shelfmark Pon Vc 1036 b (2).

work of the birth is God's alone ... it would not be possible for a human to come living into world, and be born, without God himself as the midwife'.[92] Fincel also reports the case of the Krakow monster in his unillustrated third volume, where it is the only entry for the year 1543. Despite the change of date, the location of its birth remains Krakow, rather than the Netherlands, further complicating the history of this creature. Fincel notes that he had previously reported it in his first book but does not note that the date has changed. While he does not specifically note its demonic appearance, he is clear that its birth was part of a pattern of dramatic signs as well as 'many wars and unrest' ('vil Kriegs vnd vnruw').[93]

The significance of this monstrous birth is particularly underlined by Lycosthenes's inclusion of it in the 'cabinet of wonders' frontispiece to his *Wunderwerck* (see Fig. 4.13). He views it as extreme, and therefore exceptional, but also emblematic of the great number of monstrous births that had occurred in his lifetime. The distinctiveness of this misbirth is also emphasized in Lycosthenes by its oversized illustration, the only one on the page and one of the largest in the book (see Fig. 4.7). The confusion about the monster's geographical origins had clearly already become entrenched by 1557, as Lycosthenes observes that it was born 'as some would have it, in the Netherlands, the others say in Krakow in Poland'. He locates the year of the birth as 1543. Lycosthenes emphasizes the fearful and dramatic physical presence of the child, which was 'entirely gruesome and shocking to see'. He also reports on the dramatic final act of the child, who declared 'Awake, your Lord and God is about to come; and [the child] immediately thereafter died'.[94] The monster is presented here, as in Fincel's *Wunderzeichen*, as apocalyptic in meaning, warning of the imminent judgement of God. This impression is emphasized by the following passage of text, which describes the terrors and dramas overwhelming Europe at that time. Not the least of these was the Turkish threat, and Lycosthenes concludes that 'there was a great plague across Europe'.[95] Even more so than Fincel, Lycosthenes presents the Krakow monster as exceptional amongst monstrous births, its many heads lending the body a frighteningly devilish aspect, and its sinister powers of speech placing it firmly within a narrative about the coming Last Days.[96]

Rueff, Fincel and Lycosthenes all drew heavily upon broadsheets in compiling their book-length studies, indicating how monstrous births pervaded all levels of print culture and fascinated people at many levels of society. By producing compilations, each emphasized the cumulative impact of the many cases of monstrous births reported in print from the late fifteenth century. In the case of Fincel and Lycosthenes, this became the basis for an apocalyptic interpretation: monstrous births, along with other wonders, were part of a proliferation of signs of the Last Days. Their dramatic bodies and sheer variety and volume were a clear warning that the pious would be advised to heed. The great number of visual images in the books examined here gave further emphasis to this message. The negative meaning of monstrous births was given considerable weight through the juxtaposition of images and descriptions of monstrous births with those of storms, insect plagues, other destructive natural wonders and the devil. This last example forms part of what H. C. Erik Midelfort has described as 'one of the most pervasive processes across the sixteenth century ... the growing demonization of the world'.[97] In the wake of the Reformation (and despite the ultimately rather different case of Rueff), monstrous births were increasingly regarded as negative, even demonic, occurrences and indications of the terrible events and signs that would precede the Last Days. The range of positive associations that seemed to be possible before 1523 is no longer in evidence. Fincel states categorically in the preface to the second volume of his *Wunderzeichen* that, while nature could make errors, in the final analysis monsters such as 'Papal Ass, the Monk Calf in Saxony with the monk's cowl, the child of Krakow and others of which I have written, always mean something terrible'.[98]

One of the most important themes to be developed in these wonder books is that of multiplicity. That is, they present monstrous births alongside other wonders as things that occur in great multitudes. The singular nature of these wonders is subordinated to the larger issue of their sheer number, except in the case of extraordinary and emblematic cases like the monster of Krakow, which represent multiplicity in one devilish body festooned with extra, unnatural heads. There is an additional new element in Fincel, in that wonders from different places, decades and even centuries are shown together in the same contiguous visual space. Lycosthenes and Rueff, too, generate an impression of proximity, bringing together wonders from many geographical regions on single pages. All three authors include some cases from outside German language borders: from Italy, Bohemia, Poland, France, the Netherlands and England. Fincel's geographical entrenchment, and personal investment in German Protestantism (as a Wittenberg student, inside Melanchthon's inner circle) evidently partly accounts for the much more vigorous prosecution of Lutheran ideals in his text, and greater focus on those groups that he characterizes as the enemies of the Lutheran Reformation – the papacy, the Jews and the Ottoman Turks. Monstrous births were not just negative portents, but offered increasingly complex possibilities for satire of the most literally graphic kind. The following chapter explores this aspect of the visual print culture of monstrous births, pushed to surprising new extremes in a broadsheet by the Catholic polemicist Johann Nas.

5 CATHOLIC PRINT CULTURE AND MONSTROUS BIRTHS: JOHANN NAS AND ANTI-LUTHERAN POLEMIC

The printed polemical religious imagery of sixteenth-century German lands is much more frequently associated with Protestants than with Catholics. Robert Scribner's seminal study *For the Sake of Simple Folk* emphasized the eagerness and facility with which Protestants seized the opportunity to communicate with audiences at all levels. The result was a wave of publications that were often in the vernacular and illustrated with striking images.[1] As the Counter-Reformation gained momentum, Catholics also started to make greater use of similar publications, although these have not been studied to the same extent as their Protestant counterparts. Scribner observed that 'the visual propaganda of the Counter-Reformation remains a gap to be filled', a sentiment most recently echoed by R. Po-chia Hsia.[2]

This chapter is focused on the work of one of the most active of the Catholic polemicists, the Franciscan Johann Nas (1534–90), and his use of monstrous births in a single, highly complex broadsheet that has never been the subject of a close iconographical study. Titled the *Ecclesia Militans* ('Militant Church'), it combines a polemical poem by Nas with an extraordinary image in which well-known monstrous births from throughout the century are jumbled together in a sequence that includes many figures from the apocalyptic Book of Revelation (Figs 5.1 and 5.2). Little is known about the artist, who can only be identified by the monogram L with a cross, and it can be assumed from the interaction of text and image that Nas was very active in directing the artist.[3] The imagery of the Apocalypse that permeates the print was widely known in sixteenth-century Germany, having been reproduced in book illustrations and broadsheets. As Robin Barnes has observed, the great proliferation of this sort of imagery – particularly in the increasingly polemical and eschatological period following Luther's death in 1546 – meant that many people were confused about the true meaning and significance of the Book of Revelation.[4] Nas proposes a topical, indeed highly political, interpretation from a Catholic perspective that

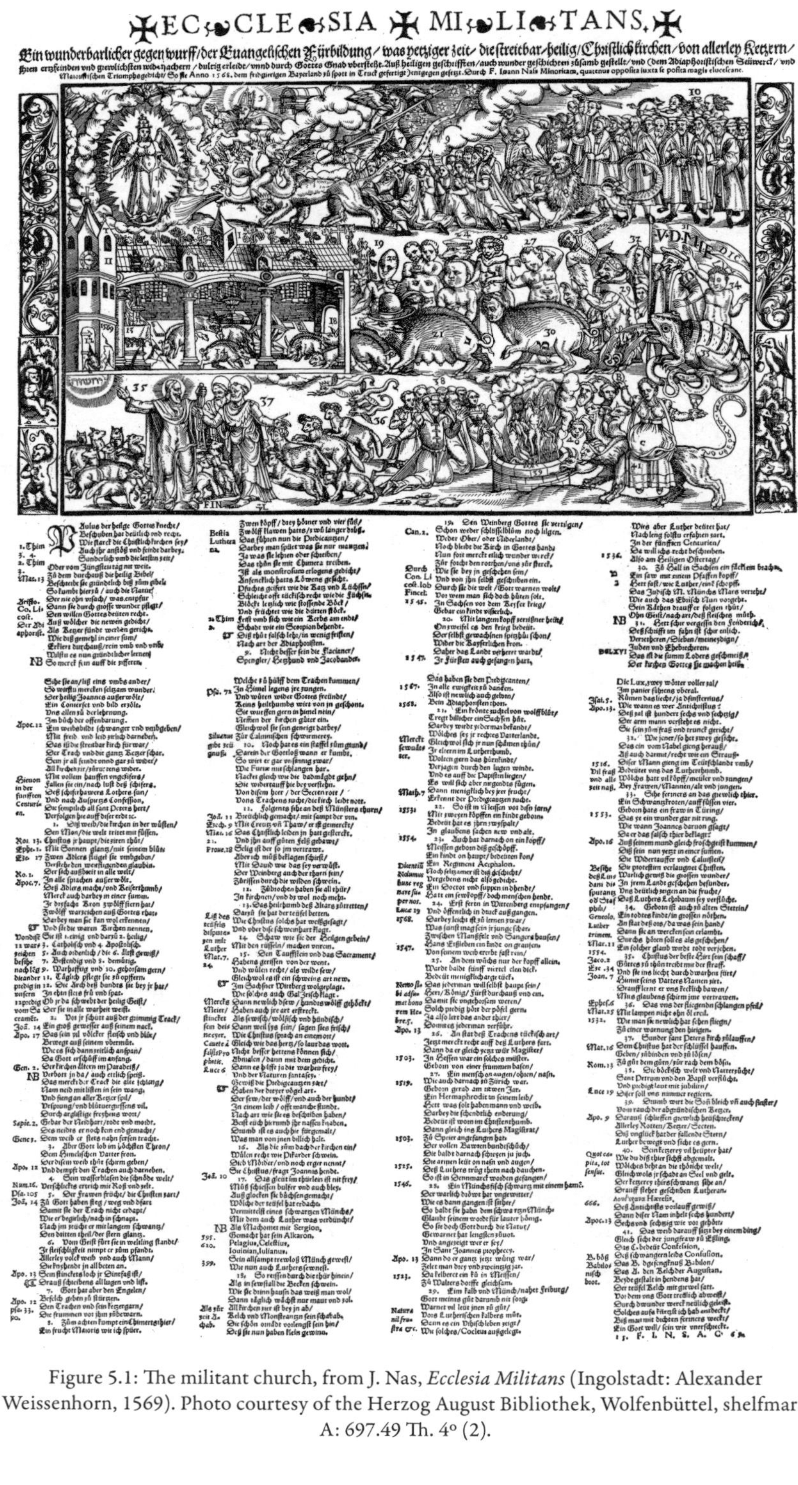

Figure 5.1: The militant church, from J. Nas, *Ecclesia Militans* (Ingolstadt: Alexander Weissenhorn, 1569). Photo courtesy of the Herzog August Bibliothek, Wolfenbüttel, shelfmark A: 697.49 Th. 4° (2).

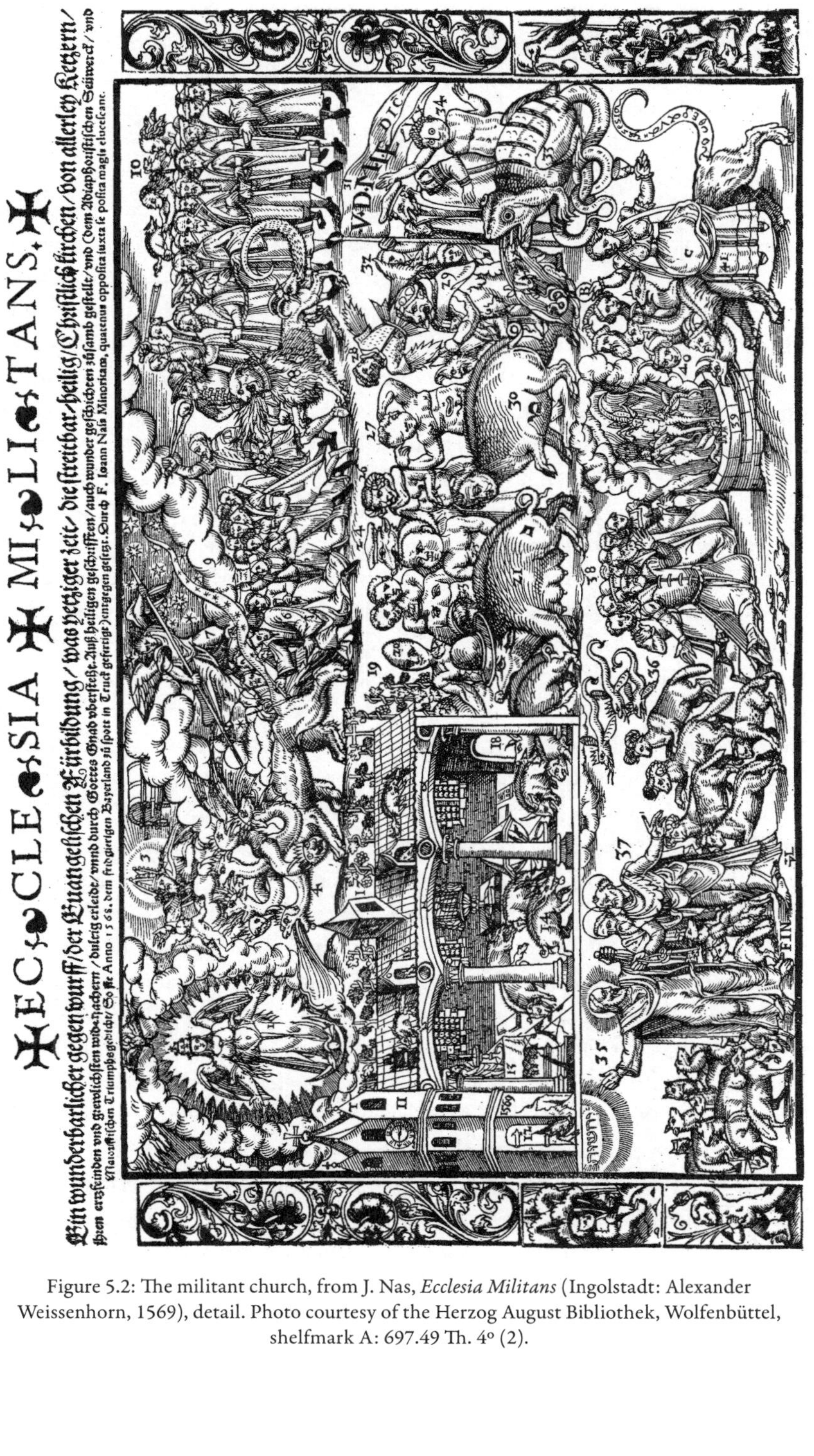

Figure 5.2: The militant church, from J. Nas, *Ecclesia Militans* (Ingolstadt: Alexander Weissenhorn, 1569), detail. Photo courtesy of the Herzog August Bibliothek, Wolfenbüttel, shelfmark A: 697.49 Th. 4° (2).

incorporates well-known monstrous births. Johannes Cochlaeus's metaphorical seven-headed Luther in the 1529 pamphlet *Sieben Kopffe Martini Luthers* was not intended to be seen as a real monstrous birth, but it was perhaps the closest that Catholics came to taking up the theme of monstrosity in a polemical fashion in the early Reformation (see Fig. 3.7).[5] In an increasingly apocalyptic Protestant world view, monstrous births were generally seen as signs of the coming Last Days, demonstrated in the Reformation pamphlets and Protestant wonder books that are the subject of the previous two chapters.

Yet the *Ecclesia Militans* broadsheet demonstrates that Catholics, like Protestants, could hold strongly developed apocalyptic views that were also bound up with the appearance of monstrous births. The broadsheet extended Nas's existing interest in monstrous births and represents his most complex and ambitious interplay of image and text. The large group of monstrous births at its centre differentiates the *Ecclesia Militans* from other sixteenth-century broadsheets on monstrous births, which tended to present them as singular phenomena. Frederick Stopp, who has studied the publication context of the *Ecclesia Militans*, does not closely analyse these monstrous births, but admits that they 'could be seen as the heart of the matter'.[6] The analysis of the *Ecclesia Militans* presented here builds upon Stopp's work. It differs in interpretation from a recent shorter analysis by Hsia, who downplays its apocalyptic content.[7] Hsia argues that attitudes towards and emotions about monstrous births during this period were 'generally split along confessional lines', and that Lutheran responses were typically fearful and apocalyptic, while Catholic responses were characterized by a sense of repugnance towards monstrous births allied with a repugnance towards heresy, along with 'the repudiation of eschatology in Catholic polemic'.[8] While the broader ramifications of this characterization are not under examination here, it could certainly be contested in relation to this broadsheet and its representation of monstrous births. Indeed, a close iconographic examination of the *Ecclesia Militans* and its visual sources – the approach taken in this chapter – demonstrates that it is entirely underpinned by an apocalyptic theme, and that this is central to Nas's deployment of monstrous births. Yet Catholic interest in monstrous births should not be overstated, as Nas's broadsheet may be the only specifically and polemically Catholic publication to take up the theme of monstrous births in German lands in this period. Nas's extraordinary broadsheet is a sign of localized, intensely personal but nonetheless deeply Catholic interest.

The *Ecclesia Militans* provides a striking case study of how German Catholics could, just like Protestants, make use of the polemical possibilities of print. Scholarly studies of German Counter-Reformation visual print culture have tended to focus on Jesuit devotional imagery in the wake of the Council of Trent.[9] Nas developed his eschatological ideas through a dialectical process of agressively appropriating and re-conceptualizing Lutheran texts and images.

Yet this is not simply a case of mimicry: Nas is not only attempting to better his Protestant opponents, but is also critically parodying his Jesuit co-religionists. While the *Ecclesia Militans* was primarily a vehicle for Nas to attack his Lutheran opponents, it also incorporates an unexpected satire of his Jesuit rival Peter Canisius – an indication of the inter-confessional strife that adds a further layer of complexity to sixteenth-century polemical print culture.

Johann Nas and the Publication History of the *Ecclesia Militans*

The *Ecclesia Militans* appears to have been first published in 1569 in Ingolstadt by Alexander Weissenhorn, and was reissued in 1588 in an almost identical edition.[10] More precisely, the first edition appeared in 1569 according to the date given at the end of the poem. However, this line also includes the acronym 'FIN SAC', that is, Frater Johannes Nas, Sedis Apostolicae Concionator. Nas was not awarded this title until 1571, according to his brief autobiography.[11] There is, therefore, the previously unremarked possibility that while the broadsheet may have first appeared in 1569, it may also have been reissued in the 1570s. While there may plausibly be some doubt about the exact dating of extant editions of the broadsheet, the principal details of its publication context have been described by Frederick Stopp.[12] It is certain that the *Ecclesia Militans* follows Nas's 1568 broadsheet representing a dream-like vision of Luther being cut up or 'anatomized' into various body parts; this is a highly polemical work in which Nas seeks to show how Luther's followers literally tear apart his corpse.[13] Further, and more importantly, it is fundamentally a response to two anti-Catholic broadsheets. The first is the *c.* 1568 *Lutherus Triumphans* ('Luther Triumphant') (Fig. 5.3).[14] The second is a specifically anti-Jesuit broadsheet from 1568 titled *Der Suiten / welche sich Jesuiten nennen* ('The "Suiten", who call themselves Jesuits') (Fig. 5.4).[15] In the title of the *Ecclesia Militans*, Nas calls his work a 'wunderbarlicher gegenwurff', that is, a literally wonder-filled riposte, and explicitly states that it responds to these two broadsheets. For the group of monstrous births that are at the heart of this broadsheet and are its most significant iconographic innovation, Nas drew upon two books in particular: Konrad Lycosthenes's *Prodigiorum ac ostentorum chronicon* (or the 1557 German translation, the *Wunderwerck*), and Job Fincel's *Wunderzeichen*.

The life story of Nas demonstrates the complexities of the second generation of the German Reformation.[16] He was born in 1534 in Eltmann am Main in Franconia, raised Catholic, and began work as a tailor from an early age after the death of his father. Drawn towards Lutheranism during his journeyman years, Nas converted decisively to Catholicism at the age of nineteen. A year later, in 1553, he entered a Franciscan cloister in Munich as a lay brother and in 1557 was ordained as a priest. In 1559 he moved to Ingolstadt where he studied

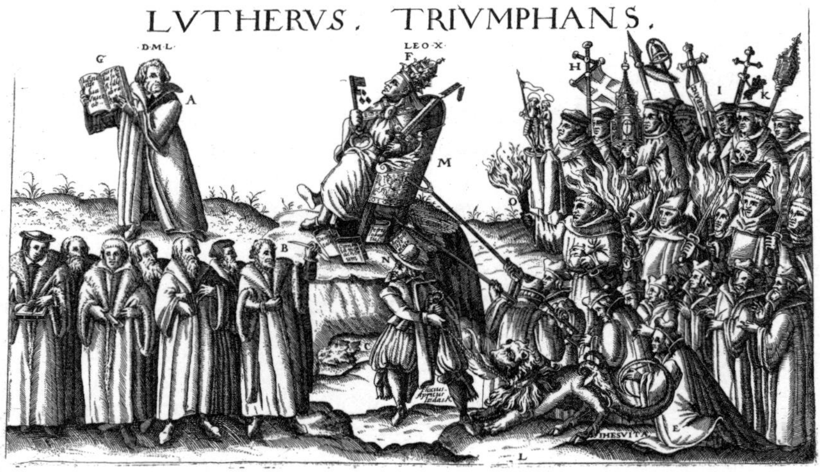

Figure 5.3: Luther triumphant, from Anon., *Lutherus Triumphans* (n.p., [*c.* 1568]), detail. Photo courtesy of the Herzog August Bibliothek, Wolfenbüttel, shelfmark A: 38.25 Aug. 2° f. 311.

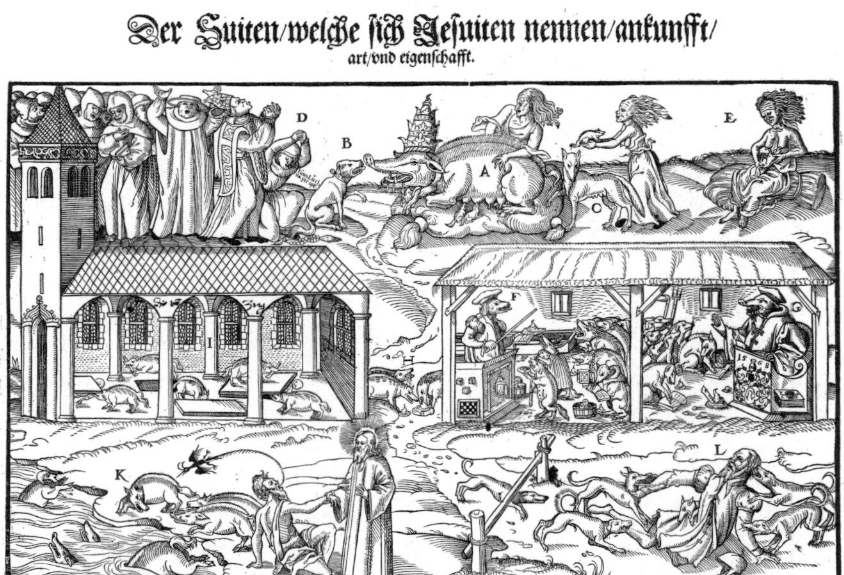

Figure 5.4: The 'Suiten' who called themselves Jesuits, from Anon., *Der Suiten / welche sich Jesuiten nennen ...* (n.p., 1568), detail. Photo courtesy of the Zentralbibliothek Zürich, shelfmark PAS 7/8 (aus F 18,160).

at university, and began preaching from 1560, with great success and often to large crowds in a number of towns across the region. From the later 1560s Nas travelled widely and was given many responsibilities and honours by his order, particularly following his 1571 journey to Rome. From 1573 he became court preacher for Archduke Ferdinand II in Innsbruck (where the previous preacher had been the Jesuit Canisius), alongside responsibilities in Brixen. Nas died in 1590 in Innsbruck. He had been a prolific writer as well as a notable preacher. His talent for vitriolic argument was primarily directed against Protestants, but he had little love for the Jesuit order, and there is an example of that conflict in this broadsheet.

In the 1560s, Nas's most substantial achievement as an author was his six-volume *Centurien*, published, not entirely in order, between 1565 and 1570, and structurally echoing or parodying Matthias Flacius Illyricus's *Centurion*.[17] Each volume was made up of a hundred points, some many pages long, refuting various aspects of Protestant and particularly Lutheran heresies and errors as identified by Nas. These volumes include passages on monstrous births as well as on Nas's great enemies within the Lutheran tradition, both useful for identifying various figures and concepts in the *Ecclesia Militans*. Nas's fifth *Centurien* includes an extended characterization of Luther as the notorious early sixteenth-century monstrous birth known as the monster of Ravenna.[18] This is one creature that does not appear in the *Ecclesia Militans*, almost certainly because it was born in Italy rather than in German lands. In the *Centurien*, Nas polemically analyses the Ravenna monster's body parts.[19] The creature's wings represent Luther's heretical books; its single clawed foot his robbery and exploitation of the church's goods; the eye on the knee his attachment to earthly things, and that 'he would not rest until he took a nun as wife'.[20] Through a complex numerological interpretation of the X and Y that mark the creature's chest, Nas associates the monster of Ravenna not just with Luther, but also with the beast of the Apocalpyse identified with the number 666.[21] Indeed, monstrous births in an apocalyptic context seem to be crucial to Nas's conceptualization of his opposition to Lutheranism. In his first *Centurien*, he states that the founding of a new religion should be accompanied by wonders and miracles, but that this was far from the case with Protestants.[22] Monstrous births were for him evidently a kind of inversion of these miracles. They were also a rich source of material for developing vivid attacks on his enemies.

The Top Row of the Illustration

Nas refers at the beginning of his poem to the 'letzten Zeit' (Last Days) and the 'Juengsten Tag' (Day of Judgement), and characterizes his own lifetime as a critical period, in which the church is under threat despite its strength. Throughout this broadsheet, Nas identifies the Catholic church with the woman clothed in the sun from the Book of Revelation. Nas emphasizes that the woman is both figure and sign, a 'weibsbild', and that she 'truly represents the valiant church'.[23] She is figure 1 in the illustration, and also the subject of much of the first column of the poem. The woman's child (at figure 5) is saved by God (at figure 3). Nas recalls with this scene the common association between this woman and Mary, and between her child and the infant Christ.[24] He compares the 'Trach' (dragon) that attacks the woman with Luther, who has led his followers astray after the 'Auspirtzs Confession': Philipp Melanchthon's 1530 *Confessio Augustana*. The following section of the poem metaphorically explains the papal tiara worn by the woman, with each star individually representing a quality of the 'wahren Kirchen' (true church). The true church is 'singular' ('einig'); 'holy' ('heilig'); 'Catholic' ('Catholisch'); 'Apostolic' ('Apostolisch'); 'orderly' ('ordentlich'); it draws upon 'traditional certainties' ('aeltst gewiß'); it is 'constant' ('Bestaendig'); 'humble' ('demuetig'); 'truthful' ('Warhafftig'); 'obedient' ('gehorsam'); and 'cares for the needy' ('pflegt sie zu opffern'). Nas finishes on a triumphal note: the woman stands beneath the Ark of the Covenant and above it hovers the Holy Ghost. The papal tiara was one of the most maligned symbols of the Roman church in the visual propaganda of the Reformation.[25] Nas here reclaims the tiara for the visual polemic of the Counter-Reformation, by setting it upon the head of the woman clothed with the sun who represents the 'Ecclesia Militans', under attack.

The specific source of the threat to the woman, and thereby the church, is the seven-headed Beast of the Apocalypse (at figure 4). The angel or 'Engelein' (Michael, at figure 7) is sent by God to fight against the beast. Yet Luther's followers ignore the angel just as they ignore the woman of the sun, and indeed God. Their focus is on the beast, and they reverently kneel behind it. Behind the seven-headed beast, at figure 6, a man dips his quill in its anus. This is Luther, and Nas curtly writes that 'its stinking hole is their inkwell / with it they all write lies and trickeries'.[26] This iconographical detail is taken and transformed from the *c.* 1568 anti-Catholic *Lutherus Triumphus* broadsheet. In that broadsheet, it was a group of Jesuits who stood behind a monstrous animal and dipped a quill into its excrement, although in that case it was a chimera-like animal.

The 'Chimersthier' does, however, make an appearance in the *Ecclesia Militans*, at figure 8. It precedes a group led by Luther, again brandishing his quill. Beside him, several other men also grasp the rope attached to the collar of the 'Chimersthier'. Nas names this group; they are 'die Flaccianer / Spengler / Hetzhund vnd Jacobander' who come to the aid of the beast. He refers here to prominent supporters of Luther: the former Wittenberg professor of Hebrew, Mathias Flacius Illyricus; the Nuremberg reformer Lazarus Spengler; the preacher and academic Tilemann Hesshus, who was from 1569 in Jena; and Jakob Andreä (Schmiedel), from 1561 professor of theology at Tübingen and here the 'Jacobander'. Nas blends his description of this monstrously hybrid creature with attacks on the 'Predicautzen' and 'Adiaphoristen' – that is, Luther and Melanchthon – who are both analagous to the beast.[27] Both the chimera and the seven-headed beast emphasize the key points that Nas is trying to make in this broadsheet, both textually and visually: that the reader should fear and distrust the variety and multiplicity of monstrosity, and that this evil multiplicity should be taken as a warning against the multiple religious groups that had sprung up as a result of the Reformation, as well as the inter-confessional strife between gnesio-Lutherans and Philippists in the previous several decades. Two female figures, 'Furies with snake-like hair / going about naked like bathhouse girls',[28] bring up the rear of this group. They give visual form to the 'senselessness' ('vnsinnig') of the 'Godless' ('Gottloß') crowd which attacks the woman and the archangel Michael, and demonstrates the ugly forces that seek to bring down the church. Again, Nas has appropriated the figures from the 1568 anti-Jesuit broadsheet. In that publication the Furies had acted as midwives and wetnurses for the hybrid offspring of a sow and a dog; Nas will push the theme of monstrous offspring considerably further in the *Ecclesia Militans*, in developing his theme of apocalyptic monstrosity.

The Central Imagery of the Broadsheet

The left hand side of the central row is taken up with a depiction of pigs invading a church. Again, the iconography is taken directly from the 1568 anti-Jesuit broadsheet. The pigs wreak havoc, and even the chalice and monstrance have been broken up.[29] One pig breaks through a wall, and several more are on the roof of the church. They do not just destroy a building, of course, but desecrate the holy space of the church. In his poem, Nas constantly alludes to the threatened position of the Catholic church in the current dangerous times. The image demonstrates that it is not just the church that is being trampled on and destroyed, but Christ himself, indicated metaphorically through the grapevines that grow up around the building. The imagery deliberately recalls Psalms 80:13, on swine in the Lord's vineyard. Explictly represented in the 1568 anti-Jesuit broadsheet, and only implicitly in Nas's *Ecclesia Militans*, is the incident in which Christ cast out demons from a man and sent them into pigs, who in their possession jumped off a cliff and drowned in a lake (Luke 8:26–39). Frederick Stopp notes a plausible connection with the *Exsurge Domine* of 1520, the papal bull against Luther, which uses similar metaphorical imagery.[30]

The small, young pigs in the church are visually linked with the two enormous pigs beside it, part of the group of monstrous births that form the most significant iconographic innovation of the broadsheet. The female is based upon the enormous papal sow from the 1568 anti-Jesuit broadsheet. In that image, the sow was giving birth with great pain and difficulty. The Furies gave their assistance, and various members of the Catholic clergy prayed over her. In Nas's reworking of that broadsheet, the sow's papal tiara has been changed to a Saxon hat, and the animal represents Katharine von Bora, the former nun and wife of Luther.[31] It is certain that both sows were inspired by the hate-filled visual tradition of the *Judensau*, generally represented as suckling Jews who also feed from her anus.[32] This association is developed by Nas, who brands the Katherine von Bora sow with the Hebrew letter 'Kaf' for Katherine, and describes her in the poem as the 'Ebrisch' (Hebrew) nun. Nas may well have been drawing on Luther's own writing here. In his rancorous *Von den Juden und ihren Lügen* ('On the Jews and their Lies') of 1543 Luther had compared a 'Hure' (whore) decorated with jewellery and fine clothing to a 'sow as it lies in excrement'.[33] Nas describes all the monstrous births in the *Ecclesia Militans* broadsheet as 'whore's children' ('Hurnkindt') and fruit or offspring ('frucht') of the monstrous sow. However, he primarily shifts the idea of abnormal pregnancy to another figure, and one strongly apocalyptic in meaning: the whore of Babylon, explored in some detail below. The sow is twinned by a male pig with a human head and a monk's tonsure. This is Luther, as figure 30, meekly trotting along behind his wife. Nas's invention is an amalgam of a caricature of Luther and a real monstrous birth born in Halle in Saxony in 1536.[34] The pig is also branded with a Hebrew letter, in this case 'Mem' for Martin.

Nas places parodies of Luther everywhere in this image. Standing behind the enormous Luther-pig is one of the most famous misbirths of the sixteenth century: the Monk Calf, a creature most successfully used by the Lutherans, notably by Luther himself in the 1523 broadsheet that he published with Melanchthon.[35] The Papal Ass is notably missing from this scene, most likely because the creature washed up on the banks of the Tiber in Rome.[36] As Hsia – the only scholar to pay attention, albeit briefly, to the individual characteristics of some of the creatures depicted here – has observed, Nas fills his broadsheet with misbirths born in Lutheran territory.[37] Nas's decision to visually combine the Luther-pig and the Monk Calf was evidently prompted by Lycosthenes's *Wunderwerck*, as this book presents the two misbirths side by side (see Fig. 4.3). Lycosthenes's succinct description includes a note that this creature was the one 'upon which Luther had written a great deal'.[38] Fincel also refers his readers to Luther's discussion, giving a full citation of where it can be found in an edition of Luther's works.[39] Both Lycosthenes and Fincel were supporters of the Reformation. Nas reclaims the interpretation of the Monk Calf for the Catholic cause. It is, not surprisingly, a particularly important monstrous birth for Nas, who devotes a long chapter to it in the fifth volume of his *Centurien*.[40] He also includes a woodcut illustration of the creature, one of very few images in the six-volume series.[41] Nas associates Luther (sometimes referred to here as 'Luder', or liar) very closely with the

Monk Calf, and draws on passages, cast in a critical light, from Luther's *Tischreden*, as well as referring directly to Luther's own text on the Monk Calf. Just as Luther had done, Nas works through a reading of the various parts of the Monk Calf's body: the tongue lies, the eyes are closed and therefore unseeing; the skin is 'torn and ripped' ('Zuorissene') in the way that the church has been. And, like Luther, Nas associates the calf with the false worship of the golden calf in Exodus 32.[42] There are several new points that are not found in Luther's interpretation: Luther is said to eat grass like a cow, which Nas presents as taking in poor nourishment, and further, Luther's teaching is 'fleshly' ('fleischlich') or worldly. The lumps on the Monk Calf are Luther's followers.[43] His opinion and argument are summed up in the pointed comment that is placed in a margin close to the end of the chapter: 'Lucifer an ox. Superbia [pride] a cow. Luther their calf.'[44]

Nas clearly had a particular interest in the disasters and devastation that had taken place in Saxony in the 1540s and 1550s. A child born in Saxony in 1545 appears at figure 20, and Nas writes that 'without a doubt it represents the war'.[45] That is, the child's birth prefigures the war of the Schmalkaldic League, which had started in 1546. In contrast, Lycosthenes's text includes the important difference that the child had 'a pointed head / as though [it] had a Turkish hat'.[46] This is in line with Fincel's *Wunderwerck*, which in the illustrated edition represents the child against a background that includes miraculous signs in the sky, including a warrior wearing a 'Turkish hat' ('Türkische huete') (Fig. 5.5). By

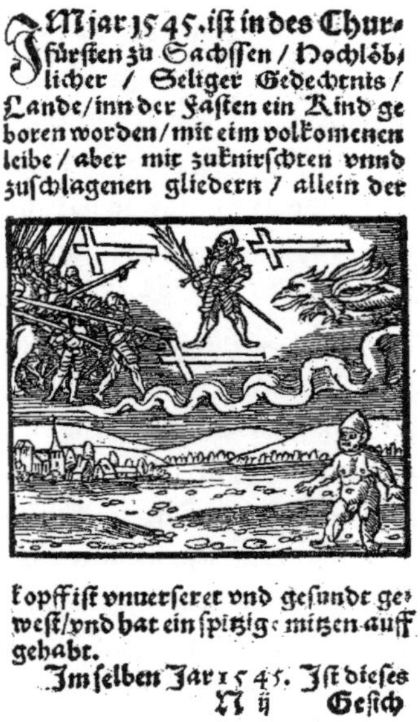
IM jar 1545. ist in des Chur-
fürsten zu Sachssen / Hochlöb-
licher / Seliger Gedechtnis /
Lande / inn der Fasten ein Kind ge
boren worden / mit eim volkomenen
leibe / aber mit zuknirschten vnnd
zuschlagenen gliedern / allein der

kopff ist vnuerseret vnd gesundt ge-
west / vnd hat ein spitzige mitzen auff
gehabt.
Im selben Jar 1545. Ist dieses
N ij Gesich

Figure 5.5: Child with a pointed head, from J. Fincel, *Wunderzeichen mit figuren* (Leipzig: Jacob Bärwald, 1557), sig. N ij r., detail. Photo courtesy of the Universitäts- und Landesbibliothek Sachsen-Anhalt, Halle (Saale), shelfmark Pon Vc 1036 b (2).

bringing in the spectre of the Turkish threat, Lycosthenes and Fincel had made the child's pointed head a reference to an externalized danger and common enemy of European Christendom. Nas, however, brings in the element of civil discord; the 'self-grown pointed hat' ('selbst gewachsen Spitzhut') that the child wears in his broadsheet is a Saxon hat set against the imperial crown. This child stands directly behind the Katherine von Bora sow with her Saxon hat, making the analogy between the two hats and heads visually stronger.

Figure 22, a child born in Meissen in 1553, continues the theme of discord in Saxony: the child's 'division [two heads] represents the old and new beliefs in Saxony'.[47] In front of the two-headed child stands figure 23, a child with no head and eyes in his chest. He was born a year later, in 1554, and again in Meissen.[48] The headless child also reveals, for Nas, the folly of Luther's followers: 'a child without a head can represent a regiment of headless creatures'.[49] This is an important misbirth for Nas, who also discusses it in the fourth volume of his *Centurien*.[50]

Figures 24, 25 and 26 all cluster behind the sow. Nas indicates that figure 24 had only been born in 1568, the year before the publication of the broadsheet, and in Wittenberg, the town most strongly associated with Luther. The figure represents a creature with a 'sow's head but human hands'.[51] The sow-headed figure seems intended as a parody, rather than the representation of a genuine misbirth. In fact, it is transposed here from the 1568 anti-Jesuit broadsheet, which explains its 'birth' in that year and its Wittenberg origins. The creature is the sow-faced teacher called Epicurus, at figure G in the anti-Jesuit broadsheet (Fig. 5.4). Epicurus teaches inside the disorderly classroom overrun by piglet-puppy hybrids at the centre of the image. Stopp identifies the sow-faced teacher as a parody of Martin Eisengrein, the 1558 convert to Catholicism and the next most influential academic in Ingolstadt after his close associate Peter Canisius.[52] Stopp does not seem to notice, however, that this figure was also included in the *Ecclesia Militans* as figure 24. Furthermore, Stopp does not observe that Eisengrein's fellow teacher Cynicus at figure F in the 1568 anti-Jesuit broadsheet has also been transposed to the *Ecclesia Militans*, as the flag-bearing figure 31. Canisius and Eisengrein preside over an unruly classroom in a parody that attacks the Jesuit focus on education. Their inclusion in the Catholic Nas's *Ecclesia Militans* is unexpected and perplexing, and will be examined when we return to the flag-waving Cynicus.

Figure 25 depicts a child born in 1547 in the region of Mansfeld and Sangerhausen. Nas continues to develop the theme of abnormal heads, but here does not draw on either Lycosthenes or Fincel. In this case, the child was not actually born physically deformed but instead developed in an unnatural way, as his head grew enormously. Nas sees this as a straightforward allegory and notes 'that everyone wants to be the leader / Lord / King / Prince, one and all / and is in doing so disobedient'.[53] That is, there are too many leaders, and the normal hierarchy of society has become dangerously disordered.

Figure 26 develops another theme. It is referred to only as 'das ander Thier', or second animal. It is given no date of birth, and does not seem to be reminiscent of any case reported in relevant broadsheets or wonder books. What, then, is this monster? The text provides a clue by its reference to the 'dragon' ('Trachen'), and the reader is directed to the Book of Revelation; a slightly misregistered marginal annotation refers the reader to 'Apo. [Apocalypse] 13'. This animal is the second beast in the Book of Revelation, the beast with lamb's horns who emerged from the earth and led people to worship the first seven-headed beast from the sea marked with the number 666. Nas suggests that it will 'seduce everyone' ('jederman verfuehr') into following Luther. Nas lifts the image from the tradition of the Luther Bible.[54] This beast's presence underlines the explicitly apocalyptic context of monstrous births.

Other monstrous births in the group demonstrate Nas's ingenious reinvention of his sources. The misbirth at figure 27 is prominently placed behind the Luther-pig, and draws the viewer's attention through a dramatic gesture at its eyeless and noseless face. Nas describes how this child was born into a 'pious' ('frommen') household in Zurich in 1519, and was a hermaphrodite missing 'eyes, ears and nose' ('Auge / Ohrn / Nasn'). Nas frames his description of this child with references to the peasant uprisings of 1503 and 1525. He links the earlier uprising to 'Luthers Magistrat', that is, Luther's rule, or magistracy. Nas draws again on Lycosthenes here, who reported a misbirth in Hessen from 1503. In Lycosthenes's *Wunderwerck*, this child stands in the same pose and gestures at his face (Fig. 5.6), which is essentially identical to that of the child in the Nas poem. Lycosthenes's text emphasizes that the 'members' or 'glider' of the child (and indeed, his entire body, except the head) were entirely normal.[55] Lycosthenes ventures a cause, or at least a meaningful context, for this misbirth: the uprisings of the *Bundschuh*, specifically in Speyer, in the wake of crop failures that affected all German lands around the year 1500. Nas redeploys this material to make an additional, and crucial point: the misguided peasant rebels became followers of Luther. By following Luther, Nas suggests, they were without eyes or ears, metaphorically blind and deaf to the true nature of Luther's Reformation.

Nas's use of figure 27 does not conclude here. In a complicated manoeuvre, he combines the case of this featureless child from 1503 with a completely different misbirth: a child born in 1519 in Zurich. This, of course, accords with Nas's own description of the child at figure 27 as born in 1519 in Zurich. This child, as reported by Lycosthenes, was a version of a hermaphrodite with a flap of skin below the navel and below that 'ein frawe[n] scha[m]' (female genitalia). Lycosthenes places his description of this misbirth closely following a description of the Diet in Augsburg in 1518, noting the condemnation there of Luther's 'teachings' ('lher') (Fig. 5.7).[56] This child is the only misbirth that Nas's other principal source, Fincel, reports for the year 1519.[57] In Nas's illustration, this child's misplaced female

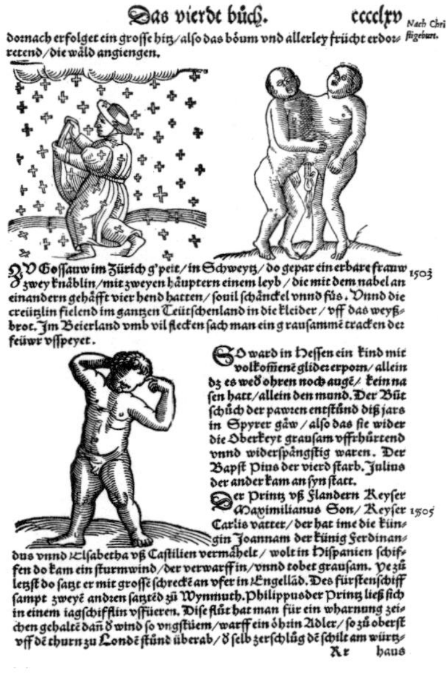

Figure 5.6: Child without eyes, from K. Lycosthenes, *Wunderwerck Oder Gottes vnergrundtliches vorbildren ... mit grossem fleiß / durch Johann Herold / vffs treüwlichst inn vier Buecher gezogen vnnd verteütscht* (Basel: Petri, 1557), p. cccclxv. Photo courtesy of the Germanisches Nationalmuseum Bibliothek, Nuremberg, shelfmark NW. 3350h.

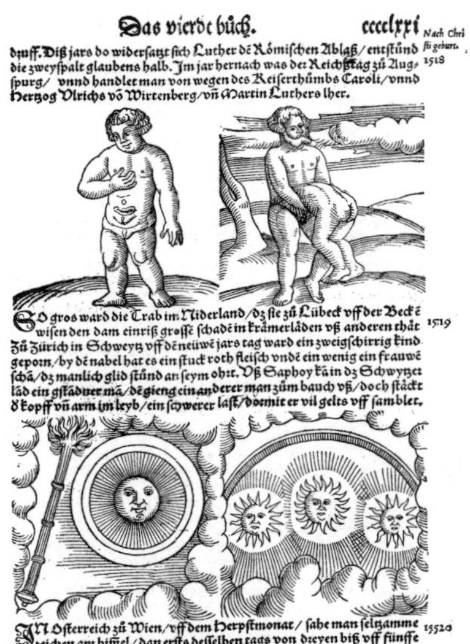

Figure 5.7: Child with male and female genitalia, from K. Lycosthenes, *Wunderwerck Oder Gottes vnergrundtliches vorbildren ... mit grossem fleiß / durch Johann Herold / vffs treüwlichst inn vier Buecher gezogen vnnd verteütscht* (Basel: Petri, 1557), p. cccclxxi. Photo courtesy of the Germanisches Nationalmuseum Bibliothek, Nuremberg, shelfmark NW. 3350h.

genitalia are transferred to the body of the child born in 1503. The boy's penis is hidden behind the Luther-pig, and so the abnormal female genitalia become visually dominant. Nas's image and text elide the two misbirths and he argues that this 'shameful change' ('schaentlich Enderung') parallels events in Christendom, and a dramatic perversion of the natural order. This, Nas emphasizes, began in Speyer in 1503 and continued through to 1525, when the *Bundschuh* rose up again, with dramatic results. Nas lays the blame for this violent disordering of society at Luther's door. This single image in the mass of figures that populate the illustration underlines the ambitious nature of the densely structured *Ecclesia Militans*, and the significance of almost every individual figure within it. Nas's strategy also points to a pragmatic attitude towards the representation of misbirths. That is, while he bases much of the argumentative force of his broadsheet on their status as true (and cumulatively threatening) events, he sees no contradiction in combining several misbirths together to make a larger point.

Only one monster in the riotous parade descending upon the church is not given an identifying number. Between the Monk Calf and the Luther-pig a bearded, demonic face is just discernable. The artist (presumably under Nas's direction) has lifted this face from a monster in Lycosthenes's *Wunderwerck* (Fig. 5.8). This wild creature was caught in a hunting expedition of 1531 by the

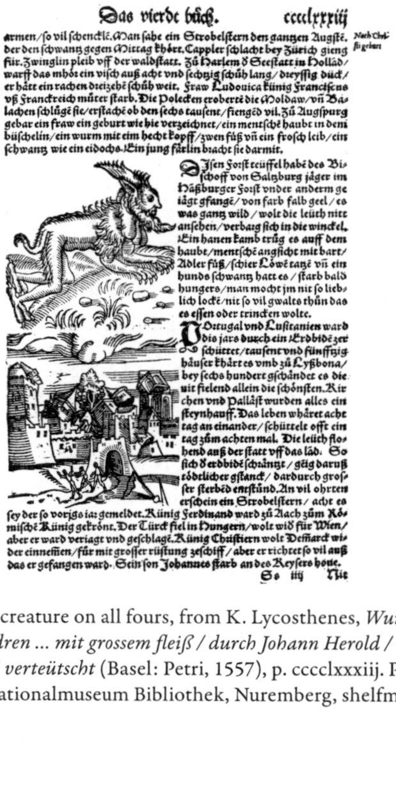

Das vierde büch. ccccl xxxiij

armen/ſo vil ſchencklẽ. Man ſahe ein Strobelſtern den gantzen Augſtẽ. der den ſchwantz gegen Mittag khört. Cappler ſchlacht bey Zürich gieng für. Zwinglin pleib vff der waldſtatt. Zů Harlem ď Seeſtatt in Hollãd/ warff das mhör ein viſch auß acht vnd ſechtzig ſchůh lang/ dreyſſig dück/ er hätt ein rachen dreizehẽ ſchůh weit. Fraw Ludouica küng Franciſcus vß Franckreich můter ſtarb. Die Polecken erobertẽ die Moldaw/vñ Walachen ſchlůgẽ ſie/erſtachẽ ob den ſechs tauſent/fiengẽd vil. Zů Augſpurg gebar ein fraw ein geburt wie hie verzeichnet/ein mentſchẽ haubt in dem büſchelin/ein wurm mit eim hecht kopff/zwen füß vñ ein froſch leib/ein ſchwantz wie ein eidochs. Ein jung färlin bracht ſie darmit.

Nach Christi geburt

DJſen Forſt teüffel habẽ des Biſchoff von Saltzburg jäger im Häßburger Forſt vnder anderm gejägt gfangẽ/ von farb falb geel/ es was gantz wild/ wolt die leüth nitt anſehen/verbarg ſich in die winckel. Ein hanen kamb trůg es auff dem haubt/mentſchẽ angſicht mit bart/ Adler füß/ſchier Löwẽ tatzẽ vñ ein hunds ſchwantz hatt es/ ſtarb bald hungers/man mocht jm nit ſo lieblich lockẽ/nit ſo vil gwalts thůn das es eſſen oder trincken wolte.

POrtugal vnd Luſitanien ward dis jars durch ein Erdbidẽ zerſchüttet/tauſent vnd fünfftzig häuſer khärt es vmb zů Lyßbona/ bey ſechs hundert gſchändet es die nit fielend allein die ſchönſten. Kirchen vnd Palläſt wurden alles ein ſteynhauff. Das leben whäret acht tag an einander/ſchüttelt offt ein tag zům achten mal. Die leüth flohend auß der ſtatt vff das lãd. So ſich ď erdbidẽ ſchräntzt/ gẽg daruß tödtlicher gſtanck/ dardurch groſſer ſterbẽd entſtůnd. An vil ohrten erſchein ein Strobelſtern/ acht es ſey der ſo vorjgs jar gemeldet. Küng Ferdinand ward zů Aach zům Römiſchẽ Küng gekrönt. Der Türck fiel in Hungern/wolt wiď für Wien/ aber er ward veriagt vnd geſchlagẽ. Küng Chriſtiern wolt Deñmarck wider einnem̃en/für mit groſſer rüſtung zeſchiff/ aber er richtet ſo vil auß das er gefangen ward. Sein ſon Johannes ſtarb an des Keyſers hove.

Ss iiij Nit

Figure 5.8: Monstrous creature on all fours, from K. Lycosthenes, *Wunderwerck Oder Gottes vnergrundtliches vorbildren ... mit grossem fleiß / durch Johann Herold / vffs treüwlichst inn vier Buecher gezogen vnnd verteütscht* (Basel: Petri, 1557), p. cccclxxxiij. Photo courtesy of the Germanisches Nationalmuseum Bibliothek, Nuremberg, shelfmark NW. 3350h.

Bishop of Salzburg.[58] It was notable for its human face combined with various animal body parts, and was starved to death. In the Lycosthenes illustration, the creature strongly recalls Nebuchadnezzar, the king of Babylon who had been divinely punished by seven years of madness, and went about on all fours like an animal (Daniel 4:31–3).[59] While Nas may have originally intended to draw a parallel along these lines, the creature's minor role, without an identifying number, makes it likely that the face was included to close up a visual gap in the group of monsters.

Behind figure 27, the creature known as the Monkfish (at figure 28) almost levitates, lifted from its water context in the illustration in Lycosthenes's *Wunderwerck*. The Monkfish was found in Denmark in 1546, and a number of extant broadsheets confirm how well known it must have been.[60] Nas presents the Monkfish as a cypher for Luther, the 'black monk' ('schwartzen Moench') who lures his followers with honey-sweet words. Again, Nas refers the reader to Apocalypse 13, and reminds them that God uses creatures like this as warning signs.

Figures 29 (the Monk Calf) and 30 (the Luther-pig) have been discussed above, and play a central role in the specific attack on Luther. There is one final cluster of monsters behind this pair. Figure 31 is a dog-headed, clothed man waving a banner. Nas is entirely silent on the identity of the figure holding the flag, described simply as a 'flag-bearer' ('Fahnrich'). This could be taken to mean that the creature is relatively unimportant. In the broadsheet catalogue edited by Wolfgang Harms it is described as a 'cynocephalous [dog-headed man] in the dress of a Protestant preacher'.[61] But, as indicated above, this creature is in fact the teacher Cynicus transposed from the 1568 anti-Jesuit broadsheet (see Fig. 5.4). That is, figure 31 in the *Ecclesia Militans* is a reversed copy of figure F in the anti-Jesuit broadsheet: the clothing and canine facial features are almost identical. The inclusion of this figure, and that of Epicurus, adds a surprising new element to the *Ecclesia Militans*. The broadsheet is overtly anti-Protestant, and especially anti-Lutheran. But it also almost certainly – and unexpectedly – includes an anti-Jesuit element.

The Cynicus figure certainly represents Peter Canisius in both broadsheets. The canine features play on Canisius's name (via the Latin *canis*), and in the anti-Jesuit broadsheet the role of teacher is a parody of Canisius's importance as a Jesuit educator. Given Nas's careful adaptation of each figure in the *Ecclesia Militans*, it is highly unlikely that he intended this to be read as a different but unspecified person. Why, then, might Nas include this parody of a co-religionist in his *Ecclesia Militans*? Nas and Canisius were in open conflict in the 1570s, when in 1573 Archduke Ferdinand II had Nas installed as the new court preacher in Innsbruck. Nas replaced the outgoing Canisius, despite Canisius's strong desire that his replacement be another Jesuit.[62] This incident led to a falling out between Ferdinand and the Jesuits, and Nas and local Jesuits attacked each other, most specifically over the issue of confession. But there were clearly larger issues relating to philosophy, approach and style behind the conflict. In a long and highly defensive letter of 30 January 1573 (1574 by the modern calendar) to the senior ecclesiatic Melchiori Parocho in Clusa, Nas dwells upon the central issue of confession and also upon his own successes as a writer, preacher and converter of souls.[63] Amongst other issues to do with confession, Nas rails against the Jesuit preference for frequent confession, declaring that Jesuits are obsessed with it just as are 'heretics [that is, Protestants] with faith alone, and Anabaptists with constant baptism'.[64] An issue that Nas does not mention, but of which he was undoubtedly aware, is the close connection between confession and political influence. Jesuit confessors had been particularly close to the extended family of Ferdinand II in the 1560s.[65]

Nas recalls his strong record of converting souls, and compares himself favourably to Canisius. The Jesuits, he declares, are jealous of his record, particularly in Munich and Ingolstadt.[66] Evidently, the conflict had its origins in Bavaria in the 1560s. As is well known, the Society of Jesus was very active in Ingolstadt in the 1550s and 1560s, and sometimes in conflict with other groups in the academic community.[67] However, existing studies place the specific conflict between Nas and the Jesuits in the 1570s. This 1569 broadsheet indicates that Nas already held virulent and personal anti-Jesuit feelings in the late 1560s. It seems likely that the broadsheet, originally issued in 1569, might have been reissued in the early 1570s, perhaps even partly to fan the flames of the debate. This would explain the mysterious 'FIN SAC' at the conclusion of the poem, an element that could have been added with little difficulty to a reissued edition in the 1570s. There is another important point to make about this attack on the Jesuits and especially Canisius: it is entirely visual. Nas may not have been imprudent enough to put his negative opinions of fellow Catholics into printed words, but it seems that he could not resist exploiting the possibilities of visual satire. That is, he pokes fun at his rival Canisius by depicting him as a ridiculous figure marching with a band of Protestant monstrous births. This anti-Jesuit element of the broadsheet has come to light as a by-product of a close analysis of Nas's use of monstrous births. Yet it underlines the complexity of sources like these, the unexpected nuances that can emerge from the most polemical publications, and the importance of carefully analysing visual as well as textual elements in broadsheets.

The Canisius figure certainly plays a very active role in the group of monstrous births, holding the flag with its cryptic message. Nas's text is concerned with the words on the banner: the phrase 'Dic Lux', and the acronym 'VDMIE'. 'Dic Lux' is best translated as 'he [that is, Luther] is said to be light'.[68] However, when rearranged by Nas and read as roman numerals, it gives the number 666, the number of the beast of the Apocalypse. To ensure that readers do not miss the connection, this number appears as a marginal annotation. Nas laments the transformation of 'the light' ('das Liecht') into 'the darkness' ('dFinsternuß'), and that what is *said* to be light is actually darkness. He reminds his readers of the Antichrist, who will seem good before his true, evil nature is revealed. The Antichrist is referred to by Nas several times in the final column of the *Ecclesia Militans* poem, and as Ingvild Richardsen-Friedrich has recently noted, Luther is presented here as a forerunner of the Antichrist and implictly also the coming Apocalypse, in an inversion of the more common Lutheran presentation of the papacy as the Antichrist.[69]

The acronym 'VDMIE', Nas writes, refers to the 'ettlich / Verraehtern' (numerous betrayers) whom he lists as 'Diebn / Meineydigen / Juden vnd auch Ehbrecherin' ('thieves / perjurers / Jews / and also adulterers'). The initials of these words give the acronym 'VDMIE'. To contemporary readers, this would have been legible shorthand for the phrase *Verbum Domini manet in eternum* ('the word of the Lord shall remain forever'). This was the motto of Philip the Magnanimous, Landgrave of Hesse and a founding member of the Schmalkaldic League, and it was closely associated with the League more generally.[70] Again, Nas transforms the meaning of a Protestant symbol. Less predictably, Nas evidently here includes Jesuits, or at least Canisius, amongst the group labelled betrayers. Conflict between the Catholic orders meant that the Catholic unity that Nas favourably compares to Protestant sectarianism and disunity was evidently something more desired and rhetorically deployed than real. Nonetheless, Nas pursues his condemnation of Protestant sectarianism strongly in the *Ecclesia Militans*. Figure 32 is almost hidden behind the elevating Monkfish and the Cynicus with the banner. It represents a man born in 1516 with a second head growing from his stomach. This unusually long-lived case of a misbirth was notable for the second head's ability to 'eat and drink' ('aß vnnd tranck'), as Lycosthenes observes.[71] For Nas, however, this two-headed man 'represents for us Lutheranism / which has many heads, mouths and tongues',[72] and acts as a metaphor for the confusing multiplicity of the voices of Luther's followers.

Figure 33, an enormous frog with a long, snake-like tail, was born in 1553 to a Thüringen woman.[73] Nas adds a striking new element to his frog. It vomits up three animals: a snake, and two smaller frogs. In doing so it takes on a malevolent aspect missing from the rather passive frog depicted in Lycosthenes's *Wunderwerck* (Fig. 5.9). These 'frog spirits' ('Froschgeist') represent for Nas the animal's speech, but also the various branches of reformed religion. The condemnation of Protestant speech here harks back to the multiple tongues condemned in figure 32. It is above all a reference to the Book of Revelation, and the 'three foul spirits ... like frogs' in Revelation 16:13 that fall from the mouths of 'the dragon, the beast and the false prophet'.[74] Nas emphasizes that these sorts of misbirths

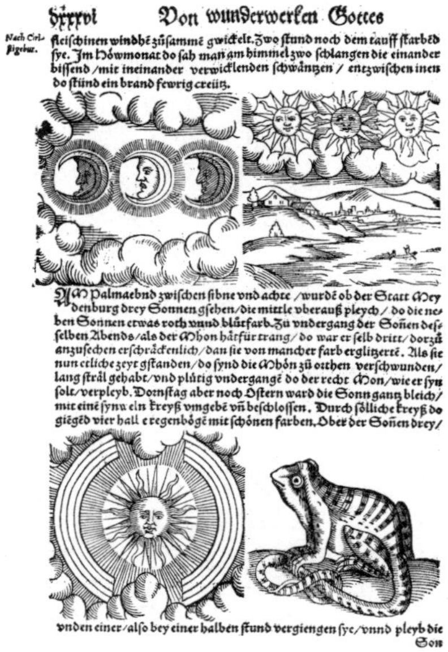
dxxxvi Von wunderwerken Gottes

Nach Cristi geburt. fleischinen windhē zůsammē gwickelt. Zwo stund noch dem tauff starbēd sye. Im Höwmonat do sah man am himmel zwo schlangen die einander bissend / mit ineinander verwicklenden schwäntzen / entzwischen inen do stůnd ein brand fewrig creütz.

AM Palmaebnd zwischen sibne vnd achte / wurdē ob der Statt Meydenburg drey Sonnen gsehen / die mittle vberauß pleych / do die neben Sonnen etwas roth vnnd blůtfarb. Zů vndergang der Soñen desselben Abends / als der Mhon hätfür trang / do war er selb dritt / dorzů anzusechen erschräckenlich / dan sie von mancher farb erglitzertē. Als sie nun etliche zeyt gstanden / do synd die Mhön zů orthen verschwunden / lang strål gehabt / vnd plůtig vndergangē do der recht Mon / wie er syn solt / verpleyb. Dornstag aber noch Ostern ward die Sonn gantz bleich / mit einē synw eln kreyß vmgebē vñ beschlossen. Durch söllliche kreyß do giēgēd vier hall e regenbögē mit schönen farben. Ober der Soñen drey /

vnden einer / also bey einer halben stund vergiengen sye / vnnd pleyb die Son

Figure 5.9: Long-tailed frog, from K. Lycosthenes, *Wunderwerck Oder Gottes vnergrundtliches vorbildren ... mit grossem fleiß / durch Johann Herold / vffs treüwlichst inn vier Buecher gezogen vnnd verteütscht* (Basel: Petri, 1557), p. dxxxvi. Photo courtesy of the Germanisches Nationalmuseum Bibliothek, Nuremberg, shelfmark NW. 3350h.

are occurring in Protestant lands, and should be taken as the 'fruit' ('Frucht') of Luther's 'tree of learning' ('Lehrbaum').

The final monstrous birth of the broadsheet is at figure 34, and is a sinister wooden figure with staring eyes. Nas explains that this child was still-born in 1554 in the town of Stettin (modern-day Szczecin). The arm that grows where the child's ear should be blocks his hearing. In his text, Nas parodies the Lutheran distrust of good works, and their theology of *sola fide* (faith alone). According to this approach, he writes, 'everything should take place through hearing',[75] but this (Lutheran) child can, in fact, neither hear nor act. The arm growing from the child's ear also gestures at the flag. Given the hidden anti-Jesuit message here in the parody of Peter Canisius, there is some possibility that Nas is also satirizing the Jesuit focus on confession, another activity entirely bound up with hearing. Both Lycosthenes and Fincel describe the physical deformities of the child – very recently born at the time that they were writing – in considerable detail.[76] Neither, however, ventures a more substantial explanation for the birth. As is the case with many of the other monstrous births that Nas discusses in this broadsheet, he pushes previous discussions of this case to a new level of interpretation through his appropriation of Lutheran textual and especially visual sources.[77]

The Bottom Row of the Illustration

The final horizontal column of figures also reads left to right, according to the numbering on the figures. However, Christ – the first figure on the left-hand side – is also labelled 'FIN'. This device makes a point about Christ as the ultimate destination of the faithful Christian, and also sets up the idea of two alternatives, developed further in this scene. Christ extends his right arm to gesture at his own name in Hebrew, blazing in the sky. Nas's text describes Christ, surrounded here by sheep, as 'the best shepherd of his sheep', who will 'lead you into light with the truth'.[78] Christ is accompanied by Peter, who holds the keys in a representation of the transfiguration on the mountain (Matthew 17:1–2). Nas reminds his audience that the keys of St Peter, and by extension the keys of the papacy, were a gift of Christ; thereby asserting the continuity and authority of tradition within the Roman church. Peter gestures with his left hand at the apocalypytic scene that unfolds beside the group. Christ and Peter's complementary gestures visually assert that there are two options available: one leading to God, and the other to damnation.

The group is threatened at its border by a group of three flying dragons at figure 36. Nas explictly connects these dragons to a case concerning a child born in 1532 'in the kingdom of Babylon' ('JM Reich Babylo[n]').[79] The child was born with teeth, had 'fiery eyes' ('fewrige augen'), began speaking when only two months old, and declared himself the son of God. One of the many signs that preceeded his dramatic birth was a dragon flying overhead. Lycosthenes saw this case as strongly apocalyptic, and writes of how at 'the hour of the birth / the end of the world is here'.[80] He makes it clear that the child was a devilish deception and a type of Antichrist. The passage is illustrated with a woodcut illustration of a double-headed fire-breathing dragon (Fig. 5.10).

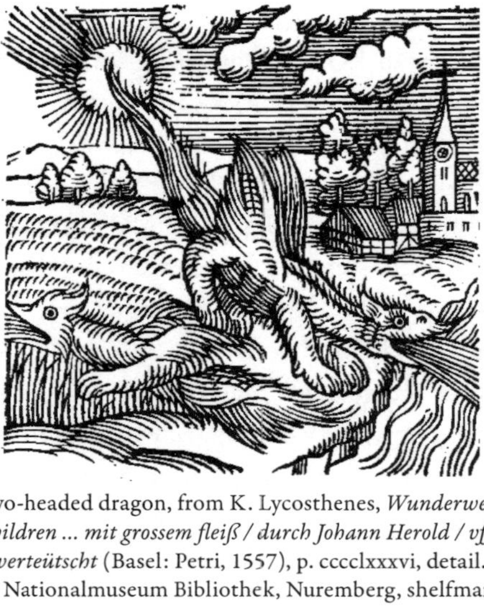

Figure 5.10: Two-headed dragon, from K. Lycosthenes, *Wunderwerck Oder Gottes vnergrundtliches vorbildren ... mit grossem fleiß / durch Johann Herold / vffs treüwlichst inn vier Buecher gezogen vnnd verteütscht* (Basel: Petri, 1557), p. ccccl xxxvi, detail. Photo courtesy of the Germanisches Nationalmuseum Bibliothek, Nuremberg, shelfmark NW. 3350h.

Nas's dragons, however, take another form, and have a different function within the image. With their crowns and stinging tails these three small dragons could be part of the swarm of apocalyptic locusts that emerge from the well at figure 39. These locusts may, according to Richardsen-Friedrich, represent Luther's heretical followers.[81] Men and women in contemporary clothing at figure 38 kneel before the well. Nas declares that they have 'Saint Peter and the Pope blasphemed',[82] but they do not yet feel the sting of the hybrid locusts that accompany the sounding of the fifth of the seven trumpets of the Apocalypse (Revelation 9:1–12). They turn away from Christ, and seem to be commanded by two figures beyond the well, located at the final point of the illustration.

These final two figures are a particularly complex element of the broadsheet, although they are easily identified as the whore of Babylon and the seven-headed beast of the Apocalypse. At figure 40, the beast is shown twice in the illustration. There are, however, some important differences in how it is represented the second time. Some of the dragon-like heads have been replaced with human heads, representing the heretics that Nas refers to in his poem. Several of these heads clearly represent tonsured monks, and the head closest to the number 40 is almost certainly Luther himself, very similarly depicted to the Luther-pig in the row above. Greek and Roman letters along the tail of the beast repeat the same phrase that Nas uses in his verse: 'Lutheran heresy'.[83] Nas emphasizes what he sees as the frightening plurality of reformed religion: 'His [Luther's] heresy has many heads / as this animal itself portrays'. He adds a marginal note to underline this point: 'however many heads, so many meanings'.[84]

The Virgin of Esslingen

While the seven-headed beast is complex and striking, it is the woman who rides upon its back who commands the viewer's attention, and is the subject of the last lines of Nas's poem. The woman is not just the 'Babylonisch Brodt' (Babylonian bread or bride) but also 'der Jungfraw zu Eßling' or virgin of Esslingen. Nas's whore of Babylon is relatively drab in appearance, with plain clothes and hairstyle, and wearing no jewellery. Further, she has a strap around her bulging, apparently pregnant stomach. She is quite distinct from the tradition of sixteenth-century illustrations of the whore of Babylon – beginning with Albrecht Dürer's version of 1496 – as a worldly woman, opulently dressed.[85] A good number of illustrations in the wake of Dürer's were anti-papal, drawing on the traditional connection between Babylon and Rome, and establishing a representation of the whore of Babylon as the personification of a worldly, wicked Roman papacy. These were images that sometimes elided the whore of Babylon and the notorious Pope Joan, supposed to have hidden her pregnancy under her papal robes and given birth during a procession in Rome, dramatically revealing both her pregnancy and her gender.[86]

Nas's plainly dressed virgin of Esslingen does not fit easily within this established iconography. However, the worldliness of the whore of Babylon could also be emphasized by representing her with a full, voluptuous figure, as in Hans Holbein the Younger's woodcut from a 1523 Basel edition of Luther's September Testament by the printer Thomas Wolff (see Fig. 3.8).[87] It is this aspect of the pictorial tradition that Nas has retained but also reinvented. In doing so he taps into the description of the whore of Babylon in Revelation 17:1–7: 'on her forehead was written a name, a cryptic name: "Babylon the Great, the mother of all the prostitutes and all the filthy practices on the earth"'. That is, he pursues the implications of the whore of Babylon being pregnant with evil deeds and creatures.

But who was the virgin of Esslingen? She was a young woman named Anna Ulmer, the perpetrator of a notorious fraud who was convicted in her home town of Esslingen in 1551 after her deceptive activities had been revealed the previous year.[88] Nas most likely encountered Anna Ulmer through Lycosthenes's *Wunderwerck*, in which she was represented with a generic woodcut (Fig. 5.11). He may also have been familiar with some of the broadsheets that discussed the case (Fig. 5.12).[89] In Lycosthenes's *Wunderwerck*, Anna is called Margreth and her mother – central to the story and the real Margreth – is left nameless. Lycosthenes tells the story of a deception perpetrated by the two women. Together, they created a huge false stomach and strapped it onto the daughter, presenting her as a wonder: a fasting virgin with an unnaturally swollen stomach. Many visitors came to see her, and the family profited financially from the fraud. There were also some less easily explained elements. Lycosthenes reported that bizarre animal noises could be heard inside the daughter's belly. Worms and snakes were also produced that, it was claimed, had been expelled from her body. Eventually Anna – here Margreth – was examined by three surgeons and a midwife who had been sent to cut open the swollen stomach, and in doing so discovered the false stomach stuffed with cushions. Lycosthenes reports that the mother was strangled and the daughter burned as legal punishment for their crimes. This is at odds with the true unfolding of events: the mother was burned in a fire made from the wood of the family home, and the daughter branded and imprisoned. In a sad irony, Anna Ulmer died in childbirth in 1564 after years spent between the prison and the poor house.[90]

To return to Nas's version of this case, the poem and illustration of the *Ecclesia Militans* incorporate an extra key at this point: the letters A, B and C guide the reader in interpreting the whore of Babylon / woman of Esslingen, whom Nas states are 'gleich' or the same. The letter A labels the communion chalice that she holds aloft in her left hand, most certainly an allusion to the bitter debates about

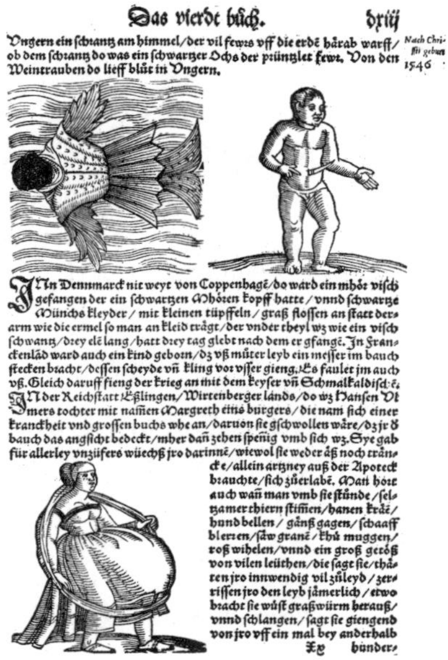

Das vierdt bůch. dxiij

Vngern ein ſchwantz am himmel/der vil fewrs vff die erdē härab warff/ ob dem ſchwantz do was ein ſchwartzer Ochs der prüntzlet fewr. Von den Weintrauben do lieff blůt in Vngern. Nach Chriſti geburt 1546

IN Dennmarck nit weyt von Coppenhagē/do ward ein mhör viſch gefangen der ein ſchwartzen Mhören kopff hatte/vnnd ſchwartze Münchs kleyder/mit kleinen tüpffeln/graß floſſen an ſtatt der arm wie die ermel ſo man an kleid trägt/der vnder theyl wz wie ein viſch ſchwantz/drey elē lang/hatt drey tag glebt nach dem er gfangē. Jn Franckenlād ward auch ein kind geborn/dz vß můter leyb ein meſſer im bauch ſtecken bracht/deſſen ſcheyde vñ kling vor vſſer gieng. Es faulet jm auch vß. Gleich daruff fieng der krieg an mit dem keyſer vñ Schmalkaldiſchē.

IN der Reichſtatt Eßlingen/Wirtenberger lands/do wz Hanſen Vlmers tochter mit nam̃en Margreth eins burgers/die nam ſich einer kranckheit vnd groſſen buchs whe an/daruon ſie gſchwollen wäre/dz jr der bauch das angſicht bedeckt/mher dañ zehen ſpeñig vmb ſich wz. Sye gab für allerley vnzüfers wüechß jro darinnē/wiewol ſie weder äß noch träncke/allein artzney auß der Apoteck brauchte/ſich zůerlabē. Man hort auch wañ man vmb ſie ſtůnde/ſeltzamer thiern ſtim̃en/hanen kräē/hund bellen/gänß gagen/ſchaaff blerren/ſäw granē/khů muggen/roß wihelen/vnnd ein groß getöß von vilen leüthen/die ſagt ſie/thäten jro innwendig vil zůleyd/zeriſſen jro den leyb jämerlich/etwo bracht ſie wůſt graßwürm herauß/vnnd ſchlangen/ſagt ſie giengend von jro vff ein mal bey anderhalb

Xy hunder-

Figure 5.11: The virgin of Esslingen, from K. Lycosthenes, *Wunderwerck Oder Gottes vnergrundtliches vorbildren ... mit grossem fleiß / durch Johann Herold / vffs treüwlichst inn vier Buecher gezogen vnnd verteütscht* (Basel: Petri, 1557), p. dxiij. Photo courtesy of the Germanisches Nationalmuseum Bibliothek, Nuremberg, shelfmark NW. 3350h.

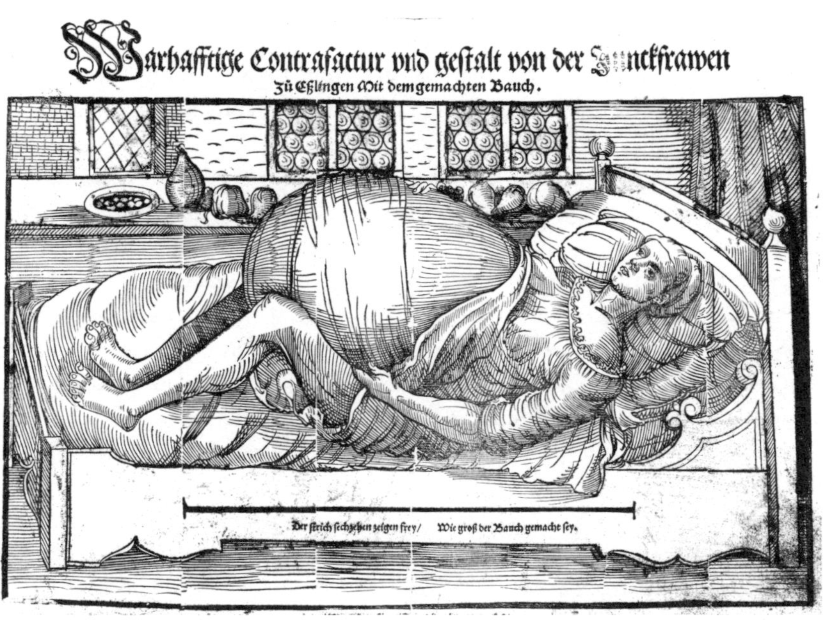

Figure 5.12: The virgin of Esslingen, from Anon., *Warhafftige Contrafactur vnd gestalt von der Junckfrawen zuo Esslingen Mit dem gemachten Bauch...* (n.p., [*c.* 1550–1]). Photo courtesy of the Zentralbibliothek Zürich, shelfmark PAS II 2/19.

communion in both kinds (that is, both bread and wine) for the laity that had raged in the early years of the Reformation, and were again debated during the Council of Trent, notably in the third sitting.[91] The chalice is filled with the 'filth of her prostitution', as it is described in the Book of Revelation 17:4. In a reference to the 1530 *Confessio Augustana*, Nas asserts that this travesty of a chalice belongs to the 'Augustan' empire, and that the devil has sated himself drinking from it.

The letter B appears on the communion wafer that the woman holds aloft. It represents for Nas 'die gfaengnuß Babylon' (the Babylonian Captivity of the church) and is thereby a reference to the famous pamphlet of 1520 which was one of Luther's earliest successes in presenting the Pope and his church as antithetical to a true Christian faith. Here, Nas reverses that idea. He also makes a play on words: the whore of Babylon is called the 'Babylonisch Brodt', which readers could simultaneously understand as bride or bread, both embodied in a perverted form. Nas makes it clear that the A and B together, in 'both forms' ('Beyde gestalt'), indicate that the Augsburg Confession is precisely the same thing as the Babylonian Captivity: they are two forms but one (perverse) essence.

In the first volume of his *Centurien*, Nas had discussed the case of the Virgin of Esslingen at some length and concluded that she embodied both what he saw as the evils of the *Confessio Augustana*, and also – as a prefiguration – the religious peace concluded at Augsburg in 1555.[92] Indeed, part of Anna Ulmer's notoriety sprang from an association made by many contemporaries between her case and the turbulent Interim that had started in 1548.[93] Richardsen-Friedrich has recently argued that Nas draws upon Friedrich Staphylus, who had already presented the whore of Babylon, traditionally utilized by Protestants as a parody of the Pope, as a personification of the *Confessio Augustana*.[94] Nas certainly did deploy the whore of Babylon as a representation of the *Confessio Augustana*. However, this point should be taken further: Nas also connects the whore of Babylon to the Interim and to the Religious Peace of Augsburg, an association strengthened through his use of the Anna Ulmer case. As Nas makes clear in his fifth *Centurien*, this case was a warning that should be interpreted and heeded, and one that was inescapably local. The virgin of Esslingen 'did not become pregnant in a foreign nation with this animal / but rather in Germany'.[95]

The concept of a monstrous, apocalyptic pregnancy underpins and concludes the *Ecclesia Militans*. The figure C appears prominently on the woman's pregnant stomach, and means, Nas explains, both 'confession' and 'confusion', two concepts that he sees as analogous. That is, the plurality of confessional approaches has led to a monstrous confusion that brews as an unnatural child inside the woman. For Nas's readers and viewers this unnaturally pregnant woman was certainly a type of evil mother brimming with monstrous births just like those that appear in the centre of the image. By concluding with the figure of the whore of Babylon, Nas returns his audience's attention to the diametrically opposing figure of the woman clothed with the sun. These two women, who had acted as female personifications of good and evil in the Book of Revelation, are adapted here by Nas to dramatically represent the Catholic church under attack by the forces of the Lutheran Reformation.

Nas, then, turned the imagery of his enemies to his own ends, and in so doing created one of the most textually dense yet still popularly oriented Counter-Reformation broadsheets of the period. The polemical print culture of the Protestants is appropriated here for Catholic ends, in an important early stage of the intensively visual form that the Counter-Reformation was to adopt. More fully comprehending Nas's heavy reliance on Protestant models, and also his aggressive reworking of his opponents' visual culture, demonstrates the complexity of this crucial period. So too does an understanding of the polemics that operated within a Catholic environment: in this case the conflicts between Franciscans and Jesuits. The broadsheet is, finally, notable within its genre, and takes the popular sixteenth-century subject of the monstrous birth to new levels of apocalyptic intensity, multiplicity and complexity within the format of a cheap and thus widely accessible publication. That it was a Catholic rather than Protestant publication doing this suggests that the apocalyptic print culture so strongly associated with Protestants in late sixteenth-century German lands should sometimes also be understood in Catholic terms.

6 'MANY HEADS, MOUTHS AND TONGUES': MONSTROUS BIRTHS IN THE LATER SIXTEENTH CENTURY

In the *Ecclesia Militans*, Johann Nas had condemned Lutheran sectarianism with its 'many heads, mouths and tongues', and added a marginal note elsewhere in his broadsheet to the same effect: 'however many heads, so many meanings'.[1] He was inspired by a two-headed man and by the seven-headed beast of the apocalypse, respectively; figures that represented the dreadful multiplicity that Nas sought to interpret and condemn. Yet in his 1495 broadsheet on the Worms twins, joined at the forehead, Sebastian Brant had observed that 'all good things come from the head'.[2] The comment was aimed at Emperor Maximilian I, and intended to flatter him as the 'head' of the Holy Roman Empire. By 1584, however, Christoph Irenaeus included an extended discussion of the meaning of multiple heads in his unillustrated but highly descriptive *De monstris* ('On Monsters'), and concluded that they always signified unhappy things: 'Such two- or many-headed monsters indicate division and discord in the spiritual and worldly orders'.[3]

By the close of the sixteenth century, the graphically striking representation of abnormal heads remained a constant theme in publications on monstrous births, but their meaning was almost entirely negative, and generally framed within an apocalyptic world view. A child might have multiple heads, recalling for the viewer and reader the seven-headed beast of the Apocalypse. It might have a dramatically deformed single head with a mouth that seemed to cry out some warning, or it might even have more extended, abnormal, prophetic powers of speech. These new publications reached for novelty, and readers and viewers were presented with increasingly extraordinary phenomena in textual and visual form. Rather than tracing the continuing fortunes of iconic monstrous births like the Monk Calf, Papal Ass or monster of Krakow – although they continued to appear in print – this chapter will look at a series of new cases from the last decades of the sixteenth century. Multiple heads, multiple births, powers of speech and a new focus on longer narratives with a greater tendency to incorporate the mothers and the communities in which monstrous births appeared were all hallmarks of the vigorous range of publications on monstrous births appearing in the final decades of the sixteenth century, and the insistently religious frameworks within which most people, at all levels of society, continued to understand monstrous births.

Second- and third-generation Protestantism became stressed and fractured during the later decades of the sixteenth century. Many of these publications depicted events that took place in towns and cities under special religious and territorial strain: areas in which Catholicism and Lutheranism, or – in a new and insistent pattern – Calvinism and Lutheranism struggled for ascendancy, as well as border towns in Inner Austria under threat during the Habsburg-Ottoman War of 1593–1606. Monstrous births still offered ways to make sense of a disordered world, and polemically to express confessional viewpoints.

By the end of the century monstrous births were increasingly presented alongside other misbirths or wonders in longer pamphlets or broadsheets containing multiple cases. The *Ecclesia Militans* would seem to have exemplified an extreme point in the interpretation and representation of monstrous births in sixteenth-century German lands. Yet broadsheets and also longer pamphlet publications (a relatively new phenomenon for this material) continued to appear.[4] Pamphlet texts and illustrations are neglected sources in the study of German monstrous births, as pamphlets do not appear in single-sheet catalogues nor do they fit within the clearly demarcated genre of longer wonder books by identifiable authors writing intellectual, religious or natural histories.[5] Yet these pamphlets appear more frequently in the latter half of the century, often containing sermon-style texts authored by Lutheran preachers, and they are a key source in this chapter, which has a smaller range of images from sources which do, however, contain lengthier and more convoluted individual narratives than has been the case in most of the previous chapters.[6] Indeed, pamphlets often provide the most extensive contemporary descriptions and interpretations of individual cases, as they are not constrained by the brief format of single-sheet prints or the compendium-style requirements of wonder books. While there are an extraordinary number of resources for examining the topic of monstrous births in early modern Germany, this chapter does not aim exhaustively to examine all possible sources, but instead to identify several central new tendencies. It does aim to contribute to the examination of the distinctive qualities of underutilized pamphlets from the latter half of the sixteenth century, not least because the intersections between religion, popular culture and print in the period between the 1555 Peace of Augsburg and the onset of the Thirty Years War in 1618 remain insufficiently studied.

This book opened with a description of a Strasbourg broadsheet reporting the birth in Italy of both a seven-headed child and a horned child in January 1578 (see Fig. I.1).[7] The apocalyptic physical features – including horns, multiple heads and hoofed feet – of these ominous, looming children were underscored by their placement in front of a terrible storm destroying the German town of Horb on the Neckar. The inclusion of three separate events – two monstrous births and a storm – in one broadsheet primarily reflects the influence of the richly illustrated wonder books that had appeared in the wake of the Reformation, particularly those by Job Fincel and Konrad Lycosthenes. In the earlier part of the century, the backgrounds to images of monstrous births were frequently either nonexistent or extremely minor. Philip Soergel argues that this helped to distance human misbirths from the domestic, everyday, interior scenes of their births, and instead emphasized their strangeness.[8] Earlier in the century, those outdoor backgrounds that were represented – for example, as in Brant's Worms twins broadsheet, Dürer's image of the Landser sow or the Papal Ass standing in front of the Tor di nonna in Rome – were there to underscore the veracity of the image by confirming the geographical location of the birth. This sense of veracity gave way, later in the century, to a desire to demonstrate the great number of wondrous and terrible events taking place. Combined together in a single publication, their multiplicity heralded the Last Days.

The broadsheet of 1578 encapsulates and distills this approach, as well as the ongoing tendency towards negative interpretations of monstrous births.[9] Examples of such interpretations of monstrous births certainly predate the Reformation. However, it took the vitriolic wave of printed materials sparked by the Reformation, the development of societies sharply divided on religious grounds and the escalation of apocalyptic fears to give full form to the representation of monstrous births as fearful signs that warned of the coming Last Days. By the seventeenth century the seven-headed monstrous birth of Eusrigo had joined the pantheon of notorious monstrous births. When it appeared in an engraving in Fortuno Liceti's *De monstris* of 1665 the large, standing creature was accompanied by a tiny, whimsical background scene – reminiscent of medieval manuscript marginalia – that showed a tiny man shooting at an equally tiny seven-headed beast.[10] But this approach was still far away, and was in any case not to become typical. In the late sixteenth century, monstrous births were unequivocally dramatic events with the power to convey increasingly complex religious and moral messages.

The Child with a Pointed Head

Heads did not need to be multiple to take on special emphasis in the later sixteenth century. A broadsheet reporting a monstrous birth in 1577 from Grevesmühlen in Mecklenburg shows a male child with a normal body but with a dramatically deformed head (Fig. 6.1).[11] His eyes and tongue are missing, and the gaping dark holes where they should be seem to freeze the face into a cry of horror. Most,

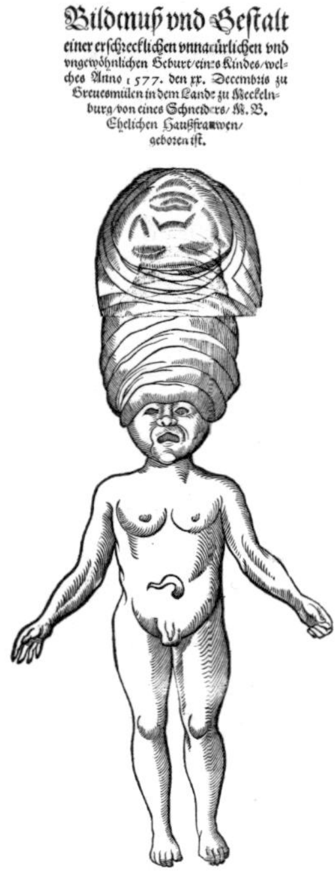

Figure 6.1: Monstrous birth with a pointed head, from S. Pauli, *Bildtnuß vnd Gestalt einer erschrecklichen ... Geburt* (n.p., 1578). Photo courtesy of the Zentralbibliothek Zürich, PAS II 15/10.

striking, though, is the over-sized turban-like head, which is in fact a large piece of skin that fell down over the face but could be lifted to reveal the horrifying features underneath. This is demonstrated in a graphic form on the broadsheet through the device of an attached flap that, like the skin, could be lifted away. The text, on a separate sheet, is made up of a numbered description of the child's body parts by the Lutheran Rostock preacher and professor of theology, Simon Pauli.[12] In what may be a sign of increasing intertextuality amongst publications on monstrous births, the text of the Strasbourg broadsheet, discussed above, included a reference to Pauli's discussion of the child with the pointed head.

Alongside this broadsheet, Pauli also prepared a much longer pamphlet on the same birth, published in 1578 and demonstrating the interaction between broadsheets and the increasingly common longer pamphlet.[13] While his fundamental message did not change, different levels of detail were made available to different audiences. As Pauli explains at the conclusion of the pamphlet, he bases his work on an image of the child sent to him by a citizen from the town of Grevesmühlen. It seems likely that this pamphlet was intended to be illustrated with a version of the same image, as Pauli refers to the child and adds that its actual 'image and form' ('bildnis vnd gestalt') can be found printed overleaf.[14]

The pamphlet includes an extended biblical analysis of the birth, and provides an apocalyptic dimension that is not explicitly developed in the broadsheet. The child reveals, Pauli tells his reader, that 'not only is the Day of Judgement nearly here, and hard at the door, but misery, great strife and plague are also coming'.[15] Pauli's text sets up a number of enemies to the faith, including Russians as well as Turks, Jews, the papacy and even his own sometimes disappointingly inadequate congregation as well as fellow preachers. Following a short descriptive list of the child's body parts (very similar to the shortened list accompanying the broadsheet), Pauli's pamphlet text is a highly detailed, numbered description and analysis of each individual body part. This approach is reminiscent of Martin Luther and Philipp Melanchthon's strategy in writing about the Papal Ass and Monk Calf, although Pauli's enemies are rather more diverse, just as the potential meanings and uses of monstrous births in print had become more complex and multi-faceted at this later stage of the century.

One of the startling facts of this case, as Pauli notes in the second paragraph of his pamphlet, is that a flap of skin across the face obscured the eyes, mouth and nose, so that it was not even possible to discern that they were there. (In his extended discussion, he presents the covering as analogous to a covering 'worn' by Jews, whose hearts are 'shielded' from the true faith. Later, he attacks them for what he describes as their inability to hear the word of God.[16]) When the flap or 'covering' ('decke') was lifted away from the monstrous child's head, the facial features were visible, and so too was the child's extraordinary pointed head, 'in the shape of a long tall Turkish or Russian hat'.[17] The facial features are also particularly horrifying in this case, as Pauli stresses. The child has no eyes, but instead bloody cavities, and no tongue, but simply a 'hideous and terrible' ('gar scheuslich vnd schrecklich') open mouth, open as though it wanted to cry out ('schreit vnd ruffet') in an equally terrible way.[18]

For Pauli, the hat recalls both the Turks and the Russians. He lists a series of territorial aggressions perpetrated by both in the preceding few years, condemning both for their 'Tyranney'.[19] Lieffland (that is, Latvia), Lithuania and Poland have been particularly subject to Russian aggression, he argues. His anxiety about Russia seems to reflect his location in Rostock in Mecklenburg, with its status as trading city and member of the Hanseatic league. Pauli then turns from international politics to morals at the community level. That the child was born to a tailor's wife is, he argues, a condemnation by God of the frivolous and luxurious fashions in clothing that had developed in recent times.[20] Pauli's railing against clothing, and also cosmetics and jewellery, dominate an extended central portion of the pamphlet, and indeed seems to overwhelm his attacks on Jews and on Russians, which seem almost mild (or more accurately, less verbose) by comparison. This aspect of the Grevesmühlen monstrous birth closely resembles a similar notorious case from 1564, of a child with a pointed head and 'ripped' skin, sometimes discussed as symbolic of excessively fashionable clothing.[21]

Pauli then turns to some of the child's individual features, and lingers on his missing ears. Here he attacks Jews again, as noted above, but also those in his own congregation and others like it, who no longer hear as they should. He specifically invokes his own status as preacher ('prediger') and pointedly remarks that it is his own words that are being ignored as well as the word of God. The child's missing tongue is a similar metaphorical indictment of those congregations who do not pray properly, preachers who do not speak properly, and 'great lords' ('grossen Herren') who also do not speak out when needed.[22] 'Where can one', he rhetorically asks, 'in this time of the church and fatherland's greatest need and danger, find tongues that will properly and earnestly pray to God the Father?'[23] Similarly, he attacks those who have eyes but are like the blind in that they do not see the terrible events that unfolding in their own lifetimes. Papal tyranny is invoked here, too, and put on a par by Pauli with Russian and Turkish tyranny.[24] Finally, the open right hand and the closed left hand of the child lead him into a discussion of preaching and other deeds performed with an open hand (good) or a closed hand (bad); the implication is that this particular event has highly negative connotations.

This child became part of the repertoire of monstrous births, and is illustrated again in a book of monstrous births prepared by physician Johann Georg Schenck (Fig. 6.2).[25] Schenck's father, also a physician, had written a very extended, multi-volume medical study that included discussions of monstrous births. The son, however, evidently recognized the continuing market for an illustrated book with relatively short texts. The elder Schenck's book forms part of a rather different attitude towards monstrous births in unillustrated publications, and lies outside the scope of this study, while the younger Schenck's book indicates the ongoing market for illustrated books of wonders that appealed to a wider, non-medical audience. The child from Grevesmühlen evidently retains his importance, as he is illustrated here with the paper flap that lifts to reveal his terrible features, with eyes and mouth as shocking cavities, and a copy of Pauli's original, shorter text. Here, the lowered flap demonstrates the ghostly appearance of the child when the skin covers his features.

Parents would seem to take on a more significant role in the later sixteenth century. In this case, the father's profession as tailor is an important issue for Pauli as he protests against luxurious clothing. But mothers became more significant in this publication genre, and while the moral culpability of the mother had featured rarely in earlier printed publications on monstrous births, they were increasingly likely now to receive some portion of implicit or even explicit blame for their child's deformity.[26] The impressionable maternal imagination had sometimes been a topic for discussion – by Martin Luther, for example – but generally in terms of protecting vulnerable women and unborn children rather than condemning the mother for her moral failings.[27] One child with four arms and legs is discussed in a broadsheet of 1578 as a reflection of the impressionability of the mother (Fig. 6.3).[28] The case is framed by a discussion of childbirth as women's painful burden after Adam and Eve's expulsion from Paradise. While this is hardly in the league of the polemic of the whore of Babylon pregnant with multiple monstrous children deployed by Johann Nas in the *Ecclesia Militans*, it does reflect a shift to a darker and more condemnatory approach to parents. Beyond this discourse on sin, mothers also appear in some later sixteenth-century publication on monstrous births in a striking new way that invites further analysis.

A broadsheet published in Cologne in 1593 relates the terrible events that took place in Rosenburg, Hungary (today in the Czech Republic), during January of that same year (Fig. 6.4).[29] The bloody suns with swords, red cross and rainbow in the sky all preceded the arrival, the text relates, of an unknown pregnant woman in the town, who did not speak a recognizable language and who went into a difficult labour. Under the signs in the sky, four monstrous births stand in a row as though orating on a stage. Their unusual bodies and proximity to other wondrous signs would certainly remind the viewer of the many cases

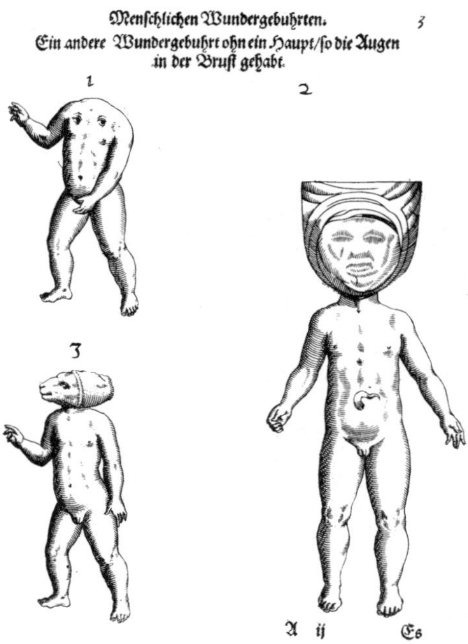

Figure 6.2: Monstrous birth with a pointed head, from J. G. Schenck, *Wunder-buch von menschlichen unerhörten Wunder- und Mißgebuhrten* (Franckfort: von Bry, 1610), p. 3. Photo courtesy of the Herzog August Bibliothek Wolfenbüttel, shelfmark A: 82.22 Quod. (1).

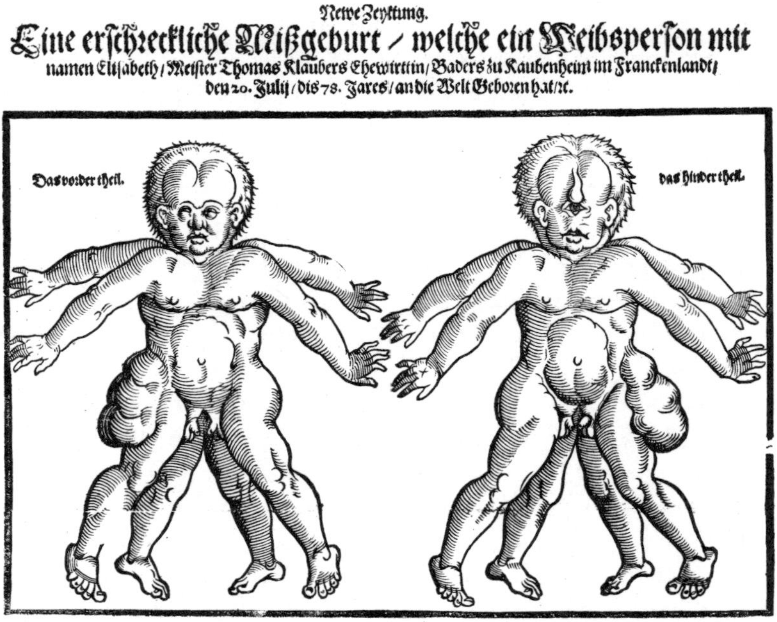

Figure 6.3: Child with four arms and four legs, from Anon., *Newe Zeyttung. Eine erschreckliche Mißgeburt* ... (Nümberg: Matthias Rauch, 1578), detail. Photo courtesy of the Zentralbibliothek Zürich, PAS II 15/36.

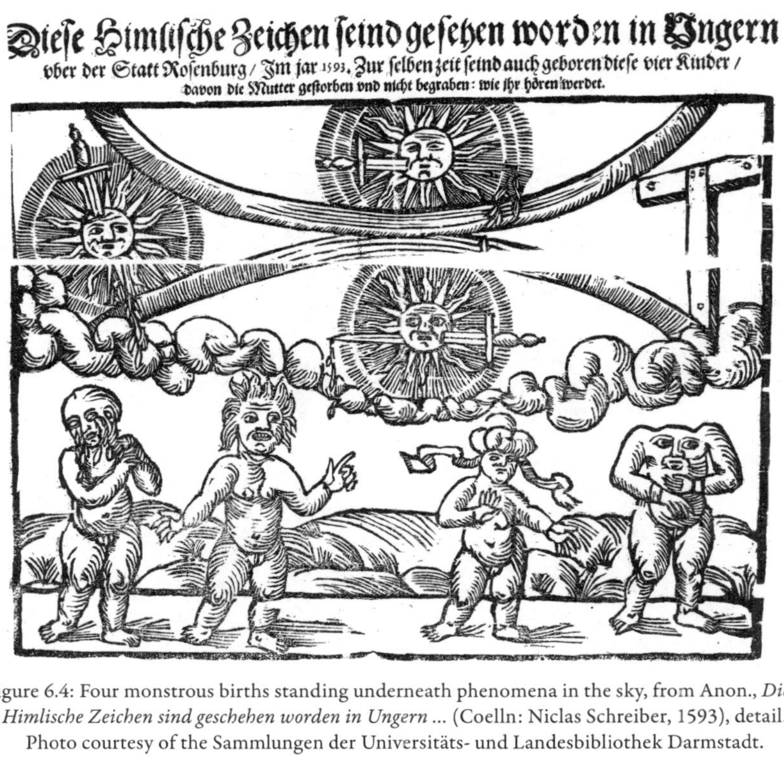

Figure 6.4: Four monstrous births standing underneath phenomena in the sky, from Anon., *Diese Himlische Zeichen sind geschehen worden in Ungern* ... (Coelln: Niclas Schreiber, 1593), detail. Photo courtesy of the Sammlungen der Universitäts- und Landesbibliothek Darmstadt.

in wonder books like Fincel's, or even the more satirical *Ecclesia Militans*. Yet these four monstrous children have a still more astonishing quality: they are quadruplets, born from one mother in a single birth, and this extraordinary new twist adds to the drama of the event. After the more fragmented, additive scenes seen so far – where different cases were brought together in sometimes unlikely combinations – this scene is presented as a cohesive contemporary event that conceptually brings together various kinds of wonders. Following the text, the first child has no head, but instead features in his chest (reminiscent of a well-known type of monstrous race known as the Blemmyae). The second child has a fleshy 'hat' in the shape of a Turkish turban, a detail perhaps prompted in this specific case by the onset of the Habsburg-Ottoman War of 1593–1606. The third child has long hair, fiery eyes, long, sharp fingernails and the appearance of a seven-year-old child rather than an infant. The fourth cries tears of blood. After this astonishing multiple birth, the mother dies. However her corpse is too heavy for even eight men to drag away into a grave; and after several days the body disappears. The children live for a further two days, and are all buried together in a grave – implausibly but dramatically dying as a group, just as they were born.

Speaking Children

This publication, particularly in its story of an itinerant pregnant woman who gives birth to wondrous children, recalls a number of other broadsheets circulating at the end of the sixteenth century.[30] From about mid-century, coincident with a wave of wonder books and increasingly complex pamphlet and broadsheet texts, a related variation of the typical monstrous birth started to appear. This was a type of monstrous human child who was not only generally physically deformed, but who also, unnaturally, had the capacity to speak. There were examples of children speaking from the womb or from a young age prior to this time.[31] However the conjunction of physical monstrosity and a prophetic voice seems highly distinctive to this period, if not unique. Alexandra Walsham observes the growing incidence of cases of wondrously prophesying children in late Tudor and early Stuart England; the earliest case that she cites is from 1555, but most are from the 1590s onwards.[32] These cases are less likely to involve monstrous births, and (while this must be a speculative point) it is possible that the phenomenon examined below was more common in German regions. These cases usually have strikingly apocalyptic dimensions. Lycosthenes, for example, in his *Wunderzeichen*, reports the case of a seven-year-old boy who spoke like an adult and preached from his home, assuring his audience that the 'Day of Judgement was at the door'.[33] However, the focus in this study is on wondrous or monstrous infants or very young children. The cases are therefore different to such stories of preaching by older children and young adults, which seem to have been reasonably common in England and also German lands.[34]

This chapter turns now to two publications that report prophetically speaking monstrous births from the close of the century. Both publications report local rather than foreign cases – one Austrian, one from northern Germany – and both are from areas where the Lutheran Reformation had been established but was under strain. The first was published in 1593 in Graz in Austria. It reported two wondrous events that had happened in January 1593 ('Jenner', in typical Austrian dialect). This simple, eight-page publication includes one woodcut illustration on the title page (Fig. 6.5), which illustrates only the events of the second case reported in the pamphlet. The first case concerns a wondrous event that took place in the town of Labach on 28 January. Labach is modern-day Laibach or Ljubljana, located in Slovenia. It lies within Carniola, at that time one of the Habsburg crown lands of Inner Austria. The region embraced the Protestant Reformation and Archduke Karl was forced to negotiate for assistance with his anti-Turkish campaigns. The latter decades of the sixteenth century saw intense struggles over religion and the ultimate triumph of the Counter-Reformation. A Jesuit college was founded in Laibach in 1597, and Lutheran priests were banned after 1598. This pamphlet therefore appeared at a high point of struggles between Catholic and Lutheran

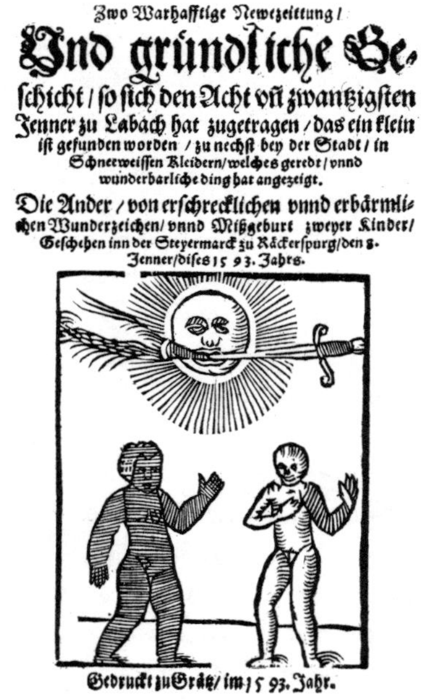
Zwo Warhafftige Newezeittung /
Vnd gründliche Ge-
ſchicht / ſo ſich den Acht vñ zwantzigſten
Jenner zu Labach hat zugetragen / das ein klein
iſt gefunden worden / zu nechſt bey der Stadt / in
Schneeweiſſen Kleidern / welches geredt / vnnd
wunderbarliche ding hat angezeigt.
Die Ander / von erſchrecklichen vnnd erbärmli-
chen Wunderzeichen / vnnd Mißgeburt zweyer Kinder /
Geſchehen inn der Steyermarck zu Räckerſpurg / den 8.
Jenner / diſes 15 93. Jahrs.
Gedruckt zu Grätz / im 15 93. Jahr.

Figure 6.5: The appearance of two strange children, from Anon., *Zwo Warhafftige Newezeittung / Vnd gruendliche Geschicht* ... (Graz: n.p., 1593), title page. Photo courtesy of the British Library. Shelfmark 717.e.42.

powers, and also early in the Habsburg-Ottoman War of 1593–1606, when the territories of Inner Austria were in particular danger.[35]

On the night of 28 January, in deep winter, a child of about three years old appeared on the road that the townspeople would normally take to church. The sex of the child is not specified, and – unlike the cases reported later in this pamphlet and in the following pamphlet – this first case is not actually an example of a monstrous birth. This nonetheless extraordinary 'child in snow-white clothing' ('Kind in schneeweissen kleidern') cried bitterly.[36] When asked why it cried, what it was actually doing there, and to whom it belonged, the child replied that it belonged to 'our Father', that it was there to shock the people of the town, and that everyone should come to see it. After several repetitions of this exchange, the child seems to have attracted a large audience and then began a monologue that lasted about eight hours. There is an evident similarity to a session of preaching, and this is emphasized by the child's appearance on the road that led to the local church. It recalls those cases of lay preaching that, as Jürgen Beyer has demonstrated, were increasingly part of the religious culture of northern Germany in the post-Lutheran Reformation.[37]

What did the child speak about? The warning nature of its speech was very clear:

> Beloved Christians, refrain from your sins and stir yourselves, since our beloved father Jesus Christ has sent me here, in order that I might warn you. He will soon forcefully bring you home [that is, the Day of Judgement comes], with terrible illness, rising prices, war and disarray, because you do not want to stir yourselves. Heed the wondrous signs that He daily sends you that you might see.[38]

The case is explicitly presented as a warning to the sinful to repent and mend their ways. Wars and misbirths are warnings sent by God, the anonymous author writes, not to cause the death or punishment of sinners, but to lead them to turn away from sin. The child repeatedly states that terrible things shall be visited upon the world, and in particular on this community. But should they mend their ways, they will be rewarded: 'the Father ... wants to mercifully grant you wine, grain, and all the fruits of the field'. Nonetheless, the crucial point is that the Last Days are coming. When one of the townsfolk asks 'how long the world will remain standing', the answer is 'a small time' ('ein kleine zeit').[39] The rewards, the reader might suspect, are above all spiritual, and intended primarily to be understood as part of the afterlife rather than the mortal present. The apocalyptic nature of the child's message about the uproar of the Last Days in emphasized by a concluding reference to the Book of Revelation. It is emphasized, too, by the unnatural appearance of a child who speaks for eight hours through the course of the long winter night, and then disappears just as mysteriously as it had appeared.

Reports of monstrous births often recall today's 'urban myths', and this case is almost certainly inspired by a related event that already in circulation. An unillustrated pamphlet from 1581 extensively reports and discusses the meaning of a monstrous birth from Havelberg, and concludes by noting how once the text was written, the authors – one a Lutheran preacher – had seen 'a sweet little child in snow-white clothing' which appeared at midnight before the feast day of Thomas the Apostle in the church of Havelberg.[40] In that pamphlet, the child in snow-white clothing had simply made an appearance in the brief concluding point, in rhetorical contradistinction to the terrible appearance, discussed in sustained detail, of the Havelberg monstrous birth. But a decade later the story of a child in white clothing had taken on more ominous, warning overtones, much more reminiscent of reports of monstrous births.

The case of the preaching child in Labach is presented in the pamphlet alongside another wondrous event from January 1593. This second case took place on 8 January in the town of Raeckerspurg in the Steyermarck, and also revolved around wondrous speaking children.[41] Raeckerspurg (or Radgona in Slovenian) is a town in the Austrian state of Styria, and at this time also a territory belonging to Inner Austria. It lies on the border between modern-day Austria and Slovenia and was made an imperial fortress in 1582, indicating its strategic importance.[42] This story of this wondrous event is presented in verse format and was probably intended to be sung, or at least to be read out loud in sing-song fashion.

The events in Raeckerspurg unfolded in several stages. First of all, at 9 o'clock in the evening of 8 January, the moon in the sky took on a blood-red cast. Taking on the appearance of a fearsome face, as the woodcut illustration demonstrates, a fiery sword appeared from one side of its mouth. The iconography is reminiscent of God the Father in the Book of Revelation, where a sword emerges from God's mouth and his face flames like the sun (Revelation 1:16). Here, however, the sword points inwards.[43] From the other side of the moon's mouth appears a 'Geissel'; that is, a whip or scourge. These visions were simply the prelude to a wondrous scene that unfolded in the sky. Soldiers on horseback appeared, with flags that portrayed a crescent moon and star, 'as in the Turkish manner'.[44] The people of Raeckerspurg, and for 7 miles (11 km) around, fell to their knees, and watched as the Turkish soldiers slaughtered a mass of Christians who had also appeared in the sky through the clouds. This marvellous and terrifying sight continued until 3 o'clock in the morning, when the light of the moon finally waned.

The townsfolk were not yet free to return to their beds and reflect upon the cosmic battle between good and evil, Turk and slaughtered Christian, that they had just witnessed in the sky. As the moon's light disappeared, a great noise was heard. It was the cries of a woman in a painful labour that continued for an extraordinary nine days. She gave birth to two sons – represented in the crude but compelling woodcut on the first page of the pamphlet – who were given to her by God, as the anonymous writer reminds the pamphlet's audience. Continuing the theme of iconography from the Book of Revelation, the events would likely have recalled for this audiences of the woman clothed with the sun and the dramatic birth of her Christ-like child while under attack from a seven-headed dragon (Revelation 12:3–4). The first of the two children was black-skinned. He wailed loudly and cried out about the terrible signs that were everywhere unfolding, and how the children were there to tell of 'murder and deathly blows'. The second child, white and with the face of a skeleton or Death, continued the refrain and warned his audience that sinners should repent and beg God's forgiveness, because the Last Days were at hand. Indeed he warned that 'we have only a short time', foreshadowing the two children's imminent disappearance as well as the onset of the Last Days.[45]

The Three-Headed Child

The second and final eight-page pamphlet to be examined here was published several years later, in 1597, in the city of Erfurt (Fig. 6.6). Erfurt is today the capital of the state of Thuringia, and figures in Reformation history as the town where Martin Luther undertook his university studies and entered the priest-

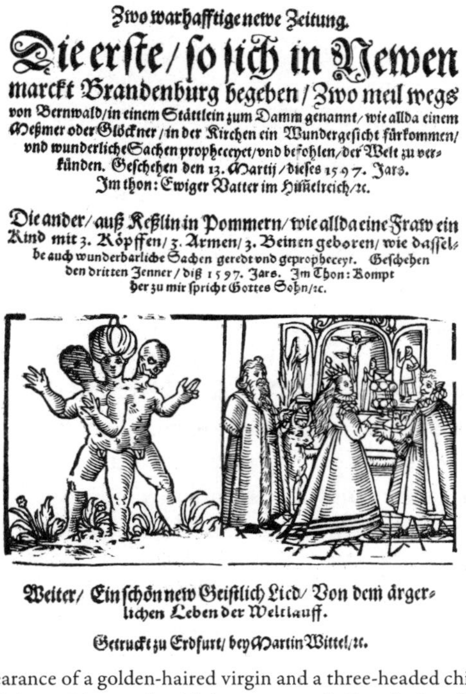
Zwo warhafftige newe Zeitung.
Die erste / so sich in Newen marckt Brandenburg begeben / Zwo meil wegs von Bernwald / in einem Stättlein zum Damm genannt / wie allda einem Meßmer oder Glöckner / in der Kirchen ein Wundergesicht fürkommen / vnd wunderliche Sachen prophecceyet / vnd befohlen / der Welt zu verkünden. Geschehen den 13. Martij / dieses 1597. Jars. Im thon: Ewiger Vatter im Hiñelreich / rc.

Die ander / auß Keßlin in Pommern / wie allda eine Fraw ein Kind mit 3. Köpffen / 3. Armen / 3. Beinen geboren / wie dasselbe auch wunderbarliche Sachen geredt vnd geprophecceyt. Geschehen den dritten Jenner / diß 1597. Jars. Im Thon: Kompt her zu mir spricht Gottes Sohn / rc.

Weiter / Ein schön new Geistlich Lied / Von dem ärgerlichen Leben der Weltlauff.

Getruckt zu Erdfurt / bey Martin Wittel / rc.

Figure 6.6: The appearance of a golden-haired virgin and a three-headed child, from Anon., *Zwo warhafftige newe Zeitung. Die erste / so sich in newenmarckt Brandenburg begeben ...* (Erdfurt: Martin Wittel, 1597), title page. Photo courtesy of the British Library. © British Library Board. All Rights Reserved. Shelfmark 11517.c.54.(6.).

hood as an Augustinian monk. This pamphlet presents its two narratives in the form of song lyrics to be sung to the tune of popular hymns; a reminder of the significance of singing and music within Protestant and especially Lutheran culture.[46] A third song reflects in more general terms on the sorry state of the world. Like the pamphlet of 1593, this one relates the story of two wondrous events. The first is of less relevance to this study, although there are some intriguing points that should be noted.[47] It concerns an event that took place in the small town of Dam, in Brandenburg. During a religious service, while the Ave Maria was being sung, a golden-haired virgin appeared to the congregation and warned them all against sin before vanishing again. This vision recalls Catholic visions of the Virgin Mary and potentially suggests that there may be Catholic sympathies behind this pamphlet.[48]

Yet Brandenburg was Lutheran territory, although there were attempts to bring back the Catholic faith. A more plausible explanation may be that this event, in the 1590s, potentially points to early stages of the existing and future debates in this region and others nearby between Lutherans and Calvinists. In Brandenburg, Elector John Sigismund's 'second Reformation', intended to institute Calvinism in 1613, was ultimately unsuccessful.[49] The rise of Calvinism in northern German areas – including Saxony during the 1580s and early 1590s – was a serious and pressing concern for Lutherans. As Thomas A. Brady, Jr, observes, 'by the early 1590s the advance of this third [after Lutheranism and Catholicism] illegal Imperial confession seemed irresistible'.[50] A chief Calvinist complaint was the laxity (that is, the unreformed nature) of Lutheran religious services.[51] The second Reformation saw particular struggles over the issue of exorcism within the ritual of baptism: Calvinists discarded it while Lutherans fought to keep it.[52] Speculatively, this point of conflict may well have been feeding into anxieties about children 'possessed' by unnatural powers and especially voices at just this time.

The second event reported in this broadsheet concerns a terrible monstrous child born on 3 January 1597 in the town of Reßlin in Pomerania (now Reszel in Poland).[53] Pomerania lay on the border between modern-day Germany and Poland, adjacent to Brandenburg. The tale, told in verse, is intended to be sung to the tune of the evidently well-known hymn 'Come to me, says the son of God'.[54] It admonishes the reader and singer about the sinful state of the world and tells of how a poor unknown woman entered the town and was admitted to the hospital where she lay in an agonizing labour, babbling in a language that no-one could understand. The similarity of this tale of an itinerant pregnant woman to the events of 1593 in Raeckerspurg indicates how stories like this were circulated, recycled and given local relevance. The woman soon gave birth to a 'terrible creature' ('schroeckliche Creatur'). As is evident in the woodcut illustration on the title page of the pamphlet, the child had three arms, three legs, two torsos and three heads. Each of the three heads had a symbolically significant deformity, and each, as the title page states, had 'spoken and prophesied wondrous things'.[55] The first has a head in the form of a Turkish hat ('Tuerckenkopff' or 'Tuerckenhutt') grown 'from flesh' ('vom Fleisch').[56] The fear of Turkish invasion was not as geographically pressing in the northern German lands as in Inner Austria but was nonetheless widely held and the Ottoman Turk was certainly the most vivid and terrifying 'other' in the Holy Roman Empire. The violence and rapaciousness of the Turk was a regular theme in the print culture of sixteenth century German and European lands.[57]

The first child, then, had a Turkish hat. The second child was red-faced and 'tyrannical' ('Tyrannisch') in appearance. The third, with its white, skeletal face, was 'just like Death' ('gleich wie der Todt'). It 'bares its teeth in an ugly manner',[58] and is again reminiscent of the second child from the Raeckerspurg case. Men and women came running from around the town to see this monstrous child, and when the room was full of people the child began to speak. Each head spoke in turn. As the first, Turk-like head began to speak, blood flowed from its mouth as though from a wound, and it proclaimed that soon 'der Tuerck' would destroy and overrun 'land and people' ('Land vnd Leuth'). The second head spoke in more general terms of the 'war and fire ('Krieg vnd Fewr') that was to come, and of the disorder and heartache that would soon overtake Christendom.[59] The third head, in a speech that seems less formulaic, laments the dead, asking 'oh, who will bury the dead in the ground, those who will soon die?'[60] Poisonous gas and smoke poured from its mouth as it spoke, sickening the people around it. Within an hour, the three-headed child had disappeared. The mother had also vanished, and although she was sought throughout the hospital and surrounding area, she could not be found. The disappearance was in itself taken as a clear sign that God had sent the woman and her children to the town. The (presumably dazed) townsfolk made their way home, the song stirringly concludes, to pray to God and ask forgiveness for their sins.

The triple heads of these children were given a sinister, leering aspect in the woodcut illustrating the pamphlet. In visual terms, the three heads would certainly have conjured up recognizable iconographical associations for contemporary readers and viewers, just as the seven-headed child of Eusrigo immediately recalled the seven-headed beast of the Book of Revelation. From the 1550s, a triple-headed dragon was a frequent means of representing the 1548 Interim in many broadsheets that reflected the anti-Interim stance epitomized by Matthias Flacius Illyricus. The heads were usually personifications of enemies of Lutheran Christianity: the Turk, the Pope and – to underscore the latter association – an angel who represented the hypocrisy of the papacy.[61] The imagery retained its currency and was reworked into new visual polemics. Johannes Praetorius of Halle wrote an illustrated pamphlet in 1592 that left aside the angel's head, and presented a three-headed Antichrist made up of a Pope, a Turk and a Calvinist;

a clear sign of how intra-confessional polemics could be just as virulent as those directed towards more obvious outsiders.[62]

Conclusion

Sixteenth-century publications on monstrous births confront modern viewers with graphically arresting images and vivid texts. Even today, these representations can be shocking and disturbing, not least because the authors, artists and publishers sought to profit or otherwise capitalize on the unfortunate children and animals that form their subject. But publishers, authors and artists also sought to provide interesting and useful information, to warn of past and future disasters, to debate important issues, and to confront pressing spiritual and confessional questions. By the close of the century, publications of various degrees of visual and textual sophistication were drawing on a wealth of existing iconographic references.

These increasingly complex publications on monstrous births offer insights into some of the most urgent issues confronting societies in a period marked by conflict, and above all by religious change. Medical issues would ultimately dominate discourse on monstrous births, but that point remains far off at the end of the century. Publications about monstrous births centred on medical issues – like the notable exception of Jakob Rueff's 1554 *Trostbüchle* – pale into insignificance during the sizteenth century beside the more pressing need to understand the messages of monstrous births in regard to the interpretation of sin, morality and God's natural signs within an apocalyptic world view.

Many of these pamphlets and broadsheets from the later decades of the sixteenth century offer particularly vivid examples of the ways in which ideas about monstrous births and popular preaching or prophesying could thematically join together. The result was the circulation in print of extraordinary scenes of monstrous infants warning townsfolk of sin and the coming Day of Judgement. To some extent, these wondrous prophetic children should be seen as the sort of false prophets that were feared to be part of the disordering of the world in the Last Days. They demonstrate that at the close of the sixteenth century the representation and interpretation of monstrous births in printed visual culture still remained fundamentally apocalyptic, even as many new elements were entering into the genre.[63] The interaction of Lutheran, Calvinist and Catholic confessions in a period of intense uncertainty, marked by new anxieties about the Turkish threat, forms the background to these new cases. This bewildering and frightening fracturing of the world found one compelling, and fundamentally visual, iconographical form in sixteenth-century monstrous births, increasingly entwined with the narrative of religious disorder that had shaken the world in which they appeared.

NOTES

Introduction

1. On this case, see I. Ewinkel, *De monstris: Deutung und Funktion von Wundergeburten auf Flugblättern im Deutschland des 16. Jahrhunderts* (Tübingen: Max Niemeyer Verlag, 1995), pp. 237–47; and W. Harms and M. Schilling (eds), *Deutsche illustrierte Flugblätter des 16. und 17. Jahrhunderts*, 7 vols (Tübingen: M. Niemeyer, 1980–2005), vol. 7; see pp. 224–33.
2. '[I]st von eyner zimlich gestandenen Matronen an die Welt gebracht worden.'
3. 'Statt Horb am Necker.'
4. '[A]lso das die Erden vnter den Lebendigen sint geschwom[m]en.'
5. '[S]olche warnungen ... ehe man noch greuliches erfahre.'
6. '[S]ihet man leyder taeglich hin vnd wider / fern vnd nahe' ('unfortunately one sees this daily here and there, far and near').
7. '[O]n bedeutnuß vnd würckung.'
8. The most significant recent analyses of monstrous births in early modern Europe are Ewinkel, *De monstris*; J. Céard, *La Nature et les prodiges: L'Insolite au XVIe siècle, en France*, 2nd edn (Geneva: E. Droz, 1996); L. Daston and K. Park, *Wonders and the Order of Nature 1150–1750* (New York: Zone Books, 1998), pp. 173–214; D. Wilson, *Signs and Portents: Monstrous Births from the Middle Ages to the Enlightenment* (London: Routledge, 1993), pp. 3–100; P. M. Soergel, 'Portraying Monstrous Birth in Early Modern Germany', in R. Dahood (ed), *The Future of the Middle Ages and the Renaissance: Problems, Trends, and Opportunities for Research* (Turnhout: Brepols, 1998), pp. 129–50; P. M. Soergel, 'The Afterlives of Monstrous Infants in Reformation Germany', in B. Gordon and P. Marshall (eds), *The Place of the Dead: Death and Remembrance in Late Medieval and Early Modern Europe* (Cambridge: Cambridge University Press, 2000), pp. 288–309; P. M. Soergel, 'Die Wahrnehmung der Endzeit in monströsen Anfängen', trans. S. Westermann, in H. Lehmann and A.-C. Trepp (eds), *Im Zeichen der Krise: Religiosität im Europa des 17. Jahrhunderts* (Göttingen: Vandenhoeck and Ruprecht, 1999), pp. 33–51; R. P. Hsia, 'A Time for Monsters: Monstrous Births, Propaganda, and the German Reformation', in L. L. Knoppers and J. B. Landes (eds), *Monstrous Bodies / Political Monstrosities in Early Modern Europe* (Ithaca, NY: Cornell University Press, 2004), pp. 67–92; and A. W. Bates, *Emblematic Monsters: Unnatural Conceptions and Deformed Births in Early Modern Europe* (Amsterdam: Rodopi, 2005).
9. Several manuscript illustrations from the very early sixteenth century are noted below, pp. 24–5, and for examples of other drawings see below, pp. 42, 52.

10. P. Findlen, 'Inventing Nature: Commerce, Art, and Science in the Early Modern Cabinet of Curiosities', in P. H. Smith and P. Findlen (eds), *Merchants and Marvels: Commerce, Science, and Art in Early Modern Europe* (New York: Routledge, 2002), pp. 297–323, on p. 297.
11. This urgency was a feature of the Italian material in the turbulent first decades of the sixteenth century. See O. Niccoli, *Prophecy and People in Renaissance Italy*, trans. L. G. Cochrane (Princeton, NJ: Princeton University Press, 1990).
12. R. Scribner, *For the Sake of Simple Folk: Popular Propaganda for the German Reformation*, 2nd edn (Cambridge: Cambridge University Press, 1994), p. 136.
13. On apocalyptic elements in broadsheets representing monstrous births in the second half of the sixteenth century, see Soergel, 'Die Wahrnehmung der Endzeit'; and Ewinkel, *De monstris*, pp. 77–102. Ewinkel does not trace the origins or course of this shift, however. Daston and Park similarly but more briefly emphasize the apocalyptic character of publications from this time. See Daston and Park, *Wonders and the Order of Nature*, esp. pp. 183, 187.
14. S. Clark, *Thinking with Demons: the Idea of Witchcraft in Early Modern Europe* (Oxford: Clarendon Press, 1997), p. 337.
15. J. Delumeau, *La Peur en Occident (XIVe–XVIII siècles)* (Paris: Fayard, 1987), p. 199, and more generally see pp. 197–231.
16. Clark, *Thinking with Demons*, pp. 335–45. On the connection between Lutheranism and the Apocalypse, see pp. 339–40; and on the topic of apocalypticism in early modern German lands, see also I. Backus, *Reformation Readings of the Apocalypse: Geneva, Zurich, Wittenberg* (Oxford: Oxford University Press, 2000); R. B. Barnes, *Prophecy and Gnosis: Apocalypticism in the Wake of the Lutheran Reformation* (Stanford, CA: Stanford University Press, 1988); I. Richardsen-Friedrich, *Antichrist-Polemik in der Zeit der Reformation und der Glaubenskämpfe bis Anfang des 17. Jahrhunderts. Argumentation, Form und Funktion* (Frankfurt am Main: Peter Lang, 2003); V. Leppin, *Antichrist und Jüngster Tag. Das Profil apokalyptischer Flugschriftenpublizistik im deutschen Luthertum 1548–1618* (Gütersloh: Gütersloher Verlaghaus, 1999); and M. Pohl, 'Exegese und Historiographie. Lutherische Apokalypsenkommentare als Kirchengeschichtsschreibung (1530–1618)', in T. Kaufmann, A. Schubert and K. von Greyerz (eds), *Frühneuzeitliche Konfessionskulturen. Nachwuchstagung des VRG Wittenberg 30.09–02.10.2001* (Gütersloh: Gütersloher Verlaghaus, 2008), pp. 289–317.
17. Clark, *Thinking with Demons*, p. 339.
18. See Z. Hanafi, *The Monster in the Machine: Magic, Medicine and the Marvellous in the Time of the Scientific Revolution* (Durham, NC: Duke University Press, 2000), pp. 7–12. On Obsequens, see Céard, *La Nature et les prodiges*, esp. pp. 161–3; R. Schenda, 'Die deutschen Prodigiensammlungen des 16. und 17. Jahrhunderts', *Archiv für Geshichte des Buchwesens*, 4 (1963), pp. 637–710, on pp. 640–1; and Ewinkel, *De monstris*, pp. 16–19.
19. Primarily in *De generatione animalium*, IV:3. For an overview of Aristotle's theories of generation in relation to monstrosity, see Wilson, *Signs and Portents*, pp. 16–21. Aristotle was of increasing interest in the sixteenth century. H. C. Erik Midelfort notes that editions of his work surged from the mid 1530s. H. C. E. Midelfort, *A History of Madness in Sixteenth-Century Germany* (Stanford, CA: Stanford University Press, 1999), p. 148.
20. Cicero, *De Senectutue, de Amicitia, de Divinatione*, trans. W. A. Falconer (London: William Heinemann, 1964), pp. 223–539. For an overview of the theme of prodigies and

portents, see R. Bloch, *Les Prodiges dans l'Antiquité Classique* (Paris: Presses Universitaire de France, 1963), and on monstrous births in particular pp. 24–5, 69–73.

21. Hanafi, *The Monster in the Machine*, pp. 7–12.
22. On recent developments in studying the 'book of nature' in early modern Europe and especially the growing scholarly interest in the religious dimensions, see the preface in A. G. Debus and M. T. Walton (eds), *Reading the Book of Nature: The Other Side of the Scientific Revolution* (Kirksville, MO: Sixteenth Century Journal Publishers, 1998), pp. vii–xvi, see esp. pp. vii–ix.
23. See Pliny, *Natural History*, trans. H. Rackham (London: William Heinman; Cambridge, MA: Harvard University Press, 1938), p. 529 (VII:3). More generally, see pp. 528–33 for multiple births. See J. F. Healy, *Pliny the Elder on Science and Technology* (Oxford: Oxford University Press, 1999), pp. 308–91. See also Céard, *La Nature et les prodiges*, pp. 12–20.
24. See Pliny, *Natural History*, p. 175 (II:3). Almost all the natural prodigies and wonders in book II are meteorological phenomena or wonders involving minerals, plants or geographical locations.
25. Julius Obsequens drew primarily upon Livy. For Obsequens's text, see Livy, *Summaries, Fragments, and Obsequens, vol. 14*, trans. A. C. Schlesinger (Cambridge, MA: Harvard University Press, 1959), pp. 283–319. On Obsequens, see P. L. Schmidt, 'Julius Obsequens und das Probleme der Livius-Epitome. Ein Beitrag zur Geschichte der lateinischen Prodigienliteratur', *Abhandlung des Geistes- und Sozialwissenschaftlichen Klasse* (1968), pp. 153–242, and on the complex issue of dating the work see pp. 229–33.
26. Hanafi, *The Monster in the Machine*, p. 12.
27. Augustine, *The City of God Against the Pagans*, ed. and trans. R. W. Dyson (Cambridge: Cambridge University Press, 1998), p. 1061.
28. Ibid., pp. 1063–4.
29. Cited in Daston and Park, *Wonders and the Order of Nature*, p. 50. For an overview of Isidore and other medieval authors, see ibid., pp. 48–59.
30. See J. B. Friedman, *The Monstrous Races in Medieval Art and Thought* (Cambridge, MA: Harvard University Press, 1981); and C. W. Bynum, *Metamorphosis and Identity* (New York: Zone Books, 2001), esp. pp. 37–76.
31. For the case of an anonymous fifteenth-century Parisian who recorded in his diary the birth of conjoined twins on 6 June 1429, see Bynum, *Metamorphosis and Identity*, p. 65. For the original text, see Anon., *Journal d'un bourgeois de Paris, 1405–1449*, ed. A. Tuetey (Paris: H. Champion, 1881), pp. 238–9. The entry was originally accompanied by a sketch, now lost.
32. One carving dates to *c.* 1120–32 and is on the capital of the Basilica of Sainte-Madeleine in Vézelay. Daston and Park, *Wonders and the Order of Nature*, pp. 52–4. Another dates from almost two centuries later, and also represents conjoined male twins. This relief carving of *c.* 1317 was formerly on the exterior of the Hospital of Santa Maria della Scala in Florence, and is now in the Museo di San Marco. Ibid., pp. 55–7.
33. Burns distinguishes this from the apocalyptic function of monstrous births. W. E. Burns, *An Age of Wonders: Prodigies, Politics and Providence in England 1657–1727* (Manchester: Manchester University Press, 2002), p. 2.
34. See Daston and Park, *Wonders and the Order of Nature*, p. 45.
35. *Gesta Romanorum*, trans. C. Swan, pref. E. A. Baker (London: George Routledge and Sons, 1905), p. 366. The passage is titled 'Of Spiritual Medicine'.

36. Daston and Park, *Wonders and the Order of Nature*; on the *Gesta Romanorum* see p. 381, n. 78; on Oresme see p. 132.
37. See Burns, *An Age of Wonders*, p. 171. See also 2 Esdras 11–12, which describes the apocalyptic beasts from the Book of Daniel.
38. H. Volz, *Vom Spätmittelhochdeutschen zum Frühneuhochdeutschen. Synoptischer Text des Propheten Daniel in sechs deutschen Übersetzungen des 14. bis 16. Jahrhunderts* (Tübingen: Max Niemeyer Verlag, 1963), p. ix.
39. L. Daston and K. Park, 'Unnatural Conceptions: The Study of Monsters in Sixteenth- and Seventeenth-Century France and England', *Past and Present*, 92 (1981), pp. 20–54; Daston and Park, *Wonders and the Order of Nature*, pp. 173–214.
40. Scribner, *For the Sake of Simple Folk*, see esp. pp. 126–33.
41. R. Scribner, 'The Reformation, Popular Magic and the "Disenchantment of the World"', in his *Religion and Culture in Germany (1400–1800)*, ed. L. Roper (Leiden: Brill, 2001), pp. 346–65, on p. 355.
42. Ibid., p. 356. While the idea that early modern societies understood dramatic natural events in entirely pessimistic terms remains dominant, some alternative readings are emerging. See, for example, P. M. Soergel, 'Portents, Disaster and Adaptation in Sixteenth Century Germany', *Medieval History Journal*, 10 (2007), pp. 303–26.
43. See these catalogues, with some images of monstrous births: F. W. H. Hollstein (ed.), *German Engravings, Etchings and Woodcuts ca. 1400–1700*, 62 vols (Amsterdam: Menno Hertzberger, 1954–95; Rotterdam: Sound and Vision Interactive, 1996–); and W. L. Strauss (ed.), *The Illustrated Bartsch*, 72 vols (New York: Abaris Books, 1978–96). More can be found in these collections of single-sheet woodcuts: M. Geisberg, *The German Single-Leaf Woodcut: 1500–1550*, rev. and ed. W. L. Strauss, 4 vols (New York: Hacker Art Books, 1974); and W. L. Strauss, *The German Single-Leaf Woodcut 1550–1600*, 3 vols (New York: Abaris Books, 1975). A more recent series of volumes edited by Wolfgang Harms and Michael Schilling catalogues broadsheets held in major German and Swiss collections and provides a new level of accessibility and scholarship. See Harms and Schilling (eds), *Deutsche illustrierte Flugblätter*.
44. A. Warburg, 'Pagan-Antique Prophecy in Words and Images in the Age of Luther', in his *The Renewal of Pagan Antiquity: Contributions to the Cultural History of the European Renaissance*, trans. D. Britt (Los Angeles, CA: Getty Research Institute for the History of Art and the Humanities, 1999), pp. 597–697, and addenda pp. 760–75.
45. See F. Saxl, 'Illustrated Pamphlets of the Reformation', in his *Lectures* (London: Warburg Institute, University of London, 1957), pp. 255–66.
46. R. Wittkower, 'Marvels of the East: A Study of the History of Monsters', *Journal of the Warburg and Courtauld Institutes*, 5 (1942), pp. 159–97, on p. 170. I make the assumption that Wittkower includes broadsheets under the term 'pamphlets', as the bulk of the primary sources are broadsheets.
47. In the English-speaking world, the work of Robert Scribner, particularly his seminal *For the Sake of Simple Folk*, has been most crucial.
48. There has been a recent wave of material on the cultural and literary history of monstrous births and wonders in early modern England. See J. Crawford, *Marvelous Protestantism: Monstrous Births in Post-Reformation England* (Baltimore, MD and London: Johns Hopkins University Press, 2005); Burns, *An Age of Wonders*; and R. Gilbert, *Early Modern Hermaphrodites: Sex and Other Stories* (Houndsmills: Palgrave, 2002).
49. Several early twentieth-century German scholars, by profession medical doctors, approached the material from a primarily medical perspective. See E. Holländer, *Wunder*

Wundergeburt und Wundergestalt in Einblattdrucken des fünfzehnten bis achzehnten Jahrhunderts (Stuttgart: Ferdinand Enke, 1921); and A. Sonderegger, *Missgeburten und Wundergestalten in Einblattdrucken und Handzeichnungen des 16. Jahrhunderts* (Zurich: Orell Füssli, 1927). For close studies of individual sources over the last several decades, see H. Schilling, 'Job Fincel und die Zeichen der Endzeit', in W. Brückner (ed.), *Volkserzählung und Reformation. Ein Handbuch zur Tradierung und Funktion von Erzählstoffen und Erzählliteratur im Protestantismus* (Berlin: Erich Schmidt Verlag, 1974), pp. 325–92; D. Wuttke, 'Wunderdeutung und Politik. Zu den Auslegungen der sogenannten Wormser Zwillinge des Jahres 1495', in K. Elm, E. Gönner and E. Hillenbrand (eds), *Landesgeschichte und Geistesgeschichte. Festschrift für Otto Herding zum 65. Geburtstag* (Stuttgart: W. Kohlhammer, 1977), pp. 217–44; V. Sack, *Sebastian Brant als Politischer Publizist. Zwei Flugblatt-Satiren aus den Folgejahren des sogennanten Reformreichstags von 1495* (Freiburg i. Br.: Stadtarchiv, 1997); K. W. Littger, 'Elßgred. Flugblätter einer Mißgeburt', *Gutenberg-Jahrbuch* (2003), pp. 74–85; and R. Schenda, 'Das Monstrum von Ravenna: Eine Studie zur Prodigienliterature', *Zeitschrift für Volkskunde*, 56 (1960), pp. 209–25.

50. Schenda, 'Die deutschen Prodigiensammlungen'.
51. Céard, *La Nature et les prodiges*.
52. C. Zika, 'Writing the Visual into History: Changing Cultural Perceptions of Late Medieval and Renaissance Germany', in his *Exorcising our Demons: Magic, Witchcraft and Visual Culture in Early Modern Europe* (Leiden: Brill, 2003), pp. 523–79.
53. P. Burke, 'Unity and Variety in Cultural History', in his *Varieties of Cultural History* (Cambridge: Polity Press, 1997), pp. 183–212, on pp. 194–8. On the new cultural history, see also P. Burke, *What is Cultural History?* (Cambridge: Polity Press, 2004). On the cultural turn in Reformation history, see S. C. Karant-Nunn, 'Changing One's Mind: Transformations in Reformation History from a Germanist's Perspective', *Renaissance Quarterly*, 58 (2005), pp. 1101–27. On the implications of the Warburg school for cultural history, see C. Ginzburg, 'From Aby Warburg to E. H. Gombrich: A Problem of Method', in his *Clues, Myths, and the Historical Method*, trans. J. and A. C. Tedeschi (Baltimore, MD: Johns Hopkins University Press, 1989), pp. 17–59.
54. Scribner, *For the Sake of Simple Folk*; R. Scribner, 'Ways of Seeing in the Age of Dürer', in D. Eichberger and C. Zika (eds), *Dürer and his Culture* (Cambridge: Cambridge University Press, 1998), pp. 93–117; and R. Scribner, 'Popular Piety and Modes of Visual Perception in Late-Medieval and Reformation Germany', and 'From the Sacred Image to the Sensual Gaze: Sense Perceptions and the Visual in the Objectification of the Female Body in Sixteenth-Century Germany', both in his *Religion and Culture in Germany*, pp. 104–28, 129–45, respectively. See, too, this new study of visual print culture: C. Zika, *The Appearance of Witchcraft: Print and Visual Culture in Sixteenth-Century Europe* (London: Routledge, 2008).
55. See especially L. Silver, 'Nature and Nature's God: Immanence in the Landscape Cosmos of Albrecht Altdorfer', *Art Bulletin*, 91 (1999), pp. 194–214; L. Silver and P. H. Smith, 'Splendor in the Grass: The Power of Nature and Art in the Age of Dürer', in Smith and Findlen (eds), *Merchants and Marvels*, pp. 29–62; D. Landau and P. Parshall, *The Renaissance Print 1470–1550* (New Haven, CT: Yale University Press, 1994), pp. 169–259; and P. Parshall, 'Imago contrafacta: Images and Facts in the Northern Renaissance', *Art History*, 16 (1993), pp. 554–79.
56. See especially D. Freedberg, *The Power of Images: Studies in the History and Theory of Response* (Chicago, IL: Chicago University Press, 1989).

57. Scribner, 'The Reformation'; and see also L. Roper, *Oedipus and the Devil: Witchcraft, Sexuality and Religion in Early Modern Europe* (London: Routledge, 1994), pp. 4–5.
58. P. Parshall, 'The Vision of the Apocalypse in the Sixteenth and Seventeenth Centuries', in F. Carey (ed.), *The Apocalypse and the Shape of Things to Come*, exhibition catalogue (London: British Museum Press, 1999), pp. 99–124, on p. 109.
59. R. Chartier, 'Texts, Printing, Readings', in L. Hunt (ed.), *The New Cultural History* (Berkeley, CA: University of California Press, 1989), pp. 154–75, on pp. 169–70.
60. C. Ginzburg, 'The High and the Low: the Theme of Forbidden Knowledge in the Sixteenth and Seventeenth Centuries', in his *Clues, Myths, and the Historical Method*, pp. 60–76.
61. Philip Soergel emphasizes this point. See Soergel, 'Portraying Monstrous Birth', p. 146.
62. The less common unillustrated or Latin publications are referred to when necessary to illuminate a particular point or group of sources.

1 From Monstrous Races to Monstrous Births

1. For a recent survey, see V. Honemann et al. (eds), *Einblattdrucke des 15. und frühen 16. Jahrhunderts. Probleme, Perspective, Fallstudien* (Tübingen: Max Niemeyer, 2000).
2. M. U. Edwards, Jr, *Printing, Propaganda, and Martin Luther* (Berkeley, CA: University of California Press, 1994), pp. 15–21.
3. See Landau and Parshall, *The Renaissance Print*, pp. 169–259; P. Parshall and R. Schoch, *Origins of European Printmaking: Fifteenth-Century Woodcuts and their Public*, exhibition catalogue (New Haven, CT: Yale University Press, 2005); and on artistic confidence and national identity, see L. Silver, 'Germanic Patriotism in the Age of Dürer', in Eichberger and Zika (eds), *Dürer and his Culture*, pp. 38–68.
4. Daston and Park, *Wonders and the Order of Nature*, pp. 64–5, 173.
5. Rudolf Wittkower's survey of this material is still very useful. See Wittkower, 'Marvels of the East', and on the specific issue of the discussion of the monstrous races in classical and medieval sources, see pp. 159–76. See also Friedman, *The Monstrous Races*; and D. H. Strickland, *Saracens, Demons and Jews: Making Monsters in Medieval Art* (Princeton, NJ: Princeton University Press, 2003), pp. 41–59.
6. Wittkower, 'Marvels of the East', pp. 176–8.
7. Friedman, *The Monstrous Races*.
8. On this tradition, see Strickland, *Saracens, Demons and Jews*, p. 49.
9. Cited and translated in Friedman, *The Monstrous Races*, p. 93. On the connection with Adam, see p. 31, and with Noah, see pp. 101–2. The original text is: 'sumeliche hêten houbet sam hunt; sumeliche hêten an den brusten den munt, / an dem ahselun dei ougen, dei mousen sich des houbtes gelouben; / sumeliche hêten sô michel ôren daz si sich dâ mite dachten. / Etlicher hêt einen fuoz unt was der vile grôz: / dâ mite liuf er sô balde sam daz tier dâ ze walde Etlichiu bar daz chint daz mit allen vieren gie sam daz rint. / Sumeliche flurn begarewe ir scônen varwe: / si wurten swarz unt egelîch, den ist nehen liut gelîch. / dei ougen in scînent, die zeni glîzent. / swenne si si lâzent blecchen sô mahten si jouch den tiufel screchen. / die afterchomen an in zeigtun waz ir vorderen garnet hêten: / also lich si wâren innen, solich wurten dise ûzzen.' From K. Smits (ed.), *Das Frühmittelhochdeutsche Wiener Genesis: Kritische Ausgabe mit einem einleitenden Kommentar zur Uberlieferung* (Berlin: Erich Schmidt, 1972), p. 135, ll. 649–60.
10. Smits (ed.), *Das Frühmittelhochdeutsche Wiener Genesis*, pp. 179–81.

11. Several Latin editions of this text did appear in print. See, for example, J. de Hese, *Itinerarius* ([Köln]: [Zierickzee], [*c.* 1500]), in the Hezog August Bibliothek, Wolfenbüttel.
12. This book was based upon Thomas Cantimpré's *De natura rerum*. Wittkower, 'Marvels of the East', p. 170, n. 9. For publishing details, see A. Schramm, *Der Bilderschmuck der Frühdrucke*, 23 vols (Leipzig: Karl W. Hiersemann, 1922–43), vol. 3, p. 14.
13. 'Wunderliche Quellen und merckwürdige Menschen'.
14. K. von Megenberg, *Hie nach volgt das buch der Natur* (Augsburg: Schönsperger, 1499), pp. 215–24.
15. The most thorough study of the Mandeville story remains J. W. Bennett, *The Rediscovery of Sir John Mandeville* (New York: Modern Language Association of America, 1954).
16. For full bibliographical details, see ibid., pp. 364–6. On this edition, see Schramm, *Der Bilderschmuck der Frühdrucke*, vol. 4, pp. 19–20, 51. For a full set of reproductions, see pp. 89–99. Schramm noted the existence of a 1478 edition but it can no longer be traced, and was possibly destroyed in the Second World War. On this, and the early Velser printed editions in general, see *Sir John Mandevilles Reisebeschreibung. In deutscher Übersetzung von Michel Velser. Nach der Stuttgarter Papierhandschrift Cod. HB V 86*, ed. E. J. Morrall (Berlin: Akademie-Verlag, 1974), pp. cxx–cxxii. For passages on monstrous races and wondrous animals, see the facsimile edition *Jean de Mandeville. Reisen. Reprint der Erstdrucke der deutschen Übersetzungen des Michel Velser (Augsburg, bei Anton Sorg, 1480) und des Otto von Diemeringen (Basel, bei Bernhard Richel, 1480/81)*, ed. E. Bremer and K. Ridder (Hildesheim: Georg Olms, 1991), pp. 105–8, 121–1*, 124–9, 154–6, 160. These references are to Michel Velser's translation.
17. For full bibliographical details, see Bennett, *The Rediscovery of Sir John Mandeville*, pp. 366–7. On von Diemeringen's translation, see *Jean de Mandeville. Reisebeschreibung. Übertragen aus dem Französichen von Otto von Diemeringen. Der Antichrist und der fünfzehn Zeichen vor dem Jungsten Gericht. Wien, Österreichische Nationalbibliothek, Codex 2838*, microfiche edn, commentary K. Ridder (Munich: Edition Helga Lengenfelder, 1992), pp. 7–15. (This publication also looks at a separate late medieval text on the coming of the Antichrist.)
18. '[V]on Cams sun ward geborn membrot [Nimrod] der was der erst künig der ÿe was ... vnd zuo des selbe[n]weib kame[n] offt die teüfel vn[d] hettent mit jr ze schaffen das dam die fraw gebar das warde volcke wider dÿe natur eins on haupt. das ander auf einem bain vnnd gar wunderlich ... vnd die seind alle von Cam kommen.' Cited in *Jean de Mandeville. Reisen*, p. 139.
19. Ibid., p. 36.
20. '[J]ch Michelfelser der dicz buoch in teütsch gepracht hat hab selber gesehen.' Ibid., p. 36.
21. '[D]er groeß als ein ganß.' Ibid., p. 37.
22. On the *Weltchronik*, see E. Rücker, *Hartmann Schedel's Weltchronik. Das größte Buchunternehmen der Dürer-Zeit* (Munich: Prestel, 1988). For a concise overview of the creation and art historical importance of the *Weltchronik*, see Landau and Parshall, *The Renaissance Print*, pp. 38–42. Schedel was, in fact, a collector of prints, including some that are amongst the earliest broadsheet reports of 'unnatural' natural phenomena. See B. Hernad, *Die Graphiksammlung des Humanisten Hartmann Schedel*, exhibition catalogue (Munich: Prestel-Verlag, 1990). Few of his prints predate the *Weltchronik*, however.
23. On this form of narrating history, see Friedman, *The Monstrous Races*, pp. 87–8.
24. For instance, the same woodcut is used for Siena and a few pages later again for Mantua. See H. Schedel, *Chronicle of the World* [facsimile of the 1493 *Weltchronik*], intro. and

appendix S. Füssel (Cologne: Taschen, 2001). For Siena, see f. LXXX r., for Mantua, f. LXXXIIII r. In another example – and these could be considerably multiplied – Plotinus and Titus Livius are also identical. For Plotinus, see f. LXXIIII v., for Titus Livius, f. LXXX v.

25. '[H]immlischen schrecklichen Zeichen, / Die Kometen, und manch greuliche Mißgestalt'. Reproduced and translated from Latin into German in S. Füssel's introduction, in ibid., p. 9.
26. Two are on ibid., f. XII v., while the remaining strip is on f. XII r., running alongside a map of the world that spreads across a double page, on ff. XII r. and v.
27. See note 94 to Chapter 3, below, p. 170, on Martin Luther's disapproval of grotesque border decorations for biblical imagery for just this reason.
28. Bynum, *Metamorphosis and Identity*, pp. 113–62.
29. Friedman, *The Monstrous Races*, pp. 197–8.
30. Daston and Park, *Wonders and the Order of Nature*, p. 24.
31. 'Mancherley wunderlicher vn[d] erschrecke[n]licher ding erschinen diser zeit in kriechischem land.'
32. This may be related to representations of Christ seated on a rainbow at the Day of Judgement.
33. '[V]nnd wen[n] ir eins aße so schlieff das ander.'
34. 'Ain weib gepare ein wu[n]der gestalt zwifachs leibs. vornen eins menschen vnnd hindten ein hundes.' Ibid., f. CXCVIII r. This page also records, although without an accompanying image, the birth of a pig with a human face and a four-footed chicken.
35. 'Ain edels weib in costnitzer bistthumb.'
36. On the upheavals of this period, see G. Strauss (ed.), *Manifestations of Discontent in Germany on the Eve of the Reformation* (Bloomington, IN: Indiana University Press, 1971).
37. Daston and Park, *Wonders and the Order of Nature*, pp. 176–7. These three categories are analysed in ch. 5 at pp. 173–214. On 'Pleasure: Monsters as Sports', see pp. 190–201.
38. Ibid., p. 177.
39. Littger, 'Elßgred', p. 79.
40. D. Kurze, 'Johann Lichtenberger. Leben und Werke eines spätmittelalterlichen Propheten und Astrologen', *Archiv für Kulturgeschichte*, 38 (1956), pp. 328–43, on pp. 338–41.
41. Warburg, 'Pagan-Antique Prophecy', pp. 622–3. Middleberg's text had been dedicated to the future Maximilian I (see p. 641).
42. D. Kurze, 'Prophecy and History: Lichtenberger's Forecasts of Events to Come (from the Fifteenth to the Twentieth Century); their Reception and Diffusion', *Journal of the Warburg and Courtauld Institutes*, 21 (1958), pp. 63–85, on p. 63; Kurze, 'Johann Lichtenberger', p. 329.
43. Kurze, 'Johann Lichtenberger', pp. 332–3. See also H. Wiesflecker, *Kaiser Maximilian I. Das Reich, Oesterreich und Europa an der Wende zur Neuzeit*, 5 vols (Vienna: Verlag für Geschichte und Politik, 1971–85), vol. 5, p. 334. On these points, and more generally on prophecies about the Last World Emperor, see M. Reeves, *The Influence of Prophecy in the Later Middle Ages*, 2nd edn (Notre Dame: University of Notre Dame Press, 1993), pp. 332–54.
44. Warburg, 'Pagan-Antique Prophecy', see p. 599 for definitions of these terms. Astrological readings were particularly important to Maximilian I. See M. Hollegger, *Maximilian I (1459–1519). Herrscher und Mensch eine Zeitenwende* (Stuttgart: Verlag W. Kohlhammer, 2005), pp. 18–19.

45. On the manuscript, see P. Kennel, 'Joseph Grünpeck. Prodigiorum interpretation. Edition der Handschrift 314 der Universitätsbibliothek Innsbruck' (Diplomarbeit, Leopold-Franzens Univeritāt Innsbruck, 2001). This useful study includes a full transcription of the text and a translation into German. Kennel also revises the date of the manuscript to December 1501, as previous studies had incorrectly dated it to 1502. See also Céard, *La Nature et les prodiges*, pp. 77–8; Wittkower, 'Marvels of the East', p. 186; and *Ausstellung Maximilian I. Innsbruck*, exhibition catalogue (Innsbruck: Verlagsanstalt Tyrolia, 1969), p. 103 and fig. 80.
46. Wiesflecker, *Kaiser Maximilian I*, vol. 3, p. 47, vol. 5, pp. 333–5, 366–7; H. Wiesflecker, *Joseph Grünpecks Commentaria und Gesta Maximiliani Romanorum Regis. Die Entdeckung eines verlorenen Geschichtswerkes* (Graz: Verlag Jos. A. Kienreich, 1965), pp. 10–11; A. Czerny, 'Der Humanist und Historiograph Kaiser Maximilians I. Joseph Grünpeck', *Archiv für österreichische Geschichte*, 73 (1888), pp. 315–64, on pp. 315–31; and Kennel, 'Joseph Grünpeck', pp. 51–6.
47. Kurze, 'Prophecy and History', pp. 65–6.
48. J. Grünpeck, 'Prodigiorum, ostentorum et monstrorum quae in saeculum Maximilianeum inciderunt, interpretation' (1501), Universitäts- und Landesbibliothek für Tirol, Cod. 314. On monstrous births, see ff. 3 v., 6 v., 7 v.–8 r., 15 v.–19 r., and on planetary conjunctions as a cause of misbirths, see ff. 22 r.–23 r.
49. On Mennel, see A. Lhotsky, 'Dr. Jakob Mennel. Ein Vorarlberger im Kreise Kaiser Maximilian I', *Alemannia. Zeitschrift für Geschichte, Heimat- und Volkskunde Vorarlbergs* (1936), pp. 1–15, and on Mennel's *De signis*, see pp. 3–4.
50. J. Mennel, 'De signis, portentis atque prodigiis' (1503), Oesterreichische Nationalbibliothek, Cod. Vindobana 4417*. See *Ausstellung Maximilian I*, p. 142. On monstrous births, see ff. 3 v., 7 v., 9 v.
51. Hollegger, *Maximilian I*, pp. 150–1. In November 1503 Maximilian founded the Order of St George for this specific purpose.
52. Daston and Park, *Wonders and the Order of Nature*, p. 173. For a recent summary of Brant's life and work, see T. Wilhelmi, 'Zum Leben und Werk Sebastian Brants', in T. Wilhelmi (ed.), *Sebastian Brant. Forschungsbeiträge zu seinem Leben, zum 'Narrenschiff' und zum übrigen Werk* (Basel: Schwabe & Co. AG, 2002), pp. 6–35.
53. See the modern edition with original illustrations, S. Brant, *Fabeln*, ed. and trans. B. Schneider (Stuttgart-Bad Cannstatt: Frommann-Holzboog, 1999).
54. For the Blemmyae, see ibid., pp. 378–9. Other strange creatures include the Sphinx (pp. 303–5) and the Basilisk (pp. 311–13).
55. Children resulting from multiple births, while not necessarily appearing to be physically abnormal, were inherently considered to be so because of the circumstances of their birth. See G. Spiegel, 'Maternity and Monstrosity: Reproductive Biology in the Roman de Melusine', in D. Maddox and S. Sturm-Maddox (eds), *Melusine of Lusignan: Founding Fictions in Late Medieval France* (Athens, GA, and London: University of Georgia Press, 1996), pp. 100–24.
56. '[E]in noch erstaunlicheres und vielleicht noch nie dagewesenes Wunder der Natur: Eine Frau aus dem östlichen Franken (das ein Teil Deutschlands ist) soll in diesem Jahr, in dem wir das hier verfaßt haben, also im Jahr 1500, im Verlauf von achtzehn Monaten zweiundfünfzig Kinder geboren haben, die (bis auf neun Fehlgeburten) alle richtig ausgebildet waren und die heilige Taufe empfingen.' Brant, *Fabeln*, p. 381.
57. P. Heitz (ed.), *Flugblätter des Sebastian Brant, mit einen Nachwort von Professor Dr. F. Schultz* (Strassburg: Heitz und Mündell, 1915), p. 5. On this point, see also W. Fraenger,

Altdeutsches Bilderbuch. Hans Weidiz und Sebastian Brant (Leipzig: Stubenrauch, 1930), pp. 12–24.

58. As Sack notes, there were a number of hands involved in the production of images for even his single publications. Sack, *Sebastian Brant als Politischer Publizist*, pp. 11–12.
59. Ibid., p. 10.
60. Heitz (ed.), *Flugblätter des Sebastian Brant*, plates 1–4 (two different editions from the same year). On this broadsheet, see D. Wuttke, 'Sebastian Brant und Maximilian I. Eine Studie zu Brants Donnerstein-Flugblatt des Jahres 1492', in O. Herding and R. Stupperich (eds), *Die Humanisten in ihrer politischen und sozialen Umwelt* (Boppard: Haraldt Boldt, 1976), pp. 141–76; and Soergel, 'Portents, Disaster and Adaptation', pp. 303–6.
61. S. Brant, *Von der Wunderbaren geburt des Kindes bei Wormß* (Augsburg: Johann Schoensperger, 1495). For details of extant copies, see Heitz (ed.), *Flugblätter des Sebastian Brant*, p. 10. This edition is reproduced at plate 7. A second German edition was published by Johann Froschauer, also in Augsburg (this one was, however, a pamphlet). It has been assumed that an original edition, now lost, was published by Brant's friend and regular publisher in Basel, Johann Bergmann von Olpe. On the history of publication, see Wuttke, 'Wunderdeutung und Politik', pp. 220–1. See also C. Kappler, 'L'interpretation politique du monstre chez Sébastien Brant', in M. T. Jones-Davies (ed.), *Monstres et Prodiges au Temps de la Renaissance* (Paris: Jean Touzot, 1980), pp. 100–10, and on the Worm twins specifically, pp. 101–4. The case of the Worms twins is most recently discussed in Hsia, 'A Time for Monsters', pp. 67–70, although Hsia mistakenly describes the twins as stillborn.
62. Wuttke, 'Wunderdeutung und Politik', p. 220.
63. See F. Hartung, 'Imperial Reform, 1485–1495: Its Course and Its Character', in G. Strauss (ed.), *Pre-Reformation Germany* (London: Macmillan, 1972), pp. 73–135. For the most thorough study of Maximilian's activities during this period, see Wiesflecker, *Kaiser Maximilian I.*
64. 'Got ordentlich gesetzt hatt / All ding in wesen. zyl unnd statt.'
65. '[K]umbt gar offt vnß rew zu spat.'
66. On Brant's anti-Turkish views, see S. Schünike, 'Zu den Antiturcica Sebastian Brants', in Wilhelmi (ed.), *Sebastian Brant*, pp. 37–81.
67. Schedel, *Weltchronik*, f. CCLVII r., and discussed in a commentary by S. Füssel, in ibid., p. 662.
68. Drawing upon ibid., f. CLI r.
69. Drawing upon ibid., f. CCXVII r.
70. Drawing upon ibid., f. CLXXXII v.
71. On Otto III and unity within the Holy Roman Empire, see E. Huant, *Otton III: La merveille du monde* (Paris: Édition P. Téqui, 1971), pp. 111–23.
72. 'Eyn kind mit zwayen leib geboren / Das vier fuß hat, vier hend vier oren / Zwen münd, vier augen, nasen zwo / Den gantzen leib getailt also.'
73. '[V]nder ain haubt samlen sich.'
74. 'Das Roemisch vn[d] dz kryechisch reich / Die yetz lang zeit zertailt sind gsein' ('The Roman and the Greek empires / That have long been separated').
75. 'Alle gutte ding auß de[n] haubt entsatn.'
76. Latin editions were also published in 1495 by Johann Froschauer in Augsburg, and Johann Prüss in Strasbourg. There are also manuscript and pamphlet versions extant, with similar illustrations. See Wuttke, 'Wunderdeutung und Politik', pp. 220–1; and for

the Bergmann von Olpe edition, see Sack, *Sebastian Brant als Politischer Publizist*, p. 45.

77. For an analysis of the Latin text, see Wuttke, 'Wunderdeutung und Politik', pp. 220–7.
78. The imperial eagle is here represented with one head, not two; while the double-headed imperial eagle was more common by this period, the single-headed eagle was still sometimes used.
79. This image, rather roughly copied, was also used to accompany a simplified, pirated poem in German, closely based on Brant's text, which was published in broadsheet form in Erfurt in 1496. See Wuttke, 'Wunderdeutung und Politik', fig. 3.
80. See Schramm, *Der Bilderschmuck der Frühdrucke*, vol. 13, pp. 7, 6 (repeated pagination).
81. The birth of physically deformed children and animals was often quickly followed by their death, an indication that they embodied some kind of message or warning and could quickly die as their role was fulfilled simply by being born. See Daston and Park, *Wonders and the Order of Nature*, p. 181.
82. On this publication, see Wuttke, 'Wunderdeutung und Politik', pp. 237–8, and fig. 5.
83. On Murner's pamphlet and his use of Augustine, see M. Sondheim, *Thomas Murner als Astrolog* (Strasbourg: Selbstverlag Elsass-Lothringische Wissenschaftliche Gesellschaft, 1938), pp. 90–126.
84. 'Do jch sie zuo Mentz gesehen Hab anno Christi tausent fünff hundert vnd eins waren sie sechs jaerig. Es waren zwey meidlin vnd seind über zehen jar nit alt worden.' S. Münster, *Cosmographei* (Basel: Henrichum Petri, 1550), f. dcclxviij. On this text, see Wuttke, 'Wunderdeutung und Politik', p. 219, n. 4.
85. Anon., *Wunderbarliche geburt vff So[n]tag Jubilate ...* (n.p., [1511]). See C. Hofmann-Randall, *Monster, Wunder und Kometen. Sensationsberichte auf Flugblättern des 16. bis 18. Jahrhunderts* (Erlangen: Universitätsbibliothek, 1999), catalogue no. A IV 2.
86. The same image was used in a broadsheet with only a brief text of the same year, prominently although most likely spuriously ascribed to Sebastian Brant. For the broadsheet, see Holländer, *Wunder Wundergeburt und Wundergestalt*, p. 343.
87. Both are reproduced in Heitz (ed.), *Flugblätter des Sebastian Brant*, figs 10–11. On this broadsheet, see also Saxl, 'Illustrated Pamphlets of the Reformation', p. 259; Warburg, 'Pagan-Antique Prophecy', p. 637; Céard, *La Nature et les prodiges*, p. 79; and Kappler, 'L'interpretation politique du monstre chez Sébastien Brant', pp. 104–6.
88. C. Eisler, *Dürer's Animals* (Washington, DC: Smithsonian Institution Press, 1991), p. 311.
89. Sack, *Sebastian Brant als Politischer Publizist.*
90. Ibid., p. 23.
91. '[W]as zu sehen grusam gnug'; 'Vß eynein hals zwo zungen'.
92. 'Was wil diß Suw uns Bringen doch'; 'Aber was dise Su bedüt / Weis ich nit gantz'.
93. '[E]s gfalt mir nüt / Das sie so zwifach zungen hat'; 'Hatt es doch menschlich gstalt vnd art'.
94. '[V]örcht ich diß Su bedüt / Ein oberkeyt der Suwschen lüt.'
95. See Sack, *Sebastian Brant als Politischer Publizist*, pp. 33–4.
96. '[E]yn wüst vnreyn thier / Die in vnflat sücht all ir zier.' Translation from I. Shachar, *The Judensau: A Medieval Anti-Jewish Motif and its History* (London: Warburg Institute, 1974), p. 57 and n. 290. Brant does not, however, pursue any Jewish connection here.
97. 'Die Su der Türcken Bruter ist.' Sack notes that to call a Turk 'brother' to the sow is to imply both a bestial and homosexual reading. Sack, *Sebastian Brant als Politischer Publiz-*

ist, pp. 28–30. See also Schünike, 'Zu den Antiturcica Sebastian Brants', pp. 60–5. On the connection with the Antichrist, see Saxl, 'Illustrated Pamphlets of the Reformation', p. 259.

98. On the Antichrist tradition, see Clark, *Thinking with Demons*, pp. 346–62.
99. Sack, *Sebastian Brant als Politischer Publizist*, see esp. pp. 31, 91.
100. '[D]is wunderschwyn ... leng nit ist in leben gsyn'; '[N]it mer dann vff eyn nacht'.
101. Sack, *Sebastian Brant als Politischer Publizist*, pp. 37, 50–1.
102. Daston and Park, *Wonders and the Order of Nature*, p. 181.
103. Sack, *Sebastian Brant als Politischer Publizist*, and on these issues see esp. pp. 11, 24, 109–11.
104. Cited in D. Wuttke, 'Sebastian Brants Verhältnis zu Wunderdeutung und Astrologie', in W. Besch, G. Jungbluth et al. (eds), *Studien zur deutschen Literatur und Sprache des Mittelalters. Festschrift für Hugo Moser zum 65. Geburtstag* (Berlin: Schmidt 1974), pp. 272–86, on p. 284, n. 25. Translation from Daston and Park, *Wonders and the Order of Nature*, p. 173.
105. '[Z]wo myl weg von Straßburg.' For these broadsheets, see Heitz (ed.), *Flugblätter des Sebastian Brant*. The German edition, *Von der zwifaltigen Gans und der Sau zu Gugenheim in Elsaß*, is reproduced as fig. 12. The Latin edition, *De monstroso Ansere atque Porcellis in villa Gugenheim*, is reproduced as fig. 13. For a brief discussion by Heitz, see p. ix. Both broadsheets were published in Basel by Bergmann von Olpe in 1496. The German edition is damaged and missing most of its third column of text.
106. 'Das die natur vns vor zeygt an / Als ich vor offt geschriben han.'

2 Visual Culture and Monstrous Births before the Reformation

1. Silver, 'Germanic Patriotism in the Age of Dürer'.
2. See P. H. Smith, *The Body of the Artisan: Art and Experience in the Scientific Revolution* (Chicago, IL: University of Chicago Press, 2004), pp. 63–7.
3. These ideas relate to northern European artists more widely; see C. Harbison, *The Art of the Northern Renaissance* (London: Everyman Art Library, 1995), pp. 11–23. Harbison argues that northern European artists were more concerned with issues of social position, pp. 22–3. For a more detailed study of the concept of the self-conscious artist (albeit in relation to Dürer only), see E. Panofsky, *The Life and Art of Albrecht Dürer*, revised edn, intro. J. C. Smith (Princeton, NJ: Princeton University Press, 2005), pp. 242–84; and see also J. L. Koerner, *The Moment of Self-Portraiture in German Renaissance Art* (Chicago, IL: Chicago University Press, 1993).
4. Harbison, *The Art of the Northern Renaissance*, p. 60.
5. R. Mellinkoff, *The Devil at Isenheim: Reflections of Popular Belief in Grünewald's Altarpiece* (Berkeley, CA: University of California Press, 1988), p. 15.
6. Zika, 'Writing the Visual into History'.
7. On secular prints, see K. Moxey, *Peasants, Warriors and Wives: Popular Imagery in the Reformation* (Chicago, IL: University of Chicago Press, 1989); and C. Grössinger, *Humour and Folly in Secular and Profane Prints of Northern Europe 1430–1540* (London: Harvey Miller Publishers, 2002).
8. Scribner, *For the Sake of Simple Folk*, pp. 164–6.
9. Scribner, 'Ways of Seeing in the Age of Dürer', p. 97.

10. On these issues, see P. O. Long, 'Objects of Art / Objects of Nature: Visual Representation and the Investigation of Nature', in Smith and Findlen (eds), *Merchants and Marvels*, pp. 63–82; and Smith, *The Body of the Artisan*, pp. 8–17.
11. See R. Schoch, M. Mende and A. Scherbaum (eds), *Albrecht Dürer: Das druckgraphische Werk*, 3 vols (Munich: Prestel, 2001–4), vol. 1, pp. 43–4; and G. Bartrum, *Albrecht Dürer and his Legacy: The Graphic Work of a Renaissance Artist*, exhibition catalogue (London: British Museum Press, 2002), pp. 112–13.
12. Schoch et al. (eds), *Albrecht Dürer*, vol. 1, p. 43.
13. 'Item darnach kon her zu ostern zwu seu, die warn anainander gewachsen oben und heten all paid neur einen kopf und heten unten ir iede vier füß und iede zwen füß uber sich gereckt, das eine sechs füß het'. Cited in ibid., vol. 1, p. 43.
14. Ibid., vol. 1, pp. 45–8.
15. Ibid., vol. 2, pp. 45–8.
16. Dürer's early mythological images often contain obscure subject matter that was developed in close consultation with his humanist friends, especially Willibald Pirckheimer. Bartrum, *Albrecht Dürer and his Legacy*, pp. 117–19.
17. Panofsky, *The Life and Art of Albrecht Dürer*, p. 224. Fedja Anzelewsky notes the existence of theories that interpret the child as a representation of 'Paidogeron', a figure simultaneously representing past and future, but prefers to see it as based upon a real child. F. Anzelewsky, *Albrecht Dürer. Das malerische Werk* (Berlin: Deutscher Verlag für Kunstwissenschaft, 1971), p. 281 and fig. 191.
18. On Dürer and the representation of the natural world, see F. Koreny, *Albrecht Dürer und die Tier- und Pflanzstudien der Renaissance*, exhibition catalogue (Munich: Prestel Verlag, 1985).
19. See Panofsky on Dürer's concept of artistic 'inventiveness'. Panofsky emphasized Dürer's belief in an artist's ability to invent new things in an almost God-like way – rather than reflect and interpret the surrounding world – and how it was modified in response to his likely conversion to Lutheranism. Panofsky, *The Life and Art of Albrecht Dürer*, pp. 280–3.
20. On this point, see D. Eichberger, '*Naturalia* and *artefacta*: Dürer's Nature Drawings and Early Collecting', in Eichberger and Zika (eds), *Dürer and his Culture*, pp. 13–37, on p. 27.
21. See *Dürer. Schriftlicher Nachlass*, ed. H. Rupprich, 3 vols (Berlin: Deutscher Verlag für Kunstwissenschaft, 1969), vol. 3, esp. sections 5, 8, p. 291, and sections 53–5, p. 295.
22. '[G]ee nit von der natur in dein gut geduncken, das du woellest meynen das besser von dir selbs zu finden; dann du wirdest verfuert.' Cited in ibid., p. 295, section 53. This passage is discussed in Silver and Smith, 'Splendor in the Grass', p. 46; and see also Smith, *The Body of the Artisan*, pp. 73, 92.
23. The original passage is 'Doch huet sich ein yedlicher, das er nichtz vnmueglichs mach, das die natur nit leyden kuen. Es wer dann sach, das einer traumwerck wolt machen, inn solchem mag einer allerley creatur vnder einander mischen.' Cited in *Dürer. Schriftlicher Nachlass*, vol. 3, p. 292, section 18. The English translation comes from W. M. Conway, *Literary Remains of Albrecht Dürer* (Cambridge: Cambridge University Press, 1889), p. 244. Jean-Michel Massing cites and discusses this passage in J.-M. Massing, 'Dürer's Dreams', *Journal of the Warburg and Courtauld Institutes*, 49 (1986), pp. 238–44, on pp. 239–40.
24. '[A]lle dag vill newer gestalt der menschen vnd andrer ding aws zw gyssenhaben, der man for nit gesehen noch ein andrer gedocht hat.' Cited in *Dürer. Schriftlicher Nachlass*, vol. 3, p. 291. English translation from R. Klibansky, E. Panofsky and F. Saxl, *Saturn*

and Melancholy. Studies in the History of Natural Philosophy, Religion and Art (London: Thomas Nelson, 1964), p. 362. This passage is discussed in Silver and Smith, 'Splendor in the Grass', p. 50.

25. *Dürer. Schriftlicher Nachlass*, vol. 1, p. 36. On the occurrence of 'blood rain' around the year 1500 and its religious meaning, see E. Gothein, *Reformation und Gegenreformation*, 2 vols (Munich: Duncker and Humblot, 1924), vol. 2, pp. 62–71.
26. 'Daz grost wunderwerck, daz jch all mein dag gesehen hab'; 'sy müst dorum sterben'. Cited in *Dürer. Schriftlicher Nachlass*, vol. 1, p. 36.
27. 'Got wende alle Ding zu besten.' On this sketch, known as *Vision of a Cloudburst*, see W. L. Strauss, *The Complete Drawings of Albrecht Dürer*, 6 vols (New York: Abaris Books, 1974), vol. 4, pp. 2280–1; and also Massing, 'Dürer's Dreams', p. 241.
28. 'Nym ein gleychnuß bey den blinden, lamen vnd verdorten kruepelen vnd hinckenden. Dergleichen solichs ist alles heßlich von des mangels wegen. Also ist auch zu fliehen der vberfluß, als das man einem drey augen, drey hend vnnd fueß wolt machen.' Cited in *Dürer. Schriftlicher Nachlass*, vol. 3, p. 296, section 61. On Dürer's theoretical texts on beauty and ugliness, see F. Anzelewsky, 'Dürers "aesthetiker Exkurse" in seiner Proportionslehre', in F. Mielke (ed.), *Kaleidoskop. Ein Festschrift für Fritz Baumgart zum 75. Geburtstag* (Berlin: Gebr. Mann, 1977), pp. 70–8.
29. 'It[em] do man zalt noch Christ gepurt 1512 Jor do ist ein solch frucht im peyrlant geporn wordn wy obn im gmell angetzeigt ist in der herren van werdenberg land in eim dorff Ertlingen genant zw negst pey riedlingen awff den zwentzigstn dag des hewmand und sy würden getawft das eine hawbt nant man eslpett das ander margrett.' Translation from Strauss, *The Complete Drawings of Albrecht Dürer*, vol. 3, p. 1312. I have altered the translation of the word 'frucht', which Strauss translated as 'growth'. However 'Frucht' was a commonly-used word for the child in the womb during this period, and is often seen in childbirth manuals published during the sixteenth century. On this term, see K. Crowther-Heyck, '"Be Fruitful and Multiply": Genesis and Generation in Reformation Germany', *Renaissance Quarterly*, 55 (2002), pp. 904–35, on pp. 913, 917–19. 'Growth' may be possible as a translation, but does not give the full flavour of the contemporary meaning and use of the word. Elsewhere, Dürer refers to pictures as the 'fruecht' created by artists. See *Dürer. Schriftlicher Nachlass*, vol. 3, pp. 295–6, sections 56–7.
30. There are copies of the broadsheet in the British Museum and also in the Bavarian State Library in Munich (the latter copy does not have the attached leaf with image). On the copy in London, see Bartrum, *Albrecht Dürer and his Legacy*, pp. 182–3. On both, see Littger, 'Elßgred', pp. 75–6.
31. For examples, see Ewinkel, *De monstris*, figs 9, 50, 51, 57, 58, 59, 61, 62, 79.
32. '[I]n der herren von Werdenberg land.'
33. 'Myßburt geschechen mengerlay / Haben bedeütnuß zwayerlay / Ungestalten bedeüt vnglick / Was wol gstalt ist mit gutem schick.'
34. '[K]rieg, unglück mit gewalt / Oder etwas anders vngefell.'
35. See H. Carl, *Der Schwäbische Bund 1488–1534* (Leinfelden-Echterdingen: DRW-Verlag, 2000).
36. J. N. Vanotti, *Geschichte der Grafen von Montfort und von Werdenberg* (1845; Bregenz: H. Lingenhöle, 1988), plate 5 (family tree).
37. 'Als ir im druck haben gesehen.'
38. In Italy, there was a considerable flourishing of interest in monstrous creatures from *c.* 1494 to 1530, coinciding with the Italian wars. On the monster of Ravenna, see Schenda, 'Das Monstrum von Ravenna'; Niccoli, *Prophecy and People*, pp. 34–52; Ewinkel, *De*

monstris, pp. 227–37; and Daston and Park, *Wonders and the Order of Nature*, pp. 177–82. On Sanuto and Luca, see Schenda, 'Das Monstrum von Ravenna', pp. 212–13.

39. Schenda, 'Das Monstrum von Ravenna', pp. 215–16.
40. For images of the monster of Ravenna, see below, pp. 92, 102.
41. '[V]nserm hailigen vatter dem bapst'; 'on speyß sterben lassen'.
42. The annotation dates the case to 1511, due to the different method for calculating the start of the new year.
43. 'Ein wunderparlichs vnd erschrockenliches ding.'
44. '[S]ussigkeyt von Zucker vnd andern suessen dingen.'
45. '[E]in horn als Moses zway het.'
46. On negative interpretations in Italy, see Schenda, 'Das Monstrum von Ravenna', p. 213.
47. 'Horn, Flügelohren, Schuppenschenkel und Vogelfuß sind Attributes des Teufel'; Schenda, 'Das Monstrum von Ravenna', p. 211. Both Rudolf Schenda and Ottavia Niccoli relate the monster of Ravenna to the negative allegorical medieval figure of *Frau Welt*. Schenda, 'Das Monstrum von Ravenna', pp. 210–11; and Niccoli, *Prophecy and People*, pp. 42–4. Lorraine Daston and Katharine Park connect it to the similarly composite *Ars memorandi* images. Daston and Park, *Wonders and the Order of Nature*, pp. 178–9.
48. '[O]b es ein meydlen oder ein knab ist.' It should be noted that the image accompanying this text seems to lack the female genitalia of other representations.
49. '[W]eder doctor geschrifft gelert, vnd vngelert.'
50. '[M]an kan auch nit wissen ob das gut oder pöß bedeut.'
51. For a discussion of 'devilish' monstrous births, although concerning cases that are all from the second half of the sixteenth century, see Sonderegger, *Missgeburten und Wundergestalten*, pp. 92–5; and also Ewinkel, *De monstris*, pp. 197–204. Daston and Park briefly discuss the broad contours of different attitudes to monstrous births in Germany (more political, and related to the Turkish threat) and Italy (associated with religious preaching by figures like Savonarola, and repeated invasions). See Daston and Park, *Wonders and the Order of Nature*, p. 180.
52. 'Die zway kindlen die sehen schon / Gar freündlichen ain ander an / In der figure sichts yderman / Do ich das kind sach/das ain wacht / Margret die mich früntlich anlacht / Elizabet lag in der wagen tieff / Dan[n] sy was klainer vnd hort schlieff.'
53. Littger, 'Elßgred', p. 78.
54. 'Wayßt nyemt was vngfel hernach kompt.'
55. '[W]ie dise figure anzeigt.'
56. 'Alle mißburt die betdeuten / Jetzund auch vor alten zeiten / Unglück krieg vnd groß zwytracht / Welches dises kündlin nit macht / Dan das sicht gar wol iederman / Das sie einander sehen an.'
57. See Littger, 'Elßgred', p. 77.
58. For examples of the use of this coat of arms in a German ecclesiastical context, see E. Zimmermann, *Bayerischen Klosterheraldik* (Munich: Zimmermann, 1930). The annotation 'Attinet Tegernsee' indicates that the broadsheet was acquired by the large Benedictine (not Cistercian) Tegernsee Abbey in Bavaria. The acquisition was almost certainly made around the time of publication. For several examples of this phrase in this hand, see, for example, the collated volume A.lat.b.708 in the Bayerische Staatsbibliothek in Munich. It includes publications acquired by Tegernsee Abbey in the first decade of the sixteenth century.
59. Littger, 'Elßgred', p. 81. Littger does not discuss the broader political situation in any detail.

60. Vanotti, *Geschichte der Grafen von Montfort und von Werdenberg*, plate 5 (family tree).
61. On tax contributions by Salem abbey, see Carl, *Der Schwäbische Bund*, pp. 355–6, and on the personal power of the abbot in this period, see ibid., p. 518.
62. See C. Hofmann-Randall, *Die Einblattdrucke der Universitätsbibliothek Erlangen-Nürnberg* (Erlangen: Universitätsbibliothek, 2003), catalogue no. A IV 3, discussed in Littger, 'Elßgred', p. 75.
63. Another case that unusually indicates something of the response of the parent is briefly discussed by H. C. Erik Midelfort: one of the many pilgrims who visited the shrine of Altötting in Bavaria was a woman from distant Kassel who made a pilgrimage there in 1497 following the birth of her child without hands, legs or feet. The shock caused the woman to have seizures, which had already been occurring for six months when she made the journey. Midelfort, *A History of Madness*, p. 296.
64. 'Waß das bedeüth weiß der almechtig got / Der vnß zu hilff komen wol fru vnd spat.'
65. Also reproduced in Geisberg, *The German Single-Leaf Woodcut*, vol. 3, p. 1371. On the artist's career, see p. viii. Traut was employed intermittently in Dürer's studio between 1505 and 1515, the last project being a contribution to Dürer's work for Maximilian I's Triumphal Arch. See J. Turner (ed.), *Dictionary of Art*, 34 vols (New York: Grove, 1996), vol. 31, pp. 287–8.
66. '[W]underlichs un[d] erschrockenlich ding.'
67. '[V]on einer frawen eines hyrtten geBoren solches kyndt. Ein haubt gehabt mit zweyen angesichten. Drey hendt / zwo gestrackt auff yetlicher seytten gewohnlich eyne. Un[d] die dritten zwischen den schultern des ruecks. Einen corper Byß auff die zwo frewlich scham auff Beyden seyten / mit vier menschlichen peynen un[d] fuessen.'
68. '[H]erren Heinrichen von Porperg. Der selbigen zeyt obgemeln Stat Spalt Pfarrer.'
69. For an analysis of the use and meaning of the concept of the 'counterfeit' in prints during this period, see Parshall, 'Imago contrafacta'.
70. Reproduced as the end page in W. Eichenberger and H. Wendland, *Deutsche Bibeln vor Luther. Die Buchkunst der achtzehn deutschen Bibeln zwischen 1466 und 1522* (Hamburg: Friedrich Wittig Verlag, 1977).
71. As the material in this and the previous chapter indicates, this is the central type of misbirth to be depicted during this period. See Sonderegger, *Missgeburten und Wundergestalten*, pp. 9–45 ('Doppelmissbildungen').
72. H.-M. Kaulbach, *Deutsche Zeichnungen vom Mittelalter bis zum Barock* (Stuttgart: Graphische Sammlung Staatsgalerie Stuttgart, 2007), pp. 94–5.
73. Landau and Parshall, *The Renaissance Print*, pp. 174, 207–11; and *Hans Burgkmair 1473–1973. Das graphische Werk*, exhibition catalogue (Augsburg: Städtische Kunstsammlungen, 1973). Unlike Dürer, however, Burgkmair has not left behind the kind of written documents that might provide insights into his attitude towards monstrosity, the natural world, or artistic creativity. Dürer is unique in this respect in the German context at this time.
74. It illustrated Balthasar Springer's famous voyage to Africa, Arabia and East India in 1505–6. For a study of this series, see M. P. McDonald, 'Burgkmair's Woodcut Frieze of *Natives of Africa and India*', *Print Quarterly*, 20 (2003), pp. 227–44.
75. R. Kroll and W. Schade, *Hans Burgkmair 1473–1531. Holzschnitte, Zeichnungen, Holzstöcke*, exhibition catalogue (Berlin: Staatlichen Museen zu Berlin, 1974), p. 7.
76. On this image, see *Hans Burgkmair 1473–1973. Das graphische Werk*, catalogue no. 95, fig. 103. It is briefly discussed in Daston and Park, *Wonders and the Order of Nature*, p. 186.

77. '[S]olich künd hat der ob bestimbt Herz vnnd Grauff seiner maller Mayster Matheysen miller Maler burger zu Lindaw mit fleyß haysen verzaychnen oder konterfenn vnd zu trucken ver ortnen wie obengesehen wirt.'
78. Vanotti, *Geschichte der Grafen von Montfort und von Werdenberg*, pp. 146–7.
79. '[D]as fießlin in der hand halten.'
80. 'So des / selbig künd wachend / seine Bain von ain ander.'
81. Geisberg, *The German Single-Leaf Woodcut*, vol. 2, p. 526. See also similar iconography in images by Erhard Schoen (vol. 3, p. 1076), and Hans (Johann) Wandereisen (vol. 4, p. 1433).
82. Schramm, *Der Bilderschmuck der Frühdrucke*, vol. 18, p. 18 and fig. 402. The most important, albeit brief, study remains P. Heitz, *Neujahrswünsche des XV. Jahrhunderts* (Strassburg: Heitz, 1900); and see also 'Jesuskind' in E. Kirschbaum (ed.), *Lexikon der Christlichen Ikonographie*, 8 vols (1970; Freiburg im Breisgau: Herder, 1994), vol. 2, pp. 400–6.
83. For examples, see C. L. Kuhn, *German and Netherlandish Sculpture 1280–1800: The Harvard Collections* (Cambridge, MA: Harvard University Press, 1965), pp. 83–4 and fig. xxxv. On the figure of the blessing infant Christ in an Italian context (although always represented together with Mary), see D. C. Shorr, *The Christ Child in Devotional Images in Italy during the XIV Century* (New York: George Wittenborn, 1954), pp. 6–30.
84. For examples, see Ewinkel, *De monstris*, figs 2, 5, 6, 10, 11, 12, 19, 23, 24, 27, 28, 48, 58, 60, 61, 62, 83, 84, 85, 87, 88, 89, 106.
85. Indeed, conjoined twins should always be the same gender, as they grow from the same fertilized egg. Yet cases of male and female twins like this were reported. This could be a case of hermaphroditism, although it was not discussed in these terms. See also Julie Crawford's analysis of an English broadsheet from the later sixteenth century, depicting two aggressively embracing conjoined twins, male and female, whose birth was interpreted as a sign of their parent's 'prohibited sexual embrace'. Crawford, *Marvelous Protestantism*, pp. 94–5.
86. To my knowledge, no misbirth broadsheet held in a major catalogued collection has this 'double frontal' structure.
87. Particularly relevant is the 1529 double portrait of the artist and his wife Anna, in which the couple are depicted, in a particularly eerie *Vanitas* allegory, with a mirror that reflects two tiny skulls. While the painting has been attributed to Burgkmair himself, it is more likely by Lucas Furtenagel. See O. Benesch, *The Art of the Renaissance in Northern Europe*, revised edn (London: Phaidon, 1965), p. 67. This painting does, however, indicate the interest in this theme in Burgkmair's artistic circle.
88. For instance, in illustrations for Balthasar Springer's travelogue of his famous voyage to Africa, Arabia and East India in 1505–6, Burgkmair's 1508 woodcuts used now-lost sources for the travel series quite differently to the other, anonymous artist who also produced woodcuts on the same subject for a 1509 publication. See McDonald, 'Burgkmair's Woodcut Frieze of *Natives of Africa and India*', p. 230.

3 Reformation Visual Culture and Monstrous Births

1. The best study remains Scribner, *For the Sake of Simple Folk*.
2. He is prompted by the incident in Genesis 30:37–9 in which Jacob uses the visual stimulus of a speckled branch to induce sheep to produce more spotted lambs. For a recent

examination of Luther's attitude towards monstrous births in ordinary domestic contexts, see Soergel, 'Portraying Monstrous Birth', pp. 133–7.

3. 'Memini me puero Isenaci formosam et pudicam matronam eniti glirem: quod eo accidit, quia ex vicinis aliquis gliri suspenderat nolam, ad cuius sonitum reliqui fugarentur. Is occurrit mulieri gravidae, quae ignara rei subito occurso et aspectu gliris ita est conterrita, ut foetus in utero degeneraret in formam bestiolae.' Cited in M. Luther, *D. Martin Luthers Werke. Kritische Gesamtausgabe*, 72 vols (Weimar: Böhlau, 1884–2007), vol. 43, p. 692. Translated in M. Luther, *Works*, 55 vols (Saint Louis, MO: Concordia Publishing House, 1955–86), vol. 5, p. 381. For a discussion of this passage, see Soergel, 'Portraying Monstrous Birth', pp. 135–6.
4. On the belief that pregnant women should not see shocking scenes or ugly or deformed people, see U. Rublack, 'Pregnancy, Childbirth and the Female Body in Early Modern Germany', *Past and Present*, 150 (1996), pp. 84–110, on pp. 93–7; and Crowther-Heyck, '"Be Fruitful and Multiply"', pp. 925–6.
5. On ideas about the maternal imagination in the early modern period, see Ewinkel, *De monstris*, pp. 151–69.
6. See Barnes, *Prophecy and Gnosis*, pp. 30–59.
7. Warburg, 'Pagan-Antique Prophecy', p. 618.
8. J. Lichtenberger, *Die Weissagunge Johannis Lichtenbergers deudsch / zugericht mit vleys. Sampt einer nutzlichen vorrede vnd vunterricht D. Martini Luthers / wie man die selbige vnd der gleichen weissagunge vernemen sol* (Wittenberg: Hans Lufft, 1527). For a description and analysis of this new edition, see H. Talkenberger, *Sintflut. Prophetie und Zeitgeschehen in Texten und Holzschnitten astrologischer Flugschriften 1488–1528* (Tübingen: Max Niemeyer Verlag, 1990), pp. 368–78.
9. '[T]hut Got ym hymel auch seine zeichen / wenn sie ein vngluck treffen sol / vnd lest schwantsterne enstehen / odder Sonn vnd Mond schein verlieren / odder sonst geborn werden / beyde an menschen vnd thieren / Wilchs alles die Engel nicht machen / sondern Gott selbs alleine / Mit solchen zeichen drewet er den gottlosen / vnd zeigt an zukunfftig vnfal vber herrn vnd lande / sie zu warnen. Vmb der frumen willen geschicht solchs nichts / denn sie durffens nicht / drumb wird yhn auch gesagt. Sie sollen sich fur des hymels zeichen nicht furchten / als Jeremias spricht / denn es gilt yhn nicht / sondern den gottlosen.' From the preface to Lichtenberger, *Die Weissagunge*, cited in A. Warburg, 'Heidnisch-Antike Weissagung in Wort und Bild zu Luthers Zeiten', in his *Gesammelte Schriften*, ed. G. Bing, 2 vols (Leipzig: B. G. Teubner, 1932), vol. 2, pp. 487–558, on p. 548. Translated in Warburg, 'Pagan-Antique Prophecy', p. 675.
10. See Warburg, 'Pagan-Antique Prophecy', pp. 603–12; and Barnes, *Prophecy and Gnosis*, pp. 141–81. On fundamental differences between Luther and Melanchthon that affected their respective approaches to the broader issue of natural philosophy, see S. Kusukawa, *The Transformation of Natural Philosophy: The Case of Philip Melanchthon* (Cambridge: Cambridge University Press, 1995), esp. p. 74.
11. 'Es ist ein dreck mit irer kunst.' Cited in Warburg, 'Heidnisch-Antike Weissagung', p. 541. Translated in Warburg, 'Pagan-Antique Prophecy', p. 607.
12. 'Sie aber, die Sternkücker, und die aus dem Gestirn wollen wahrsagen und verküngdigen, wie es einem gehen soll, erdichten, dass sie die Erde verfinstern und betrüben und schädlich sein. Denn alle Creaturen Gottes sind gut, und von Gott geschaffen, nur zum guten Brauch. Aber der mensch machet sie böse mit seinem Mißbrauchen. Und es sind Zeichen, nicht Monstra, Ungeheuer. Die Finsternisse sind Ungeheuer und Monstra, gleichwie Mißgeburten.' Cited in Warburg, 'Heidnisch-Antike Weissagung', p. 544.

Translated in Warburg, 'Pagan-Antique Prophecy', p. 661. I have altered the translation slightly, so that the word 'Ungeheuer' is translated as 'terrible things' rather than the perhaps overly precise 'evil omens'.

13. Midelfort, *A History of Madness*, p. 91.
14. '[E]in Kind allhie zu Wittenberg ohne Häupt geboren, und noch eins mit umbgekehrten Füßen.' Cited in Warburg, 'Heidnisch-Antike Weissagung', p. 522. Translated in Warburg, 'Pagan-Antique Prophecy', p. 690.
15. 'Vnd vnter diesem Maximiliano sind im himel wunderbarliche Zeichen / vnd derselben viel / geschehen / dazu auch auff erden / vnd in wassern / von welchen Christus sagt / Es werden grosse zeichen sein etc. / Also / das von keiner zeit gelesen wird / darin mehr vnd groeßere zugleich geschehen weren / Die vns gewisse hoffnung geben / das der selige tag hart fur der thuer sey.' From M. Luther, *Chronica deudsch* (Wittenberg: Hans Lufft, 1559), cited in Warburg, 'Heidnisch-Antike Weissagung', p. 523. Translated in Warburg, 'Pagan-Antique Prophecy', p. 636.
16. On Lutheran apocalyptic thought in the first half of the sixteenth century, see T. Kaufmann, *Konfession und Kultur. Lutherischer Protestantismus in der zweiten Hälfte des Reformationsjahrhunderts* (Tübingen: Mohr Siebeck, 2006), pp. 29–66.
17. Philip Soergel emphasizes the negative meaning of monstrous births during the Reformation. See Soergel, 'Portraying Monstrous Birth', p. 132.
18. On the Antichrist in Reformation print culture, see Richardsen-Friedrich, *Antichrist-Polemik*, pp. 78–133; and Scribner, *For the Sake of Simple Folk*, pp. 148–89. Luther saw the devil as being more active in the world (an impression that was to grow and be increasingly widely held in the second half of the sixteenth century), and connected this to the coming Apocalypse. See Midelfort, *A History of Madness*, pp. 97–8.
19. Barnes, *Prophecy and Gnosis*, p. 4.
20. For an overview of the nature, quantity and circulation of these pamphlets, see Edwards, *Printing, Propaganda, and Martin Luther*, pp. 15–21. On the public for pamphlets, see H.-J. Köhler (ed.), *Flugschriften als Massenmedium der Reformationzeit* (Stuttgart: Ernst Klett Verlag, 1981).
21. See Edwards, *Printing, Propaganda, and Martin Luther*, p. 17.
22. P. Melanchthon and M. Luther, *Deuttung der czwo grewlichen Figuren, Bapstesels czu Rom und Munchkalbs zu Freijberg ijnn Meijszen funden* (Wittenberg: Johann Grunenberg, 1523). A number of editions were printed in this year. Various editions from the Herzog August Bibliothek have been examined for this chapter. For the texts by Melanchthon and Luther cited in this chapter, see Luther, *D. Martin Luthers Werke*, vol. 11, pp. 357–85. The Melanchthon text is referred to below as 'Der Bapstesel durch Philippen Melanchthon deuttet', and the Luther text is referred to below as 'Deuttung des Munchkalbs zu Freyberg'.
23. While Luther frequently wrote in German, this was less common for Melanchthon.
24. The Reformation 'culture of persuasion' as Pettegree terms it, has been analysed recently in P. Matheson, *The Rhetoric of the Reformation* (Edinburgh: T. and T. Clark, 1998); and A. Pettegree, *Reformation and the Culture of Persuasion* (Cambridge: Cambridge University Press, 2005).
25. The literature on the Monk Calf and Papal Ass is extensive. Important studies include Scribner, *For the Sake of Simple Folk*, pp. 127–33; Niccoli, *Prophecy and People*, pp. 126–9; Soergel, 'Portraying Monstrous Birth', pp. 133–5; Saxl, 'Illustrated Pamphlets of the Reformation', pp. 259–62; Richardsen-Friedrich, *Antichrist-Polemik*, pp. 113–18; and N. R. Smith, 'Loathly Births off Nature: A Study of the Lore of the Portentous Monster

in the Sixteenth Century' (PhD dissertation, University of Illinois at Urbana-Champaign, 1978), pp. 351–87. However, the most thorough study of the Papal Ass remains K. Lange, *Der Papstesel. Ein Beitrag zur Kultur- und Kunstgeschichte des Reformationszeitalters* (Göttingen: Vandenhoeck and Ruprecht's Verlag, 1891).

26. 'Ein Christliche vnn vast wolgegrundete beweysung von dem Jüngsten Tag Vnnd von seinen zeichen, das er auch nit ferr mer sein mag.' See Warburg, 'Pagan-Antique Prophecy', p. 762.
27. 'So wird auch kein Stern Kündriger thüren sagen, daß des Himmels Lauf habe verkündiget das schrecklich Thier, das die Tiber zu Rom tot auswarf vor kurzen Jahren, welchs hatte einen Eselkopf, eine Frauenbruste und Bauch, einen Elephantenfuß an der rechten Hand und Fischschuppen an den Beinen, und ein Drachenkopf am Hintersten. Darin das Papsttum bedeutet ist, der große Gottes Zorn und Strafe. Solcher Haufen zeichen will etwas Größeres bringen, denn alle Vernunft denket.' Cited in Richardsen-Friedrich, *Antichrist-Polemik*, p. 115. Translated in Warburg, 'Pagan-Antique Prophecy', p. 763.
28. For a discussion of the circulation of this imagery, see Niccoli, *Prophecy and People*, p. 122.
29. This broadsheet is reproduced in Geisberg, *The German Single-Leaf Woodcut*, vol. 4, p. 1549.
30. See Scribner, *For the Sake of Simple Folk*, pp. 127–33; Niccoli, *Prophecy and People*, pp. 126–9; Soergel, 'Portraying Monstrous Birth', pp. 133–5; and Saxl, 'Illustrated Pamphlets of the Reformation', pp. 259–62.
31. On Cranach's graphic work, see J. Jahn, *Lucas Cranach d.Ä. 1472–1553. Das gesamte graphische Werk* (Berlin: Rogner und Bernhard, 1972), and on these prints see pp. 784–7.
32. Another version, published in Erfurt by Wolfgang Stürmer in 1523, has rather hastily copied images and splits the pamphlet into two separate publications, each with its respective full-page image. This approach was presumably spurred by the publisher's desire to double his profits.
33. For a detailed overview of the various forms in which the pamphlet was published, see Luther, *D. Martin Luthers Werke*, vol. 11, pp. 361–8.
34. See ibid., p. 358 (in the introductory passage).
35. 'Gott hatt alweg sein gnade oder zorn durch ettliche zeichen und sonderlich die herschaften wunderlich damit furgebildet, wie wir sehen Danielis viij.' Melanchthon, 'Der Bapstesel durch Philippen Melanchthon deuttet', p. 375. This particular passage of English translation is from Saxl, 'Illustrated Pamphlets of the Reformation', p. 260.
36. 'Und also eygentlich alles weßen Bepstliches reichs abmalet und furbildet, das nicht muglich were eynigem menschenn solchs zuertichten, Sondern man sagen muß, das got selb disen grewel also abcontrofeyt habe.' Melanchthon, 'Der Bapstesel durch Philippen Melanchthon deuttet', p. 375.
37. The meaning is essentially the same, depsite the prefix 'ab-'. See J. Grimm and W. Grimm, *Deutsches Wörterbuch*, 16 vols (Leipzig: S. Hirzel, 1854–1960), vol. 1, p. 18.
38. 'Auffs erst bedeutt der Esels kopff den Bapst.' Melanchthon, 'Der Bapstesel durch Philippen Melanchthon deuttet', p. 375.
39. '[G]leich einem Elephanten fuß, bedeut aber das geystlich regiment des bapsts'; '[D]enn er verderbt die seelen mit seynen unzelichen und untreglichen gesetzen'; 'Gleich wie das grosse schwere thier der Elephant zu tritt und zuknyrst alles, waruber er kompt'. Ibid., p. 376.

40. '[D]ie bepstliche lerer, prediger, pfarrer und beychtvetter, sonderlich aber die Theologi Scolastici'; 'Es werdenn falsche Christen unnd falsche propheten auff komen.' Ibid., p. 377.
41. '[B]edeut des Bapsts corper, das sind Cardinal, bischoff, pfaffen, munch, studenten ... denn yr leben ist nur fressen, sauffen, unkeuscheit, wollust und alles gut leben habenn auff erden.' Ibid., p. 378.
42. On the gendered quality of this image, see the introduction in U. Rublack (ed.), *Gender in Early Modern German History* (Cambridge: Cambridge University Press, 2002), pp. 1–18, on p. 3.
43. Melanchthon, 'Der Bapstesel durch Philippen Melanchthon deuttet', p. 378.
44. Ibid., pp. 378–9.
45. Scribner, *For the Sake of Simple Folk*, p. 131.
46. '[T]odt funden ist, bestettiget, das des Bapstums ende da sey.' Melanchthon, 'Der Bapstesel durch Philippen Melanchthon deuttet', p. 379.
47. 'Die Prophetische deuttung dises Munchkalbs wil ich dem gehst lassen, denn ich kein prophet bin'; 'Mein wundsch und hoffnung ist, das der Jungst tag sey'. Luther, 'Deuttung des Munchkalbs zu Freyberg', p. 380.
48. Scribner, *For the Sake of Simple Folk*, p. 130. Scribner's analysis (pp. 127–32) has guided my own interpretation and translation.
49. 'Auffs erst und zursumma dises zeychens laß dir das keyn schimpff seyn: Das Gott eym kalb das geystlich kleyd, die heilige kutten hatt angezogen. Damit hatt er on zweyfell auff eym hauffen bedeut: das es bald offenbar werden muß, wie die ganze Muncheren und Nonneren nichts anders sey denn ein falscher lugenhafftiger schein und eußerlich gleyssen eyns geystlichen gottlichens lebens.' Luther, 'Deuttung des Munchkalbs zu Freyberg', p. 381.
50. Ibid., p. 381.
51. 'Was ist denn das kalb? Es ist yhr falscher abgott yn yrem lugenhafftigen herzen.' Ibid., p. 382.
52. Ibid., p. 385.
53. Ibid., p. 383.
54. 'Als das das ore an der kutten die untregliche Tiranney der beycht bedeutte.' Ibid., p. 384. Robert Scribner further notes 'that the knobs are on the "tonsure" shows that the Gospel must conform to the tonsure, that is, to the will of the monks'. Scribner, *For the Sake of Simple Folk*, p. 130.
55. Scribner, *For the Sake of Simple Folk*, p. 130. See Luther, 'Deuttung des Munchkalbs zu Freyberg', p. 384.
56. Luther, 'Deuttung des Munchkalbs zu Freyberg', p. 385.
57. '[F]uret das kalb aller dinge die geperde eins predigers: es streckt die hinterbeyn, als stunds und reckt auß die rechte pfotte wie ein prediger sein rechte hand und zeucht die lincke zu sich, wirfft den kopff auff und hat die zunge ym maul, und ist alles gestalt, als stund es und predigest.' Ibid., p. 383.
58. The implied connection with the world of human action is made explicit in a related image that places the Monk Calf, in exactly the same pose, in an audience with Pope Adrian. Scale is as distorted as context, as the deformed foetus would have been a fraction of the size of its portrayal. See H. Koegler, 'Das Mönchskalb vor Papst Hadrian und das Wiener Prognostikon. Zwei wiedergefundene Flugblätter aus der Presse des Pamphilius Gengenbach in Basel', *Zeitschrift für Bücherfreunde*, 11 (1907), pp. 411–16.

Koegler provides the full text of the broadsheet. On this broadsheet, see also Harms and Schilling (eds), *Deutsche illustrierte Flugblätter*, vol. 6, pp. 18–19.

59. On this point, see Scribner, *For the Sake of Simple Folk*, p. 132.
60. 'Darum wie der Bapstesel das Bapstum abmallt, So malet eygentlich dis Munchkalb die Apostel und schuler des Bapsts, das alle wellt sehe, was sie bisher fur prediger und lerer gehort und noch hoeren.' Luther, 'Deuttung des Munchkalbs zu Freyberg', p. 383.
61. On this verb, and its use by Luther in particular, see R. R. Anderson, U. Goebel and O. Reichmann (eds), *Frühneuhochdeutsches Wörterbuch*, 11 vols– (Berlin: Walter de Gruter 1986–), vol. 1, part 2, pp. 246–8; and Grimm and Grimm, *Deutsches Wörterbuch*, vol. 1, 76.
62. On this text and the relationship drawn by Emser with the Landsberg-born calf, see Harms and Schilling (eds), *Deutsche illustrierte Flugblätter*, vol. 1, pp. 448–9.
63. Although the sheet does not give publication details, Michael Schilling surmises the date on the basis of the language used. See Harms and Schilling (eds), *Deutsche illustrierte Flugblätter*, vol. 1, p. 448.
64. 'Der ander / zu Freiberg ist auch eins gborn.'
65. On the fundamentally oral nature of broadsheet culture in a society where most people could not read, see R. Scribner, 'Oral Culture and the Diffusion of Reformation Ideas', *History of European Ideas*, 5 (1984), pp. 237–56.
66. See Niccoli, *Prophecy and People*, pp. 43–4; Daston and Park, *Wonders and the Order of Nature*, pp. 178–9, 182.
67. It was published by Georg Glockendon in Nuremberg, and this copy comes from the collection of the influential Nuremberg publisher Hartmann Schedel. See Hernad, *Die Graphiksammlung des Humanisten Hartmann Schedel*, pp. 280–1.
68. On this broadsheet, and for a translation of the text, see S. Ozment, *When Fathers Ruled: Family Life in Reformation Europe* (Cambridge, MA: Harvard University Press, 1983), pp. 66–7.
69. See C. C. Christensen, *Art and the Reformation in Germany* (Columbus, OH: Ohio University Press, 1979); and L. P. Wandel, *Voracious Idols and Violent Hands: Iconoclasm in Reformation Zurich, Strasbourg, and Basel* (Cambridge: Cambridge University Press, 1995).
70. For a concise summary of the topic of Luther and his attitude to visual images, see R. Bergmann, 'A "tröstlich picture": Luther's Attitude in the Question of Images', *Renaissance and Reformation/Renaissance et Réforme*, 5 (1981), pp. 15–25.
71. Scribner, 'Ways of Seeing in the Age of Dürer', pp. 103, 113.
72. Christensen, *Art and the Reformation in Germany*, p. 123.
73. The major study is P. Martin, *Martin Luther und die Bilder zur Apokalypse* (Hamburg: Friedrich Wittig Verlag, 1983). On Luther's attitude towards illustrating the Bible, see also Bergmann, 'A "tröstlich picture"', pp. 19–20.
74. See Carey (ed.), *The Apocalypse*.
75. B. Moeller, 'Was wurde in der Frühzeit der Reformation in den deutschen Städten gepredigt?', *Archiv für Reformationsgeshichte*, 75 (1984), pp. 176–93.
76. Both titles underline the visual and prophetic nature of the book.
77. On this image, see Scribner, *For the Sake of Simple Folk*, pp. 232–3; and G. Bartrum, catalogue entry in Carey (ed.), *The Apocalypse*, p. 190.
78. For detailed explanations of these personas, see P. N. Brooks (ed.), *Seven-Headed Luther: Essays in Commemoration of a Quincentenary 1483–1983* (Oxford: Clarendon Press, 1983).

79. See Scribner, *For the Sake of Simple Folk*, p. 233. Scribner notes that this image 'failed to develop the apocalyptic overtones of the monster theme'. Both the seven-headed beast and the Pope were, in turn, associated with the figure of the Antichrist, and with the Whore of Babylon (see ch. 6, 'Antichrist and the World Turned Upside-Down', pp. 148–89, and esp. pp. 169–74). See, for example, the complex illustration known as *The Seven-Headed Papal Beast*. The best-known version appeared in 1543 with a text by the Nuremberg satirist Hans Sachs. Earlier versions of the work were published as a broadsheet, and as a book illustration. For an analysis of this image, and the tradition it fits within, see Scribner, *For the Sake of Simple Folk*, pp. 100–4; and also P. Burschel, 'Das Monster. Katholische Luther-Imagination im 16. Jahrhundert', in H. Medick and P. Schmidt (eds), *Luther zwischen den Kulturen. Zeitgenossenschaft – Weltwirkung* (Göttingen: Vandenhoeck and Ruprecht, 2004), pp. 33–48.
80. '[W]ider Apostolisch noch prophetisch.' Cited in Luther, *D. Martin Luthers Werke*, vol. 7, p. 404. Translated in M. Luther, 'Preface to the Revelation of St. John [I]' (1522), reprinted in Luther, *Works*, vol. 35, pp. 398–9, on p. 398. On the ways in which the text was accorded secondary status in this edition (through the form of listing on the contents page, and a relative lack of glosses), see Edwards, *Printing, Propaganda, and Martin Luther*, pp. 113–14. The major study of Luther's use and interpretations of the Book of Revelation is H.-U. Hofmann, *Luther und die Johannes-Apokalypse* (Tübingen: J. C. B. Mohr, 1982); on Luther's preface, see pp. 251–98.
81. '[M]eyn geyst kan sich ynn das buch nicht schicken ... bleyb ich bey den buchern, die myr Christum hell vnd reyn dar geben.' Cited in Luther, *D. Martin Luthers Werke*, vol. 7, p. 404. Translated in Luther, 'Preface to the Revelation of St. John [I]', p. 399.
82. '[D]ie Apostell nicht mit gesichten vmbgehen, sondern mit klaren vnd durren wortten weyssagen, wie Petrus, Paulus, Christus ym Evangelio auch thun, denn es auch dem Apostolischen ampt gepurt, klerlich vnd on bild odder gesicht von Christo vnd seinem thun zur eden. Auch, so ist keyn Prophet ym allten testament, schweygg ym newen, der so gar vnd durch mit gesichten vnd bilden handelt.' Cited in Luther, *D. Martin Luthers Werke*, vol. 7, p. 404. Translated in Luther, 'Preface to the Revelation of St. John [I]', p. 398.
83. Bergmann, 'A "tröstlich picture"', p. 19.
84. Parshall, 'The Vision of the Apocalypse', pp. 102–5, and for catalogue entries on the prints, see pp. 144–6 in Carey (ed.), *The Apocalypse*. See also P. Schmidt, *Die Illustration der Lutherbibel 1522–1700* (Basel: Verlag Friedrich Reinhardt, 1962), pp. 93–136.
85. Martin, *Martin Luther und die Bilder zur Apokalypse*, pp. 60–2, 78–81, 67–70. The last detail is oddly reminiscent of the Monk Calf's cowl.
86. G. Bartrum, catalogue entries, in Carey (ed.), *The Apocalypse*, pp. 145–6. On the antipapal elements in this series and some that followed, see also Scribner, *For the Sake of Simple Folk*, pp. 169–77.
87. Parshall, 'The Vision of the Apocalypse', p. 106. For catalogue entries on these, see pp. 147–63 in Carey (ed.), *The Apocalypse*.
88. See Edwards, *Printing, Propaganda, and Martin Luther*, p. 127.
89. See Schmidt, *Die Illustration der Lutherbibel*, pp. 122–7, and for this image specifically see p. 125.
90. On this second preface and the possible causes for Luther's change of heart, see Hofmann, *Luther und die Johannes-Apokalypse*, pp. 395–455; Martin, *Martin Luther und die Bilder zur Apokalypse*, pp. 129–35; Parshall, 'The Vision of the Apocalypse', p. 111; and Barnes, *Prophecy and Gnosis*, p. 41.

91. Barnes, *Prophecy and Gnosis*, p. 42.
92. Schmidt, *Die Illustration der Lutherbibel*, pp. 179–216.
93. '[D]iese ist dreierley. Die erste thuts mit ausgedruckten worten, on bilde vnd figuren, wie Moses, David vnd der gleichen Propheten mehr, von Christo weissagen, Vnd wie Christus vnd die Apostel, von dem Endechrist vnd falschen lerer etc. Die andere thuts mit bilden, aber doch setzt daneben auch die auslegung mit ausgedruckten worten, wie Joseph die trewme auslegt, Vnd Daniel, beide trewme vnd bilder auslegt. Die dritte, die es on wort odder auslegung, mit blossen bilden vnd figurn thut, wie dis buch der offenbarung, vnd vieler heiligen leute, trewme, gesichte vnd bilder, welche sie vom heiligen geist haben, wie Act. ij. Petrus aus Joel predigt. Ewre sone vnd tochter sollen weissagen, vnd ewre juenlinge sollen gesichte sehen, vnd ewer Eltesten sollen trewme trewmen. Vnd so lange solche weissagungen, vngedeut bleibt, vnd kleine gewisse auslegung kriegt, ists eine verborgene, stumme weissagung, vnd noch nicht zu jrem nutz vnd frucht komen, den sie der Christenheit geben sol.' Cited in Luther, *D. Martin Luthers Werke*, vol. 7, pp. 406–8. Translated in Luther, 'Preface to the Revelation of St. John [II]' (1546; 1530), reprinted in Luther, *Works*, vol. 35, p. 400.
94. Peter Parshall notes how Luther's contemporary, Christoph Walther, commented upon his condemnation of inappropriately printed and decorated Bibles. See Parshall, 'The Vision of the Apocalypse', p. 105, and see n. 8 at pp. 122–3.
95. Barnes, *Prophecy and Gnosis*, pp. 74–5.
96. P. Melanchthon, *Der BapstEsel / durch M. Philippum Melanchthon gedeutet und gebessert* (Wittenberg: Schirlentz, 1535).
97. On Lutheran attitudes to conciliar issues, see M. U. Edwards, Jr, *Luther's Last Battles: Politics and Polemics, 1531–46* (Ithaca, NY: Cornell University Press, 1983), pp. 68–96, and esp. p. 77, on the 'first of a growing number of published attacks by Luther on past councils' from 1535 onwards.
98. Melanchthon, *Der BapstEsel*, see sigs B i r.–B ij r.
99. Ibid., see sig. B iiij v.
100. 'Der BapstEsel ist an jm selbs / ein scheuslich / heslich / grewlich bilde / Vnd jhe lenger mans ansihet / jhe schrecklicher es sihet / Aber nichts ist so vber aus schrecklich daran / als das Gott selbs / solche wunder vnd vngehewer bilde / gemacht vnd offenbaret hat / Denn wo es ein mensch also ertichtet / geschnitzet odder gemalet hette / mochte mans wol verachten odder daruber lichen / Aber weil es die Hohe Goetliche maiestet / selbs geschaffen / vnd dargestellt hat / Solche billich die gantze welt sich dafuer entsetzen vnd erzittern / als daraus man wol mercken kan / was er gedenckt vnd jm synn hat.' M. Luther, 'Amen', in ibid., sig. C r.
101. On this pamphlet, see Scribner, *For the Sake of Simple Folk*, pp. 79–94, 132–3; see fig. 99, p. 133, for a reproduction of the Papal Ass woodcut.
102. For the illustration, see Edwards, *Luther's Last Battles*, fig. 6, p. 195.
103. On this publication, see ibid., pp. 182–200.
104. Noted in ibid., p. 4.
105. P. Melanchthon, M. Flacius Illyricus and M. Luther, *Ein grausame Meerwunder / den Bapst bedeutende / zu Rome gefunden / vnd zu Wittenberg erstlich Anno 23. uvd darnach abermal Anno 46. mit der ausleguug Philippi gedruckt / mit einer Vorrede Matthiae Flacij Illyrici* (Magdeburg: Rödinger, 1549). The reference to 1546 is uncertain, but may possibly be to one of Luther's 1545 publications.
106. On Matthias Flacius Illyricus, see W. Killy (ed.), *Literaturlexikon: Autoren und Werke deutscher Sprache*, 15 vols (Gütersloh: Bertelsmann-Lexikon-Verlag, 1988–93), vol. 3,

pp. 404–6; and O. K. Olsen, *Matthias Flacius and the Survival of Luther's Reform* (Wiesbaden: Harrassowitz Verlag, 2002).

107. His choice of this text is somewhat puzzling, particularly given Melanchthon's increased emphasis on the belly and breasts of the Papal Ass in the 1535 edition. It is possible that Flacius only had access to the 1523 edition during the time that he was preparing this version in Magdeburg.
108. Melanchthon et al., *Ein grausame Meerwunder*, sig. A v. The issue of adiaphora is particularly strongly associated with Philipp Melanchthon and the Interim. See H. Oelke, *Die Konfessionsbildung des 16. Jahrhunderts im Spiegel illustrierter Flugblätter* (Berlin: Walter de Gruyter, 1992), pp. 307–11
109. Melanchthon et al., *Ein grausame Meerwunder*, sigs A ij r.–A iij r.
110. Ibid., sigs B ij r.–B ij v, B iiij r.

4 Wonder Books and Protestants

1. '[I]m jar vnnd anfang als Martinus Luther hat das Euangelium anfahen predigen.' J. Rueff, *Ein schön lustig Trostbüchle von den empfenknussen und geburten der menschen* (Zürich: Christoph Froschauer, 1554), f. LXXII v.
2. J. Fincel, *Wunderzeichen mit figuren* (Leipzig: Jacob Bärwald, 1557), sigs E iiij r.–E iiij v.
3. See above, p. 61.
4. '[D]oruon Luther vil gschriben.' K. Lycosthenes, *Wunderwerck Oder Gottes vnergrundtliches vorbildren ... mit grossem fleiß / durch Johann Herold / vffs treüwlichst inn vier Buecher gezogen vnnd verteütscht* (Basel: Henrichum Petri, 1557), p. cccclxxiij. Note that, unusually, the pagination shifts from a signature style in the early part of the book to roman numerals on every page in the latter part of the book.
5. It should be noted that Fincel does bring in earlier examples in a comparative way.
6. Fincel, *Wunderzeichen mit figuren*, sigs c vi r.–v. Oddly, however, Fincel does not refer to fact that Melanchthon wrote the text, but instead simply directs the reader to the 1555 edition of Luther's collected works, published in Jena. This edition reprinted Melanchthon's text along with the 1545 image. M. Luther, *Der ander Teil aller Bücher vnd Schriften des thewren, seligen Mans Doct. Mart. Lutheri* (Jena: Rödinger, 1555), see ff. 286 r.–292 v.
7. '[B]eschreibt das Bapstumb eigentlich.' Fincel, *Wunderzeichen mit figuren*, sigs c vi r., d vij r.
8. Some unillustrated German wonder books also appeared during this decade, notably C. Goldwurm, *Wunderwerck und Wunderzeichen Buch* (Franckfurt am Main: Zephelius, 1557), although they are not examined here due to their lack of illustrations. See Schenda, 'Die deutschen Prodigiensammlungen', pp. 653–7.
9. Barnes, *Prophecy and Gnosis*, p. 87, and on wonder books see pp. 87–92.
10. Schenda, 'Die deutschen Prodigiensammlungen'.
11. See ibid., pp. 657–69.
12. On these publications, see R. Schenda, *Die französische Prodigienliteratur in der zweiten Hälfte des 16. Jahrhunderts* (Munich: Max Hueber Verlag, 1961); and Céard, *La Nature et les prodiges*. Céard includes some comparative material on German authors.
13. On Aldovandri, see P. Findlen, *Possessing Nature: Museums, Collecting, and Scientific Culture in Early Modern Italy* (Berkeley, CA: University of California Press, 1994), esp.

pp. 17–31. On Liceti, see Daston and Park, *Wonders and the Order of Nature*, pp. 217–28.

14. Schenda, 'Die deutschen Prodigiensammlungen', p. 668.
15. A. G. Debus, *Man and Nature in the Renaissance* (Cambridge: Cambridge University Press, 1978), pp. 35–53; and on the rise of publications, see P. Findlen, 'Natural History', in K. Park and L. Daston (eds), *The Cambridge History of Science. Volume 3. Early Modern Science* (Cambridge: Cambridge University Press, 2006), pp. 437–68.
16. On the differences between Philippists and gnesio-Lutherans in terms of understanding the natural world and, specifically, monstrous births, see Soergel, 'Die Wahrnehmung der Endzeit', esp. pp. 34–44; and Soergel, 'The Afterlives of Monstrous Infants', pp. 292–3.
17. On apocalyptic Lutheran print culture, see Leppin, *Antichrist und Jüngster Tag*; and on apocalyptic Lutheran thought in the second half of the sixteenth century, see Pohl, 'Exegese und Historiographie'.
18. J. Fincel, *Der ander teil Wunderzeichen* (Franckfurt am Mayn: Thomam Rebart, 1566), sigs B viij v.–C i v.
19. See Ewinkel, *De monstris*, pp. 77–84.
20. For an interpretation along these lines, see Wilson, *Signs and Portents*, p. 15.
21. On Rueff's life, see H. E. Keller (ed.), *Jakob Ruf, ein Zürcher Stadtchirurg und Theatermacher im 16. Jahrhundert* (Zurich: Chronos, 2006); and H. M. Koelbing, 'Einführung zu Jakob Reuffs "Trostbüchle"', in J. Rueff, *Ein schön lustig Trostbüchle von den empfenknussen und geburten der menschen* (1554), facs edn, 2 vols (Zurich: Verlag Bibliophile Drucke von Josef Stocker, 1980), vol. 1, pp. 5–7. There is some debate about the correct spelling of his name (see Keller (ed.), *Jakob Ruf*, pp. 30–4). I follow Koelbing, who has produced a facsimile edition of the *Trostbüchle* and the most important studies of this text, in calling the author Jakob Rueff.
22. The main study of the text is Koelbing, 'Einführung zu Jakob Reuffs "Trostbüchle"'.
23. E. Rößlin, *Der swangern Frauwen vnd Hebamen Rosegarten* (Argentine: Martinus Flach, 1513).
24. J. Rueff, *De Conceptv et Generatione Hominis* (Tigvri: Christophorvs Frosch, 1554). For an analysis of the differences between the two texts, generally minor in relation to the sections relevant to this chapter, see H. M. Koelbing, '"De conceptu et generatione hominis": die lateinische Fassung von Jakob Rueffs "Trostbüchle", Zürich 1554', *Gesnerus*, 38 (1981), pp. 51–8. Koelbing makes only a brief reference to the passages on monstrous births (p. 56).
25. V. Nutton, 'The Anatomy of the Soul in Early Renaissance Medicine', in G. R. Dunstan (ed.), *The Human Embryo: Aristotle and the Arabic and European Traditions* (Exeter: University of Exeter Press, 1990), pp. 136–57, on p. 142.
26. See R. J. Durling, 'A Chronological Census of Renaissance Editions and Translations of Galen', *Journal of the Warburg and Courtauld Institutes*, 24 (1961), pp. 230–305, on p. 259. On the uptake of Galenic theories about the formation of the foetus, see Nutton, 'The Anatomy of the Soul'. For the late fifteenth and first half of the sixteenth centuries, see esp. pp. 139–42. For the best study of the distinctions between Galenic and Aristotelian theories in the late medieval period, see J. Cadden, *Meanings of Sex Difference in the Middle Ages: Medicine, Science and Culture* (Cambridge: Cambridge University Press, 1993), pp. 117–30.
27. See Durling, 'A Chronological Census of Renaissance Editions and Translations of Galen', p. 280. Huldrych M. Koelbing suggests that Gessner had some influence on the

preparation of the Latin edition. See Koelbing, '"De conceptu et generatione hominis"' p. 54.

28. Rueff, *Ein schön lustig Trostbüchle*, ff. LV v., LVI r.
29. For this broadsheet, see Harms and Schilling (eds), *Deutsche illustrierte Flugblätter*, vol. 6, pp. 58–9; and Keller (ed.), *Jakob Ruf*, p. 212.
30. On this common visual strategy, see Soergel, 'The Afterlives of Monstrous Infants', pp. 300–1.
31. '[D]erglychen zwey kind an einanderen gewachsen.' Rueff, *Ein schön lustig Trostbüchle*, f. LXVI v.
32. Lycosthenes, *Wunderwerck*, pp. ccccclxiiij, ccccclxv (facing page), ccccclxxxix, dvi.
33. For the corresponding images, see J. Obsequens, *Prodigiorum liber*, ed. K. Lycosthenes (Basel: Oporinus, 1552). See 50, 63, 69, 71, 75, 76, 81, 83, 88, 98, 102, 103 (several used twice).
34. Koelbing, '"De conceptu et generatione hominis"', p. 55.
35. A. Vesalius, *De humani corporis fabrica libri septem* (Basel: Joannis Oporini, 1543), p. 478.
36. See Rueff, *Ein schön lustig Trostbüchle*, ff. LXIIII v.–LXXVI v.
37. '[K]inder so jre glider verkeert vnd nit alle habe[n]d / oder aber deren zuo vil'; '[K]rotten/ würm / oder andere vergifftige thier'; '[N]it kochet/ zuobereit/ vnd zuo einem rechten kind werde[n].' Ibid., f. LVIII v.
38. Ibid., f. LXX r.
39. On Rueff's interest in natural causes, see Ewinkel, *De monstris*, pp. 123–4.
40. Paracelsus is a notable exception, although his work had a limited readership until the second half of the century in any case. See G. Scholz Williams, *Defining Dominion: The Discourses of Magic and Witchcraft in Early Modern France and Germany* (Ann Arbor, MI: University of Michigan Press, 1995), pp. 45–63.
41. For a discussion of monstrous births as part of the plenitude of nature, see A. W. Bates, 'Good, Common, Regular, and Orderly: Early Modern Classifications of Monstrous Births', *Social History of Medicine*, 18:2 (2005), pp. 141–58. The connection between the diversity of nature and monstrosity is also an important theme throughout Céard, *La Nature et les prodiges*.
42. '[D]er zyt als Marcellus vn[d] Hanibal mit einanderen stryt oder krieg gehebt habe[n]d.' Rueff, *Ein schön lustig Trostbüchle*, f. LXXIII r.
43. Obsequens, *Prodigiorum liber*, illustrated at p. 36 and briefly discussed at pp. 36–7. The elephant-headed boy was also one of several classical monstrous births illustrated in F. Nausea, *Libri Mirabilium Septem* (Coloniae: Petrem Quentell, 1532), illustrated at f. XXV r. and briefly discussed at f. XXII v.
44. '[S]ollend wir des ewigen Gottes wunderwerck erlernen ... vnd die zuo vnserer besserung vfnem[m]en.' Ibid., f. LXXVI v.
45. Schilling, 'Job Fincel und die Zeichen der Endzeit'; on Fincel's biography, see pp. 327–32. For a recent discussion of Fincel, and especially his attraction to Philippist understandings of natural history, and specifically monstrous births, see Soergel, 'Die Wahrnehmung der Endzeit', pp. 39–42. Soergel tends to characterize Fincel as a Philippist because of his interest in reading the natural world as filled with signs from God (as oposed to the gnesio-Lutheran tendency to represent monstrous births as embodiments of sin), see pp. 41–4. Schilling suggests that while Fincel was certainly a follower of Melanchthon, he does not forcefully come down on either side in his publications (p. 329).

46. '[V]berfluessige oder zu wenig Glieder in geburten etc. geschen natuerlich. Darumb sind sie nicht Wunderzeiche[n].' Fincel, *Der ander teil Wunderzeichen*, sigs B vij r.–B vij v. On Fincel's interest in natural causes of misbirths, see Ewinkel, *De monstris*, pp. 141–3.
47. For an anlysis of causal theories in the early modern period, see L. S. Joy, 'Scientific Explanation from Formal Causes to Laws of Nature', in Park and Daston (eds), *The Cambridge History of Science. Volume 3*, pp. 70–105.
48. Fincel, *Der ander teil Wunderzeichen*, sig. B viij r.
49. Schilling, 'Job Fincel und die Zeichen der Endzeit', p. 379.
50. Fincel, *Wunderzeichen mit figuren*. The three unillustrated volumes consulted for this chapter are as follows: J. Fincel, *Wunderzeiche[n]. Warhafftige Beschreibung vnd gruendlich verzeichnus schrecklicher Wunderzeichen vnd geschichten* (Franckfurt am Mayn: Thomam Rebart, 1566); Fincel, *Der ander teil Wunderzeichen*; and J. Fincel, *Der dritte theil Wunderzeychen* (Franckfurt am Mayn: Weygand Hanen Erben, 1567). Contemporary editions also appeared with other publishers, notably through Jacobus Berwald in Leipzig. For full bibliographical details, see Schilling, 'Job Fincel und die Zeichen der Endzeit', pp. 390–1.
51. Fincel, *Wunderzeichen mit figuren*, sig. B viij r.
52. Ibid., sigs A v r.–D i v.
53. Ibid., sig. B iiij v. On this point see also sig. C v v.
54. '[M]it Sodomittischen suenden vberschuettet vnd erfuellet.' Ibid., sig. B v v. He repeats this assertion in the foreword to his second volume. Fincel, *Der ander teil Wunderzeichen*, sig. B iiij v. Helmut Puff argues that during this period 'sodomitische' activity was not restricted to the modern-day definition of sodomy, but could be a way of describing any sexual practice that was outside the norm, unproductive in terms of producing children, and most particularly same-sex acts. See H. Puff, *Sodomy in Reformation Germany and Switzerland, 1400–1600* (Chicago: University of Chicago Press, 2003). The metaphor of escaping the city of Sodom also had particular currency in German Reformation polemic (p. 139).
55. 'Aus diesem verdampten Sodom hat vns der heilige Man / Doctor Luther / gefurt.' Fincel, *Wunderzeichen mit figuren*, sig. B vi v.
56. See, for example, ibid., sigs F viij r., M v r.
57. See, for example, ibid., sig. O viij r.
58. On war in Fincel's *Wunderzeichen*, see Schilling, 'Job Fincel und die Zeichen der Endzeit', pp. 339–40.
59. Fincel, *Wunderzeichen mit figuren*, sig. C vi r.
60. 'Solch Wehklangen ist auch etlich Jar zuuor offt des ortes gehoeret worden.' Ibid., sigs Y viij r.–v.
61. Ibid., sig. R vi r.
62. Ibid., sigs B iij r.–B iij v., C vi v., C vij v.
63. Ibid., sigs C viij r.–C viij v. On this point, see Schilling, 'Job Fincel und die Zeichen der Endzeit', p. 359. Fincel returns to this point in his second volume, see Fincel, *Der ander teil Wunderzeichen*, sigs Bij v.–Biij r.
64. '[D]er Juengstetag [ist] fuer der thuer.' See, for example, Fincel, *Wunderzeichen mit figuren*, sig. O i r.
65. See A. Burckhardt, *Johannes Basilius Herold. Kaiser und Reich im protestantichen Schrifttum des Basler Buchdrucks um die Mitte des 16. Jahrhunderts* (Basel and Stuttgart: Verlag von Helbing und Leichtenhahn, 1967). See pp. 156–72 on Herold's interest in German history, and specifically pp. 165–7 on the German language and translating from Latin.

66. Lycosthenes, *Wunderwerck*, sigs a v r.–b iiii r.
67. K. Lycosthenes, *Prodigiorum ac ostentorum chronicon* (Basilae: Henricum Petri, 1557). On this book, see Schenda, 'Die deutschen Prodigiensammlungen', pp. 649–52; Wilson, *Signs and Portents*, pp. 62–7; J.-C. Margolin, 'Sur quelques prodiges rapportés par Conrad Lycosthenes', in Jones-Davies (ed.), *Monstres et Prodiges*, pp. 42–54; Céard, *La Nature et les prodiges*, pp. 186–91; and Daston and Park, *Wonders and the Order of Nature*, pp. 182–7.
68. Killy (ed.), *Literaturlexicon*, vol. 12, pp. 412–13. See also Margolin, 'Sur quelques prodiges rapportés par Conrad Lycosthenes', pp. 42–54.
69. Obsequens, *Prodigiorum liber*.
70. On the Reformation in Switzerland, see B. Gordon, *The Swiss Reformation* (Manchester: Manchester University Press, 2002), and on the broader intellectual culture, especially in the 1550s and including figures such as Conrad Gessner and Sebastian Münster, see pp. 317–42. On Johann Jakob Wick's contemporary collection of prints and drawings of wondrous and dramatic events see pp. 278–80.
71. Lycosthenes, *Prodigiorum ac ostentorum*, sigs b iiii v.–b vi r. This section does not appear in the German edition.
72. Lycosthenes, *Wunderwerck*, p. ccccl v.
73. On the development of scientific cabinets of wonders in early modern Europe, particularly Italy in the seventeenth century, see Findlen, *Possessing Nature*.
74. For one significant example related to a birth in 1532, discussed in the next chapter in relation to Johann Nas's complex *Ecclesia Militans* broadsheet of 1569, see Lycosthenes, *Wunderwerck*, pp. cccclxxxv–cccclxxxvi.
75. See, for example, ibid., pp. ccccxcij–ccccxciij.
76. Ibid., p. dlvij.
77. For a contemporary broadsheet that reports this birth, see Harms and Schilling (eds), *Deutsche illustrierte Flugblätter*, vol. 6, pp. 60–1. This monster, born on 25 January in the town of Winterswijk in the Netherlands, is associated in this broadsheet with the civil conflict in the Netherlands between 1538 and 1543.
78. 'Das ist ja warlich ein abschewlich Monstrum oder Wundergeburt gewest.' C. Irenaeus, *De monstris. Von seltzamen Wundergeburten* (Ursel: Henricus, 1584), sig. M ii v.
79. These points to do with representation are discussed in Harms and Schilling (eds), *Deutsche illustrierte Flugblätter*, vol. 6, p. 60. On the representation of devils and demons, see *Diables et diableries. La représentation du diable dans la gravure des XVe et XVIe siècles*, exhibition catalogue (Geneva: Cabinet des estampes, 1976).
80. Daston and Park, *Wonders and the Order of Nature*, p. 185.
81. On Rueff's interest in the question of whether or not the devil can engender children, see B. Gordon, 'God Killed Saul: Heinrich Bullinger and Jacob Ruef on the Power of the Devil', in K. A. Edwards (ed.), *Werewolves, Witches and Wandering Spirits: Traditional Belief and Folklore in Early Modern Europe* (Kirksville, MO: Truman State University Press, 2002), pp. 155–79.
82. Rueff, *Ein schön lustig Trostbüchle*, ff. XCIII v.–XCIIII r. For the section on 'demonic' births in its entirety, see ff. XCII r.–XCVII r.
83. '[V]nd dergleichen ding.' Ibid., f. XCIIII r. This is a theme taken up another physician, Johann Weyer, who wrote in his groundbreaking 1563 treatise on witchcraft of various hard objects placed in the body by the devil and expelled from the mouth or other orifices. Weyer, nonetheless, also refutes the idea that devils can engender children. J. Weyer, *Witches, Devils and Doctors in the Renaissance*, trans. J. Shea [translation of *De praestigiis*

daemonum] (Binghampton, NY: Medieval and Renaissance Texts and Studies, 1991), see especially pp. 295–6.

84. On the devil as a dominant cultural figure in the second half of the sixteenth century, see Midelfort, *A History of Madness*, pp. 53–9; and Clark, *Thinking with Demons*, pp. 161–78.
85. '[E]in menschliche gestalt / wol geformiert.' Rueff, *Ein schön lustig Trostbüchle*, f. LXXII r.
86. Both Céard and Bates emphasize the issue of God's anger in relation to this monster; see Céard, *La Nature et les prodiges*, p. 294; and Bates, *Emblematic Monsters*, p. 74. Bates, in particular, emphasizes this point in order to downplay Rueff's interest in natural causes.
87. Pliny was primarily concerned with enumerating the great and wondrous variety of possible types in the world, rather than fully accounting for their cause or meaning. See Pliny, *Natural History*, p. 175 (II:3).
88. '[V]nglyche geburten vnnd Monstra wider den gemeinen bruch der natur.' Rueff, *Ein schön lustig Trostbüchle*, f. LXXII r.
89. Ibid., f. LXXII r.
90. Fincel, *Wunderzeichen mit figuren*, sigs O iiij r.–O v r.
91. 'Das es ein Androgynus gewest / bedeute die aller schendlichste / Sodomische vnzucht'. Ibid., sig. O v v.
92. 'Es hat drey stunde gelebt vnd gesagt / Wachet / ewer Gott ist fuer der thuer'; 'das werck der geburt allein Gottes werck ist ... es were nicht mueglich / das ein mensch lebendig zur Welt kommen koendt / vnd geborn warden / so nicht Gott selbs Hebam vnnd Wehemutter were'. Ibid., sig. O iiij v.
93. Fincel, *Der dritte theil Wunderzeychen*, sig. E iiij v.
94. '[W]ie ettlich woelle[n] / im Niderla[n]d die andern sage[n] zuo Crackauw in Polen'; 'gantz grausam vn[d] erschrockenlich anzuosehen'; 'Wachend / eüwer Herr vnd Gott ist vorhanden / vnd gleich doruff gestorben'. Lycosthenes, *Wunderwerck*, p. dvij.
95. '[E]in grosser sterbend war im gantzen Europen'. Ibid., p. dvij.
96. For more on monstrous children with unnatural powers of speech in the later sixteenth century, see below, pp. 139–45.
97. Midelfort, *A History of Madness*, p. 53, and, on this theme more broadly, see pp. 53–9.
98. '[D]er Bapstesel / das Kalb in Sachssen / mit der Muench kutten / das Kind zu Cracaw vnd andere deren ich viel beschrieben habe / bedeute[n] sie doch allwege was schrecklichs.' Fincel, *Wunderzeichen mit Figuren*, sigs B vi v.–B vij r.

5 Catholic Print Culture and Monstrous Births

1. Scribner, *For the Sake of Simple Folk*, pp. 229–39.
2. Ibid., p. 261; R. P. Hsia, *The World of Catholic Renewal 1540–1770*, 2nd edn (Cambridge: Cambridge University Press, 2005), p. 248.
3. On this point, see Harms and Schilling (eds), *Deutsche illustrierte Flugblätter*, vol. 2, p. 38.
4. Barnes, *Prophecy and Gnosis*, pp. 74–5.
5. See above, pp. 74–5, and also Scribner, *For the Sake of Simple Folk*, pp. 232–3. For a discussion of Catholic attitudes, see Ewinkel, *De monstris*, pp. 34–8, although she does not seem to be aware of the *Ecclesia Militans*.
6. '[D]iese monströsen Wunderzeichen können als Kern der Sache angesehen warden.' F. Stopp, 'Der religiös-polemische Einblattdruck "Ecclesia Militans" (1569) des Johann

Nas und seine Vorgänger', *Deutsche Vierteljahrsschrift für Literaturwissenschaft und Geistesgeschichte*, 39 (1965), pp. 588–638, on p. 623.

7. Hsia, 'A Time for Monsters'; on the *Ecclesia Militans* see pp. 84–7.
8. Ibid., p. 71, and on this issue see also p. 87.
9. The most important recent discussion of this printed material can be found in J. C. Smith, *Sensuous Worship: Jesuits and the Art of the Early Catholic Reformation in Germany* (Princeton, NJ: Princeton University Press, 2002), pp. 11–55.
10. The most important study of the *Ecclesia Militans* is Stopp, 'Der religiös-polemische Einblattdruck "Ecclesia Militans"', although the broadsheet is only discussed in detail on pp. 622–6, and Stopp is mostly concerned with its publication context. See also Harms and Schilling (eds), *Deutsche illustrierte Flugblätter*, vol. 2, pp. 38–9 (and for a second edition of the broadsheet, published in 1588, see ibid., vol. 2, pp. 40–1); Hsia, 'A Time for Monsters', pp. 84–7; and Richardsen-Friedrich, *Antichrist-Polemik*, pp. 321–31.
11. I. Zingerle, 'Selbstbiographie des Johannes Nasus', *Zeitschrift für deutsche Philologie*, 18 (1886), pp. 488–90, on p. 489. The article includes a transcription of the autobiography, found in a prayer book in the Konventsbibliothek of the Franziskanerkloster in Innsbruck. Nas does not use the title in his six-volume *Centurien* series, published between 1565 and 1570 (see below, note 17). However, the date may possibly be 1570, as Lutheran polemicist Georg Nigrinus's attack on Nas's title was published in 1570 according to the *Verzeichnis der im deutschen Sprachbereich erschienenen Drucke des 16. Jahrhunderts (VD 16)*, see http://www.vd16.de/. However, the date does not appear on the Nigrinus publication and this could potentially also indicate a need to consider redating Nigrinus's text to 1571. See G. Nigrinus, *Uon Bruder Johan Nasen Esel vnd seinem rechtem Tittel, F.I.N.S.A.C. oder F.I.N.S.C.E.* ([Oberursel]: [Henricus], [*c.* 1570]).
12. Stopp, 'Der religiös-polemische Einblattdruck "Ecclesia Militans"'.
13. See Harms and Schilling (eds), *Deutsche illustrierte Flugblätter*, vol. 2, pp. 32–3; and Stopp, 'Der religiös-polemische Einblattdruck "Ecclesia Militans"', pp. 597–602. For Catholic parodies of Luther, see Burschel, 'Das Monster'.
14. See Harms and Schilling (eds), *Deutsche illustrierte Flugblätter*, vol. 2, pp. 36–7; and Stopp, 'Der religiös-polemische Einblattdruck "Ecclesia Militans"', pp. 613–20.
15. The word 'Suiten' is a play on words intended to remove the reference to Jesus, and to show how the Jesuits draw upon the 'Sitten' or morals of their mother, a sow ('Sus') who represents the Pope. See Harms and Schilling (eds), *Deutsche illustrierte Flugblätter*, vol. 6, pp. 320–1. See also Stopp, 'Der religiös-polemische Einblattdruck "Ecclesia Militans"', pp. 602–13.
16. For a more extended biography, see G. Pointner, 'Das Luthertum vom Teufel erdacht hat alles Unglück in die Welt bracht. Die polemische Publizistik des J. Nas' (PhD dissertation, University of Vienna, 1996), pp. 19–29; and Zingerle, 'Selbstbiographie des Johannes Nasus'.
17. The editions used here are: *Das Antipapistisch eins vnd hundert* (Ingolstadt: Alexander Weissenhorn, 1568 [slightly revised second edition of the first volume]); the *Secvnda Centvria* (Ingolstadt: Alexander Weissenhorn, 1568); the *Tertia Centvria* (Ingolstadt: Alexander Weissenhorn, 1569); the *Qvarta Centvria* (Ingolstadt: Alexander Weissenhorn, 1570); the *Qvinta Centvria* (Ingolstadt: Alexander Weissenhorn, 1570); and the *Sextae Centvriae* (Ingolstadt: Alexander Weissenhorn, 1569). The most substantial studies of Nas's polemical writing are Pointner, 'Das Luthertum vom Teufel erdacht'; H. Lukasser, 'Die Centurien des Johannes Nas. Ihre Waurzeln und Formen. Ein Beitrag zur Prosa des 16. Jahrhunderts' (PhD dissertation, University of Innsbruck, 1952); and H.

Oelke, 'Konfessionelle Bildpropaganda des späten 16. Jahrhunderts: Die Nas-Fischart-Kontroverse 1568/71', *Archiv für Reformationsgeschichte/Archive for Reformation History*, 87 (1996), pp. 149–200. Pointner simply reproduces the *Ecclesia Militans*, Lukasser does not seem to have been aware of it, and Oelke discusses it briefly (pp. 172–4).

18. Nas, *Qvinta Centvria*, ff. 83 v.–86 r.
19. Ibid., ff. 83 v.–86 r.
20. '[D]as er kein rhuo wür haben / biß er ein Nunnen zuom Weib krieget'. Ibid., f. 84 r.
21. Ibid., f. 84 v.
22. Nas, *Das Antipapistisch eins vnd hundert*, ff. 42 v.–48 r.
23. 'Dast ist die streitbar Kirch fuer war.'
24. See G. Schiller, *Ikonographie der christlichen Kunst*, 5 vols (Gütersloh: Gütersloher Verlagshaus, 1966–91), vol. 4, part 2, pp. 192–3.
25. There are many examples in Scribner, *For the Sake of Simple Folk*, see esp. pp. 148–89.
26. 'Sein stinckets Lock jhr Dintfaß ist / Drauß schreibens all Luegen vnd List.'
27. 'Predikant' is a negative term used here in contrast to 'Prediger'. See Pointner, 'Das Luthertum vom Teufel erdacht', pp. 44–5. On adiaphora see above, p. 79.
28. 'Furiæ mit Schlangen Haar. / Nacket gleich wie die Badmaegd gehn.'
29. 'Kelch vnd Monstrantzen seyn schabab.'
30. Stopp, 'Der religiös-polemische Einblattdruck "Ecclesia Militans"', p. 623.
31. This is one of the few specific iconographical identifications made by Stopp. Ibid., p. 624.
32. Shachar, *The Judensau*.
33. 'Saw, wie in Kot liege.' Luther, *D. Martin Luthers Werke*, vol. 53, pp. 417–552, see p. 444.
34. Lycosthenes, *Wunderwerck*, p. cccclxxiij. On this case see also the sixth volume of Nas's *Centurien*. Nas, *Sextae Centvriae*, ff. 54 r.–54 v., where Nas discusses a similar misbirth with a Luther-like face that was born in Halle in 1524.
35. See above, pp. 69–72.
36. Nas did discuss the Papal Ass elsewhere. See Nas, *Qvinta Centvria*, ff. 319 v.–324 v.
37. Hsia, 'A Time for Monsters', p. 85.
38. '[D]oruon Luther vil gschriben.' Lycosthenes, *Wunderwerck*, p. cccclxxiij.
39. Fincel, *Wunderzeichen mit figuren*, sig. Eiiij v.
40. Nas, *Qvinta Centvria*, ff 166 v.–179 v.
41. Ibid., f. 169 r.
42. Ibid., ff. 170 r., 171 v., 175 r., 172 r., see also ff. 177 v.–178 r.
43. Ibid., ff. 175 v.–176 r.
44. 'Lucifer ein ochs superbia ein kueh. Luther jr kalb.' Ibid., f. 179 r.
45. 'Ohn zweifel es den Krieg bedeut.'
46. '[E]in spitzkopff / als ob ein Türckische[n] hut vff haet.' Lycosthenes. *Wunderwerck*, p. dx.
47. 'Bedeut hat es ihren zwy spalt / Jn Glaubens Sachen new vnd alt.' Lycosthenes gives only a brief description of this child. Lycosthenes, *Wunderwerck*, p. dxxxvij.
48. Ibid., p. dxlvi; and Fincel, *Wunderzeichen mit figuren*, sig. a ij r.
49. 'Ein Kind ohn Haupt. bedeuten kan / Ein Regiment Acephalon.'
50. Nas, *Qvarta Centvria*, f. 69 r. Nas also refer his reader here back to the *Ecclesia Militans*.
51. 'Saewkopff / doch menschen haend.'
52. Stopp, 'Der religiös–polemische Einblattdruck "Ecclesia Militans"', pp. 603, 612.

53. 'Daß jederman wil selbst Haupt seyn / Herr / Koenig / Fuerst durchauß vnd ein / Damit sie vngehorsam waeren.'
54. See Martin, *Martin Luther und die Bilder zur Apokalypse*, pp. 67–70.
55. Lycosthenes, *Wunderwerck*, p. ccccIxv.
56. Ibid., p. ccccIxxi.
57. Fincel, *Wunderzeichen mit figuren*, sig. D vii v.
58. Lycosthenes, *Wunderwerck*, p. ccccIxxxiij.
59. See Kirschbaum (ed.), *Lexikon der Christlichen Ikonographie*, vol. 3, pp. 303–7.
60. I. Faust, *Zoologische Einblattdrucke und Flugschriften vor 1800*, 5 vols (Stuttgart: Anton Hiersemann, 1998–2003), vol. 5, pp. 214–21. Lycosthenes, *Wunderwerck*, p. dxiij; and Fincel, *Wunderzeichen mit figuren*, sigs R i r.–Riij r.
61. 'Kynokephale in der Tracht eines protestantischen Predigers.' Harms and Schilling (eds), *Deutsche illustrierte Flugblätter*, vol. 2, p. 38.
62. See J. Hirn, *Erzherzog Ferdinand II von Tirol. Geschichte seiner Regierung und seiner Länder*, 2 vols (Innsbruck: Verlag der Wagner'schen Universitäts-Buchhandlung, 1885–8), vol. 1, pp. 227–62.
63. J. M. Wagner, 'Johannes Nas und die Jesuiten', *Archiv für die Geschichte deutscher Sprache und Dichtung*, 1 (1874), pp. 51–66. The letter is transcribed in the article and makes up the bulk of it (pp. 53–66). On the conflict between Nas and the Jesuits, see also J. Brodrick, *Petrus Canisius 1521–1597*, trans. K. Telch, 2 vols (Wien: Verlag Herder, 1950), vol. 2, pp. 450–3; and B. Duhr, *Die Jesuiten und den deutschen Fürsthöfen des 16. Jahrhunderts* (Freiburg im Breisgau: Herdersche Verlagshandlung, 1901), pp. 90–1.
64. '[W]ie ketzer allain auf den glauben, wie die widertauffer allain auf daß vil und offt tauffen.' Johann Nas to Melchiori Parocho, 30 January 1573, cited in Wagner, 'Johannes Nas und die Jesuiten', p. 59.
65. Duhr, *Die Jesuiten und den deutschen Fürsthöfen*, pp. 71–82.
66. Johann Nas to Melchiori Parocho, 30 January 1573, cited in Wagner, 'Johannes Nas und die Jesuiten', p. 63.
67. See A. Seifert, *Die Universität Ingolstadt im 15. und 16. Jahrhundert. Texte und Regesten* (Berlin: Duncker und Humblot, 1973), pp. 169–238.
68. For examples of the persistent use of imagery of the metaphoric light of the gospel used in relation to Luther by Reformers, see C. Zika, 'The Reformation Jubilee of 1617: Appropriating the Past in European Centenary Celebrations', in his *Exorcising our Demons*, pp. 197–236.
69. Richardsen-Friedrich, *Antichrist-Polemik*, p. 322.
70. Ibid., p. 325. Nas explicitly connects the acronym to the Schmalkaldic War in the fourth volume of his *Centurien*. Nas, *Qvarta Centvria*, f. 311 r.
71. Lycosthenes, *Wunderwerck*, p. ccccIxx.
72. 'Bedeuttet vns das Lutherthumb / Welchs hat vil Koepff / Maeuier vn[d] Zungen.'
73. Ibid., pp. dxxxvi–dxxxvij; and Fincel, *Wunderzeichen mit figuren*, sig. Z i v.
74. See Richardsen-Friedrich, *Antichrist-Polemik*, p. 325. Richardsen-Friedrich argues that Nas is drawing here upon Catholic convert Friedrich Staphylus's unillustrated book of 1565, *Vom letzen und großen Abfall / so vor der zukunfft des Antichristi geschehen soll.*
75. 'Durchs hoeren soll es alls geschehen.'
76. Lycosthenes. *Wunderwerck*, pp. dxxxviij–dxxxix; and Fincel, *Wunderzeichen mit figuren*, sigs a iii v.–a iiij r.
77. Monstrous births evidently remained important to Nas's conception of Lutheranism. His 1577 book *Wiedereinwarnung* presents the reader with an embodied representation

of Luther's central concept of *sola fide*: it is represented as a monstrous birth. J. Nas, *Widereinwarnung / An alle from[m]e Teutsche[n]* (Ingolstadt: Alexander Weyssenhorn, 1577), pp. 82–4.

78. '[D]er beste Hirst sein Schaff'; 'sie ins Liecht durch dWarheit fuehrt'.
79. Lycosthenes, *Wunderwerck*, pp. cccclxxxv–cccclxxxvi.
80. 'Die stund der geburt / der welt end ist hie.'
81. Richardsen-Friedrich, *Antichrist-Polemik*, p. 327. Again, Nas is drawing upon Staphylus.
82. 'Sanct Petrum vnd den Bapst verflucht.'
83. Richardsen-Friedrich, *Antichrist-Polemik*, p. 328. Once again, this comes from Staphylus.
84. 'Sein Ketzerey vil Haeupter hat / Wie diudiß Thiers sichst abgemahlt'; 'Quot capita, tot sensus'.
85. For Dürer's version, see Carey (ed.), *The Apocalypse*, p. 138.
86. Scribner, *For the Sake of Simple Folk*, pp. 171–3.
87. Schmidt, *Die Illustration der Lutherbibel*, pp. 122–7, and for this image specifically see p. 125.
88. Harms and Schilling (eds), *Deutsche illustrierte Flugblätter*, vol. 6, pp. 92–4.
89. See Geisberg, *The German Single-Leaf Woodcut*, vol. 3, p. 1066; Harms and Schilling (eds), *Deutsche illustrierte Flugblätter*, vol. 6, pp. 92–7.
90. See Harms and Schilling (eds), *Deutsche illustrierte Flugblätter*, vol. 6, p. 92.
91. Hsia, *The World of Catholic Renewal*, p. 20. This issue remained a heated topic within the Catholic church at the time that Nas was preparing the *Ecclesia Militans*: for example, communion in both kinds was still offered in Catholic churches in some Austrian areas. See Hirn, *Erzherzog Ferdinand II. von Tirol*, vol. 1, pp. 140–1, 170.
92. Nas, *Das Antipapistisch eins vnd hundert*, f. 73 r., and for the entire passage see ff. 72 v.–74 v. Nas also connects the Augsburg Confession to the whore of Babylon and the seven-headed beast of the Apocalypse in the third volume of the *Centurien* (Nas, *Tertia Centvria*, ff. 56 r.–56 v.) and also in the fifth columе (Nas, *Qvinta Centvria*, ff. 394 v.–395 r.).
93. Harms and Schilling (eds), *Deutsche illustrierte Flugblätter*, vol. 6, p. 94.
94. Richardsen-Friedrich, *Antichrist-Polemik*, pp. 321, 326–8.
95. '[N]icht inn ainer frembden Nation mit disem Thier schwanger gewesen / sonder in Teütschland.' Nas, *Das Antipapistisch eins vnd hundert*, f. 74 r.

6 'Many Heads, Mouths and Tongues'

1. '[V]il Koepff / Maeuier vn[d] Zungen.' 'Quot capita, tot sensus'. See above, p. 122.
2. 'Alle gutte ding auß de[n] haubt entsatn.' See above, p. 30.
3. 'Solche zwey oder vielkoepffichte Monstra haben gemeiniglich vneinigkeit / zwytracht / im Geistlichen vnd Weltlichen Regiment bedeutet.' Irenaeus, *De monstris*, sig. I i v. For Irenaeus's chapter on 'what children born with two, three or more heads signify' ('Was die Kinder / so mit zweyen / dreyen / oder mehr Koepffen geboren warden / bedeuten'), see sigs Iii 1 v.–Kkk 4 v.
4. For a representative selection of broadsheet reproductions, see Harms and Schilling (eds), *Deutsche illustrierte Flugblätter*, vol. 6; and Ewinkel, *De monstris*. A number of new wonder books appeared in the second half of the sixteenth century, but they were unillustrated. The most important examples are Irenaeus, *De monstris*; and A. Engel,

WiderNatur und Wunderbuch (Franckfurt am Mayn: Brachfeld, 1597). See Schenda, 'Die deutschen Prodigiensammlungen', pp. 657–69.

5. Soergel is one of few authors to have examined such pamphlets on monstrous births in his articles 'Die Wahrnehmung der Endzeit', and 'The Afterlives of Monstrous Infants'.
6. Excepting the Monk Calf and Papal Ass, German pamphlets on monstrous births in key research libraries including the Herzog August Bibliothek and the British Library generally date from the later part of the sixteenth century.
7. See the discussion above, pp. 1–3. On this broadsheet and its publication context, see Ewinkel, *De monstris*, pp. 237–47. For reproductions of Italian broadsheets that individually depict the two monstrous births see pp. 330–1; for German broadsheets depicting the seven-headed child alone and against a plain background see pp. 332, 334; for the broadsheet discussed here see p. 333; and for a seventeenth-century version of this monstrous birth see pp. 335–6. The second German broadsheet reproduction (p. 334) reports that the child was born in the Netherlands. As was the case with the monster of Krakow, confusion evidently developed around the geographical location of the birth. Later in the century, see Irenaeus, *De monstris*, sig. S iiij r., where Irenaeus also locates the birth in the Netherlands. Several broadsheets reporting the birth of the same seven-headed child also appear in Harms and Schilling (eds), *Deutsche illustrierte Flugblätter*, vol. 7; see pp. 224–33, and see pp. 230–1 for the version examined here.
8. Soergel, 'Portraying Monstrous Birth', p. 138.
9. It should be noted that the text refers the reader to another monstrous birth born that same year and discussed by the preacher Simon Pauli of Rostock (see below, pp. 133–6, for this case).
10. See Ewinkel, *De monstris*, fig. 116, p. 396.
11. On this case, see Harms and Schilling (eds), *Deutsche illustrierte Flugblätter*, vol. 7, pp. 220–1.
12. On Simon Pauli, see the *Allgemeine Deutsche Biographie*, 56 vols (1875–1912), facs edn (Berlin: Duncker and Humblot, 1967–71), vol. 25, pp. 273–4.
13. S. Pauli, *Bildnis vnnd Gestalt einer erschrecklichen vnnatuerlichen vnd vngewoenlichen Geburt / eines Kindes / welches Anno 1577. den 20. Decembris zu Greuesmuelen im Land zu Meckelnburg / von eines Schneiders / M. B. ehelichen hausfrauwen/ geboren ist* (Rostock: Jacobus Lucius, 1578). This was reprinted again at least once that same year in Hamburg by the publisher Löw.
14. Ibid., sig. A 4 r.
15. '[D]as nicht allein der jungste tag bald verhanden vnd hart fuer der thuer sey/ sondern auch das vngeluecke vnd grosse straffen vnd plagen komen werden'. Ibid., sig. A 4 r.
16. Ibid., sigs A 4 r., C 3 r.
17. '[E]ines hohen langen Tuerckischen oder Reussischen huts / gestalt'. Ibid., sig. A 2 r.
18. Ibid., sigs A 2 r.–A 2 v.
19. Ibid., sigs B 3 r.–B 3 v.
20. Ibid., sig. B 4 r. Pauli prepared another pamphlet, published in Rostock by Ferber in 1579, on a child born in December 1578. The sermon-like text is about clothes and their Christian meaning, beginning with a discussion of Adam and Eve. The child, born with skin that appeared like clothing, is discussed in only one paragraph, and seems simply to have been a jumping-off point for Pauli's text, which ends with a warning about the coming Day of Judgement. S. Pauli, *Bildnis und Gestalt einer erschrecklichen unnatürlichen und ungewöhnlichen Geburdt eines Kindlins / welches Anno 1578. den 15. Decembris zu*

Rostock geboren ist (Rostock: Ferber, 1579). For another 1579 case also concerned with clothing, see Soergel, 'The Afterlives of Monstrous Infants', pp. 305–6.

21. On this case, see Harms and Schilling (eds), *Deutsche illustrierte Flugblätter*, vol. 6, pp. 274–7.
22. Pauli, *Bildnis vnnd Gestalt einer erschrecklichen*, sigs C 3 r., C 4 r.
23. 'Wo findet man zungen die zu Gott dem HERRN / in dieser / der kirchen vnd des vaterlands eussersten not vnd gefahr / recht vnd mit ernst beten?' Ibid., sig. C 4 v.
24. Ibid., sig. C 4 v.
25. A Latin edition of this work had been published in 1609. On Schenck the Elder, see Midelfort, *A History of Madness*, pp. 169–72.
26. This tendency increased in seventeenth-century England. See Crawford, *Marvelous Protestantism*.
27. See above, p. 60.
28. On this broadsheet, see Harms and Schilling (eds), *Deutsche illustrierte Flugblätter*, vol. 7, pp. 273–4.
29. On this broadsheet, see Harms and Schilling (eds), *Deutsche illustrierte Flugblätter*, vol. 4, pp. 396–7.
30. For a 1594 case involving a woman in labour for five days, her abnormal child adorned with jewellery, and a lengthy exposition of the birth by Johannes Cuno, see Soergel, 'The Afterlives of Monstrous Infants', pp. 307–8.
31. In the same decade, Andreas Engel devoted a short chapter to this phenomenon in his *WiderNatur und Wunderbuch*, pp. 202–4.
32. Walsham links these cases to a rise in similar prophetic activity by the elderly. See A. Walsham, *Providence in Early Modern England* (Oxford: Oxford University Press, 1999), p. 207, and on lay and youthful prophesying see pp. 207–18. See also A. Walsham, '"Out of the Mouths and Babes and Sucklings": Prophecy, Puritanism and Childhood in Elizabethan Suffolk', in D. Wood (ed.), *The Church and Childhood* (Oxford: Blackwell, 1994), pp. 285–99.
33. '[J]üngst tag waer vor der thür.' Lycosthenes, *Wunderzeichen*, p. cccclxxxvi.
34. On popular prophecy and lay preaching in Reformation Germany, see J. Beyer, 'Lutheran Lay Prophets, 1550–1700' (PhD dissertation, Cambridge University, 2002); J. Beyer, 'A Lübeck Prophet in Local and Lutheran Context', in R. Scribner and T. Johnson (eds), *Popular Religion in Germany and Central Europe, 1400–1800* (Basingstoke: Macmillan, 1996), pp. 166–82, pp. 264–72; and J. Beyer, 'Lutheran Popular Prophets in the Sixteenth and Seventeenth Century: The Performance of Untrained Speakers', *Arv: Nordic Yearbook of Folklore*, 51 (1995), pp. 63–86.
35. On territorial issues in this region, see G. Pálffy, 'The Origins and Development of the Border Defence System against the Ottoman Empire in Hungary (up to the Early Eighteenth Century)', in G. Dávid and P. Fodor (eds), *Ottomans, Hungarians and Habsburgs in Central Europe: The Military Confines in the Era of Ottoman Conquest* (Leiden: Brill, 2000), pp. 3–69.
36. The text for this case can be found at anon., *Zwo Warhafftige Newezeittung / Vnd gruendliche Geschicht ...* (Graz: n.p., 1593), sigs A i v.–A ii v.
37. Beyer, 'Lutheran Lay Prophets'; Beyer, 'A Lübeck Prophet in Local and Lutheran Context'; and Beyer, 'Lutheran Popular Prophets'.
38. 'Lieben Christen / steht ab von ewren suenden / vnd bekehret euch / dan[n] vnser lieber Vatter Jhesus Christus / hat mich her gesandt / ich soll euch warnen / er will euch schwerlich in kutzer zeit heimsuchen / mit schweren kranckheiten / Theurung / Krieg /

Auffruh / weil jr euch je nicht bekehren wolt / noch achtet der Wunderzeichen / die er euch taeglich zuschickt / vnd sehen lest.' Anon., *Zwo Warhafftige Newezeittung*, sig. Aii r.

39. '[D]er Vatter ... woll euch mit Wein / Getraeid / vnd allerley Fruecht auff dem Feldt / gnadenreich begaben'; 'wir lang der Welt noch stehn soll'. Ibid., sig. Aii r.
40. '[E]in leibliches Kindlein inn schneeweissen Kleidern.' P. Rinovius and P. Victorius, *Beschreibung und deutung der zweyen Mißgeburten / so Anno Christi 1580 12. Decembris nach Mittage / zwischen 7. vnd 8. uhrn zu Hauelberg inn der Marck / von einer Frawen geboren* (n.p., 1580); on the child see sig. E i v.
41. The text for this case can be found at anon., *Zwo Warhafftige Newezeittung*, sigs A iii r.–Aiiii r.
42. On this region, see R. Pörtner, *The Counter-Reformation in Central Europe: Styria 1580–1630* (Oxford: Clarendon Press, 2001).
43. Suns and moons pierced by swords, and sometimes bleeding, appear in other woodcuts of meteorological wonders. For a recent study of Revelation imagery in the early modern period, see Parshall, 'The Vision of the Apocalypse'.
44. '[G]leich auff die Tuerckisch manier.' Anon., *Zwo Warhafftige Newezeittung*, sig. A iii v.
45. 'Moerederey und Todtschlag'; 'wir haben gar kleine zeit'. Ibid., sigs A iii v.–A iiii r.
46. On popular Lutheran music, see R. W. Oettinger, *Music as Propaganda in the German Reformation* (Aldershot: Ashgate, 2001).
47. The text for this case can be found at anon., *Zwo warhafftige newe Zeitung. Die erste / so sich in newenmarckt Brandenburg begeben ...* (Erdfurt: Martin Wittel, 1597), sigs A i v.–A ij v.
48. On wonders in the German Counter-Reformation, see P. M. Soergel, *Wondrous in his Saints: Counter-Reformation Propaganda in Bavaria* (Berkeley, CA: University of California Press, 1993).
49. See B. Nischan, *Prince, People and Confession: The Second Reformation in Brandenburg* (Phildelphia, PA: University of Pennsylvania Press, 1994).
50. T. A. Brady, Jr, 'Settlements: the Holy Roman Empire', in T. A. Brady, Jr, H. A. Oberman and J. D. Tracy (eds), *Handbook of European History, 1400–1600*, 2 vols (Leiden: Brill, 1994–5), vol. 2, pp. 349–83; on the spread of Calvinism in German lands see pp. 355–8, and for this quotation see p. 355. See also H. Schilling (ed.), *Die Reformierte Konfessionalisierung in Deutschland – Das Problem der 'Zweiten Reformation'* (Gütersloh: Gütersloher Verlaghaus Gerd Mohn, 1986).
51. Nischan, *Prince, People and Confession*, pp. 46–9.
52. See B. Nischan, 'Ritual and Protestant Identity in Late Reformation Germany', in B. Gordon (ed.), *Protestant History and Identity in Sixteenth-Century Europe*, 2 vols (Aldershot: Scolar, 1996), vol. 2, pp. 142–58; and B. Nischan, 'The Exorcism Controversy and Baptism in the Late Reformation', *Sixteenth Century Journal*, 18 (1984), pp. 31–50.
53. The text for this case can be found at anon., *Zwo warhafftige newe Zeitung*, sigs A ij v.–A iij v. The fact that many monstrous births occurred in January is clearly significant, and may well be an inversion of the German tradition of the *Neujahrskind*: a representation of the Christ child that was specific to the new year period. On the *Neujahrskind*, see Heitz, *Neujahrswünsche*.
54. 'Kompt her zu mir spricht Gottes Sohn.' Anon., *Zwo warhafftige newe Zeitung*, title page.
55. '[W]underbarliche Sachen geredet und geprophecyt'. Ibid., title page.
56. Ibid., sig. A iij r.

57. See, for some examples, M. Dimmock and A. Hadfield (eds), *The Religion of the Book: Christian Perceptions, 1400–1660* (Houndmills: Palgrave Macmillan, 2008), and, in relation to the specific issue of monstrosity, see M. Dimmock, '"A Human Head to the Neck of a Horse": Hybridity, Monstrosity and Early Christian Conceptions of Muhammad and Islam', in ibid., pp. 66–88, esp. pp. 67, 83.
58. '[B]leckt gar heßlich seine Zaehn.' Anon., *Zwo warhafftige newe Zeitung*, sig. A iij r.
59. Ibid, sig. A iij r.
60. 'Ach wer will doch die todten Leuth / die sterben werden in kurtzer zeit / vergraben in die Erden'. Ibid, sig. A iij r.
61. On this iconography, see Harms and Schilling (eds), *Deutsche illustrierte Flugblätter*, vol. 7, pp. 10–11; and Olsen, *Matthias Flacius and the Survival of Luther's Reform*, pp. 176–83, 213–14.
62. J. Praetorius, *Dreykoepffichter Antichrist / Darinnen des Bapstes Grewel / der Tuerckische Alcoran / vnd der Calvinistischen Lesterschwarm / Allen frommen Gotteskindern zu Trost vnd Warnung abgebildet vnnd widerleget wird* (n.p., 1592). See sig. A iiij v. for the woodcut illustration. The text is framed in terms of the coming of the Last Days and the most lengthy and vitriolic attack is reserved for Calvinism.
63. The terrible birth scenes that draw mothers of monstrous births into increasingly complex narratives and explanatory texts, for example, seem to draw on the polemical iconography of the whore of Babylon and the woman clothed with the sun from the Book of Revelation that had been current earlier in the century.

WORKS CITED

Primary Sources

Anon., *Journal d'un bourgeois de Paris, 1405–1449*, ed. A. Tuetey (Paris: H. Champion, 1881).

—, *Eyn. soelich kint ist geboren ein meil von W[o]rms* ... (Erfurt: Hans Sporer, 1500).

—, *Wunderbarliche geburt vff So[n]tag Jubilate* ... (n.p., [1511]).

—, *Zu wissen. Ein wunderlichs vn[d] erschrockenlich ding* ... (n.p., 1511).

—, *Anno domini Millesimo quingetesimo duodecimo* ... (n.p., 1512).

—, *Im iar als man zalt tausent fünff hundertvnd zwolften ist geboren ain solichs kind* ... (n.p., 1512).

—, *Disz künd ist geboren worden zu Tettnang* ... (n.p., 1516).

—, *Dis wunderlich Thier hat man auß einer Kuehe geno[m]men* ... (n.p., 1522).

—, *Als Man zelt. xv hundert. xxiij iar* ... (n.p., 1523).

—, *Warhafftige Contrafactur vnd gestalt von der Junckfrawen zuo Esslingen Mit dem gemachten Bauch*... (n.p., [*c*. 1550–1]).

—, *Der Suiten / welche sich Jesuiten nennen* ... (n.p., 1568).

—, *Lutherus Triumphans* (n.p., [*c*. 1568]).

—, *Newe Zeyttung. Eine erschreckliche Mißgeburt* ... (Nümberg: Matthias Rauch, 1578).

—, *Warhaftige vnd schroeckliche bildnuß vnd gestalt zwoern neuer leydigen vngewonlichen Mißgeburt* ... (Strasbourg: n.p., 1578).

—, *Diese Himlische Zeichen sind geschehen worden in Ungern* ... (Coelln: Niclas Schreiber, 1593).

—, *Zwo Warhafftige Newezeittung / Vnd gruendliche Geschicht*... (Graz: n.p., 1593).

—, *Zwo warhafftige newe Zeitung. Die erste / so sich in newenmarckt Brandenburg begeben* ... (Erdfurt: Martin Wittel, 1597).

Augustine, *The City of God Against the Pagans*, ed. and trans. R. W. Dyson (Cambridge: Cambridge University Press, 1998).

Biglin (?), *Elsbeth / Elisabethen* (n.p., 1512).

Brant, S., *De Monstruoso partu apud Wormacium* (Basel: J. Bergmann von Olpe, 1495).

—, *Von der Wunderbaren geburt des Kindes bei Wormß* (Augsburg: Johann Schoensperger, 1495).

—, *An den grosmechstigsten aller durchlichtigsten herren Maximilianu[s] ... Von der wuderbaren Su zuo Landser* (n.p., 1496).

—, *Fabeln*, ed. and trans. B. Schneider (Stuttgart-Bad Cannstatt: Frommann-Holzboog, 1999).

Cicero, *De Senectutue, de Amicitia, de Divinatione*, trans. W. A. Falconer (London: William Heinemann, 1964).

[Dürer, A.], *Dürer. Schriftlicher Nachlass*, ed. H. Rupprich, 3 vols (Berlin: Deutscher Verlag für Kunstwissenschaft, 1969).

Engel, A., *WiderNatur und Wunderbuch* (Franckfurt am Mayn: Brachfeld, 1597).

Fincel, J., *Wunderzeichen mit figuren* (Leipzig: Jacob Bärwald, 1557).

—, *Der ander teil Wunderzeichen* (Franckfurt am Mayn: Thomam Rebart, 1566).

—, *Wunderzeiche[n]. Warhafftige Beschreibung vnd gruendlich verzeichnus schrecklicher Wunderzeichen vnd geschichten* (Franckfurt am Mayn: Thomam Rebart, 1566).

—, *Der dritte theil Wunderzeychen* (Franckfurt am Mayn: Weygand Hanen Erben, 1567).

Gesta Romanorum, trans. C. Swan, pref. E. A. Baker (London: George Routledge and Sons, 1905).

Goldwurm, C., *Wunderwerck und Wunderzeichen Buch* (Franckfurt am Main: Zephelius, 1557).

Grünpeck, J., 'Prodigiorum, ostentorum et monstrorum quae in saeculum Maximilianeum inciderunt, interpretatio' (1501), Universitäts- und Landesbibliothek für Tirol, Cod. 314.

Hese, J. de, *Itinerarius* ([Köln]: [Zierickzee], [*c.* 1500]).

Irenaeus, C., *De monstris. Von seltzamen Wundergeburten* (Ursel: Henricus, 1584).

Lichtenberger, J., *Die Weissagunge Johannis Lichtenbergers deudsch / zugericht mit vleys. Sampt einer nutzlichen vorrede vnd vunterricht D. Martini Luthers / wie man die selbige vnd der gleichen weissagunge vernemen sol* (Wittenberg: Hans Lufft, 1527).

Livy, *Summaries, Fragments, and Obsequens, vol. 14*, trans. A. C. Schlesinger (Cambridge, MA: Harvard University Press, 1959).

Luther, M., 'Preface to the Revelation of St. John [I]' (1522), in Luther, *Works*, vol. 35, pp. 398–9.

—, 'Preface to the Revelation of St. John [II]' (1546; 1530), reprinted in Luther, *Works*, vol. 35, p. 400.

—, *Der ander Teil aller Bücher vnd Schriften des thewren, seligen Mans Doct. Mart. Lutheri* (Jena: Rödinger, 1555).

—, *Chronica deudsch* (Wittenberg: Hans Lufft, 1559).

—, *D. Martin Luthers Werke. Kritische Gesamtausgabe*, 72 vols (Weimar: Böhlau, 1884–2007).

—, *Works*, 55 vols (Saint Louis, MO: Concordia Publishing House, 1955–86).

Lycosthenes, K., *Prodigiorum ac ostentorum chronicon* (Basilae: Henricum Petri, 1557).

—, *Wunderwerck Oder Gottes vnergrundtliches vorbildren ... mit grossem fleiß / durch Johann Herold / vffs treüwlichst inn vier Buecher gezogen vnnd verteütscht* (Basel: Henrichum Petri, 1557).

[Mandeville, J.], *Sir John Mandevilles Reisebeschreibung. In deutscher Übersetzung von Michel Velser. Nach der Stuttgarter Papierhandschrift Cod. HB V 86*, ed. E. J. Morrall (Berlin: Akademie-Verlag, 1974).

—, *Jean de Mandeville. Reisen. Reprint der Erstdrucke der deutschen Übersetzungen des Michel Velser (Augsburg, bei Anton Sorg, 1480) und des Otto von Diemeringen (Basel, bei Bernhard Richel, 1480/81)*, ed. E. Bremer and K. Ridder (Hildesheim: Georg Olms, 1991).

—, *Jean de Mandeville. Reisebeschreibung. Übertragen aus dem Französichen von Otto von Diemeringen. Der Antichrist und der fünfzehn Zeichen vor dem Jungsten Gericht. Wien, Österreichische Nationalbibliothek, Codex 2838*, microfiche edn, commentary K. Ridder (Munich: Edition Helga Lengenfelder, 1992).

Melanchthon, P., *Der BapstEsel / durch M. Philippum Melanchthon gedeutet und gebessert* (Wittenberg: Schirlentz, 1535).

Melanchthon, P., and M. Luther, *Deuttung der czwo grewlichen Figuren, Bapstesels czu Rom und Munchkalbs zu Freijberg ijnn Meijszen funden* (Wittenberg: Johann Grunenberg, 1523).

—, *Deuttung der zwo grewlichen figuren Bapstesels zu Freyburg in Meyssen funden, mit anzaygu[n]g des jungstentags* (Wittenberg: n.p., 1523).

Melanchthon, P., M. Flacius Illyricus and M. Luther, *Ein grausame Meerwunder / den Bapst bedeutende / zu Rome gefunden / vnd zu Wittenberg erstlich Anno 23. uvd darnach abermal Anno 46. mit der ausleguug Philippi gedruckt / mit einer Vorrede Matthiae Flacij Illyrici* (Magdeburg: Rödinger, 1549).

Mennel, J., 'De signis, portentis atque prodigiis' (1503), Oesterreichische Nationalbibliothek, Cod. Vindobana 4417*.

Münster, S., *Cosmographei* (Basel: Henrichum Petri, 1550).

Murner, T., *Invetiua contra Astrologos* ([Strasbourg]: [Hüpfuff], 1499).

Nas, J., *Das Antipapistisch eins vnd hundert* (Ingolstadt: Alexander Weissenhorn, 1568).

—, *Secvnda Centvria* (Ingolstadt: Alexander Weissenhorn, 1568).

—, *Ecclesia Militans* (Ingolstadt: Alexander Weissenhorn, 1569).

—, *Tertia Centvria* (Ingolstadt: Alexander Weissenhorn, 1569).

—, *Sextae Centvriae* (Ingolstadt: Alexander Weissenhorn, 1569).

—, *Qvarta Centvria* (Ingolstadt: Alexander Weissenhorn, 1570).

—, *Qvinta Centvria* (Ingolstadt: Alexander Weissenhorn, 1570).

—, *Widereinwarnung / An alle from[m]e Teutsche[n]* (Ingolstadt: Alexander Weyssenhorn, 1577).

Nausea, F., *Libri Mirabilium Septem* (Coloniae: Petrem Quentell, 1532).

Nigrinus, G., *Von Bruder Johan Nasen Esel vnd seinem rechtem Tittel, F.I.N.S.A.C. oder F.I.N.S.C.E.* ([Oberursel]: [Henricus], [*c.* 1570]).

Obsequens, J., *Prodigiorum liber*, ed. K. Lycosthenes (Basel: Oporinus, 1552).

Pauli, S., *Bildnis vnnd Gestalt einer erschrecklichen vnnatuerlichen vnd vngewoenlichen Geburt / eines Kindes / welches Anno 1577. den 20. Decembris zu Greuesmuelen im Land zu Meckelnburg / von eines Schneiders / M. B. ehelichen hausfrauwen/ geboren ist* (Rostock: Jacobus Lucius, 1578).

—, *Bildtnuß vnd Gestalt einer erschrecklichen ... Geburt* (n.p., 1578).

—, *Bildnis und Gestalt einer erschrecklichen unnatürlichen und ungewöhnlichen Geburdt eines Kindlins / welches Anno 1578. den 15. Decembris zu Rostock geboren ist* (Rostock: Ferber, 1579).

Pliny, *Natural History*, trans. H. Rackham (London: William Heinman; Cambridge, MA: Harvard University Press, 1938).

Praetorius, J., *Dreykoepffichter Antichrist / Darinnen des Bapstes Grewel / der Tuerckische Alcoran / vnd der Calvinistischen Lesterschwarm / Allen frommen Gotteskindern zu Trost vnd Warnung abgebildet vnnd widerleget wird* (n.p., 1592).

Rinovius, P., and P. Victorius, *Beschreibung und deutung der zweyen Mißgeburten / so Anno Christi 1580 12. Decembris nach Mittage / zwischen 7. vnd 8. uhrn zu Hauelberg inn der Marck / von einer Frawen geboren* (n.p., 1580).

Rößlin, E., *Der swangern Frauwen vnd Hebamen Rosegarten* (Argentine: Martinus Flach, 1513).

Rueff, J., *De Conceptv et Generatione Hominis* (Tigvri: Christophorvs Frosch, 1554).

—, *Ein schön lustig Trostbüchle von den empfenknussen und geburten der menschen* (Zürich: Christoph Froschauer, 1554).

[Rueff, J.] 'I.R.', *Anno a Christo nato 1543. sexto Februarij ...* (Tiguri: Eustachium Froschouerum, 1543).

Schedel, H., *Chronicle of the World* [facsimile of the 1493 *Weltchronik*], intro. and appendix S. Füssel (Cologne: Taschen, 2001).

Schenck, J. G., *Wunder-Buch von menschlichen unerhörten Wunder und Mißgeburten* (Franckfort: von Bry, 1610).

Vesalius, A., *De humani corporis fabrica libri septem* (Basel: Joannis Oporini, 1543).

Von Megenberg, K., *Hie nach volgt das buch der Natur* (Augsburg: Schönsperger, 1499).

Weyer, J., *Witches, Devils and Doctors in the Renaissance*, trans. J. Shea [translation of *De praestigiis daemonum*] (Binghampton, NY: -Medieval and Renaissance Texts and Studies, 1991).

Secondary Sources

Allgemeine Deutsche Biographie, 56 vols (1875–1912), facs edn (Berlin: Duncker and Humblot, 1967–71).

Anderson, R. R., U. Goebel and O. Reichmann (eds), *Frühneuhochdeutsches Wörterbuch*, 11 vols– (Berlin: Walter de Gruter 1986–).

Anzelewsky, F., *Albrecht Dürer. Das malerische Werk* (Berlin: Deutscher Verlag für Kunstwissenschaft, 1971).

—, 'Dürers "aesthetiker Exkurse" in seiner Proportionslehre', in F. Mielke (ed.), *Kaleidoskop. Ein Festschrift für Fritz Baumgart zum 75. Geburtstag* (Berlin: Gebr. Mann, 1977), pp. 70–8.

Ausstellung Maximilian I. Innsbruck, exhibition catalogue (Innsbruck: Verlagsanstalt Tyrolia, 1969).

Backus, I., *Reformation Readings of the Apocalypse: Geneva, Zurich, Wittenberg* (Oxford: Oxford University Press, 2000).

Barnes, R. B., *Prophecy and Gnosis: Apocalypticism in the Wake of the Lutheran Reformation* (Stanford, CA: Stanford University Press, 1988).

Bartrum, G., *Albrecht Dürer and his Legacy: The Graphic Work of a Renaissance Artist*, exhibition catalogue (London: British Museum Press, 2002), pp. 112–13.

Bates, A. W., *Emblematic Monsters: Unnatural Conceptions and Deformed Births in Early Modern Europe* (Amsterdam: Rodopi, 2005).

—, 'Good, Common, Regular, and Orderly: Early Modern Classifications of Monstrous Births', *Social History of Medicine*, 18:2 (2005), pp. 141–58.

Benesch, O., *The Art of the Renaissance in Northern Europe*, revised edn (London: Phaidon, 1965).

Bennett, J. W., *The Rediscovery of Sir John Mandeville* (New York: Modern Language Association of America, 1954).

Bergmann, R., 'A "tröstlich picture": Luther's Attitude in the Question of Images', *Renaissance and Reformation/Renaissance et Réforme*, 5 (1981), pp. 15–25.

Beyer, J., 'Lutheran Popular Prophets in the Sixteenth and Seventeenth Century: The Performance of Untrained Speakers', *Arv: Nordic Yearbook of Folklore*, 51 (1995), pp. 63–86.

—, 'A Lübeck Prophet in Local and Lutheran Context', in R. Scribner and T. Johnson (eds), *Popular Religion in Germany and Central Europe, 1400–1800* (Basingstoke: Macmillan, 1996), pp. 166–82, pp. 264–72.

—, 'Lutheran Lay Prophets, 1550–1700' (PhD dissertation, Cambridge University, 2002).

Bloch, R., *Les Prodiges dans l'Antiquité Classique* (Paris: Presses Universitaire de France, 1963).

Brady, T. A., Jr, 'Settlements: The Holy Roman Empire', in T. A. Brady, Jr, H. A. Oberman and J. D. Tracy (eds), *Handbook of European History, 1400–1600*, 2 vols (Leiden: Brill, 1994–5), vol. 2, pp. 349–83.

Brodrick, J., *Petrus Canisius 1521–1597*, trans. K. Telch, 2 vols (Wien: Verlag Herder, 1950).

Brooks, P. N. (ed.), *Seven-Headed Luther: Essays in Commemoration of a Quincentenary 1483–1983* (Oxford: Clarendon Press, 1983).

Burckhardt, A., *Johannes Basilius Herold. Kaiser und Reich im protestantichen Schrifttum des Basler Buchdrucks um die Mitte des 16. Jahrhunderts* (Basel and Stuttgart: Verlag von Helbing und Leichtenhahn, 1967).

[Burgkmair, H.], *Hans Burgkmair 1473–1973. Das graphische Werk*, exhibition catalogue (Augsburg: Städtische Kunstsammlungen, 1973).

Burke, P., 'Unity and Variety in Cultural History', in P. Burke, *Varieties of Cultural History* (Cambridge: Polity Press, 1997), pp. 183–212.

—, *What is Cultural History?* (Cambridge: Polity Press, 2004).

Burns, W. E., *An Age of Wonders: Prodigies, Politics and Providence in England 1657–1727* (Manchester: Manchester University Press, 2002).

Burschel, P., 'Das Monster. Katholische Luther-Imagination im 16. Jahrhundert', in H. Medick and P. Schmidt (eds), *Luther zwischen den Kulturen. Zeitgenossenschaft – Weltwirkung* (Göttingen: Vandenhoeck and Ruprecht, 2004), pp. 33–48.

Bynum, C. W., *Metamorphosis and Identity* (New York: Zone Books, 2001).

Cadden, J., *Meanings of Sex Difference in the Middle Ages: Medicine, Science and Culture* (Cambridge: Cambridge University Press, 1993).

Carey, F. (ed.), *The Apocalypse and the Shape of Things to Come*, exhibition catalogue (London: British Museum Press, 1999).

Carl, H., *Der Schwäbische Bund 1488–1534* (Leinfelden-Echterdingen: DRW-Verlag, 2000).

Céard, J., *La Nature et les prodiges: L'Insolite au XVIe siècle, en France*, 2nd edn (Geneva: E. Droz, 1996).

Chartier, R., 'Texts, Printing, Readings', in L. Hunt (ed.), *The New Cultural History* (Berkeley, CA: University of California Press, 1989), pp. 154–75.

Christensen, C. C., *Art and the Reformation in Germany* (Columbus, OH: Ohio University Press, 1979).

Clark, S., *Thinking with Demons: the Idea of Witchcraft in Early Modern Europe* (Oxford: Clarendon Press, 1997).

Conway, W. M., *Literary Remains of Albrecht Dürer* (Cambridge: Cambridge University Press, 1889).

Crawford, J., *Marvelous Protestantism: Monstrous Births in Post-Reformation England* (Baltimore, MD, and London: Johns Hopkins University Press, 2005).

Crowther-Heyck, K., '"Be Fruitful and Multiply": Genesis and Generation in Reformation Germany', *Renaissance Quarterly*, 55 (2002), pp. 904–35.

Czerny, A., 'Der Humanist und Historiograph Kaiser Maximilians I. Joseph Grünpeck', *Archiv für österreichische Geschichte*, 73 (1888), pp. 315–64.

Daston, L., and K. Park, 'Unnatural Conceptions: The Study of Monsters in Sixteenth- and Seventeenth-Century France and England', *Past and Present*, 92 (1981), pp. 20–54.

—, *Wonders and the Order of Nature 1150–1750* (New York: Zone Books, 1998).

Debus, A. G., *Man and Nature in the Renaissance* (Cambridge: Cambridge University Press, 1978).

Debus, A. G., and M. T. Walton (eds), *Reading the Book of Nature: The Other Side of the Scientific Revolution* (Kirksville, MO: Sixteenth Century Journal Publishers, 1998).

Delumeau, J., *La Peur en Occident (XIVe–XVIII siècles)* (Paris: Fayard, 1987).

Diables et diableries. La représentation du diable dans la gravure des XVe et XVIe siècles, exhibition catalogue (Geneva: Cabinet des estampes, 1976).

Dimmock, M., '"A Human Head to the Neck of a Horse": Hybridity, Monstrosity and Early Christian Conceptions of Muhammad and Islam', in Dimmock and Hadfield (eds), *The Religion of the Book*, pp. 66–88.

Dimmock, M., and A. Hadfield (eds), *The Religion of the Book: Christian Perceptions, 1400–1660* (Houndmills: Palgrave Macmillan, 2008).

Duhr, B., *Die Jesuiten und den deutschen Fürsthöfen des 16. Jahrhunderts* (Freiburg im Breisgau: Herdersche Verlagshandlung, 1901).

Durling, R. J., 'A Chronological Census of Renaissance Editions and Translations of Galen', *Journal of the Warburg and Courtauld Institutes*, 24 (1961), pp. 230–305.

Edwards, M. U., Jr, *Luther's Last Battles: Politics and Polemics, 1531–46* (Ithaca, NY: Cornell University Press, 1983).

—, *Printing, Propaganda, and Martin Luther* (Berkeley, CA: University of California Press, 1994).

Eichberger, D., '*Naturalia* and *artefacta*: Dürer's Nature Drawings and Early Collecting', in Eichberger and Zika (eds), *Dürer and his Culture*, pp. 13–37.

Eichberger, D., and C. Zika (eds), *Dürer and his Culture* (Cambridge: Cambridge University Press, 1998).

Eichenberger, W., and H. Wendland, *Deutsche Bibeln vor Luther. Die Buchkunst der achtzehn deutschen Bibeln zwischen 1466 und 1522* (Hamburg: Friedrich Wittig Verlag, 1977).

Eisler, C., *Dürer's Animals* (Washington, DC: Smithsonian Institution Press, 1991).

Ewinkel, I., *De monstris: Deutung und Funktion von Wundergeburten auf Flugblättern im Deutschland des 16. Jahrhunderts* (Tübingen: Max Niemeyer Verlag, 1995).

Faust, I., *Zoologische Einblattdrucke und Flugschriften vor 1800*, 5 vols (Stuttgart: Anton Hiersemann, 1998–2003).

Findlen, P., *Possessing Nature: Museums, Collecting, and Scientific Culture in Early Modern Italy* (Berkeley, CA: University of California Press, 1994).

—, 'Inventing Nature: Commerce, Art, and Science in the Early Modern Cabinet of Curiosities', in Smith and Findlen (eds), *Merchants and Marvels*, pp. 297–323.

—, 'Natural History', in Park and Daston (eds), *The Cambridge History of Science. Volume 3*, pp. 437–68.

Fraenger, W., *Altdeutsches Bilderbuch. Hans Weidiz und Sebastian Brant* (Leipzig: Stubenrauch, 1930).

Freedberg, D., *The Power of Images: Studies in the History and Theory of Response* (Chicago, IL: Chicago University Press, 1989).

Friedman, J. B., *The Monstrous Races in Medieval Art and Thought* (Cambridge, MA: Harvard University Press, 1981).

Geisberg, M., *The German Single-Leaf Woodcut: 1500–1550,* rev. and ed. W. L. Strauss, 4 vols (New York: Hacker Art Books, 1974).

Gilbert, R., *Early Modern Hermaphrodites: Sex and Other Stories* (Houndsmills: Palgrave, 2002).

Ginzburg, C., *Clues, Myths, and the Historical Method*, trans. J. and A. C. Tedeschi (Baltimore, MD: Johns Hopkins University Press, 1989).

—, 'From Aby Warburg to E. H. Gombrich: A Problem of Method', in Ginzburg, *Clues, Myths, and the Historical Method*, pp. 17–59.

—, 'The High and the Low: the Theme of Forbidden Knowledge in the Sixteenth and Seventeenth Centuries', in *Clues, Myths, and the Historical Method*, pp. 60–76.

Gordon, B., 'God Killed Saul: Heinrich Bullinger and Jacob Ruef on the Power of the Devil', in K. A. Edwards (ed.), *Werewolves, Witches and Wandering Spirits: Traditional Belief and Folklore in Early Modern Europe* (Kirksville, MO: Truman State University Press, 2002), pp. 155–79.

—, *The Swiss Reformation* (Manchester: Manchester University Press, 2002).

Gothein, E., *Reformation und Gegenreformation*, 2 vols (Munich: Duncker and Humblot, 1924).

Grimm, J., and W. Grimm, *Deutsches Wörterbuch*, 16 vols (Leipzig: S. Hirzel, 1854–1960).

Grössinger, C., *Humour and Folly in Secular and Profane Prints of Northern Europe 1430–1540* (London: Harvey Miller Publishers, 2002).

Hanafi, Z., *The Monster in the Machine: Magic, Medicine and the Marvellous in the Time of the Scientific Revolution* (Durham, NC: Duke University Press, 2000).

Harbison, C., *The Art of the Northern Renaissance* (London: Everyman Art Library, 1995).

Harms, W., and M. Schilling (eds), *Deutsche illustrierte Flugblätter des 16. und 17. Jahrhunderts*, 7 vols (Tübingen: M. Niemeyer, 1980–2005).

Hartung, F., 'Imperial Reform, 1485–1495: Its Course and Its Character', in G. Strauss (ed.), *Pre-Reformation Germany* (London: Macmillan, 1972), pp. 73–135.

Healy, J. F., *Pliny the Elder on Science and Technology* (Oxford: Oxford University Press, 1999).

Heitz, P., *Neujahrswünsche des XV. Jahrhunderts* (Strassburg: Heitz, 1900).

— (ed.), *Flugblätter des Sebastian Brant, mit einen Nachwort von Professor Dr. F. Schultz* (Strassburg: Heitz und Mündell, 1915).

Hernad, B., *Die Graphiksammlung des Humanisten Hartmann Schedel*, exhibition catalogue (Munich: Prestel-Verlag, 1990).

Hirn, J., *Erzherzog Ferdinand II von Tirol. Geschichte seiner Regierung und seiner Länder*, 2 vols (Innsbruck: Verlag der Wagner'schen Universitäts-Buchhandlung, 1885–8).

Hofmann, H.-U., *Luther und die Johannes-Apokalypse* (Tübingen: J. C. B. Mohr, 1982).

Hofmann-Randall, C., *Monster, Wunder und Kometen. Sensationsberichte auf Flugblättern des 16. bis 18. Jahrhunderts* (Erlangen: Universitätsbibliothek, 1999).

—, *Die Einblattdrucke der Universitätsbibliothek Erlangen-Nürnberg* (Erlangen: Universitätsbibliothek, 2003).

Holländer, E., *Wunder Wundergeburt und Wundergestalt in Einblattdrucken des fünfzehnten bis achzehnten Jahrhunderts* (Stuttgart: Ferdinand Enke, 1921).

Hollegger, M., *Maximilian I (1459–1519). Herrscher und Mensch eine Zeitenwende* (Stuttgart: Verlag W. Kohlhammer, 2005).

Hollstein, F. W. H. (ed.), *German Engravings, Etchings and Woodcuts ca. 1400–1700*, 62 vols (Amsterdam: Menno Hertzberger, 1954–95; Rotterdam: Sound and Vision Interactive, 1996–).

Honemann, V., et al. (eds), *Einblattdrucke des 15. und frühen 16. Jahrhunderts. Probleme, Perspective, Fallstudien* (Tübingen: Max Niemeyer, 2000).

Hsia, R. P., 'A Time for Monsters: Monstrous Births, Propaganda, and the German Reformation', in L. L. Knoppers and J. B. Landes (eds), *Monstrous Bodies / Political Monstrosities in Early Modern Europe* (Ithaca, NY: Cornell University Press, 2004), pp. 67–92

—, *The World of Catholic Renewal 1540–1770*, 2nd edn (Cambridge: Cambridge University Press, 2005).

Huant, E., *Otton III: La merveille du monde* (Paris: Édition P. Téqui, 1971).

Jahn, J., *Lucas Cranach d.Ä. 1472–1553. Das gesamte graphische Werk* (Berlin: Rogner und Bernhard, 1972).

Jones-Davies, M. T. (ed.), *Monstres et Prodiges au Temps de la Renaissance* (Paris: Jean Touzot, 1980).

Joy, L. S., 'Scientific Explanation from Formal Causes to Laws of Nature', in Park and Daston (eds), *The Cambridge History of Science. Volume 3*, pp. 70–105.

Kappler, C., 'L'interpretation politique du monstre chez Sébastien Brant', in Jones-Davies (ed.), *Monstres et Prodiges*, pp. 100–10.

Karant-Nunn, S. C., 'Changing One's Mind: Transformations in Reformation History from a Germanist's Perspective', *Renaissance Quarterly*, 58 (2005), pp. 1101–27.

Kaufmann, T., *Konfession und Kultur. Lutherischer Protestantismus in der zweiten Hälfte des Reformationsjahrhunderts* (Tübingen: Mohr Siebeck, 2006).

Kaulbach, H.-M., *Deutsche Zeichnungen vom Mittelalter bis zum Barock* (Stuttgart: Graphische Sammlung Staatsgalerie Stuttgart, 2007).

Keller, H. E. (ed.), *Jakob Ruf, ein Zürcher Stadtchirurg und Theatermacher im 16. Jahrhundert* (Zurich: Chronos, 2006).

Kennel, P., 'Joseph Grünpeck. Prodigiorum interpretation. Edition der Handschrift 314 der Universitätsbibliothek Innsbruck' (Diplomarbeit, Leopold-Franzens Univerität Innsbruck, 2001).

Killy, W. (ed.), *Literaturlexikon: Autoren und Werke deutscher Sprache*, 15 vols (Gütersloh: Bertelsmann-Lexikon-Verlag, 1988–93).

Kirschbaum, E. (ed.), *Lexikon der Christlichen Ikonographie*, 8 vols (1970; Freiburg im Breisgau: Herder, 1994).

Klibansky, R., E. Panofsky and F. Saxl, *Saturn and Melancholy. Studies in the History of Natural Philosophy, Religion and Art* (London: Thomas Nelson, 1964).

Koegler, H., 'Das Mönchskalb vor Papst Hadrian und das Wiener Prognostikon. Zwei wiedergefundene Flugblätter aus der Presse des Pamphilius Gengenbach in Basel', *Zeitschrift für Bücherfreunde*, 11 (1907), pp. 411–16.

Koelbing, H. M., 'Einführung zu Jakob Reuffs "Trostbüchle"', in J. Rueff, *Ein schön lustig Trostbüchle von den empfenknussen und geburten der menschen* (1554), facs edn, 2 vols (Zurich: Verlag Bibliophile Drucke von Josef Stocker, 1980), vol. 1, pp. 5–7.

—, '"De conceptu et generatione hominis": die lateinische Fassung von Jakob Rueffs "Trostbüchle", Zürich 1554', *Gesnerus*, 38 (1981), pp. 51–8.

Koerner, J. L., *The Moment of Self-Portraiture in German Renaissance Art* (Chicago, IL: Chicago University Press, 1993).

Köhler, H.-J. (ed.), *Flugschriften als Massenmedium der Reformationzeit* (Stuttgart: Ernst Klett Verlag, 1981).

Koreny, F., *Albrecht Dürer und die Tier- und Pflanzstudien der Renaissance*, exhibition catalogue (Munich: Prestel Verlag, 1985).

Kroll, R., and W. Schade, *Hans Burgkmair 1473–1531. Holzschnitte, Zeichnungen, Holzstöcke*, exhibition catalogue (Berlin: Staatlichen Museen zu Berlin, 1974).

Kuhn, C. L., *German and Netherlandish Sculpture 1280–1800: The Harvard Collections* (Cambridge, MA: Harvard University Press, 1965).

Kurze, D., 'Johann Lichtenberger. Leben und Werke eines spätmittelalterlichen Propheten und Astrologen', *Archiv für Kulturgeschichte*, 38 (1956), pp. 328–43.

—, 'Prophecy and History: Lichtenberger's Forecasts of Events to Come (from the Fifteenth to the Twentieth Century); their Reception and Diffusion', *Journal of the Warburg and Courtauld Institutes*, 21 (1958), pp. 63–85.

Kusukawa, S., *The Transformation of Natural Philosophy: The Case of Philip Melanchthon* (Cambridge: Cambridge University Press, 1995).

Landau, D., and P. Parshall, *The Renaissance Print 1470–1550* (New Haven, CT: Yale University Press, 1994).

Lange, K., *Der Papstesel. Ein Beitrag zur Kultur- und Kunstgeschichte des Reformationszeitalters* (Göttingen: Vandenhoeck and Ruprecht's Verlag, 1891).

Leppin, V., *Antichrist und Jüngster Tag. Das Profil apokalyptischer Flugschriftenpublizistik im deutschen Luthertum 1548–1618* (Gütersloh: Gütersloher Verlaghaus, 1999).

Lhotsky, A., 'Dr. Jakob Mennel. Ein Vorarlberger im Kreise Kaiser Maximilian I', *Alemannia. Zeitschrift für Geschichte, Heimat- und Volkskunde Vorarlbergs* (1936), pp. 1–15.

Littger, K. W., 'Elßgred. Flugblätter einer Mißgeburt', *Gutenberg-Jahrbuch* (2003), pp. 74–85.

Long, P. O., 'Objects of Art / Objects of Nature: Visual Representation and the Investigation of Nature', in Smith and Findlen (eds), *Merchants and Marvels*, pp. 63–82.

Lukasser, H., 'Die Centurien des Johannes Nas. Ihre Waurzeln und Formen. Ein Beitrag zur Prosa des 16. Jahrhunderts' (PhD dissertation, University of Innsbruck, 1952).

McDonald, M. P., 'Burgkmair's Woodcut Frieze of *Natives of Africa and India*', *Print Quarterly*, 20 (2003), pp. 227–44.

Margolin, J.-C., 'Sur quelques prodiges rapportés par Conrad Lycosthenes', in Jones-Davies (ed.), *Monstres et Prodiges*, pp. 42–54.

Martin, P., *Martin Luther und die Bilder zur Apokalypse* (Hamburg: Friedrich Wittig Verlag, 1983).

Massing, J.-M., 'Dürer's Dreams', *Journal of the Warburg and Courtauld Institutes*, 49 (1986), pp. 238–44.

Matheson, P., *The Rhetoric of the Reformation* (Edinburgh: T. and T. Clark, 1998).

Mellinkoff, R., *The Devil at Isenheim: Reflections of Popular Belief in Grünewald's Altarpiece* (Berkeley, CA: University of California Press, 1988).

Midelfort, H. C. E., *A History of Madness in Sixteenth-Century Germany* (Stanford, CA: Stanford University Press, 1999).

Moeller, B., 'Was wurde in der Frühzeit der Reformation in den deutschen Städten gepredigt?', *Archiv für Reformationsgeshichte*, 75 (1984), pp. 176–93.

Moxey, K., *Peasants, Warriors and Wives: Popular Imagery in the Reformation* (Chicago, IL: University of Chicago Press, 1989).

Niccoli, O., *Prophecy and People in Renaissance Italy*, trans. L. G. Cochrane (Princeton, NJ: Princeton University Press, 1990).

Nischan, B., 'The Exorcism Controversy and Baptism in the Late Reformation', *Sixteenth Century Journal*, 18 (1984), pp. 31–50.

—, *Prince, People and Confession: The Second Reformation in Brandenburg* (Philadelphia, PA: University of Pennsylvania Press, 1994).

—, 'Ritual and Protestant Identity in Late Reformation Germany', in B. Gordon (ed.), *Protestant History and Identity in Sixteenth-Century Europe*, 2 vols (Aldershot: Scolar, 1996), vol. 2, pp. 142–58.

Nutton, V., 'The Anatomy of the Soul in Early Renaissance Medicine', in G. R. Dunstan (ed.), *The Human Embryo: Aristotle and the Arabic and European Traditions* (Exeter: University of Exeter Press, 1990), pp. 136–57.

Oelke, H., *Die Konfessionsbildung des 16. Jahrhunderts im Spiegel illustrierter Flugblätter* (Berlin: Walter de Gruyter, 1992).

—, 'Konfessionelle Bildpropaganda des späten 16. Jahrhunderts: Die Nas-Fischart-Kontroverse 1568/71', *Archiv für Reformationsgeschichte/Archive for Reformation History*, 87 (1996), pp. 149–200.

Oettinger, R. W., *Music as Propaganda in the German Reformation* (Aldershot: Ashgate, 2001).

Olsen, O. K., *Matthias Flacius and the Survival of Luther's Reform* (Wiesbaden: Harrassowitz Verlag, 2002).

Ozment, S., *When Fathers Ruled: Family Life in Reformation Europe* (Cambridge, MA: Harvard University Press, 1983).

Pálffy, G., 'The Origins and Development of the Border Defence System against the Ottoman Empire in Hungary (up to the Early Eighteenth Century)', in G. Dávid and P. Fodor (eds), *Ottomans, Hungarians and Habsburgs in Central Europe: The Military Confines in the Era of Ottoman Conquest* (Leiden: Brill, 2000), pp. 3–69.

Panofsky, E., *The Life and Art of Albrecht Dürer*, revised edn, intro. J. C. Smith (Princeton, NJ: Princeton University Press, 2005).

Park, K., and L. Daston (eds), *The Cambridge History of Science. Volume 3. Early Modern Science* (Cambridge: Cambridge University Press, 2006).

Parshall, P., 'Imago contrafacta: Images and Facts in the Northern Renaissance', *Art History*, 16 (1993), pp. 554–79.

—, 'The Vision of the Apocalypse in the Sixteenth and Seventeenth Centuries', in Carey (ed.), *The Apocalypse*, pp. 99–124.

Parshall, P., and R. Schoch, *Origins of European Printmaking: Fifteenth-Century Woodcuts and their Public*, exhibition catalogue (New Haven, CT: Yale University Press, 2005).

Pettegree, A., *Reformation and the Culture of Persuasion* (Cambridge: Cambridge University Press, 2005).

Pohl, M., 'Exegese und Historiographie. Lutherische Apokalypsenkommentare als Kirchengeschichtsschreibung (1530–1618)', in T. Kaufmann, A. Schubert and K. von Greyerz (eds), *Frühneuzeitliche Konfessionskulturen. Nachwuchstagung des VRG Wittenberg 30.09–02.10.2001* (Gütersloh: Gütersloher Verlaghaus, 2008), pp. 289–317.

Pointner, G., 'Das Luthertum vom Teufel erdacht hat alles Unglück in die Welt bracht. Die polemische Publizistik des J. Nas' (PhD dissertation, University of Vienna, 1996).

Pörtner, R., *The Counter-Reformation in Central Europe: Styria 1580–1630* (Oxford: Clarendon Press, 2001).

Puff, H., *Sodomy in Reformation Germany and Switzerland, 1400–1600* (Chicago, IL: University of Chicago Press, 2003).

Reeves, M., *The Influence of Prophecy in the Later Middle Ages*, 2nd edn (Notre Dame: University of Notre Dame Press, 1993).

Richardsen-Friedrich, I., *Antichrist-Polemik in der Zeit der Reformation und der Glaubenskämpfe bis Anfang des 17. Jahrhunderts. Argumentation, Form und Funktion* (Frankfurt am Main: Peter Lang, 2003).

Roper, L., *Oedipus and the Devil: Witchcraft, Sexuality and Religion in Early Modern Europe* (London: Routledge, 1994).

Rublack, U., 'Pregnancy, Childbirth and the Female Body in Early Modern Germany', *Past and Present*, 150 (1996), pp. 84–110.

— (ed.), *Gender in Early Modern German History* (Cambridge: Cambridge University Press, 2002).

Rücker, E., *Hartmann Schedel's Weltchronik. Das größte Buchunternehmen der Dürer-Zeit* (Munich: Prestel, 1988).

Sack, V., *Sebastian Brant als Politischer Publizist. Zwei Flugblatt-Satiren aus den Folgejahren des sogennanten Reformreichstags von 1495* (Freiburg i. Br.: Stadtarchiv, 1997).

Saxl, F., 'Illustrated Pamphlets of the Reformation', in F. Saxl, *Lectures* (London: Warburg Institute, University of London, 1957), pp. 255–66.

Schenda, R., 'Das Monstrum von Ravenna: Eine Studie zur Prodigienliterature', *Zeitschrift für Volkskunde*, 56 (1960), pp. 209–25.

—, *Die französische Prodigienliteratur in der zweiten Hälfte des 16. Jahrhunderts* (Munich: Max Hueber Verlag, 1961).

—, 'Die deutschen Prodigiensammlungen des 16. und 17. Jahrhunderts', *Archiv für Geshichte des Buchwesens*, 4 (1963), pp. 637–710.

Schiller, G., *Ikonographie der christlichen Kunst*, 5 vols (Gütersloh: Gütersloher Verlagshaus, 1966–91).

Schilling, H., 'Job Fincel und die Zeichen der Endzeit', in W. Brückner (ed.), *Volkserzählung und Reformation. Ein Handbuch zur Tradierung und Funktion von Erzählstoffen und Erzählliteratur im Protestantismus* (Berlin: Erich Schmidt Verlag, 1974), pp. 325–92.

— (ed.), *Die Reformierte Konfessionalisierung in Deutschland – Das Problem der 'Zweiten Reformation'* (Gütersloh: Gütersloher Verlaghaus Gerd Mohn, 1986).

Schmidt, P., *Die Illustration der Lutherbibel 1522–1700* (Basel: Verlag Friedrich Reinhardt, 1962).

Schmidt, P. L., 'Julius Obsequens und das Probleme der Livius-Epitome. Ein Beitrag zur Geschichte der lateinischen Prodigienliteratur', *Abhandlung des Geistes- und Sozialwissenschaftlichen Klasse* (1968), pp. 153–242.

Schoch, R., M. Mende and A. Scherbaum (eds), *Albrecht Dürer: Das druckgraphische Werk*, 3 vols (Munich: Prestel, 2001–4).

Scholz Williams, G., *Defining Dominion: The Discourses of Magic and Witchcraft in Early Modern France and Germany* (Ann Arbor, MI: University of Michigan Press, 1995).

Schramm, A., *Der Bilderschmuck der Frühdrucke*, 23 vols (Leipzig: Karl W. Hiersemann, 1922–43).

Schünike, S., 'Zu den Antiturcica Sebastian Brants', in Wilhelmi (ed.), *Sebastian Brant*, pp. 37–81.

Scribner, R., 'Oral Culture and the Diffusion of Reformation Ideas', *History of European Ideas*, 5 (1984), pp. 237–56.

—, *For the Sake of Simple Folk: Popular Propaganda for the German Reformation*, 2nd edn (Cambridge: Cambridge University Press, 1994).

—, 'Ways of Seeing in the Age of Dürer', in Eichberger and Zika (eds), *Dürer and his Culture*, pp. 93–117.

—, *Religion and Culture in Germany (1400–1800)*, ed. L. Roper (Leiden: Brill, 2001).

—, 'From the Sacred Image to the Sensual Gaze: Sense Perceptions and the Visual in the Objectification of the Female Body in Sixteenth-Century Germany', in Scribner, *Religion and Culture in Germany*, pp. 129–45.

—, 'Popular Piety and Modes of Visual Perception in Late-Medieval and Reformation Germany', in Scribner, *Religion and Culture in Germany*, pp. 104–28.

—, 'The Reformation, Popular Magic and the "Disenchantment of the World"', in Scribner, *Religion and Culture in Germany*, pp. 346–65.

Seifert, A., *Die Universität Ingolstadt im 15. und 16. Jahrhundert. Texte und Regesten* (Berlin: Duncker und Humblot, 1973).

Shachar, I., *The Judensau: A Medieval Anti-Jewish Motif and its History* (London: Warburg Institute, 1974).

Shorr, D. C., *The Christ Child in Devotional Images in Italy during the XIV Century* (New York: George Wittenborn, 1954).

Silver, L., 'Germanic Patriotism in the Age of Dürer', in Eichberger and Zika (eds), *Dürer and his Culture*, pp. 38–68.

—, 'Nature and Nature's God: Immanence in the Landscape Cosmos of Albrecht Altdorfer', *Art Bulletin*, 91 (1999), pp. 194–214.

Silver, L., and P. H. Smith, 'Splendor in the Grass: The Power of Nature and Art in the Age of Dürer', in Smith and Findlen (eds), *Merchants and Marvels*, pp. 29–62.

Smith, J. C., *Sensuous Worship: Jesuits and the Art of the Early Catholic Reformation in Germany* (Princeton, NJ: Princeton University Press, 2002).

Smith, N. R., 'Loathly Births off Nature: A Study of the Lore of the Portentous Monster in the Sixteenth Century' (PhD dissertation, University of Illinois at Urbana-Champaign, 1978).

Smith, P. H., *The Body of the Artisan: Art and Experience in the Scientific Revolution* (Chicago, IL: University of Chicago Press, 2004).

Smith, P. H., and P. Findlen (eds), *Merchants and Marvels: Commerce, Science, and Art in Early Modern Europe* (New York: Routledge, 2002).

Smits, K. (ed.), *Das Frühmittelhochdeutsche Wiener Genesis: Kritische Ausgabe mit einem einleitenden Kommentar zur Uberlieferung* (Berlin: Erich Schmidt, 1972).

Soergel, P. M., *Wondrous in his Saints: Counter-Reformation Propaganda in Bavaria* (Berkeley, CA: University of California Press, 1993).

—, 'Portraying Monstrous Birth in Early Modern Germany', in R. Dahood (ed), *The Future of the Middle Ages and the Renaissance: Problems, Trends, and Opportunities for Research* (Turnhout: Brepols, 1998), pp. 129–50.

—, 'Die Wahrnehmung der Endzeit in monströsen Anfängen', trans. S. Westermann, in H. Lehmann and A.-C. Trepp (eds), *Im Zeichen der Krise: Religiosität im Europa des 17. Jahrhunderts* (Göttingen: Vandenhoeck and Ruprecht, 1999), pp. 33–51.

—, 'The Afterlives of Monstrous Infants in Reformation Germany', in B. Gordon and P. Marshall (eds), *The Place of the Dead: Death and Remembrance in Late Medieval and Early Modern Europe* (Cambridge: Cambridge University Press, 2000), pp. 288–309.

—, 'Portents, Disaster and Adaptation in Sixteenth Century Germany', *Medieval History Journal*, 10 (2007), pp. 303–26.

Sonderegger, A., *Missgeburten und Wundergestalten in Einblattdrucken und Handzeichnungen des 16. Jahrhunderts* (Zurich: Orell Füssli, 1927).

Sondheim, M., *Thomas Murner als Astrolog* (Strasbourg: Selbstverlag Elsass-Lothringische Wissenschaftliche Gesellschaft, 1938).

Spiegel, G., 'Maternity and Monstrosity: Reproductive Biology in the Roman de Melusine', in D. Maddox and S. Sturm-Maddox (eds), *Melusine of Lusignan: Founding Fictions in Late Medieval France* (Athens, GA, and London: University of Georgia Press, 1996), pp. 100–24.

Stopp, F., 'Der religiös-polemische Einblattdruck "Ecclesia Militans" (1569) des Johann Nas und seine Vorgänger', *Deutsche Vierteljahrsschrift für Literaturwissenschaft und Geistesgeschichte*, 39 (1965), pp. 588–638.

Strauss, G. (ed.), *Manifestations of Discontent in Germany on the Eve of the Reformation* (Bloomington, IN: Indiana University Press, 1971).

Strauss, W. L., *The Complete Drawings of Albrecht Dürer*, 6 vols (New York: Abaris Books, 1974).

—, *The German Single-Leaf Woodcut 1550–1600*, 3 vols (New York: Abaris Books, 1975).

— (ed.), *The Illustrated Bartsch*, 72 vols (New York: Abaris Books, 1978–96).

Strickland, D. H., *Saracens, Demons and Jews: Making Monsters in Medieval Art* (Princeton, NJ: Princeton University Press, 2003).

Talkenberger, H., *Sintflut. Prophetie und Zeitgeschehen in Texten und Holzschnitten astrologischer Flugschriften 1488–1528* (Tübingen: Max Niemeyer Verlag, 1990).

Turner, J. (ed.), *Dictionary of Art*, 34 vols (New York: Grove, 1996).

Vanotti, J. N., *Geschichte der Grafen von Montfort und von Werdenberg* (1845; Bregenz: H. Lingenhöle, 1988).

Volz, H., *Vom Spätmittelhochdeutschen zum Frühneuhochdeutschen. Synoptischer Text des Propheten Daniel in sechs deutschen Übersetzungen des 14. bis 16. Jahrhunderts* (Tübingen: Max Niemeyer Verlag, 1963).

Wagner, J. M., 'Johannes Nas und die Jesuiten', *Archiv für die Geschichte deutscher Sprache und Dichtung*, 1 (1874), pp. 51–66.

Walsham, A., '"Out of the Mouths of Babes and Sucklings": Prophecy, Puritanism and Childhood in Elizabethan Suffolk', in D. Wood (ed.), *The Church and Childhood* (Oxford: Blackwell, 1994), pp. 285–99.

—, *Providence in Early Modern England* (Oxford: Oxford University Press, 1999).

Wandel, L. P., *Voracious Idols and Violent Hands: Iconoclasm in Reformation Zurich, Strasbourg, and Basel* (Cambridge: Cambridge University Press, 1995).

Warburg, A., 'Heidnisch-Antike Weissagung in Wort und Bild zu Luthers Zeiten', in A. Warburg, *Gesammelte Schriften*, ed. G. Bing, 2 vols (Leipzig: B. G. Teubner, 1932), vol. 2, pp. 487–558.

—, 'Pagan-Antique Prophecy in Words and Images in the Age of Luther', in A. Warburg, *The Renewal of Pagan Antiquity: Contributions to the Cultural History of the European Ren-*

aissance, trans. D. Britt (Los Angeles, CA: Getty Research Institute for the History of Art and the Humanities, 1999), pp. 597–697, and addenda pp. 760–75.

Wiesflecker, H., *Joseph Grünpecks Commentaria und Gesta Maximiliani Romanorum Regis. Die Entdeckung eines verlorenen Geschichtswerkes* (Graz: Verlag Jos. A. Kienreich, 1965).

—, *Kaiser Maximilian I. Das Reich, Oesterreich und Europa an der Wende zur Neuzeit*, 5 vols (Vienna: Verlag für Geschichte und Politik, 1971–85).

Wilhelmi, T., (ed.), *Sebastian Brant. Forschungsbeiträge zu seinem Leben, zum 'Narrenschiff' und zum übrigen Werk* (Basel: Schwabe & Co. AG, 2002).

— 'Zum Leben und Werk Sebastian Brants', in Wilhelmi (ed.), *Sebastian Brant*, pp. 6–35.

Wilson, D., *Signs and Portents: Monstrous Births from the Middle Ages to the Enlightenment* (London: Routledge, 1993).

Wittkower, R., 'Marvels of the East: A Study of the History of Monsters', *Journal of the Warburg and Courtauld Institutes*, 5 (1942), pp. 159–97.

Wuttke, D., 'Sebastian Brants Verhältnis zu Wunderdeutung und Astrologie', in W. Besch, G. Jungbluth et al. (eds), *Studien zur deutschen Literatur und Sprache des Mittelalters. Festschrift für Hugo Moser zum 65. Geburtstag* (Berlin: Schmidt 1974), pp. 272–86.

—, 'Sebastian Brant und Maximilian I. Eine Studie zu Brants Donnerstein-Flugblatt des Jahres 1492', in O. Herding and R. Stupperich (eds), *Die Humanisten in ihrer politischen und sozialen Umwelt* (Boppard: Haraldt Boldt, 1976), pp. 141–76.

—, 'Wunderdeutung und Politik. Zu den Auslegungen der sogenannten Wormser Zwillinge des Jahres 1495', in K. Elm, E. Gönner and E. Hillenbrand (eds), *Landesgeschichte und Geistesgeschichte. Festschrift für Otto Herding zum 65. Geburtstag* (Stuttgart: W. Kohlhammer, 1977), pp. 217–44.

Zika, C., *Exorcising our Demons: Magic, Witchcraft and Visual Culture in Early Modern Europe* (Leiden: Brill, 2003).

—, 'The Reformation Jubilee of 1617: Appropriating the Past in European Centenary Celebrations', in Zika, *Exorcising our Demons*, pp. 197–236.

—, 'Writing the Visual into History: Changing Cultural Perceptions of Late Medieval and Renaissance Germany', in Zika, *Exorcising our Demons*, pp. 523–79.

—, *The Appearance of Witchcraft: Print and Visual Culture in Sixteenth-Century Europe* (London: Routledge, 2008).

Zimmermann, E., *Bayerischen Klosterheraldik* (Munich: Zimmermann, 1930).

Zingerle, I., 'Selbstbiographie des Johannes Nasus', *Zeitschrift für deutsche Philologie*, 18 (1886), pp. 488–90.

INDEX